DIVINE MAGNETIC LANDS

Timothy O'Grady was born in the USA and has
lived in Ireland, London and Spain. He is the
author of the novels *Motherland*, which won the
David Higham award for best first novel in 1989,
I Could Read the Sky, which won the Encore
award for best second novel of 1997 and *Light*.
His book *On Golf* was published by Yellow Jersey
to superb reviews in 2003.

TIMOTHY O'GRADY

Divine Magnetic Lands

A Journey in America

VINTAGE BOOKS
London

Published by Vintage 2009

2 4 6 8 10 9 7 5 3 1

Copyright © Timothy O'Grady 2008

Timothy O'Grady has asserted his right under the Copyright, Designs
and Patents Act 1988 to be identified as the author of this work

First published in Great Britain in 2008 by Harvill Secker

The author is grateful for financial help from the Author's
Foundation and Arts Council England

Vintage
Random House, 20 Vauxhall Bridge Road,
London SW1V 2SA

www.vintage-books.co.uk

Addresses for companies within The Random House Group
Limited can be found at: www.randomhouse.co.uk/offices.htm

The Random House Group Limited Reg. No. 954009

A CIP catalogue record for this book
is available from the British Library

ISBN 9780099469537

Mixed Sources

Product group from well-managed
forests and other controlled sources
www.fsc.org Cert no. TT-COC-2139
© 1996 Forest Stewardship Council

Typeset by Palimpsest Book Production Limited,
Grangemouth, Stirlingshire

Printed and bound in Great Britain by
CPI Cox & Wyman, Reading RG1 8EX

for Eduardo and Beatriz O'Grady

Come, I will make the continent indissoluble,
I will make the most splendid race the sun ever shone upon,
I will make divine magnetic lands,
    With the love of comrades,
    With the life-long love of comrades.

                – Walt Whitman, 'For You O Democracy'

God save America! That's what I say too, because who else is capable of doing the trick?

              – Henry Miller, *The Air-Conditioned Nightmare*

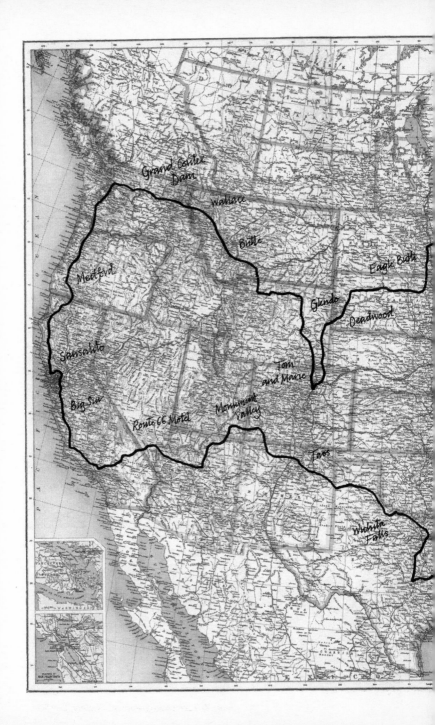

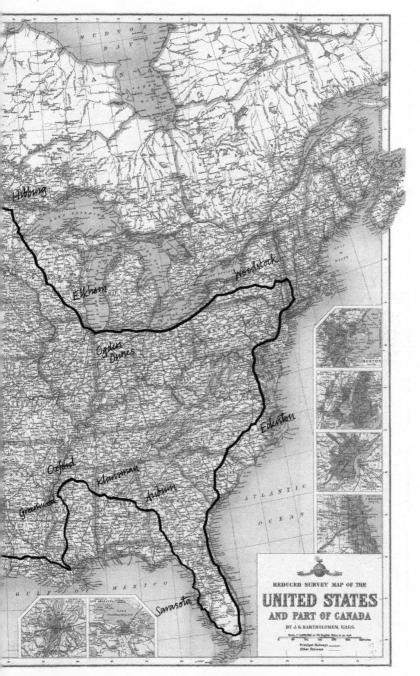

Hibbing

Elkhorn

Oglala Dunes

Woodstock

Edenton

Oxford

Stimman

Auburn

Greenwood

ATLANTIC

OCEAN

GULF OF MEXICO

Sarasota

REDUCED SURVEY MAP OF THE

UNITED STATES

AND PART OF CANADA

BY J. G. BARTHOLOMEW, F.R.G.S.

Contents

Introduction

When I was a child I had a feverish dream. I was in an open field on a low wooden stage, American flags draped in pendulous crescents across the front, a military band standing by. White clouds rolled and churned in the air as though boiling in vats. Men in suits and hats sat on the stage, others stood with women in the field. I was on a box making a frantic speech amid all this Americana that seemed to be from the era of steam trains and Abraham Lincoln.

I was around nine years old at the time. I had bronchitis and a temperature of 104 degrees. During the afternoon my mother had put me to bed in her and my father's bedroom in order to keep an eye on me. This is where the dream came upon me. Some time in the early evening she heard a shout and came in to find me standing on her bed, sweat running down my face and soaking my pyjamas, my arms upraised and a tormented expression on me as I called out, 'EVERY MAN SHOULD BE PRESIDENT!' It was the end of a long thought, and seemed the most urgent thing that had yet happened to me.

Where had the dream come from? Countries tend to be made of conglomerations of personages and events, clashing and flowing together as time moves on. From any point their pasts are visible to their people – pasts made of the evolution of language and customs and diet and of ill- or well-accomplished attempts at fiscal control and the maintenance or gaining of power. An individual may be dwarfed by the vast scale of this past, but he feels too an intimacy with it. Its things are well worn and familiar.

America is different. From the Puritans on, America has presented itself as an abstraction, born fully formed in an instant. It is made and ever remade by people who throw off their pasts upon arrival and begin at Ground Zero, their eyes fixed brightly on the future. If they navigate with skill they can get to the Promised Land. America is an experiment, a revelation, the place elected by God to be an example to the world. It lives in a continuous present of the invention and reinvention of the ill-fitting and sometimes contradictory concepts of absolute liberty and absolute equality. These concepts were proclaimed in the Declaration of Independence, worked out in terms of the architecture of government in the Constitution and guaranteed in the Bill of Rights. The rest for most is cartoon or waxworks or theme park. Americans are generally not very interested in their history. It has no tangibility for them. They are interested in the wondrous now. Liberty and equality do not evolve. They simply are. The America that is defined by them is not a process, but is rather an idea set out in philosophical tracts that grabs its people, enters their subconsciousnesses and becomes their point of reference for things both political and personal.

In his preface to *Leaves of Grass* Walt Whitman writes with a breathless, stuttering awe of the wonder of his nation and of what qualities a poet must have in order to rise to the occasion of writing about it. 'In the history of the earth hitherto,' he writes, 'the largest and most stirring appear tame and orderly to [the United States'] ampler largeness and stir. Here at last is something in the doings of man that corresponds with the broadest doings of day and night. Here is not merely a nation but a teeming nation of nations . . . The United States themselves are essentially the greatest poem.' He writes of America's rivers and the 'blue breadth of its inland sea', its trees and mines and pasturages, the songs of its birds, its 'wharf hem'd cities and superior marine', its 'rapid stature and muscle', the 'haughty defiance' of its Revolution and 'its long amativeness' and of how the poet must incarnate it all in its variety and breadth as he tries to write 'the great psalm of the republic'. He will find its tone, its vocabulary and its meaning in the people themselves, for in America as in no other place the nation and the people are one. 'Other states indicate themselves in their deputies, but the genius of the United States is not best or most in its executives or legislatures, nor its ambassadors or authors or colleges or churches or pastors, nor even in its newspapers or inventors . . . but always most in the common people. Their manner speech dress friendships – the freshness and candour of their physiognomy – the picturesque looseness of their carriage . . . their deathless attachment to freedom – their aversion to anything soft or mean . . . the fierceness of their roused resentment – their curiosity and welcome of novelty . . . their susceptibility to a slight – the air they have of persons who never knew how it felt to stand in the presence of superiors . . . These too,' says Whitman, 'are unrhymed poetry.'

There have always been, and still are, Americans who have elevated their fellow citizens to the status of gods and seen the nation itself as an instrument of Divine Will. Europeans can, and do, find this simply hysterical, but there were Europeans nevertheless who travelled to America in its first century as a democracy to look at it. They perhaps sensed in it an answer to a question it had never before been possible to ask. What might a nation do if it could just make itself up? In the last quarter of the eighteenth century, within a single generation, there had been created in America the economic and political template for the modern nation-state. It was the first country to emerge successfully from colonialism, the first republic and the first secular state. Francis Grund and Francis Lister came from Germany, Adam G. de Gurowski from Poland and Dickens and Frances Trollope from England. Around two hundred travel books about America were published between 1815 and 1860. Alexis de Tocqueville and his friend Gustave de Beaumont came from France in 1831 and travelled more than seven thousand miles by stagecoach, horseback, steamer and canal. Afterwards de Tocqueville wrote his vast and monumental analysis of the American system, which he called *Democracy in America*. In it he wrote, 'In America the sovereignty of the people is not, as with certain nations, a hidden or barren notion; it is acknowledged in custom, celebrated by law. It expands with freedom and reaches its final aims without impediment . . . The people reign in the American political world like God over the universe. It is the cause and aim of all things, everything comes from them and everything is absorbed in them.'

There was, then, a logic to my dream, even though it was brought on by a fever. It came out of those elemental concepts of liberty and equality I had been absorbing since infancy in the way that land absorbs rain. I had by then read nothing of de Tocqueville or Whitman, but the idea that every man should be president could be seen as an irreducible endpoint towards which the awed observations of the one and the passions of the other could, perhaps must, eventually lead.

I grew up in Chicago and left for Europe when I was twenty-two. I had never been out of America before and have thus far never lived there again, at least not permanently. It was an accidental journey, the consequence of a chance encounter with a poet named Anthony Kerrigan. He was passing through Chicago and stopped in the office of a literary magazine I was working at while I was a student. He was an exotic figure there in the Midwest, wild, whiskey-drinking, ribald, with white hair, white beard and white clothes out of the Cuba period of Hemingway. He smoked short cigars. He lived with his large family in Gertrude Stein's old house in Palma de Mallorca, but had bought for a few hundred pounds an abandoned house on an island called Gola off the coast of Donegal in the north-west of Ireland that had been forsaken by its inhabitants. He stayed in Chicago for a couple of days and I took him around the city. Before he left he offered me the use of the house in Ireland if ever I happened to be near it. I hadn't anything else in mind, so I took him up on it.

I flew out of Chicago for Dublin on a June day, seated between an Antrim Protestant and a west-of-Ireland Catholic, like the white stripe on the Irish flag. It was 1973. I'd been a student for the previous four years. It was a good time to be doing that – clamorous and epoch-making, or so it seemed. Things came and went as though in a pageant – reputations, fortunes, values, towns, history happening before our eyes, burning up and being remade. Everything seemed both critical and hilarious. And fast. There was no room or time for sober reflection, the building of a career, the virtue of modesty, or anything that took you out of the moment. Everything was about now, the new man, the new time, true justice, true equality, true liberty, the intensity of experience. In all the time I was there I never heard anyone speak about the job they would do.

Anthony Kerrigan's house had broken windows, no plumbing or power and a damp bed that hadn't been slept in for thirteen years. Sheep walked along the paths and through the houses. A pair of donkeys came through my door in the mornings looking for bread. I wrote letters, cooked, read, walked, had dreams of looking at a blank page and not filling it. I watched a spider weaving his web on a window. In the evenings I'd walk over to a rock and listen to ferocious lectures in Irish history by a former school-teacher who'd been born on the island and returned to pass the summers there with his wife. He had a little dog named Oscar that ran around nipping at the legs of the cows. He'd had to retire early due to a shredded throat caused by screaming at his students for thirty-five years. In doing so he raised the educational level of this impoverished district and gathered to his school an improbable number of scholarships. He told me about the island too, the life there and its vanquishment. I'd walk around then and look through the windows of homes at this life suspended at the point of departure – a jacket on the back of a chair, a tin of soup with a spoon in it, a discarded shoe. Like Macondo, Gola had lived in solitude for one hundred years, and then died.

I was in the mainland town one afternoon buying food and I saw a young woman with long, thick dark hair and a face for the ages sitting in a beam of sunlight on the ledge of the post-office window. She had on a long dress, boots and a shawl full of colours. She was looking towards the sun. That night I went into a bar and watched it fill with nationalists from the cities over the border, their raucous urban energy entering this quiet arena of sips and whispers like a marching band. Then musicians arrived. She came in too and somehow we met before the closing bell, jigs and reels and Republican ballads around us. Her name was Teresa. The next day we walked up a hill in the rain and back down again, and the day after she and the couple she was travelling with came out to my little house on the island. She and I went for a long walk in the evening light, out through the bog, along the cliffs and back through the fields, with me helping her over the stone walls as the night closed slowly in and the anticipation grew. Two days later she and her friends left for London, where they lived. She forgot her boots and I posted them to her.

I moved to Dublin when the cold autumn winds made life on the island no longer possible. The bus climbed the coast road and I looked back at the island, a bright disc in the grey sea. At the border two nervous British soldiers walked down the centre aisle with a Rolodex of photographs of IRA suspects, their fingers on the triggers of their rifles. The air seemed made of glass as they looked into our faces. They got down after a while and waved the driver through. A little further on the town of Strabane was in flames.

In Dublin I lived in a borrowed flat at the top of a rose-bricked Georgian house in Fitzwilliam Square and went out to Dun Laoghaire a few days a week to work for the *Dublin Magazine* in a caravan in the editor's garden. Elderly men of letters who had known Yeats would drive up on bicycles to deliver their manuscripts. I hadn't a clear plan. I thought of going back to Donegal in the winter to get work on the herring boats. I'd heard the money was good and wanted to stay a while longer. I had nothing else to do apart from looking at and thinking about Ireland. I loved being there. It excited and intrigued me. Everything about it was unprecedented for me – its traditions, its sense of time, its landscapes, speech, music, war. It was a seductive mystery. I thought if I read, talked, thought about and moved around in it enough, I would somehow get hold of it.

My visa had expired when I was in Donegal. I took my passport to a policeman in the mainland town. He held it for a while in his extended palm like it was a stranger's baby, passed it back and told me I'd have to bring it to Dublin. When I got there I went to the Department of Foreign Affairs, the old Guinness house on Stephen's Green, and said that I was hoping to renew my visa. I was led up a grand staircase and along corridors to a long room with eighteenth-century portraits on the walls and a walnut table that glowed like a hotplate. Forty people could have sat around it. Tea was served. Did no one else want to stay in this country? I thought of a photograph I'd seen of a holding room at a border station along the Rio Grande in Texas, six drenched Mexicans in handcuffs. After a while a civil servant came in, his glasses askew, wearing a suit the colour of curaçao. He had all the time in the world, it seemed, for this discussion about the renewal of my visa. He drank his tea and told me how great he thought it was that young people were travelling the world, and what did I think of Ireland? After a while he asked me if I had an Irish-born grandparent. I told him I did. 'If you can prove it, you can be entered into the Registry of Foreign Births. That would make you an Irish citizen,' he told me.

I took a train to Killarney and hitchhiked the fifty miles to Waterville, where a cousin of my father's named Sheila Clifford lived. She'd last seen me as a baby when she looked down at me as I was being changed and I urinated all over her blue dress. She went back to Ireland after that and had three boys. Two farmers in a truck with no floor took me into Waterville and pointed her out to me, a tiny woman praying before a grotto. We went from grotto to bar and then out the twisting, mountainous coastal road to Caherdaniel, the village of my grandfather. I was there to get a record of his birth. With that, along with my father's and my birth certificates, I could be inscribed as a citizen. From a high point in the road I looked down at this place where he had been born, a breathtaking spectacle of rock and sand and sea, mountain peaks rising out of the glittering water, the village just a church, a river and a scattering of houses around a narrow, gullet-shaped inlet. On one side was a rocky headland called Lamb's Head, and on the other a beach, grassland and oaks. Daniel O'Connell, the great nineteenth-century orator known as the Liberator, grew up among the oaks, and my grandfather among the rocks. Mountains pressed in at the back. At the end of the O'Connell head-land is a sandy rise surrounded by sea with the ruins of a monastery and an ancient graveyard. A stone marked the grave of Timothy and Teresa O'Grady. From Lamb's Head my grandfather had set out for America in the 1890s. How could he leave? But for him the question would have been: How can I stay? There were many people, little room.

We went down to the house where he'd been born. Another cousin of my father's was there, Crohan O'Grady, a tall, raw-boned man with hands the size of spades and a rope for a belt. 'O'Gradys have been in this house for three hundred years,' he told me. We'd lived in one Chicago apart-ment until I was five and another one after that and I had no idea who was in them before or after. Buildings, people, whole towns coming and going all over America, history being erased step by step by the people making it, like prey covering their tracks. Three hundred years getting a living out of the sea and some tiny pieces of land among the rocks of Lamb's Head. I seemed to be looking into a long tunnel of time, into which I was being drawn.

I got my grandfather's birth certificate and brought it back with me on the train to Dublin. There I was inscribed into the Registry of Foreign Births. The idea of a Foreign/Native

Birth is the kind of paradox the Irish are scorned and celebrated for, but it derives from a law that acknowledges the cruelties in the country's history, and that if people emigrated it was more likely through necessity than by choice. It is both a sensible and a generous law. Scores of millions of people in the world can avail themselves of it. Muhammad Ali, whose great-grandfather was an O'Grady from County Clare, only misses it by a single generation. I left the Department of Foreign Affairs and walked across Stephen's Green. It was 1 November 1973, one hundred years to the day, I noticed, after the registration of my grandfather's own birth. I was now a citizen of two countries, already slowly decanting myself from my original citizenship into the more recent one. I didn't know that at the time, however.

I had to leave the flat I was in for a couple of weeks, for it was needed by a friend of its owner, and went to London to see Teresa. She worked in a bank and lived in a compact little room in Shepherd's Bush that looked out onto an enormous tree in the back garden. We walked through the leaves along the avenue to Notting Hill for dinner and back again. There seemed nothing else for me after that, just the world of that room, the music and coal fires at night, her long hair. I forgot about the herring boats in Donegal or the idea of seeing Paris and Rome or of returning to America. I got a job putting together cash registers in a factory in the Barbican. I walked out one evening onto Waterloo Bridge, all the great edifices of British royal, political, religious and cultural life visible from it, hordes of office workers streaming around me in tones of grey. One wore lavender socks. I thought that no matter how long I tried I'd never get to the bottom of this place. I didn't understand warm bitter, Marmite, seigniorial rights, pantomime dames, pomp and circumstance, policemen's hats, ukulele music. I didn't get the colours or the gestures or the obliqueness in relations. The house I lived in with Teresa filled with South Africans pursuing a sybaritism they could not pursue at home. When the landlord, a victim of psoriasis, saw that the coin-operated gas meters had been raided for money for drugs, he sang 'Rule, Britannia' at the top of his lungs, flakes of skin flying from his face. Of what was his mind made, I wondered, and how did it work? When I asked English people questions thought normal in America, they'd look at me as though I'd defiled their homes. Chesterton had said that of the three principles of the French Revolution, the English adhered only to the first. But how could anyone with a belief in liberty think of themselves as a subject rather than a citizen? I would in time change in my feelings about England, but I thought then that it would be forever inscrutable to me. Nor was I at that point animated to try to understand it. England both made me feel more American and drove me further towards Irishness. Teresa lived utterly in an Irish world. We went to sessions where accordionists and fiddlers played wild tunes and where at closing time everyone stood for the Irish national anthem. We went on political marches and acted in plays at a theatre in the back of an Irish pub. I remember a long Sunday after-noon in north London where an American was attempting to record a legendary fiddler from County Clare, pints on tables all around, talk rising and falling, drinks being called for, bets being laid, the American spinning the dials of his recording machine and pleading for silence and order, while songs and tunes started up in various regions of the room and the fiddler swallowed another glass of whiskey. I would see other things about Ireland in time to come, but then it seemed all about camaraderie, wild tales, political justice, eloquence, catching a rising current of energy and, as Sean O'Faolain put it in his essay on the Celts, 'the final realisa-tion of the passions'. Everything was pursued to the end – of the bottle, of the music, of the story. I found something else there that I'd seen little of in America – perhaps it was present in the south, or in the Latin and black worlds of Chicago – the idea that chaos and helplessness are never far away from anyone, that they just take you as a strong wind takes a tree, and that their victims are to be commiserated with rather than scorned. That's something that can relax you. A year went by like this, then another and another. I'd imagine going back to America sometimes. I'd think of what it would be like to get off the plane and step on that land again, to be with the people I had known and tell them what I had seen. But I didn't do it.

My American life had coincided with perhaps the most prosperous, optimistic and idealistic period in the history of the country. The energy was high, the vistas vast and the sense of possibility seemingly without limit. Never before had there been such wealth, or such velocity of expansion. It did not touch everyone, but it touched more people than ever before. There was social experiment, but also security. If you were somewhere in the middle classes or above, it seemed that no matter what you did you could not fall too far.

Then came a darkening. Of this I saw only the first shadows. By the time I left in 1973, the Watergate hearings had begun and the Vietnam War was ending in a military defeat by a tiny country armed with unsophisticated weaponry and its own desire. The oil crisis would strike the following year. The great gulf between rich and poor, which had been narrowing for forty years, again began to open. The epoch known as the Sixties was over. All over America those who had been offended by its social and political mores of liberation now stood in wait, determined to bury them for ever.

During my first ten years in Europe I went back to the United States only once, in 1977. Teresa and I drove from Chicago, across Canada to Maine, then down the east coast, turning inland at Washington, through the Shenandoah Valley to Nashville, the Ozarks, north Texas, New Mexico, then north to Boulder, Colorado and east from there back to Chicago. Ten thousand miles, twenty-five states. When we were driving across Ontario with a Salvation Army hitch-hiker in the back seat we heard that Elvis had died. My father nearly died too after an operation on his gall bladder, but seemed to decide not to. Jimmy Carter was in office, a presidency characterised by lack of ostentation.

– 11 –

I went back six years later, again due to an operation on my father, this time on his heart. It was a different country to me then. I had gone one way, it seemed, and it another. Ronald Reagan was president. He had moved around on the outer margins of the primaries for some years. It had been inconceivable that he would ever be president, but there he now was. After the disgrace of Nixon, the country had voted for modesty and sobriety. Jimmy Carter had walked to his inauguration. He went around the White House in jeans and an open-necked shirt. It was like a period of penance after the hubris. Now they wanted a king, and an actor was playing the part on a grand scale. Flags flew and bugles sounded wherever he went. Every national act seemed like the half-time show at the Superbowl, with fighter-plane flyovers, operatic renditions of patriotic songs and colours out of Disney. With Reagan were Nixon administration people who had long been harbouring a grudge against the New Deal and the Sixties and also wanted to restore the presidency to its previous kingly dimensions. Now, at last, they had their man and their moment.

I began to go more regularly then. On each visit I moved around the neighbourhood I had known in granular detail, feeling a stranger. Things looked familiar, but far away. I'd lost the sense of intimacy with the place. People had different aims, different ways of enjoying themselves. They used different words. They even moved differently, it seemed, pimp rolls, struts like pecking birds, slouching grunge shuffles and, for the brash executive, or those aspiring to be one, a stride like a bowling ball headed for the pins.

And then there were people who could barely move at all. I went with my mother to a shopping precinct and waited in the car while she went to buy something. A procession of huge, slow-moving men and women came out of the supermarket like ships being launched, labouring their way with shortened breath with their shopping bags to their cars, dollops of flesh like melting ice cream hanging from their arms. Their trousers bulged like water balloons. When they got into their vehicles, the carriages descended on their springs nearly to the ground.

'What's going on?' I asked my mother when she arrived.

'With what?'

'With all these people. Look at that man. He'd need four of my shirts to cover himself. There are so many of them.'

She sighed. 'It's a shame,' she said.

Occasionally a thought would run into my mind of the life I might have lived had I stayed, and I'd shudder, drive the thought away. I may have been fooling myself that I was in a prolonged adventure in Europe, but it was working, nevertheless.

The American road is a great seduction. People have gone out onto it in search of knowledge, gain, obscurity, revelation, the meaning of America, or of themselves. Because of this it generates a feeling of myth in a way that no other road I have ever been on has done. The myths are of freedom, anonymity and discovery, the fundamental myths of America itself. You are out under the open sky, devouring the continent, lost to the world, every stage a piece in an allegory. You are free. No one knows who you are. No one knows where you are going. Long journeys elsewhere tend to carry the sense of function, or trial. On the American road you go higher, become more liberated.

People have walked, crawled, bicycled, Harley-Davidsoned, trucked, driven in cars and, if their road was a river, swam or boated through or over America as a rite of passage, sometimes the great rite of passage of their lives. Many have written of it. De Tocqueville and Beaumont persuaded the French Minister of the Interior to fund their study of the American penitentiary, but what they really yearned for was the American road, as it then was. Charles Dickens travelled through what might now be regarded as some of the dullest terrain in the country in order to produce *American Notes* for an English public curious about the experiments in democracy in Jackson's America. Lewis and

Clark, among many other explorers, kept journals. That great novel of rage and pity, *Huckleberry Finn*, perhaps the great American novel of its century, was a road book on a river. Henry James came back after a prolonged stay in Europe, as did Gertrude Stein. Both wrote of the experience.

The form really began to be realised in the mid-twentieth century. *On the Road* was published in 1957. Henry Miller, long in Europe, came back to get out of the way of the Nazis, drove across the country in a shuddering, twittering, overboiling car and wrote the damning *Air-Conditioned Nightmare*. John Steinbeck constructed a kind of houseboat on wheels and drove around with his dog and some whiskey during the 1960 election campaign to write *Travels with Charley*. *The Grapes of Wrath* is another kind of road book, wreathed in pain, as, in their ways, are *Lolita* and Kafka's *Amerika* and even *As I Lay Dying*. Simone de Beauvoir had a political, philosophical and hedonistic journey, accompanied by a letter of introduction from Jean-Paul Sartre, around the country in 1947. She kept a journal, which was later published under the title *America Day by Day*. Like the Joads, Woody Guthrie left a desiccating Oklahoma, travelled in boxcars and wrote *Bound for Glory*, a book that in turn propelled Bob Dylan out of Minnesota and into the great wide world. Robert Pirsig set out on a motorcycle and wrote *Zen and the Art of Motorcycle Maintenance*. Tom Wolfe watched Neal Cassady and Ken Kesey in a multicoloured bus travelling from coast to coast and wrote *The Electric Kool-Aid Acid Test*. William Least Heat-Moon, having lost both his job and his wife, left Columbus, Missouri in his van and made a loop around the country on its back roads, afterwards writing the beautiful, melancholic and revelatory *Blue Highways*. More recently Bill Bryson looked all over America for the ideal small town he'd developed in his mind from watching 1960s television shows, Jonathan Raban took a boat down the Mississippi, Christopher Hitchens drove a convertible Corvette, Edmund White set out looking for gay America and Joseph O'Connor for the immigrant Irish. Nik

Cohn was going to go around the world, but instead inched his way up Broadway from the Battery to Times Square, tarrying with the broken and the exotic. 'It's the world within itself,' a friend told him. They all wrote books. There are photography books, films and songs in great number. 'They've all gone to look for America,' as one of them says.

When I was living in Europe I'd think often of people I had known in Chicago, and miss them. I missed certain foods, and sports. But when I thought of America what I most yearned for was the open road. I'd think of the vastness and silence of the west, red earth and mesas, air shimmering in the heat, the radio on. When my father died in 1993 I drove around our old neighbourhood in his nearly twenty-year-old Chevrolet and had the inclination to keep going, out of the city and southwards, maybe all the way to Guatemala. I was writing a book. I could drift along, stop in motels for a few days, try to finish it. But I didn't do it.

With the election of George Bush, Jr, the attack on New York and the invasion of Afghanistan and Iraq, America entered a new epoch. A cold fear ran through the market. Debt rose and the dollar crashed like a drunk falling downstairs. The idea of government was transformed by the most radical administration in my lifetime. The country was invaded from behind its own lines and appeared vulnerable to the point where burning cities, poisons running through the country's veins and roads filled with confused refugees were not merely the visions of the mad. Scenes from the Middle Ages seemed suddenly proximate. All the world was suddenly looking at America, wondering what it now was, and where it would go.

I wondered too. And I kept thinking of the small-town bars, the neon-lit motels, the road striking out among skyscrapers, through cornfields, mountain and desert. I decided to go. What might come of it? An obituary? A celebration? A reacquaintance? And should I in any case add to the already great pile of American road books? Well, it was an unusual time, I thought, a time unlike any other. And there might be a certain starkness to my perspective, given my particular circumstances. At this point I had been in Europe for thirty years. I knew far more of Irish history than I knew of my own country's, and more about the politics of London than of Washington. I sounded somewhat different than I had, people sometimes said. British spellings were more familiar to me than American. And I had three European children – a girl, Aoife, born in 1981; and, after marrying Maria Ruiz on American Independence Day, 1998, two others born in Valencia, Spain: Beatriz, who was then four, and Eduardo, who was two. What part of me, I wondered, was still defined by America? I didn't know. I'd hold on to my prejudices, I supposed, and see if they dissolved.

Matsuo Basho, Japanese poet and traveller, wrote, 'The gods seemed to have possessed my soul and turned it inside out, and roadside images seemed to invade me from every corner . . . Even when I was getting ready, mending my torn trousers, fixing a new strap to my hat, and applying *moxa* to my lips to strengthen them, I was already dreaming of the full moon rising over the islands of Matsushima.'

Basho had seen the moon rising over the islands before, which heightened his yearning. I'd seen the bayous and mountains, the red-earth deserts and mesas of the American road. I'd seen the blue neon signs rising over the roadside bars, and a softer, warmer, more enticing light falling on the pavement by the door. In Valencia I prepared for it all – booked tickets, fixed appointments, called friends – and thought with a quickening appetite of the road. I hadn't been out on it for more than twenty-five years. And I'd never been on it alone, at least not for more than a day or two. How much could I see? How much could I hold on to?

I made two cross-country journeys by car, the first from New York to San Francisco through the north and the other eight months later from San Francisco back to New York through the south. This is what happened.

New York City

In a concrete-block holding room at the airport a policeman searched my bags and me, then slid his hands down the back of my trousers and squeezed my testicles. 'You can go now,' he said. I walked out through passport control and customs into the arrivals hall. Trolleys three dollars each. No information desk. I found the stop for buses going to the Port Authority. The sky was grey, the air heavy. A bus came along after a while and I got on. As we rolled along the freeways through Queens, girders growing out of rockland and riverbed all around, the Pakistani bus conductor keeping up a jarring banter like a Coney Island hot-dog vendor, I thought finally of all the things I might have said to that first American who had spoken to me since my arrival, his policeman's shirt rolled up over his biceps, his badge and gun sparkling in the fall of the strip light. He had a physique like a hammer thrower's. I'd long grown used to the late arrival of my devastating ripostes and stopped making them up by the time we got to the Bronx, but the question remained for a long time and remains now as I write this: Why did he do that?

I remember two of my arrivals in New York City, far apart in time and both curative in the moment of their happening. The first was when I was twenty. I'd gone to southern New Jersey to see a high-school friend who was visiting his father there and, when I could no longer tolerate the fastidious tidiness and sternness and punitive silence of this house, I got into my car and headed for New York, pulling into a parking space in Greenwich Village late that night. Blue and red lights flashed over the bars in MacDougal Street, old men played chess under the trees in Washington Square, there were musicians with guitars and violas, a lady in a ballgown dancing a waltz and, under floodlights in the centre of the square, a volleyball game of tremendous athleticism and exuberance. So much energy, so much life, all for nothing other than itself. It had all the freshness and delight and hilarity of spring after the cavernous air of that New Jersey house where, five years later, oppressed by failed investments, bank foreclosure and impossible debt, the father of my friend put a pistol to his head and shot himself.

The other time was just over twenty years later. I'd been visiting my widowed father in Chicago and on my last night there had gone from bar to bar with a childhood friend until we could find nothing open and had sat then on the back steps of my father's apartment building, drinking beer while the sun rose on our disgrace. I slept a few hours on a sofa and then got onto a plane to New York. The hangover entered like a reptile there, steadily spreading its venom into every part of my system. A plane is a bad place for that – nowhere to escape or lie down, the air unable to disguise its artificiality, everyone well presented and in their own private worlds, with no interest in or tolerance for your barely containable crisis. I laid my head against the window in pale distress, barely breathing. It seemed like some molten, radiated mineral was moving in a deadly crawl along my conduits. I was to meet a friend that night at a theatre, but could think of nothing but bed. I got off the plane and onto a bus. I put my head against the window again. I hoped for some deliverance from this, but it wasn't shifting. The bus rattled and groaned through the foul air of the Queens Midtown Tunnel and came up into the east side of Midtown Manhattan. The city lights glittered, the traffic hummed and bleated a kind of music off the walls of the buildings, people strolled along the streets and avenues as though in the corridors of their own homes. There is nowhere at all like this, I thought, so concentrated, so intimate, so dynamic, so much yearning and power and intellectual energy, every few hundred yards some iconographic landmark out of the mythology of America, the whole of Manhattan a living drama with every citizen a skilled and willing actor. Anything could happen here, it seemed. You could not fail to want to enter it. I got off the bus at Grand Central Station and walked to the theatre to see my friend, who was acting in a play. My hangover had vanished like fog burned off by the morning sun. There was a little party going on in his dressing room. The daughter of Eli Wallach invited me to another one in SoHo. The night kept tumbling out like dice thrown from a cup.

New York: cure for disenchantment and hangovers.

I was on a raised, viaduct-like freeway, still moving towards Manhattan, looking down at cemeteries and neighbourhoods. American flags and flowers decorated the graves. There were flags too sticking out from the porches of the houses and on poles in front yards, the lawns clipped. It had been two years since New York had been attacked by air. Afghanistan and Iraq had already been invaded. Much of the world watched appalled, another part with vows of vengeance. On whom would America fall next and at what point would it be too weak to rise again? What could decency and defiance, expressed by these houses and flags, do in the face of the rage of millions? Would it all be washed away? 'New York', Henry Miller wrote once, 'may come to resemble Petra, the cursed city of Arabia.'

We arrived at the Port Authority, just a few blocks up from my destination on West 43rd Street, where my friend Laralu Smith lived with her husband Joe. They'd bought an inflatable mattress and I was going to sleep on it during my stay in New York.

I'd known Laralu between the ages of five and eight. She was, like me, an only child, and lived on the first floor of our apartment building in Chicago. I remember her in pink satin dresses, Buster Brown shoes with white socks and long cylindrical ringlets like those worn by Hassidic Jews. She was a child actress. We all went to see her doing a turn in a school revue. Her father gave me his Army-issue shirt and ration bag from the war. He died at work one terrible summer morning and we all heard about it later that day. Laralu and her mother packed up and moved to Ohio. My mother stayed in touch with them through the ensuing decades and, through her, Laralu and I met again in London thirty years after I'd last seen her. It is given to some to know their calling early. She was now an actress and living in New York, she told me, and was married to another of the same profession.

She and Joe live in Manhattan Plaza on 43rd between 9th and 10th, a twin-towered luxury development with a swimming pool in the middle. It was built during the 1970s when the neighbourhood was full of peep shows and strip bars and hookers hailing down cars. Crack was sold openly. Hell's Kitchen, just to the north, had started low and gone lower. The real estate was cheap. It could have been a good bet. But halfway through construction there were no takers for the apartments and the city was facing the prospect of a huge bankrupt shell in Midtown. A group of theatre people, Helen Hayes among them, lobbied for a scheme to give the building over to performing-arts professionals as affordable housing. A deal was worked out, the federal government came in with the promise of a subsidy and the building is now full of actors, musicians, stagehands and, in one case, a circus animal trainer, paying thirty per cent of their gross incomes in rent. A typical rent at the lower end could be $370 per month, while two-bedroomed flats in the commercial market nearby are let for ten times that. As the actors moved in, the junkies and hookers drifted away and coffee houses and gourmand food shops came in. Dexter Gordon lived there, and Tennessee Williams. Samuel L. Jackson was a doorman. *Seinfeld* was conceived on the fourth floor.

I took a high-speed lift up twenty-five storeys to their apartment.

'How was the trip?' asked Laralu.

A trip, if it's by aeroplane, usually passes within narrow, predictable parameters. In my case there was one singular detail.

'I did some work, then read Dickens' *American Notes*,' I said. 'He went on about the courtesy and smiles of American customs officials compared to what he called the "ill-conditioned curs snarling around the gates of Britain". I was goosed by a policeman at the airport.'

She poured some wine and we sat at a table and talked, looking out over Hell's Kitchen, where Irishmen once brawled with blades and lead pipes. Then I went out into the night, the hours later here and, as Dickens said, 'more rakish'.

I walked up 10th and then went right on 44th, passing the studio where Jimi Hendrix recorded *Electric Ladyland*. I went on through dappled lamplight past the string of little bars tucked into the buildings on 44th as I headed towards Times Square, so called in honour of the great and sober newspaper that was once headquartered at its southern end, its presses in the basement for the easy loading of papers onto the subway. Times Square has long been known for its neon signage and once had a huge billboard advertising cigarettes, on which was a man who blew real smoke rings around the clock. When Chesterton saw all the signs he said that it would look beautiful to a person who didn't know how to read. This is a region where once lived and operated those who gnawed at the feet of the entertainment industry, scavenging its dead cells – street musicians, hopeful crooners, the eternally auditioning, star-struck courtesans, one-man bands, talking dogs, strippers, those at the end of the chorus line. Frank Sinatra vaulted clear of them all on New Year's Eve, 1942, at the Paramount Theatre just here at 43rd and Broadway, the girls in bobby socks screaming and hyperventilating and rolling their eyes, bringing the tent revival to the music theatre. Invented for him, this collective hysteria was also granted to Elvis and the Beatles, and then mysteriously disappeared.

Times Square had been an area of blacksmiths and stables called Longacre. Then Oscar Hammerstein I opened the Olympia Theatre in 1895 and its successor the Victoria in 1900, where Houdini, the Marx Brothers, Charlie Chaplin and

Lillie Langtry all played and where a net was stretched across the front of the stage to protect some song-and-dance acts from fruit hurled by the audience. This is when the area thickened with show people. Eugene O'Neill was born in a Times Square hotel called the Cadillac. Diamond Jim Brady and Lillian Russell ate at Rector's. Vaudeville was succeeded by burlesque. In the Gatsby era it became a playground of swooping limousines, lobster and champagne, showgirls leaping naked from birthday cakes. Down it went then, through the decades, until it became a region of the mad, the predatory, the obscene, and others who could not find a space elsewhere in America in which to fit. I saw a shaven-headed woman running up 8th near here in the 1980s, calling out like an auctioneer, trying to throw her dress off as if it were in flames. But as the world knows, they were all, or nearly all, swept away by Mayor Giuliani and his planners, beginning in 1996, and Times Square is now dominated by Madame Tussaud's and Disney and tourists wearing the same clothes you can see in Orlando or Las Vegas. It is safe now, but some would say it has hit its lowest mark yet.

I went north up Broadway, the Great White Way. The streets grew cleaner, less garishly illuminated. There were fewer people and their faces were less lined and shadowed. At 52nd Street I passed the Brill Building, a hit factory in the 1960s where Leiber and Stoller wrote songs for Elvis. A little further on, where the Letterman show is recorded now, is the theatre where the Beatles made their first appearance on American television on the *Ed Sullivan Show* before seventy-four million people, of which I, crouched down on the floor under a pool table in the house of friends of my parents, was one. The towers of central and east Midtown sparkled like carnival prizes.

I kept going north, the city's pageantry ever changing. The street population again grew a little more dense, the buildings were of more intimate proportions, the street-level shops were open and catering for the domestic. Couples united after a day at work walked hand in hand, ties loosened, heels clicking on the pavement, carrying their takeaway dinners and a bottle of wine in plastic bags. Keys came out of pockets, walk-up doors were unlocked.

I saw a bar advertising music and went in. Inside, the walls were painted pink. The owner, according to a newspaper article in a frame on a wall, had been in a band that had a hit in the Seventies. It had that air of anticipation a bar has an hour or so before it awakens into life – the doorman adjusting his tie and rolling his neck, a technician twiddling the dials of the amps on the stage and setting the guitars in their racks, early customers stepping tentatively in.

I took a seat at the bar. Next to me were a man and woman, both spectacularly plastered. The man was giggling as though he'd been locked in a closet inhaling laughing gas. When he tried to speak, each word seemed to arrive to him like a stranger. The woman was far worse. Every once in a while she'd start rotating on her bar stool, going down slowly like George Foreman in Kinshasa, until the man tipped her up by the elbow. 'Manhattanick', I'd read, is an old Indian word meaning 'island of drunkenness', and there they were.

They were drinking white wine. Her glass for the most part remained untouched, for when she reached for it she usually missed. She talked to the man, then to herself, and then suddenly turned to me, already speaking.

'. . . and I think it's wonderful, it's *truly wonderful*. You've gone through so much, you've waited for so long and now you've found the person of your life, your great love, someone who out of all the people in the world is just *perfect* for you. That doesn't happen to many people. But it's happened to you! I'm so happy for you, really *happy*. It's *great!*'

She turned back to the man. Again I couldn't get what she was saying. I looked over my shoulder to see if she had been speaking to someone else the previous moment, but there was no one near. She got hold of her glass and took two sips, then turned to me again, her head drifting from side to side, her eyes taking a long time to focus.

'Who are you?' she said.

I introduced myself and looked around the bar. It was a quarter full of mainly young, loud, prankish men, traders, perhaps, or bank officials. In a minute I got another visit.

'. . . and I know they say it's easier now,' she was saying. 'But then you still have to *do* it. A *person* has to do it, not a social trend. And you've done it!' She took hold of my hand. 'It's wonderful. It's a beautiful, very moving story. To be so lost, so broken, to then find this person, *your* person, your beautiful wonderful person, and then to come out before the world and tell everybody that *he's a man*! A great, big, glorious man! You're so brave. I'm proud of you. I really am. It's absolutely . . . *noble*.'

What was this? Did she know about the policeman?

She seemed to fade for a moment like a thing with its batteries running down, then looked suddenly startled.

'*Who are you?*' she said again. Then she slumped on her seat and seemed to doze.

I walked back downtown and found an Irish place where I could get a hamburger. It had an ellipsoid bar in the centre with wooden tables beyond the perimeter and a few televisions on the walls as if thrown there by centrifugal force. Carnegie Hall was just across the street. On one of the televisions was the fourth game of a play-off series between the Atlanta Braves and the Chicago Cubs baseball teams. The Cubs, and in particular their great home-run-hitting short-stop Ernie Banks, had largely defined my childhood summers. I went to games often, taking the elevated train with a few friends down to Wrigley Field and paying sixty cents for a grandstand seat. Afterwards we'd wait at the players' parking lot to get autographs. Everyone wanted Ernie's, the great shining light in this heartbreaking team. The *Chicago Tribune* ran a cartoon around this time with Ernie at every position and everyone else on the team looking out from the bench. The other players also knew why we were there. They'd arrive, the kids would scurry over with their scorecards and pencils. 'Ernie's on the way out now,' they'd say, and hop into their cars and drive away, unmolested. When he got

there he'd stand in the sun and sign every last one. 'Let's play two today,' he'd say when he arrived at the park, as if one game could not be enough to satiate him. The Cubs had a tradition of starting fast, sometimes leading their division until halfway through the season, then going into a decline. I'd walk around my neighbourhood with a transistor radio up to my ear, mourning their slow demise. At the time, weekday afternoon games only drew a few thousand people. There had been a drift out to the suburbs in a search for status and security and comfort. Baseball was a little tainted with the inner city and the plebeian. The players had hick accents and chewed tobacco. But in the 1980s many of the young and affluent began to come back into town. They disavowed the leafy serenity of the suburbs. They wanted neighbourhood bars, blues music and sand-lot softball leagues. Professional baseball boomed as one of the last refuges of American authenticity and Wrigley Field, one of the only ball parks still set down in an urban neighbourhood, was regularly sold out. And now the Cubs were winning. If they won this five-game series against the Braves, which they were leading by two games to one, they would go on to play for the National League title. If they won this final play-off series they'd go into the World Series against the American League champions for the first time since 1938.

Forty thousand people were in Wrigley Field for the game. The rooftops of the buildings beyond the stadium walls were full of people barbecuing and drinking beer. The Cubs' new manager, Dusty Baker, was in every respect like the managers of my youth – well worn, hyper-realistic, kindly and shrewd, with fast-working jaws – except that he was black and chewed sunflower seeds instead of tobacco. He couldn't prevail that night, however, and the Braves, hitting well, won the game 6–4. The series was tied 2–2.

I walked out into the street, drifting south and a little westwards. The subways exhaled up through the grilles, the smell of food billowed from the exhaust fans over restaurant doors, and currents of perfume floated like streamers behind striding ladies. I can't remember ever feeling bad here, or even indifferent. The city gives you energy and desire. It seems that anything can happen, and is just about to. Everything lures you: a drawn blind, neon over a bar, a glass sparkling in the shadows, an ankle disappearing through a revolving door.

I held my course until I got to 43rd and 10th. On one side of the street was the entrance to Laralu's building and on the other side a bar where a karaoke contest was going on. It was around one o'clock. I hadn't been in a bed for nearly twenty-four hours. I stood still for a while wondering what to do, then went into the bar. This wasn't the kind of karaoke you'd find in a Butlin's in Clacton-on-Sea. Anyone

I saw that night could have fronted a band and made you remember them. They were all girls. One from Texas sang Hank Williams' 'You Win Again' with coquettish irony. A black girl moved all around the room with a liquid litheness singing 'Don't You Feel My Leg', her voice soaring and then restricting to short, ecstatically pained gasps, down on her knees at the end, bent over and holding the microphone up to her mouth with both hands. No one knew what to do after that. The air seemed to ache with yearning. I went up to the bar for another beer. The possible was rattling around the room like a roulette ball. When I came back she was at the table where I'd been sitting. She looked at me as though there was some injustice in my presence there.

'Who are *you*?' she said then.

That was the third time in the same night.

In the morning Laralu and I walked along 43rd a block west to the Market Diner for breakfast. I'd been here before. It was the kind of place I could never tire of – snake-skin booths, world-weary waiters, a seven-page poly-ethnic menu. 'Manhattan's Only Diner With Its Own Parking Lot', it called itself. This drew cab and limousine drivers. It looked like it had been ready-made somewhere and dropped down on the tarmac, a flat, wavy-edged hat set on top. Inside it displayed the decorative taste of a 1960s bowling alley. The traffic flowed along 11th Avenue, once known as Death Row because of the railroad that ran up its centre. Perhaps around forty years earlier a Greek left his labyrinthine, white-painted village on an island, with its smells of oregano, lime and Aegean sea salt, with his life savings to set up this restaurant and thereafter flip hamburgers among the spitting grease and exhaust fumes. A long while later the Siren Women's Motorcycle Club of New York began to dispense bikers' permits for the motorcycle section of the Gay Pride march here in the Market Diner. Next door is Club Edelweiss, 'the only transgenderist club in New York with its own parking lot and valet service'. Perhaps they share with the Market Diner.

I had French toast, Laralu an omelette. Joe had been on a nervous search for an honest car mechanic, or the nearest equivalent, and joined us after making his choice. He ordered eggs sunny side up. There was a whole language for this sort of food evolved by cooks in sweat-drenched T-shirts and gum-chewing waitresses with beehive hairstyles – 'Two cows and kill 'em' for well-done hamburgers, for instance – which I never learned. Places like the Market Diner have long been giving way to Subways and Starbucks, and this language of the short order is vanishing, like Cornish. You leave places like this with reluctance.

Joe and Laralu told me that a couple of years earlier a friend working in a bank let them know about a new online stock-trading service her company was starting up. 'You can't miss with this,' she said. Joe did some painting and decorating. Laralu was a part-time secretary for a maverick lawyer. They got par.s in commercials and television dramas every now and then and very occasionally there were films. They acted in plays, sometimes for a living wage, sometimes for nothing. With all of this they had managed to save a few thousand dollars. They saw the date for the offering of the online trading service shares in a list in the *New York Times* and decided to put their savings in them. The value of it went up, as their friend said it would, precipitously. Almost hysterically. 'The numbers looked good,' said Joe. 'They kept going up for the first two or three weeks. I thought we should sell, but then I had to go upstate to Albany to see my mother and I lost track of the prices. I'm not very alert about this kind of thing.' The prices levelled while he was away. Then the investment bank that had started the online trading company was bought by another investment bank, whose directors were then offered the online trading company's stock for prices well below market level. They dumped them all at once, the stock crashed and the company vanished. All those walls painted, those legal briefs typed, those auditions successfully passed, deleted like a misprint from a screen. A question of alertness. Or aspiring speculators armed with a little privileged information vanquished by those who couldn't lose.

I took a subway down to Union Square and walked south in the sun towards Greenwich Village. It was a Sunday. The cars were eerily scarce, the pace slow, people out on the terraces with their croissants and heaped newspapers. Many were alone. New York is a city, like London, replete with single people briefly colliding. Unattached women between the ages of twenty and thirty-five, I was told, stand in relation to unattached, straight men of the same age at a ratio of four to one. It has perhaps long been thus. Federico García Lorca wrote to his parents about the women flocking around him everywhere he went, lamenting, 'It is a plague I have to endure.'

I crossed 14th on 5th. Henry James' father used to walk around here on his cork leg, having lost the original in a fire. I was making for Washington Square, as he often did. The Village passed from the rural to the urban when refugees from the yellow-fever epidemic of 1822 fled to it from downtown. It was almost made into the administrative centre of the city, but it escaped this. It had a prolonged bohemianism. John Reed and Emma Goldman spoke of revolution in a house on 5th I passed on my walk. It belonged to an heiress named Mabel Dodge, another of whose houses I was to encounter later in Taos, New Mexico. Eugene O'Neill lived at 38 Washington Square and wrote *The Iceman Cometh* there. He drank gallons of intoxicants at the Golden Swan Bar, headquarters of his friends the Hudson Dusters, an Irish gang. Even Tom Paine lived in the Village, already spurned as an atheist and enemy of society by the government born of the revolution for which he had provided the intellectual structure. On this balmy day in Washington Square old men were greeting each other before moving off to the chessboards. There was an air among them of lightly born affection. My mother's cousin Bob, a reformed alcoholic, lived with his wife a hundred yards from here and filled the time he used to spend drinking with bird banding, Boy Scout leading and tree labelling. Trees in the square bore his metal plaques for decades. Alcoholics have such a void to fill when they stop drinking. For money he tended the bar in cummerbund and bow tie at the grand Racquet and Tennis Club. 'You'd be surprised how many ex-alcoholics are bartenders,' my father once told me. 'They're thought to be highly trustworthy.'

I headed west and crossed Sheridan Square, named for the marauding, scorched-earth Civil War cavalry commander, then entered Christopher Street. In 1969 New York City police entered a gay bar called the Stonewall here and started to eject patrons. A call went out and there ensued an hour-long street brawl between gay men and the police, which is commemorated annually on the last Sunday in June in the Gay Pride march. For years marches have also taken place in cities all over America on the same day. One afternoon I sat with my father in the back room of his apartment and we watched the Chicago Gay Pride march, a long sequence of transvestite marching bands, drag acts on fairy-castle floats, Judy Garland impersonators, old men holding hands, lesbians on Harley-Davidsons. In all other respects it was like the St Patrick's Day Parade. There was a troupe of moustachioed men who all looked like Freddie Mercury wearing sequined catsuits and thigh-high boots twirling batons and high-stepping to Nancy Sinatra's 'These Boots Are Made for Walking' and just behind them, smiling and waving from the back seat of a little red convertible, was Mayor Richard M. Daley, son of another Mayor Richard Daley, the legendary Boss, who had held the job from 1955 until 1976, when he died in office, a block-built, syntax-mangling Irish-American ward fixer who probably thought that transvestites were advanced mathematical equations. The son, a couple of decades on, knew that he needed the gay vote.

I had an early lunch with the writer Edmund White at an Italian restaurant. Like many before him, he'd left the Midwest and gone to Paris. There was a time when it was thought there was no American culture, that it was a place only of vulgarians and businessmen, that the themes for the great poems and novels were to be found in the drama and subtlety and richness of Europe, and that it was there that anyone wishing to dance, compose, act, paint or sculpt must go if they were to learn best how to do it. It is difficult to imagine T.S. Eliot or Ezra Pound doing what they did had they stayed in St Louis or Idaho. Or Gertrude Stein in California. Americans did not perceive their country in these limited terms by the time Edmund White went to Paris, but go he did nevertheless for seven years, before returning with his boyfriend Michael. I wondered what he had seen there, and how it was to come back.

'I had lunch with George Plimpton's sister when I arrived. It was Lotusland. You couldn't leave. I walked directly into its embrace. I chose writing and hedonism over civic duty. I'd have stayed, but Michael wanted to come back, which we did in 1990.'

What, I asked, was his first impression?

'I was shocked at the Political Correctness. I got a job at Brown. I was teaching a course in Gay and Lesbian Literature. The lesbians got together to protest that I was "denying them their oppression". That's how they put it. That was a new concept for me. It wasn't as though we weren't more or less on the same side. Older women are in charge of ethics committees at the universities. They're terrified of professors falling in love with their students. They see themselves as the only line of defence against lubriciousness. You can't have a conference with a student with the door closed. It extends throughout life here, including of course the political world. No one will forgive anything. Everything is on a personal level. It is all about character, so called, rather than deeds. When I was a child no one even knew that Roosevelt was crippled. They didn't know he had three lovers in the White House, or that Mrs Roosevelt had two men and a woman. Think of that compared to the way Clinton was treated. Nixon's disgrace took away the

– 31 –

immunity. Gary Hart introduced sex, or rather the media elected to work this theme with him as the focus. It's happened before. Marie Antoinette was accused in pamphlets of lesbianism and incest. Respect was so lowered that it was only a short step to cutting off their heads.

'I was also struck by the nakedness of the proclamations about status and success. There's so much criticism and envy in Europe. People tend not to boast for fear of being knocked down. Irony and self-deprecation are the modes of speech. I'd got accustomed to that in Paris. But in America if you make a self-deprecatory remark they say, "So you're not very good at your job?" Ninety per cent of Americans think they're middle-class. The top thirty per cent think they're in the top two per cent. And they will as readily applaud others as themselves. Frank Sinatra wasn't just a singer, he was a "song stylist". Helen Hayes was the "First Lady of American Theatre". Can you imagine the English speaking like that? Europeans accustomed to getting knocked down feel liberated when they come to live in America.'

He asked me what I'd noticed. I told him I'd only been in the country for a day. One thing I'd wondered about from afar was the profusion of therapists. I'd heard of an heiress in California who collected them as others might face creams or recipes and had reached the point where it was costing her $10,000 per month. They'd been around for a long time, I knew, but there hadn't been so many, nor did they follow so many different theories. Many were without degrees or even any training in their fields. And the language of therapy had got into everything.

'Proper therapy is on the wane,' he said. 'That is, personal, sustained, introspective therapy, the kind that tells you your problems will never be wholly resolved and that you must cut your losses and get on with life. This hasn't disappeared, but it is diminishing in the face of the Oprah fallout. Why spend so much time and money and accept irresolution when you can have instant catharsis on a television show or in a therapist's office? It's all tied up with the evangelical movement, as the other type of therapy was tied up with the other great strand of religion in America, the Puritans, whose religious life was based on meditative examination of the self and a strong sense of personal responsibility. The evangelical movement began in 1730 with the Great Awakening. It's all about faith, being saved. You are reborn and have a personal relationship with Jesus. Good works count for nothing. It really caught on in America. It was a convulsive, communal form of Christianity that suited isolated, rural life. They'd set up a camp in a clearing in the woods for a week some time between planting and harvesting. It was very emotional, and it was also very louche. They were drinking up in the hills. There were prostitutes who came in for business. Preachers would touch the girls while they were swooning. Now you can confess, convulse and be saved all at once in front of a therapist or on TV. A girl weeps about being abused as a child. They bring out the father. He's also weeping. There follows a traumatic, tear-drenched, but cathartic meeting. You're saved, somehow. There's been no need for sustained introspection. Or at least apparently not.'

I'd been told by an American in Valencia that I wouldn't be able to cross America without repeated collisions with fundamentalist Christians and quack therapists, the former concentrated in the vast centre and the latter on the coasts. Sometimes I would meet both in the same person. Redemptive, quick-fix therapy, I was to learn, has grown in importance not only because of television and religion, but also for economic reasons. A psychologist in San Francisco told me that insurance companies won't pay for long-term treatment of mental ailments. They prescribe time limits for the treatment of various categories of illness and won't cover anything that exceeds them, no matter what the psychologist feels the patient needs. Another source of the decline of in-depth psychoanalysis, a journalist told me, has been the mass manufacture and vigorous marketing of anti-depressants and other psychotropic drugs. Collectively, the pharmaceutical companies spend $25 billion annually on marketing and have more lobbyists working for them in Washington than there are legislators. They have come to control how and by whom medical research is conducted, how they are regulated and what is published about the effects of their products and which conditions are included in the American Psychiatric Association's manual of mental disorders. Since this manual was first published in 1952 hundreds more conditions have been added to the list, including states once thought to be a normal part of living, such as worrying, sadness or shyness, all of them treated by drugs prescribed by GPs. The redundancy of psychologists and psychoanalysts increases.

I was to take a train that night to New Haven, Connecticut. The first step in a long journey. I got the subway back uptown towards Laralu's and when I came up onto the street a tall black man not far from panic asked me for help in getting a place for the night. He'd been in jail. He had a daughter. 'There was a time when everything was going along nicely and then all of a sudden it just went straight to hell,' he told me. We talked a little while, then shook hands. I thought he might cry. 'This is just so bad,' he said, and walked away. He was forty-eight years old, he told me, and had been in several different jails for fourteen of them.

I still had some time left before the train. I went into a bar and sat at a window. A cab rolled by with an electric screen mounted on the side displaying baseball scores. In Atlanta the Cubs had beaten the Braves 5–1 and won the series 3–2. If they could beat the Florida Marlins over seven games, they'd go to the World Series. Men were lined up along a wall waiting to get into the toilet, clutching their groins. In many American bars there is only one cubicle for each sex, containing a single toilet. Space is cash, it would seem, and for ingesting rather than the reverse. A lean young man, luminous in the eyes and a little jumpy from the beer, asked me what I was doing in New York. I told him I was going to drive to California.

'You're going to what?'

'I'm going to drive across the country.'

'Haven't you ever heard of airplanes?' he asked.

'Well, I thought I'd like to take a look at it.'

He looked at me as if he'd never heard anything as foolish as this before.

'But there's nothing between here and California except gas stations!' he said.

New Haven, Connecticut

I got off the train at what seemed the disproportionately grand Union Station, renovated not so long before in New Haven's exhausting and expensive battle to hold on to itself in the face of industrial collapse and the flight of the middle class. There were several ill-tempered commuters in my carriage, shoving each other to get space for their newspapers and laptops. The belligerence of New York still hung in the air, though it had lost the witty theatricality it had *in situ*. It's a long way to travel, twice each day, I suppose.

I got into a cab and gave the driver an address in Orange Street, where I was to have the use of an apartment belonging to a couple who taught at Yale and were to be away during the time I was there. The driver seemed hard of hearing. Whenever I said something he cocked his head like a bird, then turned around and squinted at me, as though the missed information might arrive visually. He overshot the destination and I had to make my way back to where I was going, dragging and kicking and heaving my bags across the lawns of Orange Street in the darkness.

I found the keys under a shrub and went upstairs, passing a flat that had been rented, I'd been told by the couple, to three Chinese students sent by their government to study computer science at Yale, one of several elite American institutions training foreigners how to usurp America's economic pre-eminence. Their shoes were lined up outside the door, neat as a window display. I put the key in the door at the top of the stairs and went through into a cultural wonderland of painting and photography on the walls, books by the thousand on the shelves, ornamental boxes, curiosities and magazines on the tables and a kitchen full of condiments, herbs and cheeses of the world. They'd left fish, stewed apples and a note of welcome for me, yet still I could sense what I've heard described as the exhilaration of the house thief as I walked around looking at everything.

I thought of a little stroll around the bars of New Haven after I ate the dinner, but gravity seemed to be drawing me down and I went to bed with the *New Yorker*. I read there that according to the American Psychological Association the second most influential psychotherapist of the twentieth century was Albert Ellis, founder of Rational-Emotive Behaviour Therapy and follower of Epictetus, the Stoic philosopher who stated that what makes an impact on people is not what has happened to them, but rather their view of those events. 'I don't damn any person,' Ellis is quoted as saying, 'including Stalin, Hitler and President Bush.' 'Second most influential' would seem to require originality, but I couldn't see any thus far. Nor did the *New Yorker* state who was ahead of him in influence. Freud? It went on to say that he was the author of more than seventy books, including *Sex Without Guilt, Sex and the Liberated Man, The Case for Promiscuity* and *How to Stubbornly Refuse to Make Yourself Miserable About Anything – Yes, Anything!* Perhaps he was the one who had moved psychotherapy into the supermarket check-out line. The article said that he'd started picking up girls in the Bronx Botanical Gardens when he was a young man and had gone on, he claimed, to become 'one of the best picker-uppers in the United States'. His next book was to be entitled *A History of the Dark Ages: The Twentieth Century*. Reading about Albert Ellis woke me up for a moment, but then in the tomb-like darkness of the room, the vastness of the bed and the perfect silence of Orange Street I slept more deeply than I had in weeks.

I woke to the news that Conan the Barbarian had been elected Governor of California. So eerie was this that it seemed I was

still dreaming. On the plane from London I'd read an interview with a girlfriend he'd had shortly after arriving in the
United States from Austria in 1967. 'One day,' he told her, 'I
will be Governor of California.' That must be one of the
oddest and most unlikely predictions in political history. He
had then only a fragile grasp of English. He had no contacts,
administrative experience, party affiliation, university degree,
evident ideology, corporate backers, training, profession or
money. He was unknown outside that camp world of steroids,
tiny swimsuits and oiled muscles where men become
outsized figurines. But he had an American dream of a kind.
'When I was ten years old, I dreamed of being an American,'
he told the oral historian Studs Terkel before the cyclone of
fame had hit him. 'I felt it was where I belonged. I didn't
like being in a little country like Austria . . . Number One in
America pretty much takes care of the rest of the world. You
kind of run through the rest of the world like nothing.'
Bodybuilding was an activity at which he could excel without
athletic ability. He put his head down and he drove. He won
championships all over Europe and then all over the world.
He was Mr Olympia six times. He went on *The Dating Game*.
Then his ascent became precipitous – Conan the Barbarian,
the Terminator, highest paid actor in the world. He married
a Kennedy. He bought watches for hundreds of thousands
of dollars and a fleet of gargantuan, custom-made four-wheel-
drive vehicles, including two that were nearly tanks. 'If the
Terminator wants something,' he said as he pointed at a
Humvee mounted on a dais, 'he's going to have it!' The
photographers' bulbs flashed like gunfire. There was applause
and the laughter of warmth and awe.

The immigrant dream, the American dream, had been
and still was of a fresh start, of religious and political freedom,
of a little house with a white picket fence, nice neighbours
and children who would grow up to be doctors. Arnold
Schwarzenegger dreamed surpassingly of a world in which
he would not only have what he wanted, but in which he
could actually *be* what he wanted. 'When I was a small boy,

my dream was not to be big physically,' he said, 'but big in a way that everybody listens to me when I talk, that I'm a very important person, that people recognise me and see me as something special. I had a big need for being singled out.' What is so uncanny is that he actually arrived there. As of that morning, and thanks to a by-election forced by a curious law that allows Californians to fire an incumbent governor before his term is up if they don't like his tax plans, he was presiding over a state with a population nearly as large as, and an economy far larger than, those of Spain. 'EVERY MAN SHOULD BE PRESIDENT!' I had called out from my dream. Where else was there for Arnold Schwarzenegger to go? Would the constitutional impediment to the foreign-born being elected president be removed on his behalf? Orin Hatch, Chairman of the Senate Judiciary Committee, was already trying to do so.

I went out onto Orange Street and headed downtown. New Haven was known as 'the place of the pink bluffs' because of the two great rock faces that in part frame the city. Two of the judges who signed the death warrant of Charles I were given refuge in these bluffs.

Quinnipiak Indians fished and farmed maize here. The Dutch visited briefly and moved on. Five hundred Puritans under the leadership of the Reverend John Davenport and a London merchant named Theophilus Eaton came from Massachusetts in 1638 in the hope of establishing a more perfect religious community than the one they had left behind. They bought land from the Quinnipiak and protected them from the Pequot and the Mohawk. After nine years of town-building, husbandry and artisanship they filled a boat they called the *Great Shippe* with the best of their products and sent it to England, hoping thereby to gain control of trade in Long Island Sound and perhaps as far south as Delaware Bay. The sailors shuddered with foreboding when, contrary to superstitious nautical practices, the boat was towed out stern-first in the fog through a path cut in the ice. As they went out they heard the Reverend Davenport intone from the shore, 'Lord, if it be Thy pleasure to bury these our friends in the bottom of the sea, take them, they are Thine.'

All through the winter and spring the town awaited the return of the boat. Finally, it is said, it appeared on the horizon on a bright June day, sailing into the wind with its square-rigger loose. A solitary figure stood in the bow pointing back out to sea with his sword. Then the maintop snapped, masts and spars blew away and the hull went down into the sea under an enshrouding mist.

New Haven never established itself as a major port after the loss of the *Great Shippe*. Boston and what was then New Amsterdam (and later New York) vastly surpassed it. But it became a city of inventions and new industrial practices. Eli Whitney, a Yale graduate, invented the cotton gin in 1793. This spread cotton growing westwards from Georgia and the Carolinas throughout the south all the way to Texas. Later, he conceived of a new method of mass manufacture. He vastly increased the call for slaves with his first innovation and put thousands of artisans out of work with the other. He set up a gun factory just outside the city where, in 1836, Samuel Colt invented the automatic revolver. It was the weapon that gave the Texas Rangers their first victory over the Comanche, who could shoot twenty arrows and ride three hundred yards in a minute. The Rangers worked with Colt to refine the weapon and the tribe's encounter with the gun stayed for ever as a cataclysm in its folk memory. Winchester Rifles moved in and New Haven became known as the 'Arsenal of America'. Slavery, genocide, unemployment. The inadvertent legacy of the innovator-scientist.

New Haven boomed during the Civil War and for long after. Rubber goods, carriages, ploughs, clocks, beer and pianos were made here. George C. Smith invented lollipops and Isaac Strouse was the first to mass-produce corsets. Great fortunes were amassed. Two waves of black Americans came, one during the colonial period and another from the Carolinas in the 1940s. There was a kosher health-food store in New Haven where Hassidic Jews shopped with the offspring of black migrants from the south who were still close enough to their rural roots to make their own medicines from herbs on sale in the shop. Europeans came in large numbers until anti-immigration laws blocked them. Italian craftsmen built houses, much of the Yale campus and put in the simple and graceful dark golden door frames in the apartment where I was staying. It is a city unusually blessed with good carpentry.

The only industries left now are a replica rifle factory in the old Winchester building and some small machine-tool companies. The windowless shells of warehouses and factories are scattered around the city like ghost ships in a bay. Out beyond the city limits descendants of the Pequot Indians who plagued the Quinnipiak and after whom Melville named Ahab's boat are using their right to transcend local laws to set up casinos. When I was living in the United States the only casinos were in Atlantic City, New Jersey and Nevada. Now you find them all across America on Indian land. Casino operators encourage the tribes to go to Washington to claim their rights under old treaties and then lease the licences to the operators. The tribes have grown rich. 'Eastern Connecticut has primarily a service economy now,' a journalist named Bruce Shapiro told me. 'And casinos and strip clubs are the fastest-growing part of it.'

Yale, like Oxford, was once no more than a significant presence in a prosperous, industrialised city. Now it and the hospitals are overwhelmingly the largest employers. Successive mayors have thrown themselves with gusto against the city's ailments and been washed back on a tide of closing businesses, middle-class migration, a declining tax base, growing unemployment, a booming drug market and gangs. Its dignity, still very evident, has become more fragile.

I arrived at the massive Green, laid out by Puritans as common land in the English manner. The Green is still more of the town than of the university, though the university lies immediately to the north and west of it. I walked through the streets to the east. There were dollar discount shops, jewellers, palm readers, nail shops, yoga classes up flights of stairs. A church advertised Alcoholics Anonymous meetings and Alpha groups. Some of the churches in town, I'd noticed, had become Korean or Chinese. The most smartly presented premises I saw on this side of the Green was a US Army recruitment office.

I made my way along the southern edge of the Green towards Yale. Men drank sherry from paper bags, students had picnics, office workers strode the paths, neckties flying. A black man with the toes gone from his shoes sold hot dogs sponsored by a law firm – CALL 1-800-LAWYERS, it said on the red umbrella over his steaming two-wheeled tin box with the hot dogs in it. A Frisbee sailed up and curved off. I'd had an antipathy towards Frisbee-throwing since I was at university, but I hadn't known then to blame Jazz Age Yale students, who started it all by throwing pie tins from Mrs Frisbie's bakery across this Green. I got to College Street, entranceway to a strip of bars and restaurants. Just along here before a Doors concert in 1967, Jim Morrison was discovered by police to be having sex in a shower backstage with a witch. They thought about it for a while before declining to arrest him, but then when he abused them from the stage they took him to the station and booked him. '. . . Blood in the streets of the town of New Haven . . .' he later sang.

I'd been to New Haven several times. An unlikely number of friends of mine had arrived here after earlier lives of varying degrees of chaos. Once I taught fiction writing at the Yale Summer School. I had a spectacularly heterogeneous class. There was an eighteen-year-old Korean who wrote stories of precocious delicacy and a young man from Georgia who was raised in a strict Baptist household, but who was growing more camp as we looked at him, coming out, it seemed, by the minute as he told us graphic stories of tequila drinking and lavatory encounters. A young woman was fleeing her marriage, a young man holding at bay the question of what he would do. An ex-*Dating Game* host and stand-up comedian closed up his flat in Los Angeles, packed a van with his belongings and drove across America to take this course.

He'd been published in both the *New York Times* and the *New Yorker*, but had become nauseated by his own verbal facility and was in search of scale and depth. There was too someone of a type I'd never before met, an eighty-year-old great-grandmother who'd grown up in New Haven in a manner that was in most respects upper-level Victorian – a newspaper-magnate father, sprawling house with servants and nannies, with long dresses and summonses by bell for dinner. Over two days after the first class I met them one by one in a bar to ask them who they were, what they had done and what they expected to get from the course. At the end of it I couldn't stand up. I felt like my blood had been drained. To teach, I then realised, you must find a means of preserving distance.

The great-grandmother was writing a novel after the manner of Trollope. But this was not what was foremost in her mind. When we sat across from each other in the bar, she dispensed with my questions within ten minutes and then proceeded to the story that had run through her life like a current in a river. When she was a girl her parents sent her to school in France. While there she fell in love with a young French officer, and he with her. They planned to elope. She confided this to her twin sister, who was in another school in Switzerland. Her sister thought it her duty to inform her parents, who immediately sailed to France, brought her back to America and arranged a marriage for her with a young lawyer, who was delighted to be marrying into one of the richest and most prestigious families in the town. They began to have children. They had twelve, in all. Around eight years after she'd been removed to America the French officer wrote to her to say that he now knew it was futile to wait for her any longer and that he was going to get married. He was doing it only to avoid having to spend the rest of his life alone. More years passed. Grandchildren arrived, then great-grandchildren. When she was in her mid-seventies she and her husband went to France. Before leaving she wrote to her French officer. They met, just the two of them, and spent the afternoon together. It was as though no time had passed at all.

'Did your husband know?' I asked.

'He did.'

'Did he mind?'

'Why would he?' she asked. 'He had all he wanted from me.'

She and the Frenchman were writing to each other now, she told me, and spoke regularly on the telephone.

'There's not another person in the whole of the world I can talk to as I do to him,' she said. 'And at least I have him now, in a way.'

The Yale Law School is in Wall Street. Many of its students are likely to wind up in the brokerage houses of its namesake in New York. I went up the steps. A group of about twenty of them had just come out of a class and were standing in this hall of sandstone and marble. Around four thousand apply each year for entry, but only six per cent are accepted. The voices of these students were pitched just above a whisper, their manners mildly ironic, their gestures minimal. They conveyed the impression that it tired them to have to put their elegant thoughts into words adjusted for those of lower rank.

They were destined for both wealth and infamy. Lawyers surpass tax collectors and bailiffs in being despised in America. These students are likely to learn early how to mock their profession as they collect their fees. Millions of Americans believe that lawyers have created a national mania for suing, that because their marketplace lies in grievance and dispute they set about encouraging enmity between individuals and their employers, their government, their neighbours, the companies that feed, clothe, transport, medicate and otherwise serve them, and their spouses, and that this process has entered so deeply into the national psyche that it's become rotten with victimhood, for in victimhood there's money. America had been made and populated by immigrants. They had given it a character of mutability, experiment, dynamism. There was at least a presumed equality of opportunity. You were free. You could make of yourself what you wished. Part of the deal was the necessity for stoicism. Now, it seemed, there was a general scramble for a niche in which victimhood could be felt, and this was, many believed, the fault of lawyers. They had driven up doctors' insurance premiums, and thereby the cost of medical treatment, with their compulsive malpractice suits. They had done the same with industry with their multi-million-dollar compensation claims for accidents at work. Everyone knew of the woman who bought a cup of coffee at McDonald's, drove off with it between her legs and then won a seven-figure compensation suit after the cup tipped over and scalded her. The claim was based on the coffee being too hot. It was difficult to imagine a judge or jury listening with seriousness to a case such as this. Had lawyers turned the United States into a nation of people who had to be led by the hand through life as they could not be expected to know that coffee could burn them if they poured it onto their legs? Lawyers were the same parasites Dickens had described with such loathing in *Bleak House*, believing in nothing apart from their own enrichment, laughing as they left businesses, local governments, families and individuals in ruins. All, or nearly all, were by instinct ambulance-chasers. I was somewhat of this opinion myself. So, it seemed, were lawyers, at least for form's sake. Self-deprecation had been integrated into their styles. 'What's a boat filled with 142 lawyers at the bottom of a lake?' a lawyer in a bar asked me. 'What?' I said. 'A good start,' he replied, then let out a dry, slow, well-practised laugh. An old friend from my neighbourhood in Chicago, one of three of a primary-school graduating class of around thirty who became lawyers, included in a letter to me the observation that when extra-terrestrials visit the decimated earth in some century to come and find a gravestone with the inscription 'Here Lies a Lawyer and a Good Man', they will conclude that our civilisation ended due to overcrowding as we had to place two corpses in each grave. Dead-lawyer jokes have some vintage. 'Why does a hearse horse snicker,' wrote the poet Carl Sandburg half a century ago, 'hauling a lawyer away?'

I went out onto Wall Street, then through the Yale campus. Mark Twain, who had briefly been a Confederate soldier, paid the tuition fees of a black student here in the aftermath of the Civil War. I passed Turnbull College, in the guest rooms of which I had stayed while teaching. I had a living room, bathroom and bedroom, everything well appointed, comfortable and serious, the walls wood-panelled and the windows leaded. My view was of rooftops and pathways lined with shrubs and bicycles. Architecturally Yale aspires to Oxford and Cambridge and succeeds in conveying antiquity, but though it was founded in 1701, much of the present campus was built by Depression-era craftsmen skilled at the distressing of stone, tiles and wood. I passed the Beinecke Library and quad after quad. The students were walking so slowly it seemed they were saving their energy for the forthcoming struggle to repay the terrifying debts from their education.

The United States is too regional in its consciousness for Princeton, Harvard and Yale to be as definitively dominant as are Oxford and Cambridge in Britain. But everyone in the country is aware of their status and they at least dominate the east, which has the greatest concentration of population and is where the intellectual energy tends most to congregate. Aspirant students need either exemplary academic records or rarefied connections to gain entry to these institutions. I heard a story about a notable alumnus, the editor of a national magazine, being given a tour of Yale by a woman from the university's public-relations office, who was from the south. The alumnus looked around the familiar grounds and listened to a recitation of some of the stellar achievements of recent graduates. 'I suppose applicants need SAT scores in around the top half per cent to get in here now,' he said. 'Why no, sir,' the woman replied. 'If that were the case, all our students would be Chaah-*neese*.' And indeed several were. And Korean, Lebanese, Croat, Russian, Nigerian, Indonesian, Polish and so on. It was similar at other elite campuses I was on – Cornell, the University of Chicago, Northwestern, Stanford. You could get the impression that America was educating the world. These institutions are expensive, but there is also a beneficence to them. Investments and endowments have made many of them very rich. Yale's endowment alone is $15.2 billion. Large amounts of these resources are allocated to the granting of scholarships to both Americans and foreigners who could not otherwise attend. I know a Serb former theatre director now delivering spectacles by van for a small optician's in Valencia. His daughter excelled at physics in her secondary school in Belgrade. She came to the attention of the Massachusetts Institute of Technology, which offered to educate, feed and house her almost entirely for free.

I walked past the Yale pool. Johnny Weissmuller, Hollywood's first Tarzan, became the first person to swim 440 yards in less than five minutes here in 1923, breaking his own record by eleven seconds. It was the forty-seventh of his career. I looped back eastward on Grove. Set obscurely and peacefully among trees, like the mausoleum it is meant to resemble, is The Tombs, headquarters of Yale's Skull and Bones Society. It was founded around a myth about Eurologia, goddess of eloquence, who ascended into heaven upon the death of Demosthenes and didn't come back to earth until 1832, when she took up residence at Yale. The Tombs has a dining room called the Boudle, a Firefly Room where hooded initiates are taken and where members wave around lit cigarettes in the dark air, and an Inner Temple where a patriarch named Uncle Toby officiates, assisted by knights called the Devil, the Pope, Don Quixote and Elihu Yale, all in costume. There are tombstones, skulls, skeletons and a mummy. The two candidates for president in the 2004 election were members. Like the Freemasons and Opus Dei, the Skull and Bones Society is a facilitator in the ascent of a career. George W. Bush was preceded as a member by his father and grandfather. He benefited from his membership in many ways, though gifts from Eurologia were not among them. He was given his first job by a member. Others invested in the baseball team he owned when his other ventures failed, and those and more contributed large sums to his campaign – $1 million in one case. In turn, he advanced members. Among his appointees, his assistant attorney general, the chairman of the Securities Exchange Commission, the general consul of the Office of Homeland Security, the associate director of the National Economic Council, the ambassador to Trinidad and Tobago, the Secretary of Defence's representative in Europe, an associate judge of the Supreme Court of the District of Columbia, and the ambassador to Hungary, a cousin of his, were all members of the Skull and Bones Society. Its mixture of the puerile, the pagan and the Mickey Mouse Club can be found in varying degrees in men's clubs and fraternities all over America, and most spectacularly in Bohemian Grove, a remote rural retreat north of San Francisco where bank heads, CEOs of multinational corporations and the politically powerful gather to form alliances, divest themselves for a while of the grievous weight of their duties and renew themselves through nature and comradeship by drinking vintage champagne, jumping naked together into a pond, worshipping tortoises, burning effigies and getting into drag to have themselves photographed in pornographic poses. Dick Cheney, James Baker, Henry Kissinger and every president since Coolidge have been to Bohemian Grove. Why do powerful men do such things? Cyril Connolly, an old Etonian, thought that membership of fraternal societies at school condemned one to a perpetual adolescence of secrecy and loyalty oaths, pranks, initiation rites and group singing.

I walked over to Berkeley College to listen to Joan Didion talk about California in a room thronged with students. Eminent cultural figures such as she can move around the universities of America, at times getting five-figure sums for their visits. When I was a student we had, among others,

Groucho Marx and Anaïs Nin. There was an annual poetry festival, which concluded on a Saturday night with a reading by four renowned poets in a thousand-seat theatre and afterwards a bacchanal with free bar and rhinestone-bejewelled country-and-western band in the basement of the Catholic students' centre. Girls I'd seen all year in work boots, dungarees and T-shirts were out in high heels and little dresses that plunged towards their waists. They didn't dress like that when the big rock groups came through, or of course for us, but they did for seventy-five-year-old poets. I looked in vain for rhyme and metre, but couldn't find them. At those festivals, becoming a poetic adept seemed an investment in a kind of libidinal pension. One year I served as driver for Kenneth Rexroth, a godfather to the Beats. As we drove around Chicago he tried to instruct me in the appropriate techniques for picking up girls in various American cities. In Denver you had to do this, in Tampa, Florida that. 'But in Detroit,' he said, 'you just open the car door, reverse and *scoop 'em up*!'

In Berkeley College that afternoon Joan Didion spoke of California with an irony that fell as slowly and delicately as the red leaves in the quad beyond the window. She seemed almost too small and frail to sustain life. Just a little over two months later, with her only daughter critically ill in hospital, her husband of forty years – the writer John Gregory Dunne – took a sip of the whiskey she had brought him, put aside a history of the First World War he was reading and took a seat for dinner in their New York apartment, then suddenly fell over and died. Shortly afterwards, her daughter also died. She reeled into a prolonged, disorienting and life-draining grief and, much later, coughed it up onto the page.

I left Yale then and passed a man on a street corner delicately clearing something from his child's eye. In Valencia, my son was turning three on that day.

Back in the apartment I read in a newspaper that the Cubs were to open their series against the Florida Marlins that night to decide the National League championship. Much of the nation, it seemed from the report, was yearning for a World Series between the Cubs and the Boston Red Sox, who were at the time playing the New York Yankees for the American League title. The Yankees were rich and dynastic and hated in the way that Real Madrid is hated in Spain, while the Florida Marlins were historyless and played in a state full of golf courses and the retired, where baseball was as out of place as a double chin in a cosmetic-surgery ad. The Red Sox and Cubs, on the other hand, were seen as Cinderella teams – old-fashioned, unpretentious, inner-city urban, evocative of a now-unreachable era of communality, family and simple pleasures in which everyone knew more or less who they were. Their stands may have been packed with corporate ticket holders, futures traders and lawyers, but in a kind of mental mist people imagined instead freckle-faced boys eating peanuts, beer-drinking firemen and factory hands in T-shirts calling out insults to opposing players, and fathers and sons amplifying their intimacy through a common devotion to the national game. I'd loved both watching and playing baseball, but had lost track of it. Yet my interest had come back as if on a tide when I saw the Cubs play the Braves on the barroom television in New York. I dearly wanted to see the game that night. That couldn't be, however, for I was to have dinner with Jill Cutler, who had been my boss when I was teaching at Yale.

I got into a cab on Orange Street. The driver was garrulous and as vast as a phone box, sweat running down the back of his neck. He sensed something alien in my voice and asked me where I was from. I told him, then said I was living in Spain. He wanted to know all I could tell him about the life there. I told him about the *paseo*, the *terrazas*, the *fiestas*, the numerous occasions during the day when they eat or drink, the *siesta*—

'The what?' he said.

'The *siesta*.'

'Is that the dinner?'

'No,' I said. 'The *siesta* is a little sleep after lunch.'

'Oh, man,' he said. 'I want some of that.'

He drove off shaking his head at the fortunes of the Spanish, and I went into Jill's house. We had rice and chicken and beer in her kitchen. She told me that one of my former students had signed a six-figure deal for a book about NASCAR, a form of car racing that is the Wal-Mart of sport.

I asked her what she thought was the main political difference between now and when she had been a student.

'It's the passivity,' she said. 'The 2000 election was a bloodless coup that should have precipitated a constitutional crisis, but didn't. There's something sick in how we regard leadership now. I saw it articulated by a very bright student I had, a right-winger who went to work for Bush. He wrote a paper about an Australian sheep farmer he idolised. He said a leader is ideally a father figure who protects us by making decisions without referring to anyone else. There's a general admiration for that kind of thing now. It's as if we're too tired for democracy.'

She'd grown up Jewish in New York and even adolescence in suburban Washington hadn't dislodged her from the bohemian left, which she found young through her parents and still retains. She remembered her mother in a panic some time in the 1950s hiding her Woody Guthrie and Red Army Chorus records and the works of Karl Marx and Earl Browder, once head of the American Communist Party, after an FBI agent came to their house to enquire about a neighbour. She went to live in Greenwich Village as soon as she was free to do so. She was at a party there in the 1960s and Bob Dylan honed in on her like a heat-seeking missile. He put forward his proposition; she declined. She married a photographer and had twin girls. Dylan moved out of New York and had children of his own. She didn't see him after the party, nor had she known him before that. One day years afterwards she was waiting at a bus stop when a van with darkened glass pulled up. A window went down and Bob Dylan looked out from behind the steering wheel.

'Changed your mind?' he asked her.

She hadn't.

We went into a large room, the walls heavy with volumes of politics and poetry. She told me she was writing a biography of her body, through the clothes she had put on it. I asked her to read some of it to me. She went out and came back in spectacles and with a chapter called 'Babe in Black'. It was about a dress she wore on a date as a teenager with a cultivated Jewish boy named Arthur Martin. At twelve she'd seen a picture of Audrey Hepburn in a magazine in a dentist's office. She'd eaten peaches for weeks in search of Audrey Hepburn's delicacy, then fainted one day. It became an impossible quest with the ripening of adolescence, and her body, compared to Audrey Hepburn's, became an outsized, ungainly, alien thing, her shape, the way she walked and the volume of her laughter seeming to her ill-fitting and wrong. When Arthur Martin asked her out, she was stricken with a dark panic over what she might wear. She decided not to look like a beatnik, which is how she usually looked. She thought she should wear a dress, but there was only one in her wardrobe – a tight-fitting black one handed down from an aunt. It had a straight skirt and ten satin buttons down the front. Her mother thought it suitable only for funerals, but she went out in it anyway, thinking with every step that the world was somehow judging her ill. She got through dinner and then a concert, Brahms and Mozart at the Constitution Hall. They left in Arthur Martin's car and he drove directly to a shady place by the Jefferson Memorial, parking near other courting couples. There he managed to bedazzle her with the words 'Probably I shouldn't be doing this; we haven't known each other so long. But you look so good', then went through the satin buttons of her dress like a chef opening oysters. Afterwards, laughter came easier to her and her gait was less hemmed-in by self-consciousness. Audrey Hepburn went away into the vapour. The dress itself became a kind of aphrodisiac. 'It was a wonderful dress,' she read out to me, 'in which to have the sex one was permitted to have.'

On the way back I stopped at the Anchor Bar, a kind of earthbound liner with chrome, wood, portholes and crescent-shaped benches around the tables, owned by a woman named Kathleen for the past forty years. I met a young golf pro and his girlfriend, who were drinking brandies with crème de menthe. They seemed to have been doing so for hours.

'Where are you living?' I asked him.

'In my car,' he said.

The news came on the television over the bar. I waited for the sports part to come on. At Wrigley Field, in the first game of the play-off series, the Cubs had scored four runs in the first inning, but then needed to score two in the bottom of the ninth to tie the game. They managed that, but then lost by a single run in the eleventh.

'The road is life,' wrote Jack Kerouac. I was finally about to hit it in a rental car I was to pick up in the morning. The flat I was in had conventional plumbing, but also a shower in the back yard, which my welcome note had advocated that I try. I decided to do it. The pipes were mounted on the side of the stairs. The water drained through stones that, in their delicate grey colour, their roundness and the care with which they were positioned, suggested a Japanese garden. The curtain was an artificial tree. The dew on the grass was nearly frost. Each breath was imprinted on the air. I left my clothes in a little heap and stepped under the water. Steam flew up as if from the chimney stack of a foundry. The soap was made from mint. I felt the heat envelop my body and looked at the last yellow and red autumn leaves against the bright sky. Each pore seemed to sing. When I came out I felt so alert and so fresh that it was almost like love.

The rental agency of my car was on Crown Street. On the way I passed a café where in July 1994, when I was teaching at Yale, an instructor I knew was sitting with two friends when one of the unattended mad of New Haven, enraged because he couldn't find his mother in the hospital and thought she'd been kidnapped, pulled a knife from his pocket and began stabbing people. My friend made for the door, but was caught in the crush. He was stabbed in the lungs and spleen. Everyone who was attacked was saved by the Yale Hospital. I wondered what it could have been like. The heat of the assailant's body. His closeness and his speed. His animal breath and adrenaline and unstoppableness. His unanswerable blade. Like being savaged by a hyena. Closer than you'd ever want to be to a force so unequivocally and impersonally focused on your death, the smell of yourself as butchered meat.

My car was in a lot behind Louis' Lunch, where the hamburger was invented by Louis Lassen in 1900. This event is accepted generally in the way that saints' bones are accepted as relics after the Vatican confers beatification. The first hamburger was a disc of ground-beef between two slices of bread prepared as an improvisation for a man in a hurry. I looked inside. People must have been smaller in 1900. It seemed like a doll's house. Many hamburger-eaters now would not pass through the door, or fit their girths between the chairs and the tables. New Haven also claims the origin of that other world-conquering, multi-billion-dollar fast food, the pizza. But this is more dubious.

I went into a little hut in the car lot, where a man in a rental-agency uniform was reading a newspaper with a large picture of Arnold Schwarzenegger on it. He looked up at me over his glasses. 'Can you imagine mature adults going into a booth and voting for him?' he asked. I filled in the papers he gave me and he brought me to the car I would be in, for up to ten hours a day, as I made my way to San Francisco. My friend Don Faulkner had advised me to select a memorable vehicle. 'All the road books have them,' he said. 'Jazzy convertibles, Kesey's bus, Henry Miller's wreck, the adapted vans that Least Heat-Moon and Steinbeck slept in. It makes for a running theme. They're like pets.' I was to be in a pale beige Chevrolet. It had a CD player and a radio and no particular distinguishing features. As I write this I can remember nothing else about it apart from that it was quiet, reliable and by European standards spacious. I drove it a little tentatively across New Haven and then set off northwards, towards Albany, New York. I felt as I would if facing a night out with someone unknown to me, yet beguiling. 'Oh highway,' chanted Walt Whitman. 'You express me better than I can express myself!' What words would it give to me?

New York State

Lost in Albany, I came to a V in the road where a madman stood waving his arms and screaming at the cars moving away to either side of him. People leaned against walls, talking, smoking cigarettes, not noticing him. Pedestrians passed by him without looking up. Perhaps it was his regular station. Like a Roman traffic policeman he stood straight-backed and wore white gloves. American traffic policemen too evidently once had this imperious demeanour, for Arnold Bennett, in 1912, mistook one for an archduke. 'WELCOME TO URBAN RENEWAL,' the madman screamed at a car. 'HOW DO YOU LIKE IT?' Then to another, 'PUT ON YOUR TURN SIGNAL, YOU BOIL-FACED LIZARD!' I watched him for a while, parked and got out of the car. 'BRING BACK NAPALM!' he called to the sky.

He was standing in front of a statue in memory of soldiers who had fought in the Spanish–American War. I took the fork in the road to the right and walked along a row of shop fronts – Rapunzel's Hair Salon, a pawn shop, a couple of Indian restaurants, a liquor store, a place where you could get your hair braided and another where you could get your teeth plated in gold. There was a tattoo and body-piercing parlour with the designation TAT2 on its window, a Caribbean record shop and the Social Justice Center for Albany. It was a block of poverty management and body decoration in the main. I glanced back at the man. He was quiet now, his arms held back and his chest out as he looked ahead. He was like the figure on the prow of a ship, the cars like waves falling to either side of him.

I went into the Capitol Mini Mart and bought a ten-dollar

phone card from a North African working there. I called London and Spain from a public phone in the street and then had to go back into the store to buy another card. I was going to have to do something about phones, but I didn't know what. About one-third of the public phones I'd tried didn't work and if you wanted to call long-distance from one, you needed to have enough quarters in your pocket to drop you to the bottom of a lake. The cut-rate cards you buy in shops offered cheap calls from fixed-line private phones, but I rarely had access to one of those. The public phones, like nearly everything else in the United States, exist in a wilderness of deregulation with all the different companies charging and functioning differently. At one point I used a cut-rate card from a public phone and, after tapping in enough numbers to fill a school blackboard, a crisp, unforgiving female voice said, 'This phone is not in the database. Please call the Gemini Center.' What was that? Finally that afternoon in Albany I bought a mobile phone with a contract from T-Mobile. I didn't know then that I would only get coverage for about eight per cent of the land I was to cover between there and San Francisco because the company restricts its transmission masts mainly to interstate highways and cities. Much of rural America, I was to discover, has no access to broadband or to mobile telephones. The United States, the prime innovator of much nanotechnology and telecommunications, has fallen behind Asia and Europe in both of these areas.

I walked back to my car. On the way a young man of mixed race with angelic features, long ringlets in his hair and biceps that had split the seam of his shirt stopped me and said he'd just come out of the state penitentiary. Could I give him some money for a meal? he asked in a near-whisper. I gave him a couple of dollars and he rolled away, taking with him a story I'd never hear. As I thought of this I still had time to stop him, but didn't. There would be many others who would pass me by, unexamined, on the road ahead. The purgatory of unheard stories.

I got into my car and drove through downtown Albany,

over the Hudson River and east out Sand Lake Road towards Averill Park. A black man named Adam Blake, the son of a freed slave who had also been the town's most spectacular dandy, opened a hotel along here in 1878. Blake was first a waiter, then a steward at the Albany Club, and, after his business in Averill Park wound down, he moved back into the city and opened the Kenmore. It became immediately fashionable. Blake died in 1881, but the hotel went on. In the 1920s and '30s they were serving nine hundred lunches per day and, at night, in the Rain-Bo Room, up to five hundred formally dressed people would listen to Rudy Vallee, Cab Calloway, Frank Sinatra and Duke Ellington, among others, while Legs Diamond sat in a corner with six bodyguards and his girlfriend Kiki Roberts.

I was on my way to see William Kennedy, author of *Legs, Billy Phelan's Greatest Game* and *Ironweed*, with whom over a nine-year period I'd intermittently played pool. Our last game had been on a table in his living room, beside a fully equipped bar. Screenplays, movie rights and a MacArthur Foundation grant can make certain youthful dreams come true.

I'd driven out of New Haven in the late morning and then up through the Naugatuck and Farmington River valleys of Connecticut on Route 8. Route 8 is sometimes a country road and sometimes motorway, but it is never motorway of the landscape-scarring and homogenising type that is the American interstate, with its wide cuts, massive green signage, roaring trucks lit up like fairgrounds and long ramps at exits with clusters of gas-station, fast-food and hotel advertisements mounted on huge poles like bloated storks. From a car on an interstate, Utah can look not so very different from Pennsylvania. Everything around – desert, mountains, lakes, farms, human life – seems far away. I'd had the idea when young that these were the roads to use over long distances in America, not because of their safety or comfort or speed, but rather because it seemed that a country so vast and open should be devoured rather than tasted, that the point of travel in America was not in the detail, but in mobility itself. I'd changed in that. I wasn't on foot or two wheels, but I wanted to feel the country, to be in it rather than moving over it. The interstates were loud and monotonous and reductive of the spirit. You could already feel the tedium of a long journey in the first hour. I'd use the interstates at night or when I had to make up ground or when there was no other option. Otherwise I'd stay on the back roads. On Route 8 there were stone bridges and the genteel exit ramps turned into little folds in the woodland. Here was once farmland and industry. Seth Thomas made clocks in Thomaston and the Stanley Company made tools. The manufacture of brass in the nineteenth century nearly killed the Naugatuck River, but it survived and provided the name for Naugahide, a thick and unsubtle vinyl invented here that was used to cover sofas and was intended to suggest leather. Now the whole of Connecticut seems covered in trees, for life in this state is less rural than it is suburban. Yet it was enticing, nevertheless. All the way to Albany I was accompanied by a rich October light that flitted over the land when a high wind blew away the clouds or fell in tremendous concentrated shafts through the trees. There were wooden houses with wide porches set into the woodland, quiet ponds, sleeping dogs, scattered crimson leaves, all illuminated as though from within by this magnificent light.

Connecticut, from the Indian name Quinnehtukgut for the great tidal river that bisects it, has given itself the title 'The Constitution State'. I'm from Illinois, called 'The Land of Lincoln' even though Lincoln was born and raised in Kentucky. American states all have their colours and flowers and mascots and slogans, as though they were high-school football teams rather than regional tiers of government. 'We're not a bad people,' an old friend said to me the night before I left New Haven. 'But we're very naïve. It makes us seem childish sometimes.' Such boostering accoutrements are intended to generate a sense of local identity where often little or none is felt. People from Vermont or Texas may have no need for this, while those from Iowa or Florida might. Intense local connections are more rarely felt in a country not so many generations old and with such a high degree of itinerancy.

Connecticut is called 'The Constitution State' because its original charter was one of the models for the national Constitution, though the state constitution of Massachusetts was probably more influential because it articulated the separation of governmental power into its judicial, legislative and executive branches, a notion at least nominally fundamental to national governance. Those who wrote the Constitution consulted a lot of documents and sources – the Magna Carta, the English Bill of Rights of 1689, the writings of Charles de Secondat, Plato and various Romans and an Iroquois treaty made in 1520 that began with the words, 'We, the people . . .' They took their time. They knew that the Constitution, once ratified, would bring an entire nation instantly into being. The word would be made flesh, and for this the document would have to have a biblical definitiveness and authority, so much so that no individual government or vested interest could supersede it. And it was to last for ever. 'Government is not reason, it is not eloquence, it is force – like fire, a troublesome servant and a fearful master. Never for a moment should it be left to irresponsible action,' wrote George Washington. They wanted the document itself to be more powerful than any such force. Tom Paine said that Dr Johnson and others like him could not fathom the distinction between a constitution and a government. 'They could not but perceive,' wrote Paine, 'that there must necessarily be a controlling power existing somewhere, and they place this power in the discretion of the persons exercising the government, instead of placing it in a constitution formed by the nation. When it is in a constitution, it has the nation for its support, and the natural and controlling political powers are together. The laws which are enacted by governments, control men only as individuals, but the nation, through its constitution, controls the whole government, and has a

natural ability so to do. The final controlling power, therefore, and the original constituting power, are one and the
same power.'

Those who wrote the Constitution were boat builders,
businessmen, stock traders, government officials, both large
and small farmers. Many were lawyers, and many of these
had been trained in England. Of the thinking about the
Constitution and the writing of it, John Adams wrote, 'It will
never be pretended that any persons employed in that service
had interviews with the gods, or were in any degree under
the influence of Heaven, more than those at work upon ships
or houses, or labouring in merchandise or agriculture – it
will forever be acknowledged that these governments were
contrived merely by the reason and the senses.' God is
invoked in the Articles of Confederation and the Declaration
of Independence, but He appears nowhere in the
Constitution. The country had been rapidly populated by
opportunists, political exiles and the poor, but also by those
persecuted for their religious beliefs, many of whom, in
consequence, were inclined towards fundamentalism. There
had been attempts to create theocracies. This, the drafters
of the Constitution perhaps thought, could be a force as inimical to democracy as a foreign imperial power or vested
commercial interests. They insisted on a permanent,
unbreachable separation of Church and State. But most presidents since then, Lincoln no less than Reagan, but perhaps
none more than George W. Bush, seem to have had God
whispering in their ears. It can leave you longing sometimes
for more prosaic language.

Route 8 becomes country road again at Winsted and shortly
after that I left Connecticut and crossed into Massachusetts a
little way to the west of Springfield. Massachusetts was the
original religious utopia, or attempt at one, founded by Puritan
pilgrims fleeing England in advance of the Civil War. Their
intention was to establish their 'city upon a hill', as their
governor John Winthrop called it. This is a favourite phrase
of political speechwriters who want to give to their employers

a patina of high eloquence and a direct line to the eternal. By 'city upon a hill' they mean a place both visible and exemplary. But in the same tract in which this was written Winthrop also declared, 'We must be willing to abridge ourselves of our superfluities, for the supply of others' necessities. We must uphold a familiar commerce together in all meekness, gentleness, patience, and liberty. We must delight in each other, make others' condition our own, rejoice together, mourn together, labour and suffer together, always having before our eyes our commission and community in the work, as members of the same body.' The Puritans' 'city upon a hill' was not to be, as it happened, for it could not long withstand the forces of disputation, secularism and other religious traditions.

I thought of turning right on 57 to Springfield, but didn't. I mightn't get to Albany in daylight if I did. I was a little curious about Springfield, though, for it was the principal destination of émigrés from the Great Blasket, an island off the Dingle coast in the south-west of Ireland, and I'd read several books by writers from there. This little island of uneducated Irish-speaking peasants had for a time a per capita rate of literary production superior to that of Saint-Germain, Greenwich Village or Hampstead. Perhaps the most powerful of these books was written by a fisherman named Tomas O'Crohan. He was teaching Irish to an English scholar who encouraged him to write a book about his life. 'Why should anyone want to read about me?' O'Crohan asked. The scholar gave him a copy of Gorky's autobiography. 'I see,' he said when he had finished it, then wrote *The Islandman*, a record of a vanishing life, for eventually Springfield won and the island was deserted. Springfield had other curiosities. The frantically rhyming children's author Dr Seuss and the apostle of LSD Timothy Leary were born there. In the 1890s Dr James Naismith invented basketball as an invigorating off-season game for the young men of the city's YMCA. George Washington selected Springfield for the National Armory and its contents came to be known as Springfield rifles.

I turned west on US 20 into the Berkshire Hills, a perfectly bucolic, rolling landscape with grand Victorian mansions and immaculate villages that some say suggests the English Lake District. Sometimes 20 took me past the Massachusetts Turnpike, with its bellowing, thundering trucks. Three very different Americans lived for periods in this corner of Massachusetts. Norman Rockwell, whose paintings of small-town American family life were put on the covers of the *Saturday Evening Post* for more than forty years, lived in Stockbridge, which now has a museum devoted to him. Arlo Guthrie, son of Woody, came to Stockbridge for high school, and wrote 'Alice's Restaurant' about the house of one of his teachers. A long while later he bought the house where the story started and turned it into a non-denominational church. North of Stockbridge, at Arrowhead, Herman Melville wrote *Moby-Dick*, then had to leave when it didn't sell. Rockwell, Guthrie, Melville – the cosy, the dissenting, the biblically dark.

Rockwell painted grandfathers, Santa Claus, baseball games, turkey dinners, tomboys, the radiant certitudes of families as organically unified as an orchestra in mid-movement. The emotions depicted generally ranged from the mildly embarrassed at one end to the convivial at the other. The tragic, the individualistic or the ecstatic were rarely, if ever, seen. If he were an orchestra he would play Christmas carols or show tunes from *Easter Parade*. He was so enormously popular and present that he came to be definitive of a certain view of American life. Some say that he painted Americans as they like to see themselves. It might even be said that some Americans in part discovered how they saw themselves and their country through Rockwell's covers for the *Saturday Evening Post*. Others said that these were lies and the essence of kitsch. But Rockwell also painted the civil-rights movement and, under commission, the 'Four Freedoms', based on the speech by Franklin Roosevelt in which he described a world in which there would be freedom of speech, freedom to worship, freedom from want and freedom from fear. 'The fourth is freedom from fear,' he said, 'which, translated into world terms, means a world-wide reduction of armaments to such a point and in such a thorough fashion that no nation will ever be able to commit an act of physical aggression against any neighbour, anywhere in the world.' He thought all this plausible 'in our time'. He was nearly right. The invention of the atomic bomb and the power it gave to the United States set the last of these freedoms back, but the idea was revived in the early 1960s, when officials from the Khrushchev and Kennedy administrations drew up an agreement to destroy offensive weapons, withdraw all armies back to within national borders and make it legally and logistically impossible for any nation to attack any other. It was at the point of being signed, but then collapsed. Gorbachev made a similar proposal, but it was to Ronald Reagan, an enthusiast for weaponry that was by then going galactic. It is difficult to imagine anyone even on the left of the Democratic Party putting all these principles together in a single speech now. But in 1943 the US Treasury took the speech and Rockwell's paintings on a tour of the nation and the Office of War Information printed 2.5 million copies. Sixty thousand Americans wrote Rockwell letters about the Four Freedoms.

William Kennedy once believed he loathed Albany, and that when he left he'd never come back to live there again. He paid a visit once and found it no more alluring than it had been. Then he was in Puerto Rico, writing a novel that was set there. Instead of letting himself be taken by the tropical winds and the words that were meant to describe them, he found himself staying at home looking at a book of old photographs of Albany, the city quickening into unlikely life within him. He let the novel go. 'I cared more about the shape of the ball returns in the Knights of Columbus alleys in Albany,' he later wrote. He was called home to family business and got a temporary job on the local paper writing about the city neighbourhood by neighbourhood – their histories, ethnic compositions, people. The fascination that was awakened in Puerto Rico acquired detail, characters, shape and story. He moved back and stayed, writing the city he had entrapped as a child and as a journalist into nine novels, two works of non-fiction and a play. It is his only setting, his only subject. Other American writers have displayed a strong sense of place, but very few such an exclusive one. His 'imagination', he has said, 'has become fused with a single place, and in that place finds all the elements that a man ever needs for the life of the soul'.

I had a late game of straight pool with him after an Italian dinner. His wife Dana was there too, a former dancer he'd met more than forty years before in Puerto Rico. He was like a praying mantis over the ball, body low to the table, elbows up, his face lean and taut as he bore down on the shot. Before dinner in a game of eight ball he'd snicked in seven balls to my two, then scratched on an ambitious attempt at the eight ball. There'd been a lot of wine at the dinner. Standards had dropped. The play was sodden, clumsy. Balls missed by half a foot. Dana said she'd see us in the morning. I had another beer from his bar and then missed a straight shot into the side pocket. 'Someone said that even a single glass of sherry is detectable in a written sentence,' I said. 'Do you think the same could be true of pool?' He tried a straight shot down the rail. It rattled in the pocket and stayed out, but the cue ball following behind stayed on its course and dropped. 'Evidently,' he said. We were going to play to fifty, but shortened it to twenty-five so that we could get to bed at some point. 'What do you think of our present government?' I asked him. He took aim. 'They're only good at plunder,' he said, then banged the ball across the length of the table smartly into the corner pocket.

In the morning at breakfast he told me about a woman named Huybertie Hamlin, née Pruyn, whom he'd interviewed in 1963. She was ninety at the time. Her Albany lineage went back to Brandt Aertsz van Slechtenhorst in the mid-seventeenth century when Albany was a Dutch settlement called Fort Orange ruled over by an aristocratic figure called the Patroon. In 1656 Dutch trappers killed thirty thousand beavers there, and the city still has places named after this animal once so sought after by the makers of hats. Huybertie grew up in a world of maids and summering by the sea and coming-out balls in which Yankees were still disdained as interlopers. J.P. Morgan and Matthew Arnold were dinner guests at her home. Also Lady Raleigh, who ate a peanut, including the shell, for the first time there, then advised her son, 'Don't try one. They're nasty things.' Once, when Huybertie was a child, she and her mother called in to see her aunt and found Herman Melville there drinking Madeira. They were toasting Melville's forthcoming book, *John Marr and Other Sailors*, a total of twenty-five copies of which were printed. He asked her about her history class and when Huybertie told him she was studying Paul Revere, he said that his grandfather had been among the 'blue-eyed Indians' at the Boston Tea Party. His grandfather's wife, with a sense for the occasion, collected tea leaves from his pockets and trouser cuffs and put them in a bottle. They are now in a museum in Boston. In William Kennedy's kitchen I was just four steps away from the opening day of the American Revolution.

Before I left he sat under a photograph of himself, Gabriel García Marquez and Fidel Castro taken in Cuba and signed a copy of his book *O Albany!* for me. Positioned just behind García Marquez's head in the picture was an ornament with spikes, making him look like a punk with a Mohican. I saw too a newspaper which said that the Cubs had won their game 12–3. They'd split the two games at Wrigley Field and would be travelling to the Pro Players Stadium in Florida for the next three. If Florida won all of them, they would be going to the World Series and the Cubs would be finished for the year. *O Albany!*, subtitled *Improbable City of Political Wizards, Fearless Ethnics, Spectacular Aristocrats, Splendid Nobodies and Underrated Scoundrels*, is William Kennedy's non-fiction evocation of the city, taking in past and present, high and low, virtually inch by inch. I have it open beside me on a rainy day in Valencia as my principal guide other than memory to Albany, but at the time I was there I knew next to nothing about this capital city of New York. I would have a couple of hours that morning before moving on, and asked him what he thought I should see.

'Take a walk around downtown. In the 1960s this area barely registered a pulse. Commerce was moribund and the people had deserted it. There were a few once-grand hotels, which came to be filled with the lost and the elderly. That was the worst feeling for me, to see the city like that. Then, when Nelson Rockefeller was governor, he expropriated ninety-eight acres there and built the South Mall, a vast, monumental administrative centre. And the city has been renovating and upgrading itself since then. Lumber, pigs, cattle, riverboat and commercial traffic have all come and gone and now the city is again remaking itself as a nanotechnology centre. The state university here has put in place a $450-million research department in this field. It looks like what happened to Austin, Texas will happen here. The old Arsenal is being turned into a centre for new technology business. They're building apartments for technocrats. Dove Street is one example of many where this has happened. I have a house at number sixty-seven where I wrote a couple of books. Legs Diamond was shot in it in 1931.'

Henry Hudson, having travelled up the river that had many names until it was finally named for him, got to what is now Albany in 1609 and was given a meal of pigeon and dog by Indians there. 'The natives are a very good people,' he recorded in his journal, 'for when they saw that I would not remain, they supposed that I was afraid of their bows, and taking the arrows, they broke them in pieces, and threw them into the fire.' The Indians called this place Penpotawitnot. Dutch traders named it Beverweyk and later Fort Orange. The English took it and in 1664 named it after the Duke of York and Albany.

The water at Albany determined not just its history, but also that of the country generally. Beaver pelts could be portaged, but prior to the railroad the great mineral, timber and agricultural wealth that lay inland could only reach markets, ports and the world beyond by water. Some speculators among the English settlers thought that the route to the Atlantic would be by the St Lawrence River and established themselves to the north of the Great Lakes. The other routes were the Mississippi, Hudson Bay and the Hudson River. Empires fought over who would control them. The last of these routes, the Hudson River, which ended upriver via the splendidly named Opalescent River at the cul-de-sac of Lake Tear in the Clouds in the Adirondack Mountains, was the least promising, but there was already a proposal in 1699 to construct a link that would connect the Hudson via the Mohawk River valley to the Great Lakes. The intersection was at Albany. This valley, a glacial meltwater, divided the Appalachian range into the Catskills and the Adirondacks and was the only cut in the mountains north of Alabama. The land rose six hundred feet from Albany to Lake Erie and the route would need at least fifty locks to make it navigable. Thomas Jefferson thought the idea preposterous, but a man named Jesse Hawley, who'd gone broke due to transport costs in the region, wrote fourteen eloquent and impassioned essays under the name of Hercules in defence of a canal from his cell in a debtors' prison. DeWitt Clinton, the governor of New York, read them and was persuaded. Among his supporters was Billy James, one of Albany's richest citizens and the grandfather of Henry and William James. He was so rich that he became known as the Patroon and when he died in 1832 left an estate of $3 million. Henry later wrote, 'We were never in a single case, I think, for two generations, guilty of a stroke of business.'

The Erie Canal took eight years to build, from 1817 to 1825. In the end it required eighty-three locks. One thousand men died from fever at the Montezuma Swamp west of Syracuse. New methods of clearing, digging and leak prevention had constantly to be invented. An eighty-foot wall of dolomitic limestone known as the Niagara Escarpment had to be crossed to get to Lake Erie. They did it with locks, an aqueduct and blasting, and without a civil engineer, for there were no civil engineers in the United States at the time. Instead, the overseers of the canal's construction were a maths teacher, a judge who had done some surveying to settle land disputes and a young enthusiastic amateur who went to England at his own expense to investigate how they were building canals there. When it was finished and operating, transport costs from Buffalo to New York City dropped to one-twentieth of what they had been. Western New York became rapidly populated. Albany boomed. The Adirondacks were cleared of trees and the city became known as the White Pine Centre of the World. Guitars made of Adirondack spruce became prized in Europe. Cattle and pigs flooded in on their way south and east to markets. Pigs wandered the streets acting as garbage collectors. In 1854 city officials rounded up fifteen thousand of them. Universities and other institutions developed departments for the training of engineers. The German masons who came to make the walls and locks stayed after the work was finished and built some of the most notable buildings in the world. The Irish navvies who had done the digging extended westwards along the water route, populating cities and creating political machines. The produce of America moved along it, rather than the St Lawrence River. Had it been the other way, as those English settlers had been expecting, Montreal would have been the centre for both export and European immigration. Instead it was New York, and a great surge in money and power and population went to the United States rather than to Canada. A three-foot eel was the first living thing through the lock at Albany. DeWitt Clinton, who had been the administrative power who made it happen, died in his home there three years after the canal was opened, owing $6,000. He turned up later on the federal tax stamp that sealed American cigarette packets. His canal, beaten into commercial obsolescence by railroads, trucks and the finally triumphant St Lawrence Seaway, is now used only by people who are in their boats for fun rather than money.

I got into Albany, parked my car and walked over to Dove Street to see where Legs Diamond had been shot. Albany had been from the beginning a city open to the louche pleasures. In 1653 a Dutch poet named Nicasius de Sille wrote, 'They all drink here, from the moment they can lick a spoon.' Years later, an uncle of William Kennedy told him, 'The last time I refused a drink I didn't understand the question.' There were slot machines in grocery stores, crap games in back alleys, casinos, numbers and horse-playing in bars. The plastic billiard ball was first manufactured in Albany. Figures out of Damon Runyon scurried around the streets of Nighttown until the dawn drove them home. During Prohibition there were speakeasies everywhere, the Downtown area was filled with cabarets and burlesque houses where you could see such spectacles as the 'Dance of Enticement' and, as William Kennedy writes in *O Albany!*, '. . . down Broadway and up State Street and over Eagle Street and up Hudson Avenue, up Colombia to North Pearl, up Broadway to Little Harlem, down Green Street into an entanglement of back alleys and shadowy streets where you could make your fortune for the week in a blind-pig game, or lose your dignity or virginity with Big Betty, or if she wasn't how you wanted to lose whatever it was you needed to lose, you could try Madge Burns's house, or Little Read's, or Davenport's, which was the expensive place, five dollars a shot. So they say.'

You could get anything you wanted in Albany, but not everyone was allowed to supply it. Dutch Schultz, one of the most prominent of the Prohibition-era gangsters in the eastern United States, was turned away at the train station when he wanted to lie low for a while in Albany, even though the request for sanctuary came from the then head of Tammany Hall in New York City. Legs Diamond, known primarily for hijacking other gangsters' moonshine and beer, was allowed for a while to relax in Albany, but when he let it be known that he wanted to start a protection racket and beer operation, one of the toughest detectives on the Albany force told him he'd be shot if he tried.

In the era of the gangster and for decades afterwards the supreme power in the city at every level was the Democratic Party political machine, run from 1920 until his death in 1977 by Daniel O'Connell, who, through a system of patronage, vote-rigging, largesse and a natural display of the common touch, created an organisation impervious to national, state, corporate or organised criminal influence that endured far longer than any other of its kind in America. I had grown up thinking that Chicago under Mayor Daley was the world's paradigm for the political machine until I read in William Kennedy's book how far it had been outstripped by what O'Connell did in Albany. He put in place three mayors, the last of whom, Erastus Corning, served eleven consecutive terms from 1941 to 1983, longer than any other mayor in United States history. O'Connell left school in the sixth grade, worked in a brickyard and in his father's bar and kept five hundred fighting chickens. One night he won $65,000 in a chicken fight in Troy, just outside of Albany. Corning was a Yale graduate, scion of a city dynasty and bon viveur said to have an effect on a room like that of Joe DiMaggio. Newspapers, Republicans, state investigators, reformers and activists tried to break or at least hobble their machine. None could. It was in the gift of this machine to determine who benefited from the gambling dens, speakeasies and brothels, and it was generally only extended to Democratic Party loyalists, rather than gangsters. And they had a police force hard and loyal enough to enforce this.

Dove and the streets around it are tree-lined with well-appointed town houses and terraces and the kinds of corner restaurants, delicatessens and specialised laundries favoured by people with money who prefer the urban to the suburban. I stood in front of number sixty-seven, which looked as closed and lifeless and turned away from the world as a pub out of hours. The Historic Albany Foundation had put a plaque on it commemorating the killing there of Legs Diamond. He had been charged with torturing a truck driver who was hauling hard cider and, when he was on trial in Troy, he booked under the name of Kelly into a rooming house at this address with a small entourage that included his wife. He was thirty-one, an habitué of fashionable bars, the most glamorous of the eastern gangsters, a subject for gossip columnists as well as crime reporters. He was, after all, supplying Americans with what the majority of them wanted. He could be casually cruel. He gave away copies of Rabelais' *Gargantua and Pantagruel* to friends. He moved in a world where enemies were easily made and where no one could be trusted.

Legs Diamond beat his charge in Troy, then came to Albany for a party at a speakeasy across from the railroad station. From there he went to an apartment where his mistress, Kiki Roberts, was staying, then went back to Dove Street and got into bed, drunk and alone. At five-thirty in the morning two men came in and three bullets were put into Legs Diamond's head. Criminals bragged about knowing who had done it. Others made accusations or put forward theories. Nothing, however, has been verifiably established about who did it or why. William Kennedy, who wrote a novel about Legs, spent more time than most thinking and asking questions about the killing. He found evidence from more than one source – one of them being Daniel O'Connell – that Diamond had been warned by the police to get out of town, and hadn't. He also found a retired reporter who'd seen Diamond's corpse before the police arrived. He wouldn't say who had told him where it was, but his office was next to police headquarters and detectives often gave him privileged information. Diamond might have been shot by William Fitzpatrick, the detective who had told him to leave town and who later was Albany's Chief of Police until he, too, was shot in the head, in his case by a friend and fellow detective. The Wild West, perhaps, lived on into the 1930s in Albany, but instead of Wyatt Earp there was the Democratic Party machine and its armed wing in the police force.

Ninety-eight acres of houses like those in Dove Street were expropriated by Nelson Rockefeller and then torn down to make way for the South Mall, or, as it is now known, the Rockefeller Empire State Plaza. He commissioned Wallace Harrison, whom he believed to be the greatest architect of the twentieth century, then showed him a drawing he made on an envelope inspired by the palace of the Dalai Lama in Tibet. He told him that that was the effect he wanted. There was a precedent in Albany for such grandeur. The state capitol building, designed by three teams of architects, including one led by the great H.H. Richardson, was modelled on the Hôtel de Ville in Paris, opened in 1899 when Teddy Roosevelt was governor, having cost $25 million. This made it the most expensive building in the United States. The Empire State Plaza is also said to achieve an ultimacy of degree in architecture by being the largest marble project ever undertaken in the history of the world. It is set on a kind of vast plinth five levels deep from which rise five blank, pitiless-looking towers, a performing-arts centre called the Egg, a trapezoid and a low marble building a quarter of a mile long, all of it surrounded by gardens and looking down on the city. It took years to finance and build and its story is one of kickbacks, thievery, arson and featherbedding, without a single arrest ever being made for any of it – 'one of the most perfectly designed perpetual opportunity machines in the history of boondogglery', as William Kennedy put it. In the end it cost just under $2 billion. I don't imagine that West Virginia, Utah or even Texas think on such a scale about their political monuments, but perhaps they do. It's a difficult spectacle to warm to. Robert Hughes in *The Shock of the New* declared it an example of 'an architecture of coercion', and said it could have been decorated with a swastika or hammer and sickle, without either being out of place. What might Rockefeller have said to this? There is a photograph of him in a room full of people, leaning forward over a microphone with a gleefully vicious smile as he thrusts his arm out and raises his middle finger to the crowd.

Eleven hundred and fifty buildings were destroyed to make Rockefeller's monument, most of them in the south Albany district known as the Gut, a one-time red-light area that had declined into, as William Kennedy describes it, a 'bedroom community for a generation of solitaires: family outcasts, night-shift nurses, semi-affluent winos, motherless gays, dishwashers aspiring to be short-order cooks, horse players doing their level best to die broke, closet hookers and other functionaries and freelancers of Nighttown who got around to putting their heads on their greasy pillows just as the sun was coming up', the types here shading through detail into implied life stories. I can think of no other city of comparable size with a chronicler so knowledgeable, so inclusive and so artful.

I left Albany and went south on Interstate 87 through the Hudson Valley. The concentration of old wealth and power grows more dense the further south one goes along the river. Vanderbilt, Roekefeller and Roosevelt family mansions are to the south of Kingston, the old state capital, and beyond Poughkeepsie is the West Point Military Academy. Bob Dylan had ambitions as a boy to go there. He thought he'd like to be a general. He never made it, but he did live for a time in Woodstock, upriver from there. That's where I was going. It was fifty miles or so from Albany, the shortest drive between stops I'd make on the entire journey.

When there was industry here, factories dumped chemicals into the river legally. General Electric poured the highly toxic polychlorinated biphenyls into it liberally and under licence for thirty years. A river that the folk singer Pete Seeger said once contained sturgeon you could spear at twelve feet, and from which caviar was once exported, became lethal. But most of the industry was now gone and, helped by the Clean Water Act, the river revived. William Least Heat-Moon came up it during his journey across America by boat, and in *River Horse* he lists some of the fish now swimming in the Hudson: 'stonerollers, horny-head chubs, comely shiners, margined madtoms, northern hogsuckers, hogchokers, short-head redhorses, four-beard rocklings, mummichogs, naked gobies, striped searobins, slimy sculpins and – more rarely – oyster toadfish, gags, lookdowns, four-eye butterfly fish, northern stargazers, freckled blennies, fat sleepers, and whole classes of bowfins, anchovies, needlefish, pipefish, silversides, jacks, wrasses, puffers, and flounders (left-eyed or right-eyed)'.

I came off 87 at the exit for Veteran and Saugerties and followed 212 into the Catskills. In West Saugerties is Big Pink, the house where The Band made *Music from Big Pink* and they and Bob Dylan recorded *The Basement Tapes*. Dylan was there after his motorcycle accident, slowing down his music and his life from the frenzy that had preceded it, when every show that he and The Band did had 'seemed like the end of the world'. He'd arrive at this house during the slower time in the morning before the rest of them were up, make a pot of coffee and write songs as quickly as if they were grocery lists. Then they'd record them in the basement. Long before that, before he knew how to write songs, he sat in his little apartment in New York studying the Kurt Weill–Bertolt Brecht collaborations and the works of Rimbaud, Woody Guthrie and Robert Johnson, writing them out on scraps of paper, seeing what was left out, placing the lines in a different order, trying to understand how the structure was formed and where they got their power, like a medical student with a cadaver. When he found out how to do it himself he couldn't, or at least didn't, stop. Joan Baez said that when they were together in Big Sur, songs came out of him 'like tickertape'.

The road wound through forest land and I pulled over for a moment to look at it. The leaves were wet from a brief rain. A breeze stirred the branches. Water moved through a stream, the rocks clicking like billiard balls. The leaves were orange as pumpkins, red as embers. Beads of rainwater moved over their veins and then fell, shafts of sunlight catching them. The road ran on before me like a body uncoiling from sleep, there was the whoosh of a bird's wings, a flash of blue as it flew beneath the branches, vines twisting around fence posts. All around the woodland floor, moss-covered boulders and tree trunks lay around like drunks after a party. I went on, passing a golf course, and then was in Woodstock.

Woodstock is strung out along a small section of 212 in a mixture of the New Age, the politically left and the bohemian, as well as shops, restaurants and hotels for those who like the gently bucolic at the weekends. A didgeridoo player was blowing into his pipe on the green. Just beyond it a woman in a long skirt was standing at the side of the road with her thumb out. She was the first hitch-hiker I saw since I arrived, and would be the last. I stopped for her and she got in.

Her name was Muffy. She was angular, deep-voiced and terse, with fast, bird-like movements. I didn't know if the terseness was because she was tough or troubled, or some other thing. She was a waitress sometimes and had sung in bands that never arrived where they were aiming. People were just getting in for the weekend. The traffic crept. We passed clothes shops, galleries, shops selling crystals and meditation guides. 'For a hundred years there have been what you could call "experiments in living" here,' she said. 'Some more interesting than others.' We passed a photography gallery that had been a café in the 1960s. 'Bob Dylan had a room above it,' she said. She told me he'd worked part-time at a place called Maggiore's Farm. Van Morrison, Jimi Hendrix and Janis Joplin had all lived here, but the legendary music festival of 1969 happened sixty miles away at Bethel. Even then Woodstock was a kind of brand name. Bethel Nation didn't resonate.

Muffy was just going a few miles along the road to Bearsville, and when we got there I hadn't heard enough of the stories I thought she could tell me.

'Do you want to eat something with me later?' I asked her.

'Yes,' she said. 'All right.'

We made the arrangements.

'Where did Bob Dylan fall off his motorcycle?' I asked.

'Just up this road, I believe,' she said, and then went into her house. That might have been a guess. I later read a different account that suggested it happened on the other side of Woodstock, on the Zena Road, south of 212. But that might also be wrong. I was unlikely to be able to ask the accident victim. I went where Muffy had directed, trying to imagine this moment when his work began its movement from electrified surrealism to parable, country and the extolling of the pleasures of family life here in this little town.

I was to pass my first night of the trip thus far in a hotel, and drove back to Woodstock to look for one. One after another was full, but I finally got into one with little cabins set among trees. The room was made of unvarnished planks. I turned on the television, sat down. There was a story on the news about the arrest of a young black girl from Brooklyn who had a twenty-three-month-old child and a job at Wendy's. She left her child in the care of a fifteen-year-old girl from her neighbourhood, who then kidnapped him. A man who had seen the child's picture on television noticed him and the babysitter on a train platform. He called out and the girl ran away. The child was restored to his mother, and then the police arrested her for negligence. There followed a story about how a couple was suing the National Football League because their son drank fourteen bottles of beer at a game. Lots of work for the law graduates. The Cubs, the news programme then announced, would be playing the third game of their series against the Marlins that evening.

I went back to Bearsville to get Muffy and we ate eastern Mediterranean food at Joshua's Café in the centre of Woodstock. The town has a population older, whiter, wealthier, better educated and politically more to the left than most others in the state, and tends to draw from a similar social stratum at the weekends. I watched them as they strolled the pavements, white-haired, pink-faced, dressed from an outdoors-wear catalogue, genially enjoying themselves and anticipating their weekends. There hadn't been a murder or rape in years and only a single robbery. They had safety, contemporary art, theatre and music, bonhomie, woodlands and mountains and looked as if they knew and appreciated it. There were clicking glasses, robust greetings and bursts of laughter around us as Muffy told me about Woodstock.

'This was all open farmland not so long ago,' she said. 'Mainly dairy farms. There would have been few trees, though it may look like virgin forest now. There was quarrying and tanning also. Tanning needs water and hemlock bark, and they had both here. There was a whole forest of hemlock. Hides were shipped from California and South America. A lot of Irish came after the Famine and worked in the quarries. Others worked on the waterways from the reservoirs and they were called sandhogs. They cut ice from the Hudson too and sent it down to New York on trains. This is named Ulster County because of them. Do you know about Byrdcliffe?'

'No,' I said.

'It was an Arts and Crafts movement that came up here in 1903.' She looked at me expectantly.

'You might be surprised at how little I know about America.'

'Ralph Whitehead and Jane Byrd McCall, his wife, started it. He was from a brewing family in England. She was the daughter of the mayor of Philadelphia. One of her ancestors was William Byrd, the founder of Virginia. She'd gone to Europe when she was young and studied under John Ruskin. She also knew William Morris. She was very influenced by them, and also by Emerson, about the idea of a simple life, close to nature, surrounded by beautiful music and beautiful things. They bought land here and invited furniture makers, metal workers, ceramic and textile craftsmen to come up and live with them. They also invited intellectuals, musicians, artists. My family came too. My grandmother was Jane's sister. They wanted more people to come from New York for weekends. They thought churches might attract them.

My grandfather built the first Catholic church in Woodstock. But mainly they were artists, bohemians. It wasn't easy for the people living here. They were farmers, very conservative, easily shocked. Isadora Duncan came and danced on their lawns at four in the morning.'

'What happened to it?'

'Well, it faded away. Is there anything that doesn't? But because of what it established, the artists kept coming here. Charlie Chaplin came to develop ideas for films. And of course all the musicians in the Sixties. Some of them stayed on after that. I saw Rick Danko and Paul Butterfield a few years ago playing in a bar. The barman told them to shut up. And the music was really glorious. They have to live with casual insults from fools. Garth Hudson, the organist from The Band, just an innocent, brilliant, talented man, had his instruments stolen. He was homeless for a while. They're surrounded by counter-culture capitalists, helpless beings who attach themselves to them and bleed them for drug money. Lesbians go from rock star to rock star, have their children and take their money. These are the kinds of people who are closest to them. The rest of the world begins to look a little twisted.'

We went out into the street. She told me there was a full-moon drum-circle gathering going on in the meadow up in the mountain. 'I don't know what you'd think of it,' she said. 'But at the very least it's harmless.'

We drove out of town and up the Rock City Road. She pointed out a Tibetan monastery set back in the trees. Then we parked, and set off on a winding, hilly path through the woods.

'This is Byrdcliffe land,' she told me. 'They handed it over on the understanding that it would be kept open for anyone who would like to use it. These people meet here every month on the night of the full moon, apart from a few of the winter months. They mightn't have anywhere to go without the Byrdcliffe provision. They get chased off land all over the country. Landowners and police have built walls of sand and trucked up tons of chicken manure to block roads and keep them off land. They're utterly immaculate. They clean up every matchstick when they're finished. They control the noise, advise new visitors about local parking regulations. You couldn't have better guests.'

People moved along the dark pathway with coolers and firewood. I could hear guitars and drums and some soft singing. Ahead was a meadow. The mountainside glowed yellow and orange from a bonfire. I could feel its heat, smell marijuana on the currents of air it pushed along.

In the meadow drummers sat in the grass beating out a gentle rhythm around the bonfire. There were around a hundred people there scattered among tents, blankets and smaller fires, smoking, singing, drinking, talking. They were in carnival wear, stripes, polka dots, glittering waistcoats, billowing trousers like those of clowns, cool blue-white moonlight on their faces, or firelight. The youngest were infants, the oldest in their seventies. There seemed to be no mystical or political purpose to it. It was just a party, held under the moon.

Muffy knew several of them and moved around from group to group. I sat down in the grass and listened to a song. A young man told me that he had been born on a commune in Oregon. His brothers and sisters had names like Sirius, Freedom and Tawort, Egyptian goddess of child-birth. They had lived in tents, school buses, improvised shacks, abandoned office buildings and numerous homes of friends and relatives in British Columbia, Toronto, Montana, Chicago and Woodstock, with barely, he said, a cross word ever uttered among them.

'Do you work?' I asked him.

'I'm doing some part-time gardening now. I do computer work sometimes too. I like to keep moving, though. These kinds of gatherings happen all over America – Vermont, Ohio, over in Massachusetts, California, Washington state. That's my community, really.'

Some children follow their parents into banking, plumbing,

the theatre or professional baseball; others, it seems, into transcendentalism and the brotherhood of itinerancy.

'Do you know what happened in the Marlins–Cubs game this evening?' I asked him.

'Yeah, I heard it on the radio. The Cubs won 5–4 in the eleventh inning. It was an intense game. Are you a Cubs fan?'

'I was, and it seems I am again. So much so that my nerves might have been wrecked by an eleventh-inning game.'

'They're a cool team,' he said. 'I hope they go all the way.'

Muffy and I came down off the mountain and had a couple of beers in an empty bar in town. She was forced by regulations to go outside to have a cigarette and was furious about it. 'It's a question of freedom,' she said.

'I suppose,' I said. 'But then there's also the freedom to have a drink without your eyes burning and being made nauseous by clouds of smoke.'

'Look, if people don't like it they can go outside to drink. You're supposed to be able to do what you want here. That's the basic idea of America. But there's people spending all their time trying to find ways to stop you.'

She looked like she wanted to put her cigarette out in my eye.

Economic libertarians, preachers, civil-rights activists, racists, advertisers, hippies, soul singers, radio talkshow hosts and politicians about to launch invasions all invoke freedom as their fundamental principle. The word always has a different stress and tone from the words around it in whichever sentence it appears. It is meant to be absolute, a priori, unassailable, and to reflect well on the person saying it. There's nearly always a sense of righteousness propelling the word from the speaker. Nowhere is this word heard more often than in the United States, where there is probably more of it than in other places – behaviourally, domestically, socially, psychologically. Social mobility can be more rapid than elsewhere. Class inhibits less. '*And there is no class*,' wrote John Butler Yeats from New York to a friend. 'You have to come to America to find out the blessedness of those words.' You can for the most part pray where you want and say what you want. But it is also clear that none of the above list of people could pursue their individual or collective freedom absolutely without quickly running into the freedom of one or more of the others. But further discussion of this was only likely to aggravate Muffy more. I watched her finish her cigarette, then we went back into the bar.

'You've had the history and you've had the tour,' she said when we were back on our stools. 'What about you?'

I gave her a very brief synopsis. It seemed I was in the wrong place, as if I'd climbed up from the audience onto the stage.

'Did you grow up here?' I asked her when I finished.

'I grew up in Mexico. My mother was looking for something there, in the nature, the culture, the ancient Indian religions. I'm not sure what it was. Maybe she picked this up from Byrdcliffe. She didn't find it, I would say. She was never easy. We lived all over the place. There was a lot of chaos. I had a hole in my appendix when I was a baby and, because it wasn't diagnosed, I was given phenobarbital to stop me from screaming. I grew up faster, perhaps, than I should have. I had a radio programme when I was ten. I was called Tinkerbell.'

I drove her back to Bearsville. She got out and stood by the car window.

'That was nice,' she said.

'Yes,' I said. 'Thank you. What's next for you?'

'I don't know. I've got to leave here by the middle of next week.'

'Why?'

'I can't make the rent.'

'But where will you go?'

'I don't know,' she said. 'I'll be all right.' She walked to her door and waved. 'Good luck!' she said.

A friend of mine in England, heir to a landowning and vastly rich entrepreneurial family and himself in the margins of the academic world, once enumerated all his failures in business. 'When a family begins to fall,' he said, 'nothing can stop it.' Muffy's had gone from the mayoralty of Philadelphia to elegant bohemianism, to a desperate search for enlightenment and finally to homelessness, each generation seeming to unwittingly contaminate the next. How could she leave without knowing where she was going? With what? Was there anyone to help her? Not I, evidently.

When I got back to my hotel I found much of the town there, steaming the windows, gyrating to music, spilling out onto the pavement and in among the trees with their drinks. This was Woodstock's latest-opening bar. I went in and made my way through air thick with sweat and breath. While I was waiting at the bar to order my drink, a round man in a bright checked shirt and skin so scrubbed it shone shouted, 'How'ya doin'?' Americans will resort to this if nothing else comes to mind. An English friend of mine living in New York finds this invasiveness intolerable. It's at its worst on planes, he says, where you can't escape. They often ask where you're from. If you name a town they'll say, 'Well, what do you know, my cousin once had the Buick dealership there,' and then beam at you as if that's the beginning of a friendship. The next question is, 'And what do you do for a living?' He has an answer ready for that one. 'I'm a worker in the sex industry,' he says. That, he says, usually sends them back to their in-flight magazine. I, being American, usually don't mind this. I turned to the man in the checked shirt. Next to him was his wife. They were up from New York City for the weekend. 'We're Republicans,' he beamed. 'An endangered species in this town!' I hadn't met any yet, so I thought I should ask them something.

'What is the biggest change in this country you've noticed over the past ten years?' I said.

'I like to look on the bright side,' the man said. 'And I would say that the biggest change is that people are taking less drugs.'

'The biggest change I've noticed is that my fifteen-year-old son feels perfectly calm saying, "Fuck you, Mom,"' his wife said. 'That was beyond imaginable when I was his age. The other thing is that more people have their hands out for benefits. Especially these veterans coming back from Iraq.'

This last complaint surprised me, but it is nevertheless consistent with her party's policy, as they have proposed to cut $15 billion in veterans' pension, medical, education, rehabilitation and housing benefits over ten years. In a single year they cut $900 million in medical benefits alone. There are twenty-eight million veterans in the United States. As with long-established companies with heavy pension obligations, it is a serious burden for the state. But it is not such an easy policy to sell when so many of the psychological and medical problems are the result of service in wars. A Pentagon official has said that these benefits are harmful to national security because the money could more usefully be spent on buying weapons. Those advocating the continuance of these benefits would, by implication, be unpatriotic, it would seem.

There was a pool table in a corner and I walked over to try to get a game. A young Englishman was seeing off everyone with despatch. Games were over in minutes. His eye was like a laser, though he seemed less than sober. A friend of his in a silk scarf who had a Dorian Gray-like languorousness and facial muscles that barely moved was reading to a girl from a page of *Romeo and Juliet*, which he had been carrying in his pocket. 'I'm making a study of this single, wonderful page!' he said to me over her shoulder. She had a red jewel in her navel and a voice that seemed to come from a penthouse on Park Avenue, though she said her parents were subsistence farmers in Ecuador. She said she occasionally cooked vegan haute cuisine for private dinner parties in the homes of the very wealthy. Was this the American Dream, or a joke in the last hour of the night? The young man reading to her from Shakespeare was, I then learned, the stepson of the novelist J.P. Donleavy. Donleavy had grown up in New York, went to study at Trinity College in Dublin, plunged head-first into the alcohol-fuelled bohemianism of the Brendan Behan era, wrote a famous book called *The Ginger Man* about it all, and then, in time, and with the profits from it and other books, bought a grand manor with land in the Irish midlands, where he wore cravats and tweeds and rode with the hounds. The young man's accent would not, I supposed, have been out of place in this house, though it might have been in the nearest town. 'You will have to admit, won't you,' he said, 'that *The Ginger Man* is one of the truly great and magnificent works of art of its century. There are parts of it, I believe, which are even on the level of *this*!' He waved his page of *Romeo and Juliet* in the damp air. I got called to the pool table to play. His friend ran in all the balls from the break. My cue never left its resting place on the floor. Then it was 4 a.m., the bar closed, the two young men and the girl with the jewel in her navel went off looking for further adventures and I went to bed in my little cabin.

In the morning I had breakfast in a place more elaborate, chic and wholefood-oriented than I was looking for. I was thinking of the kind of place that had on the menu eggs sunny-side up or Pigs in Blankets – what are known as choles-terol bombs. I'd have to leave Woodstock for that. The music was from Afghanistan. People leaned back and read the *New York Times*, as in Greenwich Village. The waiters looked like out-of-work dancers. I heard one say to a customer, 'I took a year off and lost my benefits. Now we find out that *she* has no insurance.' The dark spectre of medical costs. It drives some into jobs they don't want for the insurance cover, and others into the woods to escape unpayable debt. 'Will Marry for Health Care,' declares a bumper sticker.

Going back to my hotel I passed the Golden Notebook bookshop. These were the titles of the books in its window: *Rogue Nation: American Unilateralism and the Failure of Good Intentions*; *Big Lies: The Right-Wing Propaganda Machine and How It Distorts the Truth*; *Gangs of America: The Rise of Corporate Power and the Disabling of Democracy*; *Fear's Empire: War, Terrorism and Democracy*; *The Great*

Unravelling: Losing Our Way in the New Century; *Bushwhacked: Life in George Bush's America*; *Thieves in High Places: They've Stolen Our Country and It's Time to Take It Back*; *One Thousand Years for Revenge: International Terrorism and the F.B.I.*; *Pigs at the Trough: How Corporate Greed and Political Corruption Are Undermining America*; *The Lies of George W. Bush: Mastering the Politics of Deception*; *Lies and the Lying Liars Who Tell Them: A Fair and Balanced Look at the Right*; *Imperial America: The Bush Assault on the World Order*; and *Dude, Where's My Country?* by Michael Moore. The Republicans I met in the hotel bar had a point.

Byrdcliffe as a living community was gone within a dozen years, but it set the tone in Woodstock for a century. The United States has been, from the beginning, particularly prone to such 'experiments in living'. Woodstock has had a concentration of them, like places such as Big Sur, Taos, New Mexico, San Francisco and parts of Vermont and Montana. But they've been found all over the country – even in Indiana, even in Texas. Many have been religious, ranging from the Puritan theocracies to ashrams. The Mormons had a state-within-a-state in Utah. There were Christian groups, ever more rarefied in their devotion to simplicity, in the country from the beginning. Hare Krishnas, Moonies and Scientologists all have their centres or even whole towns. There have been other organising principles, such as survivalism, organic farming, white power, environmentalism, even particular colours in clothing. There are groups armed like commando units whose principal objects of devotion are guns. Sex occupies this place elsewhere. Charismatic leaders like Charles Manson, David Koresh of the Branch Davidians and Elizabeth Clare Prophet formed their own tribes in, respectively, California, Texas and Montana. Not in every case, but very often, the motivating idea behind these groups has been to throw off the artificiality of life in society, to return to the land, to discover the spiritual essence of life, to begin again. America is predicated upon this idea of beginning again. This is the immigrant experience. This is the Constitution. The entire country was an exercise in beginning again. This was meant never to cease. There is an innocence and idealism about this which Europeans, particularly the English, can find ludicrous. You find your life, they say, in what you've been given, you 'make do', you 'get on with it'. Spectacular displays of effort or enthusiasm driven by an ideal are embarrassing. E.M. Forster went with a *New Yorker* journalist and a few other people to visit the dwindling Shaker community in Mount Lebanon, New York. This was a group founded in New England by a former Quaker. Their motto was 'Hands to work and hearts to God', and in this spirit they invented the flat broom, the washing machine and the clothespeg. They lived simply, practised celibacy and attended meetings where, seized by a spirit, they shook. One man and a few elderly women were then living there, each in their own compartment. Forster wrote of it, 'The experience was more romantic for [the other visitors] than it was for me, and the idea of home-made chairs hanging from pegs on a wall filled [them] with nostalgia. It was part of the "dream that got bogged", the dream of an America that should be in direct touch with the elemental and the simple. America has chosen the power that comes through machinery but she never forgets her dream ... They were a symbol of something which America supposes herself to have missed.' G.K. Chesterton, writing in 1931, said, 'There is nothing wrong with Americans except their ideals. The real American is all right; it is the ideal American who is all wrong.'

I left Woodstock and got onto 28, then drove west through the Catskills. It was like parts of Wisconsin where I'd gone on vacation as a child. There were log-cabin motels, bait-and-tackle shops, stands on the roadside selling apple cider and honey. A Cub Scout troop, all in uniform, was selling pumpkins. Houses had hammocks on their front porches. Someone had hammered sheet metal and parts of old cars into the shapes of a rocket and a jet fighter and set them down in their yard facing the road. Bands of bikers near retirement age roamed over the mountain roads, their moustaches white, their handles high, but the bikes wide and low to the ground, like rhinos. A pickup truck moved slowly along filled with dark objects the size of bowling pins in the back. They looked like smiling, varnished bears. Towns began not, as is customary in America, with long concrete approachways of pizza places and muffler shops, but rather with houses. There was a Main Street in the centre. They looked serene, intimate, welcoming. I didn't see a fast-food place or a mall, and wouldn't until I got to Ithaca. I thought this was an America that had vanished, but here it was, mile after mile.

I left the Catskills, which more or less marked the western limit of early English settlement. Thoreau wrote, 'The English were very backward to explore and settle the continent they had stumbled upon . . . Prairie is a French word, as Sierra is a Spanish one . . . Within the memory of the oldest man, the Anglo-Americans were confined between the Appalachian Mountains and the sea, "a space not two hundred miles broad".' I entered Delaware County and, as I did, saw agriculture for the first time since landing. To the east, where people have second homes and take vacations, those working the land were in forestry or were landscape gardeners. Here were cows and men in baseball caps on tractors, dust and chaff rising into the sky. I was on my way to Ithaca, but was stopping first to have lunch with a friend named Charlie Cendrars I'd known in London and hadn't seen in more than a decade. He was a photographer, born not far from where we were to meet, trained in New York City, and who had afterwards roamed the world and stopped for a while in London, where I'd had some long lunches with him. Now we were to have another.

He was sitting in a booth with a small glass of beer, dressed like a farmer. In these things he was of a piece with everyone else there. 'This is the America of fifty years ago,' he said to me as we ate. 'You'd have seen that on your way here. It's the poorest county in the state, but – or because of that – people are kind. They have time for you. These are qualities about which much can be said. But the demographics are changing. Since 11 September the property prices have tripled. People are fleeing Long Island and the Hudson Valley because they're afraid they're going to get bombed. They could be right. We've rapidly made lethal enemies of a quarter of the world's population. And our defence for the kind of attack they might launch is weak. When the enemy has no standing army or visible weaponry or even land, and is already behind your lines, the riposte has to be diplomatic on the one hand and covert on the other. But the diplomats are bureaucratic, hierarchic. Their biggest aim is to cover their asses. There's no courage, no vision. There's no capacity to make a large gesture. And nobody with power listens to diplomats anyway, bad or good. As for the CIA, they were always stupid. I saw them when I was in South-East Asia. They actively repel information that might make us understand these places we're attacking.'

He'd been away for twelve years. I asked him how it was to return.

'I felt elation,' he said. 'Everything was speaking to me. Even the salt shakers. I'd been living with the unfamiliar, and liking it, and now I was in this ceaseless flow of the familiar. I revelled in it. But I see mental illness everywhere. In my daily routine of buying and service-seeking I see people speaking like they're on television. They assume this volume of speech and set of expressions and complete belief system based on material goods and seem unaware how horribly inauthentic it looks. You can't even call it materialism. It's so deep in the being, in the thinking and perception, everything turning to, or trying to be made into, cash. And they get screwed every day by people who are quicker at it than they are. Then they applaud their victimisers. The victimisers have never been better placed. We have a government made up of stenographers for the corporations.'

A shadow fell across our lunches. I looked up and saw a large man around eighty years old in a plaid woollen shirt and a face as grave and a voice as stentorian as a tribal elder's. He was looking down at us from the edge of our table.

'I'm a registered Republican and I've been listening to

what you've been saying,' he said, his voice booming around our little cubicle. 'And I want you to know that I agree with every word of it. This man we have now as president, he inherited surplus. He inherited goodwill. We were not loathed in the world. Now we're in a war without justification. Our debts are so serious it's difficult to see how they can be repaid. Our jobs and our wealth and our credibility in the world are being dissipated. This man is like the wastrel son who takes generations of carefully husbanded resources and squanders it all in a frivolous and idiotic spree. He is a disgrace.' He nodded once. 'Thank you,' he said, then returned to his table and sat down with his wife, picking up a spoon for his pie.

'That's the Heartland,' said Charlie. 'They can see through the lies. They wouldn't believe that in New York or London.'

I was eating an all-American meal, connecting, as he had, with the familiar forms and tastes. A prize-winning fish was mounted on the wall. There was a photograph of an Aegean village. People came and went, tipping their caps to one another and smiling, then stepping out into the sunshine. Three generations of a single family ran the restaurant. There was a nudge, a squeeze, an imparting of news or a joke whenever they intersected.

'I'm in retreat here,' said Charlie. 'That sounds a little self-important. I should just say that I'm not living the way I did when I knew you in London. I don't have television. There are no long lunches with the wine bottles lined up. When I was in Asia in the late 1960s I encountered Buddhism for the first time. I became interested in it, and stayed with it in my way. You wouldn't have noticed that because it wasn't so present for me then. There's a teacher I have faith in. He's the reason my family and I came down here to live. That makes the structure of my day now. In the morning I give my mind to thinking or praying. We have lunch and dinner communally. I don't know how this sounds to you. Maybe you think it's like the Moonies. Work and ambition, and maybe you could say hedonistic pursuits, were in the ascendant position before. But not now. I've given myself to this. When

11 September happened I didn't think that action was required, certainly not the aggressive military thing that they think they do so well. The only thing I could think of offering was prayer. I can imagine what thought this might provoke in some people here. But, well, that's the way my life moved. Before I'd get up in the morning, read newspapers and magazines. I'd call galleries and agents and plan trips. It suddenly was no longer interesting. I stopped taking pictures virtually in the middle of a roll of film. And there's not a thing I miss about it.'

We left the restaurant and he walked with me to my car. He pointed the way towards Ithaca and we said goodbye. I left town on state highway 10, but stopped a little while later to look at a huge American flag that had been painted on the side of a barn. Then I wrote down some of the things he had said. What was the culmination of his long spiritual quest? What had it brought him? Solidity? Radiance? Simple joy? It looked that way. I seemed to get some of it as I looked out again at what was in front of me – wooded hills full of colour rolling away, a maple sapling, cows moving slowly over the vibrantly green grass, the red barn with the American flag in the afternoon light. 'There's nothing between here and California except gas stations,' I'd been told.

I arrived in Ithaca at twilight. I found a strip with a lot of bars, picked one with a television and sat down to watch the fourth game of the Marlins–Cubs series. I watched the players trot out for their pre-game warm-up, the announcers injecting extra gravity and urgency into the spectacle we were about to witness, the 65,829 Florida fans strolling around, buying hot dogs, venting their opinions, the sound like a far-off, long-breaking wave. Finally the Marlins ran out onto the field, a roar went up and the game got under way. The Cubs came out swinging, scoring four runs in the first inning, and never let the Marlins get ahead of them. If they won the following night they'd go to the World Series. If not, they'd be back in Chicago for game six of the best-of-seven series. What a fine thing it would be to run through the streets of my home town with hundreds of thousands of others celebrating something unimaginable when the great Ernie Banks was still playing shortstop.

Glaciers cut through here, gouging out deep gorges now filled with waterfalls and eleven long slender bodies of water that came to be known as the Finger Lakes. Cayuga Lake, named for the dominant Native American tribe, is forty miles long and three and a half miles across at its widest point and is in places four hundred feet deep. This makes it deeper than Lake Ontario. Ithaca, not too far from Ulysses, Syracuse and Troy, was built in a valley on silt that collected at the southern end of the lake. A far higher proportion of school-children read *The Odyssey* here than elsewhere in the country. Oak, maple, ash, hemlock, chestnut and beech once covered this area, but the Iroquois cleared it in parts for buffalo grazing. When they were compromised by having acted as mercenaries for the British during the Revolutionary War, they were despatched from the land and it was given to war veterans. Now Amish and Mennonites have dairy farms, and grapes for the New York wine industry are grown here.

I found a bed and breakfast and was given a room on the ground floor that looked out to a pond and had its own bath and a bed like a throne, cloud-white, piled with pillows, airy, luxuriant and warm. You would not find a bed such as this in a hotel costing less than five hundred dollars per night. I could never get a bed to look like that. In the morning I asked the owner how it was done. She demonstrated, primping and beating and smoothing until it was light as a soufflé. 'There isn't a trick,' she said. 'You just have to spend a little time.'

Cornell University is in Ithaca. I'd had the idea when eighteen of applying to go to school there myself, but for reasons that I cannot precisely remember I didn't do it. I might have had a good time. Others seem to have had. Kurt Vonnegut was a student there in the 1940s before going to Europe to fight in the war. He later referred to it and to Ithaca several times in his novels. William Gass got his PhD there. Richard Fariña, later a friend of Bob Dylan and husband of Joan Baez's sister Mimi, got expelled in the 1950s for taking part in a demonstration against the university's excessive chaperoning, but was later reinstated and set some of his only novel, the legendary *Been Down So Long It Looks Like Up to Me*, at Cornell. Two days after it was published he died in a motorcycle accident. Vladimir Nabokov, who wrote *Lolita* while teaching there, was one of his professors. Thomas Pynchon was a fellow student and helped carry the coffin at his funeral. The Nobel Prizewinner Pearl S. Buck, the former Superman Christopher Reeve, attorney general Janet Reno and presidential advisor Paul Wolfowitz all studied there. Wolfowitz's father Jacob, a professor of statistics at the university, was a Polish Jew, many of whose family had died in concentration camps. He, like his son, was a Zionist. In the midst of his studies at Cornell the future foreign-policy planner and head of the World Bank went on the March on Washington where he heard Martin Luther King give his 'I have a dream' speech. He was a member of the Telluride Institute at the university, where an elite group of students were in a living experiment of intellectual enquiry and demo-cratic principles, voting, collaborating and collectively organising events in the house where they all lived. Later he went to the University of Chicago, where his mentor was Albert Wohlstetter, a friend of his father who believed in American world supremacy through advanced weapons. He also advocated the strict monitoring and containment of other countries' nuclear-power programmes to prevent them from using plutonium by-products in the development of nuclear weapons. It was around this time that he met Richard Perle, with whom, among others, he would later write the Project for the New American Century, which became the basis for America's global strategy after the 2000 election. Zionism, the spread of democracy, the development of American lethal weapons and the limiting of everyone else's – all these ideas were set in place before Wolfowitz left university.

Cornell, the youngest of the Ivy League universities – 139 years old at the time of my visit – was from the beginning non-sectarian, devoted in large part to the applied sciences rather than the classics, and open to women. Any one of these made Cornell very unusual at the time. It was founded by two men, Andrew Dickson White and Ezra Cornell. White was sent by his father to an Episcopal college, but dreamed all the while about Oxford and Cambridge. He eventually went to Yale, but felt a more open and ambitious institution than that was needed by a new and growing nation. Cornell was the son of a potter. He used to walk from Maine to Georgia selling ploughs. He made a fortune in Western Union stock from his business stringing telegraph cables on poles for Samuel Morse and then fretted over what to do with it. 'My greatest care now is how to spend this large income to do the greatest good to those who are properly dependent on me, to the poor and to posterity,' he wrote. It occurred to him to establish a college where people who had grown up as he had could study agriculture, veterinary medicine, engineering and other applied sciences. It is the decline in enrolment in such programmes, and the increase in exercise and sports-injury-treatment students, that led Jeffrey Immelt of General Electric to declare, 'If you want to be the massage capital of the world, you're well on the way.' Cornell met White in the New York state legislature, they combined their ideas and, with money from Cornell and a federal land grant for education, they set up their university. American history is full of such visionary philanthropic acts by its millionaires. Like other towns I'd passed along the way, Ithaca was once known for its manufacture of guns and its clocks, but now the university is by five times the town's largest employer.

Mark Twain had lived not far away at Elmira, where he had started writing *Huckleberry Finn*. Somehow I had managed not to read this book in childhood, at university or during the decades after that. I had supposed it full of genial, folksy humour and river talk. Then, just before leavng for New York, I read it. I was unprepared for its chastising fury and the completeness of its damning vision. Here was an abused boy and a runaway slave who could live only on the moving water, for every time they touched the solid ground of America they met with cruelty, hypocrisy, greed, mindless hatred, exploitation and murder. Both as allegory and as story it shocks you.

That night I woke around an hour after I had gone to bed. I got up in blackness as complete as a coma and groped for a light switch, but couldn't find one. I moved around the walls with my hands. Finally I found a space that was the entrance to the bathroom. I turned the light on, took a drink of water. A bit of it spilled over the floor. I turned to reach for a towel, my feet slid on a waterslick on the finely buffed concrete, my lower part went up and my upper part went down, my descending head cracked on the edge of the sink and I hit the floor, V-shaped. I got up after a moment, unmaimed, it seemed. Then a bead of blood scurried like an insect around from the back of my neck down onto my chest, and more kept flowing behind it. It came from a small cut at the back of my head. These kinds of cuts are neither grave nor painful, but they produce spectacular results. When I looked in the mirror it seemed I was wearing a necktie made of blood. I tried to staunch the wound with toilet paper, then a towel. I used up one and went on to another. Finally, after half an hour of this, the flow stopped. I rinsed the two towels in the sink and hung them over the shower rail. I'd rinsed them repeatedly, but still they were suffused with pink, like an early morning sky. Then I went back to bed.

I woke early. A mist shot through with gold light crept and billowed on the grass. I had a long drive ahead of me, all the way to Chicago, or very nearly. I turned around to get dressed and then saw it – smears of blood daubed over the pillowcases with droplets and finger marks trailing over the duvet. It looked like an action painting, or as if someone had been shot there. I imagined a little dent in the pillow where my head rested during a sweet and troublesomeless sleep, a thank you and farewell and then the road again, but it was too late for that. What was there was uncleanable, at least by what was to hand in the room. It would need chemicals and a machine. Maybe they wouldn't work, either. I got dressed in a hurry, yearning for confession and absolution. No one was up. Finally the owner came down, then her husband. I told them that I had bled all over their sheets. 'I tried for half an hour to stop the bleeding. I thought I had,' I said. Both were dismissive. They did nothing to encourage my embarrassment.

'I'm afraid the Cubs lost last night,' said the man. 'They were shut out 4–0. Maybe they can get the job done in Chicago.' He handed me a newspaper so that I could read the report about the game.

They gave me directions to the road west. On the way out of Ithaca I stopped at a bank with a cash machine in a side wall. Written in small black letters where someone may have had some time to think while waiting to extract money was the message, 'You are not a unique and beautiful snowflake.'

Chicago

I stayed away from interstates all morning as I drove west, until 86 became inevitable just to the west of Olean; 86 hit 90 over the Pennsylvania border and I submitted myself to it all the way to the Indiana sand dunes. Before I left Ithaca I telephoned my friend Pat Mongoven, in whose house I was to stay, to ask him for a more appealing route. 'Don't bother,' he said. 'I tried US 20 once and it was uglier than the interstate.'

I stopped for lunch just west of Erie, Pennsylvania. I was almost due north of Pittsburgh, a city I'd always passed by to the south or the north without ever visiting it. Pittsburgh has seen the accumulation of some of the largest fortunes in America, the Mellons', from banks, the Fricks', from coal, and the Heinz's, from soup and ketchup. In 1870 the money Andrew Carnegie made from his expansion of the steel industry there made him the richest man in the world. As a consequence it is a city of foundations, endowed institutes and private museums, one of which is dedicated to Andy Warhol, a native of Pittsburgh.

Three rivers come together in its centre – the Ohio, the Allegheny and the Monongahela. 'Monongahela,' wrote Whitman, '– it rolls with venison richness upon the palate.' Could anyone else have thought of 'venison richness'? He loved what he called the 'aboriginal names', and wanted them to replace all the saints' names in California. Another name that had to go, he said, was Baltimore. So polluted was the Monongahela once that it used to catch fire. Much of Pittsburgh's heavy industry was gone, but the city and its rivers had, I read, found new life. I wouldn't see them, though, as I'd spent too much time in the east.

I drove on into Ohio. It was twilight by the time I passed Cleveland and I still had more than half the journey to go. I drifted on through an undifferentiated landscape, trying to find a way to use the time to some purpose. Sam Shepherd once wrote half a play on his steering wheel while driving on Highway 40 to Los Angeles. I couldn't seem to follow a single thought for more than three miles, if that. Every effort disintegrated in the face of the monotonous and trivial distractions of the road. The air in the car felt thick with mental inertia. I turned on the radio and went through bands of static and fragments of song and speech, an aural print of my mind. Jackie Brenston's 'Rocket 88' came through the speakers with crystalline clarity. I listened to him disparage the half-wrecked bangers of his rivals and then ask the ladies to allow him to introduce them to his beautiful, gleaming, irresistible Oldsmobile Rocket 88. That lifted me, but then the station faded two songs later. I heard local news, country-and-western music, heavy metal and politicians and announcers repeatedly talking about 'the greatest country in the world' in ways that sounded either as if they were about to cry or else strangle the person next to them. A Christian radio station came on just after I reached Indiana. The presenter, as softly spoken as a therapist, was interviewing a minister who was on a rampage about the marriage of homosexuals and divorce and abortion law. 'The American family is under assault!' he shouted. 'It's in the crosshairs! It's worse than the Black Plague! We're modelling our family laws on Canada and Europe. PAGAN CANADA! PAGAN EUROPE!' These stations would crackle, tune in, then fade away. It all added to the claustrophobia in the car. I wondered how truck drivers stood it.

I got off Interstate 90 at Portage and made my way to Marko's Bar. It was in a strip mall, perhaps the most desolate form of American commercial life. It wasn't late, just a little after ten o'clock, but the bar was already at the latter end of its cycle of activity for the night. People were putting on their coats, tables were being wiped by a tired waitress. A Mexican busboy leaned on the door frame of the kitchen, its light throwing his face into silhouette. I'd arranged to meet Marcella, the wife of my friend Pat, and she came in when I was just two sips into my beer, thinner than I'd ever seen her.

'He's come back all the way from Spain to look at our country,' she said to three men in baseball caps and with Fu Manchu moustaches.

'When did you leave?' one asked me. His voice seemed to come out of a cement mixer.

'1973.'

'The Seventies! You must have been smoking weed back then.'

'I never really took to it,' I said.

'Well, we never stopped!' he said, and the three of them toasted me with their beers.

We didn't stay long. I followed her by car into Ogden Dunes, a gated community for the middle class with a Volunteer Fire Department and houses built along the shore-line of Lake Michigan and beside the roads that slinked through the dunes. That's where she and Pat lived. It was developed in 1925, initially for just twenty-four residents, but before that it achieved national fame as the home of a mysteri-ous and beautiful woman who lived alone in an abandoned fisherman's hut, made wine from berries and swam naked in the lake. Fishermen saw her in 1916, the story spread and newspapers named her 'Diana of the Dunes'. She knew, they said, every plant, animal, mood and colour of the dunes, but fled whenever anyone came near her. It was claimed that she was the daughter of a Chicago doctor and had gone to the dunes after her heart had been broken by a man. Offers of marriage arrived by post and by messenger. It's not diffi-cult to see why, just from these details. She finally accepted one that arrived from Texas, but died while making her prepar-ations to leave for the wedding.

Ogden Dunes stands between a sulphurous, flaming industrial sprawl to the west and, to the east and curving northwards into Michigan along the lake shore, one of Chicago's vacation lands, a place of rentable cabins in the dunes and second homes. The dunes that run from here northwards up the eastern shore of the lake at times reach hundreds of feet in height and extend up to a mile inland. They form the largest network of freshwater dunes in the world. This vast quantity of sand is the result of millions of years of the grinding of granite by the same glaciers that dug out the Great Lakes. It was heaved and blown into hills by water and wind, fixed into dunes by the root system of marram grass, the first stage of vegetation that would later give way to dogwood, sand cherry and cottonwood, then finally to oak, maple and pine. State and national parks protect the dunes in places, but there has been a lot of property development and the sand has also been mined for such things as glass, toothpaste and bunkers for golf courses, but above all to make moulds for the engine blocks manufactured in Detroit. Around 2.5 million tons of sand are hauled away each year.

Muhammad Ali lived for many years on a farm over the Michigan border, near Benton Harbor, where 'King Ben' Franklin Purnell and his Holy Rollers of the Israelite House of David established a colony in the early years of the twentieth century. King Ben started as a broom maker, then opened his church. It followed the most well established of lines: members lived communally, observed various dietary prescriptions, handed over all their money to their leader and were told by him that, in exchange for their dedication, they would be transported bodily into heaven. They had a bearded baseball team that had some success semi-professionally playing without gloves. After two girls accused Purnell of sexually abusing them under the cover of religious ritual, he vanished for three years and then appeared in court on a stretcher after his colony was raided. He listened to the charge lying down and then whispered a denial. Stories of this kind are as repetitive as those of rock musicians and drugs, but this has not deterred people from continuing to pledge themselves and their cash to such organisations. King Ben said he was immortal, but died in 1927. The Holy Rollers kept this hidden for a while to see if there would be a resurrection, then mummified him and interred him in their Diamond House, which was designed to sparkle in the sun.

I'd known Pat since I was five. He was the eldest of what were eventually seven children whose mother had won a beauty pageant and was, at the time I met Pat, just in her mid-twenties. All of us liked her, because she was pretty and would sit down and talk with us as though she were one of us. She even had a slight helplessness in the face of the domestic onslaught brought on by a household full of small children. Helplessness can be very endearing, certainly more so than the mastery of domestic appliances, cleaning products and the maintenance of monogrammed guest towels aspired to by many women of the time. These were the years when the magazine *Housekeeping Monthly* could publish an article called 'The Good Wife's Guide', which suggested, 'Take fifteen minutes to rest so you're refreshed when he arrives. Touch up your make-up, put a ribbon in your hair ... Minimize all noise ... Make the evening his ... Don't complain if he's late home for dinner or even if he stays out all night. Count this as minor compared to what he might have gone through that day. Arrange his pillow and offer to take off his shoes. Speak in a low, soothing and pleasant voice.'

Pat was the class hedonist. His primary-school class prophecy had him becoming the Man from U.N.C.L.E., a low-budget television James Bond played by Robert Vaughn. We went to primary and secondary schools together, then went different ways for university. When I came back to America for the first time four years after having left, he was married to a woman who was, on the day I saw him, pregnant and annoyed with him. Six years later I came back again and went to see him in a basement apartment in our old neighbourhood, which was knee-deep in toys and pizza boxes and clothes and where he was living with his two children, Matt and Melissa, having got custody of them in his divorce. He was shooting wedding videos, working in a bar and going out with a good-looking nurse, buoyant, cheerful and true to his class prophecy, it appeared. On my next visit he introduced me to Marcella. She'd done postgraduate work at the University of Chicago, then had gone west to Washington state where she cut down trees and picked cherries and had come back to Chicago with an infant daughter named Annie. Soon they were all living together in Ogden Dunes. I'd go out to see them each time I visited Chicago. They all ate together every night and told their stories and held debates. The children accepted each other as siblings, the wedding-video business had evolved into a production company and was prospering, and Pat and Marcella, from all evidence known to me, found each other fascinating and hilarious. It seemed a grand life, unlikely yet viable, one found after disappointment and restlessness.

'Where's Pat?' I'd asked her in Marko's Bar.

'He had a long day,' she said. 'He's staying in the apartment we have in Chicago tonight. He'll see you tomorrow, he says.'

In the morning Marcella and I went into Portage to meet her friends Karen Tallian and Mary Pont for breakfast. I read the placemat while they looked at the menu. Dream Maker Bath and Kitchen . . . Amish Handcrafted Furniture . . . a mortgage consultant's which proclaimed that it had not changed its name five times in the past year, as other more dubious competitors presumably had . . . American Concrete Raising . . . Start Your OWN HOME Business Ask Me How, Lee Simmons, Independent Consultant, Quint Signs . . . Soto's for bodywrap, a tan and nails . . . Indiana University Northwest, where you can Earn a Degree Close to Home . . . and a legal partnership that specialised in bankruptcy: 'Stop foreclosures! Get Debt Relief!' The restaurant offered customers the opportunity to enter a weekly raffle for $10 meal vouchers if they answered questions on each of the advertisers on the placemat. They really wanted you to concentrate on them. 'Where can you get High Performance Tires and Wheels?' 'Who offers Custom Designed Granite Monuments?' 'Whose quote is . . . "If That Special Touch Means Something To You, Call Us"?' Each ad was in a small rectangle filled with slogans and lists of services and printed in bright blue, green or red, their stridency and desperation more evident, the more marginal the service on offer. Rogge Insurance and Portage Tire and Service Center were soberly announced, but the decibels seemed to rise with C.H. Kremble Enterprises CUSTOM DESIGNED QUALITY WATCHES: 'Show Your Team Spirit . . . When It's Time for a Fund Raiser, Time for an Award or Time to Show Your Appreciation . . . We Can Help!' Was there some connection between this shrillness and the bankruptcy ad? Had these people selling knick-knacks, used furniture or home-decoration advice emerged from the ruin of other businesses? Were they headed back into this condition in this town of sinking employment?

'Have you seen this?' I said, pointing to the bankruptcy ad.

'Didn't you know?' said Marcella. 'There's a bankruptcy in the United States every twenty seconds.'

'Children are likely to live through their parents' bankruptcy before their divorce,' said Karen, who is a lawyer.

'I've been there, or nearly,' said Mary. 'It was for a debt that wasn't mine. My husband ran a small business from home. Each year I signed his tax return. We separated a while ago. After that I found out there was a particular tax that he had neglected to pay. They kept sending him letters, but he didn't reply. This went on for a few years. The original assessment was for $4,500, but they compounded the interest on the debt hourly. It got to $90,000 and when they didn't get it from him, they came after me because I'd signed the tax return. I lost my credit rating. They put a lien on the house. I had to pay $400 per month hazard insurance because of this debt. The government hires mercenaries who come around at 2 a.m. and tell you you've got eight hours to get out of your house. My best friend is a tax lawyer, and eventually through him I came to an agreement with the government. I still can't get credit, though.'

Between 1980 and 1997 individual bankruptcies increased by 369.5 per cent. They continue to rise. Much of it is from credit-card debt. Nearly every person in the United States over sixteen is avalanched by offers of new credit cards, loans and the restructuring of their mortgages by post, on television, in magazines and on the Internet and many succumb, repeatedly. Spending and debt increase at a time when salaries are falling, with bankruptcy always a possible solution. 'We have no right to the standard of living we have,' an IBM executive named Nicholas Donofrio has said.

But far more significant in the increase of bankruptcy filings is the precipitous rise in costs that in most other developed countries are borne by the state. Government research in 2003 found that families were spending twenty-six per cent less on clothing, twenty-three per cent less on food and forty-four per cent less on appliances than they had a generation earlier, but sixty-one per cent more on health insurance and one hundred per cent more on university education. American per capita medical costs are almost double those of the rest of the industrialised world. Yet there are fewer doctors, fewer hospital visits, fewer child immunisations and fewer CT scanners. Around a fifth of this cost is in administration costs, more than triple that of Canada, which has a national health service. Health-insurance premiums go up by around fifteen per cent per year. Many elect for less coverage, bargaining with both their finances and their health. They avoid dentistry and any treatments that fall within their deductible amounts. Preventive care gets practised less. Forty-five million go without health insurance altogether. Some get sick and then can't pay the bills they have incurred. Some of these go on the run, middle-class outlaws. There is a vast machinery of law, accountancy, insurance and banking dealing with and feeding off this situation, including a growth industry of companies that buy debt.

Many of the things that determine how much life, or at least some lives, cost – petrol, food, property, beer, cars, golf clubs, clothes, hotels – are cheap in America. Why must medical care cost vastly more than anywhere else? I asked David Danone, a professor at the Northwestern University School of Business and author of *The Economic Evolution of American Health Care*.

'From the point of view of demand,' he said, 'we are the most obese, the most violent, the most polluting and the most drug-consuming of all the countries of the world. Until recently we were the largest consumers of cigarettes. All of these things obviously increase the demand for healthcare. We have a heterogeneous society. This increases the incidence of various diseases which are racially specific. Because of drugs and the availability of life-extending operations often not offered by national health services, we have a large proportion of elderly people who need care. And because of the geographical disparateness of families there is a higher expenditure on long-term care.

'As for supply costs, they are certainly going up. Many people think this is just a recent phenomenon, but forty years ago we also led the world in health spending and in the proportion of uninsured. Costs go up because of technological change. We can do more than ever before. A private-insurance market adds around ten per cent to costs. The practice of defensive medicine because of fear of malpractice suits adds five to ten per cent, though the American Medical Association would tell you it's twenty-five per cent. The increase in drug costs alone can account for four to five per cent of inflation generally. The providers have the market power and they are raising the prices. Companies have seven years to exploit exclusively the drugs they develop, but they extend this by fiddling with the formula. Most of the health-care industry's spending is on drugs. The amounts generated can be stupendous. Two anti-cholesterol drugs have made $13 billion worldwide. Such amounts may be thought excessive. There is a push from various quarters for government control. The Canadian government negotiates prices with the industry and there the drugs are cheaper, to the extent that some people cross the border to get them. Another factor is the amount we pay doctors, administrators and nurses. They all get more than elsewhere. Lawyers also get more and this gets figured into healthcare costs. These wages and fees may account for half the difference in cost between our system and those of other developed countries. Paediatricians make around $120,000 per year after overheads and they are the lowest paid among the specialists. A paediatrician's office costs will be around $120,000 and his malpractice insurance $20,000. An average doctor makes around $150,000. This may be thought high, even excessive, but at the same time it is a prestigious occupation, our medical schools are excellent and the good ones have the pick of the better students and generally the quality of our doctors is high. We've scared everyone out of the teaching profession with poor wages. What would happen if we did that with doctors?'

Obtaining health insurance, which costs around $600 per month, doesn't always guarantee a person access to healthcare, no matter how comprehensive their policy may seem. The insurance industry employs private detectives to examine claimants' pasts for any evidence that would justify the denial of treatment. A woman who'd said on her application form that she'd never been treated for a serious illness and was discovered by a detective to have once had cystitis was denied treatment for cancer on the basis that she'd provided false information. Doctors employed by the insurance companies, and who recommend that an expensive treatment be denied on the basis that it is not necessary or too innovative, find their salaries going up. Preventable deaths of people who have regularly paid their premiums have been the consequence.

In Portage that morning I ate a vast breakfast that spilled

over the limits of the plate and talked about books, travel and children with Karen, Mary and Marcella. Then we all left. The following year Karen ran for mayor of Ogden Dunes, lost and subsequently became a state senator. Mary was going to Florida to start a new life. I drove back with Marcella to Ogden Dunes. We sat in her kitchen, the door open, pools of autumn light falling through the pine trees onto the dunes. She didn't stop moving as we talked, small, fidgety movements without purpose, her smile fixed. Yet the light was soft, and the birdsong peaceful. She told me about her and Pat's children. Melissa had a job in tourism in Arizona and a precarious relationship with a boyfriend. Matt, handsome, winning and chivalrous, was also, she said, a 'metrosexual'. That was the first time I ever heard that term. What does it mean? I asked. 'It means he's even more appealing to women because of his use of pumice stone on his calluses and his knowledge of the thread count of sheets.' With her daughter Annie we returned to the subject of what it costs to live a middle-class life in America.

Annie was a prodigy. I remember her singing torch songs and blues on the Ogden Dunes beach when she was eight and being indignant if anyone appeared amused that such grave and passionate songs could come from a body so small. I remember her reading long nineteenth-century novels until dawn each night as a fourteen-year-old when we were all on holiday together in Ireland. At school she was placed in accelerated programmes for the gifted. In her SAT exam she was a National Merit finalist, which placed her in the top one per cent of the country.

She applied to Brown, Vasser, Dartmouth and Yale in the east, and two independent Midwestern colleges, Oberlin and Macalester. Her first choice was Dartmouth, in New Hampshire, but fees and other costs there amounted to $41,000 per year and the school declined to offer a grant or scholarship or even a low-interest loan. Pat had been inclined to live in the present, class hedonist that he was, and hadn't laid anything by for Annie's education. He still had $25,000 to pay for Matt and Melissa's fees at the University of Indiana, a state school. He was paying $440 per month for a health-care policy that required him to pay the first $2,500 of any medical treatment received by his family. This is more a bulwark against bankruptcy than genuine insurance cover. He was never in a position to pay out $41,000 per year in school fees, but now he could not afford to borrow it.

Yale was their next choice. They had hope of some form of scholarship, but the school only offered a work-study-loan combination totalling $2,500 per year. With fees and other costs similar to those at Dartmouth, this left $38,500 to pay. 'You could remortgage your home,' a school official suggested. It was too late for that, however, as they'd already done it to finance building work.

In the end Annie went to Macalester, which is on the outskirts of Minneapolis. Fees there amounted to $36,000 per year, but the college offered her a grant of $5,000 for being a National Merit finalist and a further $5,000 for financial need. Pat took out a loan for $26,000.

The Catholic primary school he and I went to cost $50 per year. He paid his own tuition fees at our Jesuit high school from money he made from summer jobs. He went to Southern Illinois University, where he received a grant for his tuition fees and paid for his room and board from part-time work. His father's job at the *Chicago Tribune* provided healthcare for the entire family. When he graduated from university, both he and his father were free of debt.

After the Second World War the American state sent eight million GIs through university for free and paid them a living wage while they were studying. Many lives were transformed for the better. No one receives such assistance now. It would cost the government one-third of what it spends annually in Iraq to provide free education for every student in a state university. But this is not on the agenda. The movement is in the other direction, away from grants and towards interest-bearing loans. Since 1975, the percentage of university students receiving the maximum federal grant has halved. In the meantime, state university fees have risen forty per cent over ten years, with a fourteen per cent rise in the year in which I sat talking about these things with Marcella in her kitchen, while the net worth of American families is declining for the first time in half a century.

I cannot recall a single conversation about debt during the time I was a student. Now students are haunted by the prospect of it even before they leave high school. Many choose programmes of study that will lead to jobs well paid enough to finance their debts, such as those offered by law or business schools. Fear of insolvency starts early and extends throughout life as university debts are compounded by house purchase, children and all the pressures of living in a society that never relents in its imprecations to buy. There is perhaps no more effective engine of social control. 'If you want an obedient populace,' the English politician Tony Benn once said, 'saddle them with debt early.'

Pat's income-tax and social-security payments amount to forty-three per cent of his income. If he were living in Britain his tax burden would be approximately equal, if not less. He would have unemployment and fully comprehensive health insurance and, eventually, a pension, all provided by the state. If he chose to have private health insurance, the cost would be far cheaper than in the United States. University fees would be less than one-fifth of what they are at the more elite American universities, and both grants and low-interest loans would be available. The fiscal part of the American social contract, such as it is, would appear to be a poor deal for the citizen. Where does all the tax revenue go? It is estimated that the war in Iraq will cost $3 trillion. The United States military budget is fifteen times that of China.

Marcella and I spoke about these things through the rest of the morning and into the afternoon, but it did not reduce the tautness in her expression or the speed of her movements. Her eyes could not rest on any of the objects in the house, where, for the first time in my experience, no one was present except her and me and no one was expected. Her fingers nudged and flicked at little things I could not see.

'Did you speak with Pat this morning?' I asked her.

'Not yet. He might have rung while we were out.'

'Do you know where he is?'

Her eyes moved in a wide arc from the door to me.

'He's with another woman,' she said. 'It started a couple of months ago. Sometimes he's here, sometimes he's there. But even if he's here I can't find him. I don't recognise him.'

'Who is she?' I asked.

'Someone who works in the office next to ours. Someone I thought was a friend.'

'What's going to happen?'

'I don't know. He says to wait. Give him some time, some room. Maybe this will go away and we can go back to where we were. But how can I do that? It's taking me apart, as the clock ticks.'

She talked for a while longer, telling this story, then broke, sobs racking her body. I'd known her to be quick to cry, but only when something moved her. I'd never see her cry for herself. This was bleak and remorseless and lacking in any consoling or redemptive light. She would of course stop in a while, and did, but later she'd come back to it. Nothing could redeem it other than time, or Pat.

'Sorry,' she said.

I told her I had to drive into Chicago. She walked me out to my car.

'Are you eating all right?' I asked her.

'More or less,' she said. 'I know I'm thinner. But that's the situation, not lack of food. Tell them all in Chicago – emotional distress is the way to weight loss.'

I drove out of Ogden Dunes and got onto US 12, going west. It comes down from Detroit, skirts Lake Michigan, then takes a wide arc around the western extremities of Chicago as it heads north. I'd meet it again a few days later in Wisconsin, and several other times along the way as it extended westwards to the Pacific. There was a railway line on my right and, to the left, woodland, then a cluster of shops and gas stations and houses. Out on its own a few miles along was a strip club with just one car in the parking lot. I was on the outskirts of Gary, home of the largest proportion of black people of any city in America. These once included Michael Jackson and his family. I could get Gary's industrial odours and hear the distant, unplaceable hum of traffic from the interstates that cross each other near here. Hookers work this quiet stretch of shadowy two-lane road. Cross-country truckers get off the interstate and employ them in the beds they keep behind the driver's seats of their cabs. Marcella told me that she and Pat picked up a high-school girl hitch-hiking as she tottered along in the rain on her heels in a mini-skirt on her way to this little strip. She told them about all the money she made from the truck drivers during the evenings after school.

I got onto Interstate 90 and began the climb onto the Chicago Skyway, a concrete and steel structure which soars 125 feet over the Little Calumet River and the stretch of steel mills, refineries, railroad tracks and urban despoliation that goes from Gary to East Chicago. The river was an industrial sewer for nearly one hundred years and tracts of land here remain embedded with lead and cyanide waste. Calumet, from the Latin *calamus*, or reed, is the pipe used by Native Americans in ceremonies, including those of peace. From the Skyway it's an unforgettably infernal spectacle – high towers pouring out black smoke and flame, the air rank with torched minerals and chemicals, its colour a sickly grey and yellow, like jaundiced skin. When I first saw it as a child I wondered what the people had done to deserve to live there. At night it can look magical, the flames coming out of the stacks seeming to dance in the sky. Carl Sandburg, in 'Smoke and Steel', saw in it a kind of zoological pageantry:

> Ears and noses of fire, gibbering gorilla arms of fire,
>   gold mud pies, gold bird wings, red jackets riding

purple mules, scarlet aristocrats tumbling from the
humps of camels, assassinated czars straddling
vermilion balloons;
I saw then the fires flash by one by one: good-by: then
smoke, smoke . . .

Steel came here in 1906. Iron ore was floated down from
the Mesabi range in northern Michigan and Minnesota. Coal
came by rail from West Virginia and southern Illinois to fire
the furnaces. There was abundant water for the cooling process
from the lake and a highly developed rail and water network
for distribution of the finished steel. The industry reached a
high point in the late 1970s, then was pushed into a decline
by a sequence of blows – a strong dollar, the collapse of the
Asian economy, stagnant technology, free-trade agreements
and cheap imports. At one point finished steel was coming in
from Kazakhstan at prices just slightly over those of American
scrap metal. The mills began to eliminate the more labour-
intensive operations and to concentrate on flat-roll steel. They
still produce six million tons, against a high point of nine
million, but thirty thousand jobs have gone from the area.
These would include workers in ancillary industries as well
as the mechanics, butchers, priests, nurses, and so on who
disappear along with a declining population of industrial
workers. Lakshmi Mittal, an Indian who started with a single
mill in Calcutta and is now worth $25 billion, bought four of
the five mills along the lake shore, one of which, Inland Steel,
once employed my mother as a secretary in their Chicago
office. US Steel, which founded Gary, still owns its mill, but
according to one worker I spoke with, they are at least as
interested in their gas stations, apartment complexes and
casinos in the area as they are in steel. Mittal runs thirty-five
mills in Third World countries, lives behind Kensington Palace
in the most expensive private home in London, threw a multi-
million-dollar wedding party for his daughter at the Palace of
Versailles and announced plans to cut 45,000 jobs in his mills
worldwide. This seems to be the kind of news that investors

like to hear. What can the unions do? Indiana has lost one hundred thousand manufacturing jobs. Companies are going bankrupt or fleeing from pension and healthcare obligations and towards lower wages in other countries. Such lobbying power as there is tends to be with the corporations or their foreign buyers, rather than with workers' organisations. The strike has become a bygone weapon, like the crossbow.

I spoke with Bill Carey, an organiser for the United Steelworkers of America, whose local headquarters are at the dead end of a road on a former dump still so toxic that worms cannot live there. 'We're smaller than we were,' he said, 'but more mobile. I think we can respond more quickly and imaginatively to issues. We react to changes in the law, such as deregulating overtime or free-trade agreements. We demonstrate, organise letter-writing campaigns to representatives. And we've made some unusual friendships. One of the big companies locked out one thousand workers. The owner was also cutting down redwoods. We were fighting him on one front, and tree-dwelling environmental activists were fighting him on the other. So we made an alliance with them. We agree on trade issues. We've got a working body organising a march on Miami. We're hoping to get thirty thousand on that. In the meantime you've got Earth First people on steel pickets and steel workers up in the trees.'

I dropped slowly down from the high point of the Skyway, paid a two-dollar toll and got onto the Dan Ryan Expressway, which runs up through the South Side of Chicago. A thief named Victor Sylvester had a great run of success robbing this toll plaza eight times in 1999 and 2000. He had a car-repair operation going on in the back yard of his house, which was within sight of the toll stop. The police didn't know it was the same man doing all the jobs because he always used his customers' cars, driving up, deftly keeping his gun out of sight of the CCTV cameras and then driving off with a drawerful of money. He was finally caught in a wild car chase through the streets and alleys of the South Side, led by Robert Erkenswick, then director of the Skyway.

It's a road I've always been pleased to get to the far side of. It quavers when trucks go over it. It was built by the City of Chicago in the late 1950s when Mayor Richard J. Daley was presiding over a circuitry of graft unrivalled in scale anywhere in America. Who knows how strictly enforced were the road-building codes on a company that may have bribed its way to a contract? I pictured a support caving in, a section of the road dropping down like a jaw in a moment of astonishment, and me sailing off it through the foul air and into a river thick with sludge and poison. Revenues from tolls dropped for a while, but picked up again when Indiana put in several casinos in its north-west corner, a solution to declining tax revenues that is used all across America. The city spent $250 million upgrading the Skyway, then leased it for ninety-nine years to an Australian–Spanish consortium for $1.83 billion. In a single moment, with Lakshmi Mittal's mills visible on the lake shore, I was passing by and over billions of dollars of American resources now in foreign ownership.

The traffic was thick and barbarous on the Dan Ryan – honking, gasping, swooping, veering and darting, each car seemingly about to mount the car in front of it. If flies moved like birds in flocks, they'd move like this. I went off a ramp and cut eastwards across the South Side to Lake Shore Drive, a genteelly flowing multi-lane highway that spans just under sixteen miles of the lake front, trees and apartments to its west, park, beach and the vast lake to the east, its sound just an airy whoosh because of the absence of trucks. If I had to choose a favourite road in the world, it would be this one, particularly on a clear summer night with the windows rolled down, coming into town from the north where Oak Street beach forces a left turn, the Magnificent Mile of Michigan Avenue stretching like a landing strip before you, the squat Drake Hotel and the Palmolive Building with its floodlit receding terraces and beacon that can be seen from the air five hundred miles away just to the left and the downtown buildings glittering beyond and the lake silent and dark to the east, like the city's collective unconscious.

I came up from the south. I passed the Museum of Science and Industry, all that remains of the boulevards, fairground, lush gardens and two hundred sparklingly white neoclassical buildings that made up the World's Columbian Exposition of 1893, an extravagant demonstration of the city's recuperative powers after the 1871 fire that supposedly began when a cow kicked over a lantern in a barn owned by a family named O'Leary on the city's West Side. The fire swept through the West Side neighbourhoods, leaped the river and went on to destroy eighteen thousand buildings in a four-mile stretch and leave one hundred thousand people without homes. The Exposition's buildings provoked the line 'thine alabaster cities gleam' in the patriotic hymn 'America the Beautiful'. Canals linked the site to the centre of the city. George Ferris exhibited his first Ferris wheel there. Buffalo Bill Cody and Annie Oakley performed feats from the Wild West, and Little Egypt danced. One of the construction workers at the Exposition was the father of Walt Disney. Both the Exposition and Disneyland had utopianism as well as entertainment in the minds of the creators.

I passed Soldier Field and the three museums of fish, stars and dinosaurs just to the south of Downtown, then was face to face with America's second most spectacular skyline, the buildings lined up like an opera company at a curtain call, the Pittsfield Building where my father had his dental practice on the thirty-first floor set down among them like a sapling in a forest. Gertrude Stein, having looked at these buildings, wrote, 'European buildings sit on the ground but American ones come out of the ground. And then of course there is the air. And that air is everywhere, everywhere in America, there is no sky, there is air and that makes religion and wandering and architecture.' When the city began to grow in the mid-nineteenth century it was a swamp in wet weather, the river flooding and the streets a mud bath; in dry weather, dust and garbage and sand from the dunes blew around. The sewers were trenches cut beside the roads and rats ran under the wooden planks of the sidewalks. After the fire the city could reconceive itself and did so according to a plan made by the visionary architect Daniel Burnham, a Swedenborgian in his youth who also designed the Columbian Exposition. It was the first comprehensive plan for the controlled growth of an American city. It specified a strip of forest along the city's western boundary and miles of continuous park along the lake front, so that every citizen would be within walking distance of outdoor recreation. This gives the city an airiness and freshness and visibility I have only rarely seen elsewhere, and which Chicago could not have had before, when docks and warehouses and commercial premises were bunched up along the lake shore. Now this most precious of the city's property is owned by its populace. 'Beneath the sun,' wrote Simone de Beauvoir, 'the water is pure silk and diamonds, and white sailboats glide back and forth – it has the serene luxury of the Côte d'Azur.' Chicago presents itself blithely and unashamedly to its waterfront in a way that almost no other cities do. New York is an island, but turns away from its rivers. Miami has handed its seashore to property developers. You could spend days in Los Angeles or Toronto without knowing you are near a body of water. But Chicago faces outward towards its lake, which in its way is an architectural as well as a natural feature.

A city so long laden with political corruption might be supposed to be stagnant, but since the fire Chicago has been, many have said, among the most architecturally dynamic cities in the world. Louis Sullivan started it. Of him, Frank Lloyd Wright wrote, 'The new in the old and the old in the new is ever principle. Principle is all and single the reality the beloved master, Louis Sullivan, ever loved . . . His loyalty to principle was the more remarkable as *vision* when all around him poisonous cultural mists hung low to obscure or blight any bright hope of finer beauty in the matter of this world.' Sullivan, Burnham, Root, Atwood and William Le Baron Jenney created the Chicago School. There was a Beaux Arts classical movement after that which produced the Art Institute, one of the country's great museums, and the lovely

Chicago Cultural Center, which was the main library when I was growing up. Frank Lloyd Wright created the Prairie Style, Mies van der Rohe the International Style and there have been many soaring and varied shapes since, including the Sears Tower, for a long while the tallest building in the world. Up at the top you feel as if you are in a plane rather than a structure resting on the ground. People come from all over the world to look at these buildings. They force you to admire them and collectively, at night, particularly from the air, they are exceptionally good-looking, but more in the manner of Cindy Crawford than Anouk Aimée. Down among them, in brutal daylight, I couldn't find the human in them, or mystery. They are too declarative. 'No author, without a trial,' wrote Nathaniel Hawthorne, 'can conceive of the difficulty of writing a romance about a country where there is no shadow, no antiquity, no mystery, no picturesque and gloomy wrong, nor anything but a commonplace prosperity, in broad and simple daylight, as is happily the case with my dear native land.'

I stayed on Lake Shore Drive until it ended just to the north of what was once the Edgewater Beach Hotel, where my parents once watched Louis Armstrong with the lake at their feet. Now there's a quarter of a mile of landfill between it and the water. There was a plan to extend Lake Shore Drive into the northern suburbs, but the residents of Roger's Park blocked it. I drove up Sheridan Road past the high-rise apartment blocks, in one of which I was briefly a janitor, past Loyola University and on into Evanston, the first of the northern suburbs and once the national headquarters of the women's temperance movement. The house of its founder, Frances E. Willard, is preserved on Chicago Avenue. It was a misfortune to be a student in a town burdened with a legacy of temperance, which it felt it had to uphold by forbidding all bars and the sale of alcohol. I stopped for a moment at the beach just to the south of Northwestern University, where I had been a student. We made bonfires here, then stayed up and watched the dawn. One evening on this beach

I met a hiker with a backpack who paused for a rest. I asked him where he was walking to. 'Oregon,' he said.

Evanston got its name from a doctor named John Evans, one of Northwestern's founders, and became incorporated only after being chosen as the site for the campus. Tinkertoys were invented here in 1914 and also, perhaps, the ice-cream sundae, a compensatory treat for those suffering under the city's temperance laws, which date to 1851. Charlton Heston, Donald Rumsfeld and Grace Slick are all from Evanston. Heston marched on Washington with Martin Luther King and spoke in favour of gun control after the assassination of Robert Kennedy, but later supported Reagan and the Bushes and became president of the National Rifle Association. Only seventeen per cent of the voting residents of his birthplace supported his preferred presidential candidate in 2004. Evanston is a leafy place of old Methodist rectitude, grand houses, serene prosperity through many of its acres, liberal beliefs and, with a quarter of its population black, relative racial harmony.

Earlier in the day I'd called Bill Glasson, the son of my parents' closest friends, and asked him if he'd like to watch the sixth and, I hoped, definitive game in the Cubs–Marlins series with me. We arranged to meet in Tommy Nevin's bar here in the once-dry Evanston, a place I would have appreciated as a student. It hadn't the exotic dilapidation we looked for then in the Chicago bars, but it had a pool table, food and drink. When I got there I saw him up at the bar with his girlfriend Carol. He was around five years older than me and had been a distant and glamorous figure when I was small, with his speedboat, his open-topped car, his friends in leather jackets and slicked-back hair and his succession of spectacular girlfriends, all at a time when I was still learning my times tables.

His parents were glamorous too. They went around in long Cadillacs, had a large second house on a lake in Wisconsin and ate in the city's best restaurants where the tail-coated maître d's all knew them. It was a high-spending manner of living a few steps too far for my father, with his Irish Catholic aversion to ostentation and his memories of the Depression. The Glassons used to stop at our house in their evening wear each New Year's Eve on their way to a ball, wafts of cologne billowing from him, gold, diamonds, sequinned dress, lipstick and teeth all glittering on her, her hairdo a piece of blonde sculpture. Bill's grandfather had started a plumbing and heating business in early twentieth-century Chicago, then died young. His grandmother ran it for a long while, then passed it to her son, Bill's father, a one-time football star at the University of Wisconsin, who augmented it with clever boiler inventions, a manufacturing plant and contracts for some of the city's biggest buildings. Bill was seen as the next step in this evolving American dream, but his poor marks in school, his interest in the less refined forms of diversion and in girls were impediments. They sent him to a crammer in New Haven, which cost $20,000 per year in 1961, around fifteen times the tuition fees of the leading universities, and guaranteed to get its pupils accepted at any university in the United States. He ran an underground beer and sandwich service there and somehow got through it, personally a little richer. His parents told him to look at Yale. Then they sent him up to Boston to look at Harvard. When he had done that, he told them he thought they were both fine places, but he didn't want to attend either of them.

'And where would you like to go, son?' they asked.

'San Marino City College,' he said. It was the least academically taxing of the leading party schools in the country.

'They would like him to be a senator,' said my father. 'But the trouble is he wants to be a plumber.'

When Bill's father got into his late seventies and thought he might like to slow down, he looked for someone who would buy his company and leave him with an office and a directorship. He thought he'd found the perfect person, someone personable, something of a bon viveur like himself, who offered a good price and as much of a continuing role in the company as he would like. A contract was signed. The man moved in, began to operate the business and purchased a car, travel, some jewellery and a fur coat for his wife, charging all of it to the company. But no money for the purchase was as yet forthcoming. There was more paper-work to be done at the bank and with the lawyers, he explained. As time went on, Bill's father saw that he was the victim of an extraordinarily audacious swindle. He notified the police. He spent thousands of dollars on lawyers to get the man off the premises. Then he had a heart attack. Bill heard about it over the phone from his mother and raced across the city to the hospital, where he found his father being wheeled on a trolley to an operating theatre, barely conscious. Bill trotted along beside him and bent low to speak to him.

'I know who's caused this,' he said to his father. 'And I promise you that if anything happens to you I'm going to kill him.'

His father raised a feeble hand.

'No, no,' he said in a whisper, then added something else in a voice too faint for Bill to hear.

'What's that?' he asked.

'Just break his legs!' his father said with all his strength.

'Amazing,' I said. 'Very self-possessed and witty, in the circumstances.'

'I thought so too,' said Bill.

'What happened to the man?'

'The embezzler?'

'Yes.'

'He went away a little while after that.'

'How did that happen?'

'I did what my dad told me to do.'

'What, you mean the legs?'

'Yeah.'

'Are you serious?'

'I went into a bar down on Rush Street. Somebody gave me a phone number. It cost $750 per leg.'

– 120 –

I hadn't expected that, but then it had been a long time since I'd been living in Chicago. If somebody tells you they're going to kill you, there's a chance they might mean it.

Bill's father died a few years later. His mother didn't know how to drive, so Bill found a driver for her, a retired widower with a complicated arrangement of pins and screws in his neck placed there to support his head. Bill was fascinated by this. 'It must look amazing inside,' he said to the man. 'It would make a great piece of sculpture.' The man drove Bill's mother around to the hairdresser, the shops, her golf club and, well into her eighties, the cocktail lounges of elite hotels she'd been going to for more than sixty years. After a period of mourning she told her son she would like an escort for her evenings out. 'Someone around your age,' she told him. He found an ex-fireman he knew from his local bar and they all went together to the Drake Hotel, where Cary Grant walked through the lobby with Eva Marie Saint in *North by Northwest*. The fireman was in his early seventies, far too old for her, Bill's mother thought, but she went anyway. When they got to the hotel the man told her he knew someone who worked there. 'Where?' she asked. 'In the kitchen,' he said, and went off to say hello. She was willing to put up with advanced age for an evening, but being friendly with the help in the kitchen was a step too far. 'Get the car,' she told Bill. 'I'm going home.'

Her closest relationship during her final years was with her driver. 'It was a *Driving Miss Daisy* scenario,' Bill said. He declined before she did. When he was close to death, he pointed to his head and said to his son, 'That's for Glasson. He wants it for a sculpture.' Bill's mother fell apart after the man died, took to her bed and never came out of it again.

Tommy Nevin's was thronged, everyone looking up at the television screens and too afraid to breathe. The Cubs went ahead 2–0 and then scored another run in the seventh. In the top of the eighth inning the Cubs' pitcher retired the first Marlin batter. By then he'd only given up three hits, all harmless singles. It was one of the finest exhibitions of pitching under pressure of the season. This could be it, we all thought – old men from the neighbourhood, travelling businessmen from the Holiday Inn across the street, firemen, law and business-school students, bikers, two priests, under-graduates, bankers in suits, construction workers, the drunk, the lonely, the scantily clad, all waiting to run out into the street with a kind of end-of-war licence to celebrate.

The next Marlins hitter got a double. Then there was a popped-up fly ball that went high up towards the lights and started its descent in foul territory off left field, adjacent to the stands. The Cub outfielder moved under it, his glove up, but just before the ball got to him, a fan reached out to grab the ball and knocked it away. It fell innocently into the stands. The outfielder cursed. The fans at Wrigley Field crashed back into their seats, their hands over their faces. Tommy Nevin's pub let out a collective wail. The Marlins hitter lived to face another pitch, the game began to lose its sense and move into the territory of nightmare, the Marlins getting hit after hit while the Cubs dropped balls and looked on aghast. By the end of the first half of the calamitous eighth inning of the sixth game of the series, the Marlins were leading 8–3, and that is how the game ended. The Cubs had lost two games in a row and the series was now tied.

I drove down to Wrigley Field. Pat and his son Matt had been at the game and I was to meet them in a bar. I parked and walked past the baseball park and the Addison Avenue elevated train station. After a round of golf when I was fifteen I teed up a ball between the wooden slats of the platform, took out a four-wood and sent the ball over the hoardings of the station and the apartment buildings on Sheffield Avenue and into Wrigley Field, empty that day. The whole area now had the look of a campaign headquarters after a lost elec-tion, paper and bottles strewn around the pavement, soli-tary drunks bumping into walls, people in a desultory march to oblivion or their homes, the feeling that the energy, recently so tangible, had fled to the opposition.

I found father and son in a bar, dancing amid the moving

beams of spotlights. We had a few beers together, Matt went home and I drove with Pat to his apartment in Marina Towers, a pair of cylindrical sixty-storey buildings known as the 'Corn Cobs'. They were built in 1959 as a 'city within a city' according to a design by Bertrand Goldberg, a student of Mies van der Rohe, and financed by trade unions who were trying to stem the flow of people out of the city. Everyone in Chicago knows these buildings, though they are by no means the tallest. They were revolutionary in their autonomy – they contain parking, shops, a bowling alley and a theatre that is now the House of Blues; in their materials – at the time of construction they were the tallest reinforced concrete structures in the world, as well as the tallest residential buildings; and in their shape – petal-shaped balconies around a central core, a thirty-five-foot-diameter service-containing 'vertical chute', as it was described by architect Paul Heyer. Goldberg himself said, 'Whereas we had been talking for years about the machine in architecture, as part of the old Bauhaus tradition, it had more potential than anything we could imagine. The post-and-beam suddenly became a hangover from the Victorian tradition where the machine had been an expression of the human arm at work, from left to right and up and down. I felt almost like a primitive looking at the machine that could create a material by a process that did not exist before – produce a magic that was not there before.'

I sat with Pat on his balcony looking out over the river at the lights of the city. The white, floodlit Wrigley Building, built with the proceeds from chewing gum, was just to our left. It was around two o'clock in the morning. We had another beer we didn't need. I asked him if he remembered our grammar-school class reunion.

'I went to a couple of them,' he said. 'You mean the big one in the school basement, the one you were at?'

'Yes,' I said. 'You wore the school uniform.'

He laughed.

'Hardly anyone brought their husband or wife, but you

brought Marcella. It had to be tedious for them, going around from group to group listening to stories about people they'd never met. People were talking a lot about those who couldn't be found, and above all they talked about Louie Dwinnell, the class wild man. Do you remember? They'd say, "Do you know where Louie Dwinnell is? Did he go back to Kentucky? Do you think he's in jail?" Marcella was going around the room hearing a lot about Louie Dwinnell. Do you remember what she did?'

'What?'

'She went over to the table at the entrance where they had a pile of blank stickers we were supposed to write our names on. She took one and wrote "Louise Dwinnell" on it, then went up to people and said, "Hi, my name is Louise. You probably remember me when I was Louie."'

He laughed again, his shoulders shaking. He'd always had the most free and infectious laugh. 'That's right,' he said. 'It was brilliant.'

I'd been thinking of what I would say to him since leaving Indiana and then tried to deliver it to him there on his balcony. I asked him to think of all he could lose, this intellectual wonder of a stepdaughter he'd once risked his life to save from drowning, this unusual wife so imaginative in thought and quick to be moved, this family of disparate parts they'd made into a single organism, but which could fall apart along its blood lines if he left. Wasn't the worst of the struggle over with? Could it be worth it to go elsewhere? He had time to answer, but seemed to be petrifying in his chair. It was the game, the beer, the lack of sleep. And anyway I'd said nothing he hadn't already thought of. These are speeches that have their origin in a feeling of grave responsibility, generate a sense of worthiness in the telling, no matter how one might struggle to avoid this, and in the end are addressed more to the self than to the other. The words drifted past him and into the night air of the city like motes of dust.

I slept on Pat's sofa and in the morning we drove to Evanston. We had breakfast in the Central Café, old clocks, coffee machines, phones, dolls and other artefacts crowding shelves and hanging from the walls. There's a strain of surrealism you meet every now and then in American restaurants, amid all the franchises. This was one of the best I found anywhere for the first meal of the day. Pat ate two cheeseburgers. I'd seen this kind of hangover remedy before, but never knew how anyone could face it. The newspaper was full of lamentation for the cataclysmic eighth inning of the Cubs game and there was nearly a page on the fan who'd interfered with the foul ball. He'd had to be escorted out of the ball park by security men, who hid him under someone else's jacket. Jeb Bush offered him asylum in Florida. Boys who played on the Little League team that the man coached stepped forward to say that he was a wonderful person and a true Cubs fan. He himself made a long, agonised statement apologising to the city of Chicago and in particular to Ernie Banks, Mr Cub, the idol of my youth. There was talk of film rights. I wondered about raising the subject of the previous night with Pat now that it was daylight, but sensed the futility of it. We played a round of golf on a small, narrow municipal course that moved behind Evanston houses and apartment buildings and along the banks of the north branch of the Chicago River, then arranged to meet later in a nearby bar to watch the final game of the Cubs–Marlins series.

That night Pat arrived with his girlfriend Barbara. She was convivial in a somewhat muted way, being perhaps a little wary of me. The game was the anticlimax that all of Chicago feared it would be. The Marlins scored three runs in the first inning, then the Cubs came back with a three-run home run in the second. Their pitcher Kerry Wood hit a home run with a man on base in the third, putting them ahead. People were there with banners and whistles and Cubs hats and there was an eruption of ecstasy at Wood's great blow, but it lacked belief. The calamitous eighth inning of the night before had maimed the city's consciousness, and the team's. The Marlins scored in the fifth, sixth and seventh and the Cubs finally went down 9–6. They'd lost the final three games of the series, and the magnificent dream of the World Series was in ruins.

Afterwards I drove south towards Ogden Dunes. On the way I stopped at the Green Mill, a late-opening jazz place on north Broadway in Uptown. It was once part of an outdoor music gardens modelled on the Moulin Rouge and then became a speakeasy in the 1920s, part owned by an Italian who gave himself the Irish name 'Machinegun' Jack McGurn in order to improve his prospects in the fight business. He once cut out the tongue of a singer named Joe E. Lewis to persuade him to renew his contract at the Green Mill instead of moving to the South Side. Al Capone had a regular booth there. You walk through the front door of this bar and into another time, grinning waiters with brillianteened hair and white aprons mixing cocktails behind the mirrored bar, velvet scythe-shaped booths with candles on the tables lighting up the undersides of faces, an aura of anticipation and pleasure and easy elegance, the soft murmur of laughter and talk rolling and gently breaking like waves on a shoreline, a jazz band up on the stage and an Art Deco statue of Ceres, goddess of grain, looking on. So artful and natural is its mixture of unpretentiousness and class that, though the customers might be in shorts and T-shirts, you nevertheless believe you are in a world of hat-check girls and starlets, men in sharp suits and hand-made shoes lighting cigarettes for glamorous women in glittering dresses. I once wrote into a novel a life-changing night I'd spent at the Green Mill, but moved it to Barcelona.

When I got back to Ogden Dunes, Marcella was in the kitchen, still taut as a cable on a bridge. After a while she asked me if I'd met Barbara. I'd told both Pat and her that I wouldn't be reporting what I'd heard from one to the other. But what were the ethics of this? 'No,' I told her, but in doing so was I protecting her or me?

Chicago has had its laureates. Carl Sandburg and Gwendolyn Brooks in poetry. David Mamet in the theatre. James T. Farrell,

Nelson Algren and Richard Wright in fiction. Their terrain, as opposed to that of the city's Nobel Prizewinners Hemingway and Bellow, has tended to be down among those at the receiving end of power rather than the bourgeois, the intellectual or the glamorous. They have written of a city of bad breaks and hard knocks, a tough and brawling city with a long history of labour, race and police riots, its streets governed by gangs, political overseers and local hard cases; a city, too, forever 'on the make', as Algren said, populated by embezzlers, power brokers, hustlers, dealers in graft, crooked lawyers and those who get used by them.

Studs Terkel is the city's laureate of the human voice. He has investigated it and celebrated if for more than seventy years on television, a daily radio show on WFMT and in fourteen books of oral history that have recorded the experience of Americans during the course of his lifetime, from the Great Depression to the Second World War to work and race and, as he got into his late eighties, death. 'They tell the story of the American century verbatim,' as one writer put it. Reading them, you think of Whitman's line, 'I hear America singing.'

The voices filled him early. His parents were Russian Jews who brought him and his two brothers to Chicago from New York when he was twelve. His father was a tailor and his mother ran a hotel called the Wells Grand, inhabited in the main by working people – engine drivers, carpenters, bakers, tool and dye makers and a Welsh scavenger named Myrd LLydgyn, 'who didn't even have a vowel to his name'. Some were members of the IWW, aspiring to create a single powerful union for all working people. Many of these were self-educated men who carried around pocket books costing five cents of works by Shakespeare or Darwin or of the speeches of Clarence Darrow. Intellectual self-improvement was part of the ethic. Others were hostile to the unions. 'I listened to their debates,' said Studs. 'That's when I began my career as a spectator and a listener.' Just a few blocks away was Bughouse Square, Chicago's version of Speakers' Corner, where he heard evangelicals, anarchists, atheists, poets and people with booklets on sexual hygiene for sale. When he was fourteen he saw Lucy Parsons there, widow of Albert, one of the Haymarket Martyrs, who was executed for his part in a demonstration in Chicago in 1886 in favour of the eight-hour day. A policeman was killed by an unidentified bomb-thrower, possibly an agent provocateur, and the state prosecuted eight of the leaders, as they were to do eighty-two years later after the demonstrations at the Democratic Convention in Chicago in 1968. In the earlier case the leaders were executed. The world's May Day celebrations were established to commemorate the Haymarket Martyrs.

Chicago is to Studs Terkel above all a 'city of hands', hands being an old word for worker. One of his favourite poems is Brecht's 'Questions from a Worker Who Reads', which begins:

Who built Thebes of the seven gates?
In the books you will find the names of kings.
Did the kings haul up the lumps of rock?
And Babylon, many times demolished,
Who raised it up so many times?

He took the name Studs, having been born Louis, from James T. Farrell's novel *Studs Lonigan*, the story of a hard-drinking South Side Irish Catholic. Chicago is proud of its plain-talking plebeianness; the name Studs is in itself a riposte to effeteness.

I went to see him in his quietly stately brick house in Castlewood Terrace in Uptown, the lake-front park to his east and a neighbourhood of working people to his west. He looked up at me through the little window on his door, his hair on end and the stub of a cigar in his mouth, then let me in. He was still in his pyjamas. 'I'm just making breakfast,' he said. I followed him through the house to his kitchen and watched him prepare orange juice, tea and toast. Three quotations were pinned to the wall: 'Too long a sacrifice

makes a stone of the heart,' W.B. Yeats; 'The executioner's face is always well hidden,' Bob Dylan; and 'He who giveth quickly, giveth twice,' Miguel de Cervantes.

I missed many things while growing up in Chicago: Hyde Park, live comedy, the Chicago Symphony under Solti, Howlin' Wolf. Another was Studs' radio show. In 1998, though, I was invited onto it along with the photographer Steve Pyke, with whom I'd produced a novel called *I Could Read the Sky*. Studs was eighty-six at the time and had just retired from his radio show, but National Public Radio let him do what he wanted, and he wanted to do something about this book as it is about a migrant worker and it reminded him of the poem by Brecht. Steve and I went to a studio at Navy Pier and waited for him. I watched through a glass door as he came in with an armful of vinyl LPs of Irish music to play during the interview, wearing a neck brace and talking with whomever passed. If no one passed he talked with himself. He laid out his hearing aids, spare batteries, a pump and miniature tools on a table, for like Beethoven, whose livelihood and passion were also based in sound, he was deaf, or very nearly. Then we went through to meet him. He swapped hearing aids and twisted dials, the little half-moon electronic prostheses letting out mournful, high-pitched wails, like cats in heat. 'God damn it!' he shouted. 'I'm the bionic man, but I'm at war with technology!' He can't drive, has never used the Internet, is baffled by telephones and self-operating lifts and even by tape recorders, the central instrument of his working life. 'And I don't mean the machinery inside it, either,' he has said. 'I mean all of it. I don't know how to put in the cassette, which way up it goes, how to close the lid when it's in, which is the button to press to get it to start . . .'

To get to work he rode the bus. Nancy Newman, a fellow passenger, said, 'We used to have long, long chats together, or at least we did the times Studs wasn't having long, long chats with someone else on the bus, or chairing a debate among all the passengers together.' His speech is voluminous, light, encircling, largely anecdotal and humorous, quick and staccato, but it can slow when he wants to savour something, and is as digressive as Tristram Shandy's, but always gets to its punch line eventually. Uniting it is a sensibility the aim of which John Kenneth Galbraith – quoting William Randolph Hearst in an attempt to summarise Studs – described as being 'To comfort the afflicted and to afflict the comfortable'. This got Studs blacklisted when he was brought before McCarthy's House Un-American Activities Committee and refused to name names, but now there is a part of Division Street named after him and the mayor declared his ninetieth birthday Studs Terkel Day.

When we went into the studio he took our book out and began to leaf through it. It was full of lines, underscores, arrows and notes in different-coloured inks and what seemed a hand-written tract at the end. Garrison Keillor has said that when Studs invites you onto his programme to discuss a book, 'he's not only read it, he can conduct a seminar on it'. On the air he's curious and celebratory rather than discursive or confrontational. For one who loves so much to talk, he's self-effacing. He tries to create an ambience of revelatory speech, all improvised, in which he can get behind what his subject has done rather than staying in front of it. He's interviewed Bertrand Russell, James Baldwin, Tennessee Williams, Dorothy Parker, Martin Luther King, Simone de Beauvoir, Bob Dylan and Billie Holiday, along with thousands known only to those around them. He looks for exemplary stories, inspired speech, a true match of word and feeling, but what he seems most to prize are examples of redemption, like the Red-hating, free-marketeering, Republican Party speechwriter who later joined the IWW, marched against the Vietnam War and named his daughters Molly Maguire, Mother Jones and Emma Goldman. Or the former Exalted Cyclops of the Ku Klux Klan who became a union organiser working on behalf of black janitors and weeping over the beauty of the speeches of Martin Luther King.

I asked him what he thought makes a good interviewer. 'Curiosity. Enthusiasm,' he said. 'And you really have to listen to a degree we usually don't when we're conversing. There can be little signs – a pause, a change of subject, a subtle tone that belies what is being said. I was on a music tour in the early 1950s with Win Stracke, Larry Lane and the great bluesman Big Bill Broonzy, three white guys and a black guy. We went into a little blue-collar restaurant in Lafayette, Indiana, and the waiter behind the counter said, "I'll serve three of you", meaning, of course, not Bill. Well, we were indignant, but I could hear a small chuckle from Bill. What was that? There was nothing going on that was funny. But it was laughter in adversity, in a moment of humiliation, the laughter of the blues that keeps you from crying, or maybe raging. That's a different tone of laughter.'

Since I was last in his house, his wife Ida had died. His

son Dan was there. We sat around the table while Studs ate his breakfast. 'I think W.C. Fields is the man of the hour,' he said. 'We're in a sinister time, a banal time, a time of forgetfulness. But it's also hilarious, and W.C. Fields is the guy who describes it. We're the beacon of freedom and democracy, but we've invaded more countries than anyone, even Rome. Remember Grenada? Two guys in the street. One says, "Grenada is a dangerous foe." "Where the hell is Grenada?" says the other. "Well, it's our *enemy*," says the first one. "Yeah, but WHERE IS IT?" That's W.C. Fields. Or Reagan saying the Sandinistas were going to invade us through Mexico. *Nobody laughed*. And Schwarzenegger, that's W.C. Fields too.'

He grew up in the Depression and was just twenty when Roosevelt took office. 'That was the turning point for me. A great hope realised. Now they preach the virtue of small government, excluding the military part of course. None did it more than Reagan. But they forget. He did too. His own father was saved by the New Deal, and he himself voted for Roosevelt four times. They vilify the Sixties too, but that was the time of the revival of the democratising principles of civil rights, anti-homophobia, international peace, feminism. These people go off their nut with rage against these things and they've been so successful with their backlash that they've completely skewed the political alignment. I'll act it out for you.'

He got up and then bent way over to the right from his waist. 'Two guys in the street, one walking normal, the other bent way over to the right. The straight one says, "How ya doin', Charlie?" The other one says, "Hey, what's happened to you? You're way over to the left." "No, I'm not, Charlie, I'm standing straight." "You're so far left you're a *terrorist*!" says Charlie. The Democratic Party is now over there with Charlie.'

At ninety-one he'd just published a book called *Hope Dies Last*. 'I've always believed in the prophetic minority,' he said. 'Thomas Paine, Sam Adams, all the people struggling down in their communities and workplaces for dignity and a fair shake, out of sight of the powerful.' The following year he became one of the oldest people ever to have open-heart surgery. He had a bad fall down his front steps afterwards that could have finished him – 'a wild, jazzy tumble,' he said, 'choreographed by Bob Fosse rather than Balanchine!' – then came back with a book about music called *And They All Sang – Adventures of an Eclectic Disc Jockey*, based on his interviews with musicians. There are many who remain lively in their nineties, but I've met no one of his age, and few of much younger ages, with his level of lucidity, wit, productivity or empathetic enthusiasm. 'His rapport with people is extraordinary,' the Chicago historian Gary Wills has said. 'They become better when they're around him.'

He had to address a meeting that lunchtime and went upstairs to change. He came down dressed as always in dark trousers and jacket with red socks and a red checked shirt. He wanted to tell another story before leaving.

'One night I was sitting in here watching a White Sox game on television. Ida was upstairs asleep. I had the windows open because it was summer. This is a street of the prosperous surrounded by the poor. A man came in through one of the windows, an amateur thief. But I didn't hear him because I didn't have my hearing aid in. Suddenly he was standing in front of me and talking to me, but I couldn't understand a thing. I turned a light on and he threw his hands up over his face. I went into the bathroom, put on a hearing aid, then turned on the hall light. Again he threw his hands up in front of his face. He told me he wanted my money. Well, that was his lucky day because I'd just cashed a cheque for $300 and had only spent twenty of it. Had I nimbler fingers, I'd have taken out just a little of it, but I could only grab the whole wad. He couldn't believe it. He stood there in front of me counting it. I said, "Wait a minute. I'm broke now. Can you give me $20?" He turned away and peeled off a twenty and gave it to me. "Thank you," I said. "You're welcome," he said, and ran away. They asked me afterwards if this experience made me more conservative. "No," I said. "The reverse. That's a perfect example of late twentieth-century capitalism. There was the hostile takeover – that was the $300. Then a moment of guilt – that was the turning away. And the $20 was the establishment of a foundation."'

I went out into Studs' 'City of Hands'. I took Lake Shore Drive all the way to 47th Street and then drove through the South Side, once known as the Black Belt, or Bronzeville, because since the First World War the population has been almost entirely black. They came up from the Mississippi Delta on the train from Memphis looking for work in the factories and stockyards and railroads, lured from their sharecropper shacks by labour agents, preachers, railroad porters who spoke of the good and dignified life to be lived in the northern cities, and above all by Robert S. Abbott, publisher of the *Chicago Defender*, the country's leading black newspaper, who launched the Great Northern Drive, comparing it to the Flight of the Israelities from Egypt and using songs such as 'Bound for the Promised Land'. Between 1910 and 1930 the black population of Chicago quintupled; then, after the introduction of the mechanical cotton picker in the 1940s, the movement of Delta sharecroppers to Chicago became part of possibly the largest ever human migration not caused by war or famine. In 1940 seventy-seven per cent of black Americans lived in the south, forty-nine per cent in rural areas. Five million went north after the cotton picker came in and thereafter black America was largely urban. At one point 2,200 black people were moving to Chicago each week. Bronzeville took over from Harlem as the capital of black America. Joe Louis and Mahalia Jackson lived there. It was a world unto itself. An anonymous New Deal Federal Writers' Project observer – it might have been Studs Terkel as he was one of the Chicago writers in the project, along with Saul Bellow and Nelson Algren – described the area around South Park Way and 47th Street: 'On adjoining side streets are small shops selling mystic charms and potions; curbstone stands with smoke rising from wood fires over which chicken and spare ribs are being barbecued; lunchrooms serving hot fish, sweet potato pie, gumbo and other Southern dishes, markets bulging with turnip tops, mustard greens, and chitterlings; taverns and nightclubs that resound with blues singing and hot-foot music.'

The migrants were hemmed in by real-estate trade practices that forbade agents from renting properties in white neighbourhoods to black people, by white mobs of thousands who gathered each time the city housing authority tried to integrate and stoned and firebombed the prospective black tenants back into the ghetto, and eventually by railroad lines and the Dan Ryan Expressway, which formed the boundaries for the parts of the city in which they were to be permitted to live. The agony and shame of the south moved northwards. A southern white lawyer named David Cohn, who'd once expressed the opinion that educating a black man 'tends to unbalance him mentally', wrote: 'The coming problem of agricultural displacement in the Delta and the whole South is of huge proportions and must concern the entire nation . . . Five million people will be removed from the land within the next few years. They must go somewhere. But where? They must do something. But what? They must be housed. But where is the housing? Most of the group are farm Negroes totally unprepared for urban, industrial life. How will they be industrially absorbed? What will be the effect of throwing them upon the labour market? What will be their reception at the hands of white and Negro workers whose jobs and wages they threaten? . . . If tens of thousands of Southern Negroes descend upon communities totally unprepared for them psychologically and industrially, what will the effect be upon race relations in the United States? . . . Will the victims of farm mechanization become the victims of race conflict? There is an enormous tragedy in the making unless the United States acts, and acts promptly, upon a problem that affects millions of people and the whole social structure of the nation.'

Richard Wright, author of *Native Son* and a migrant himself, wrote similarly: 'We, who were landless upon the land; we, who had barely managed to live in family groups; we, who needed the ritual and guidance of institutions to hold our atomized lives together in lines of purpose; we, who had only known relationships to people and not relationships to things; we, who had our personalities blasted with two hundred years of slavery and had been turned loose to shift for ourselves – we were such a folk as this when we moved into a world that was destined to test all we were, that threw us into the scales of competition to weigh our mettle.'

When I was growing up, the racial lines had been drawn absolutely and the South Side was the Heart of Darkness to white Chicago, a place where every male was said to be armed and wishing you ill.

I drove over to 48th and Indiana to see if a bar named Theresa's was still there. It wasn't, and the corner looked nothing like how I'd remembered it. I'd gone there one night with some friends when I was a student to hear Junior Wells play the blues. It was a small, narrow bar with a tiny dance floor in front of a stage. We were the only white people in it. There was a house band with which various guitarists and singers appeared. Junior Wells was to come on around midnight. We sat at a long table with three middle-aged black ladies in frilly dresses who offered us shots from their flasks. 'You don't want to pay no Saturday-night prices at the bar, sugar,' one said as she tipped some whiskey into my glass.

In front of the stage a moustachioed man with his shirt open moved like a firestorm among the dancers, clucking, strutting, pirouetting, his arms waving as though in a religious convulsion. Finally he had the dance floor to himself. He threw off his shirt, mopped his brow, then picked up a chair with his teeth and danced with it. I saw a tall young woman wearing spectacles, rather prim-looking, watching him through narrowed eyes. Then she got up and moved towards the stage. She began to dance, first by herself in a corner, then with the man. She might have been a school-teacher. The man held his arms above his head and, hips thrust forward, moved towards her in short hops. With each one he let out a yelp, 'Yeah! . . . All right! . . . I'm comin' for ya!' They met, pelvis to pelvis. He ground his hips into her in wide loops, his back arched. She moved forward like a ship entering a harbour, forcing him back towards a wall. He stepped latterly to avoid being trapped, but she cut him off. Soon he was flat against the wall. With a quick leap she turned around and shimmied down to the floor and back up again, then bent over, her hands on her knees, and screwed her bottom into his pelvis. He looked around at everybody and tried to laugh, but seemed unable to make a sound. It was all running away from him now. She turned around to face him and pinned him to the wall, her hands planted above his shoulders. The guitar player and drummer drove harder into the tune for they wanted to get the most they could out of this. Sweat ran down over the man's eyes and off the tip of his nose. He looked like he couldn't breathe. She slid down his front and back up again, her whole body pressed to his, the music driving still louder and more insistent. Then they went at it together, shoulder to shoulder, hip to hip in a shuddering frenzy, him letting out a long wail and her driving on until finally he could take no more and reached into his pocket, took out a white handkerchief and waved it before her in surrender, then collapsed against the wall. His chest heaved as he struggled to get his breath. The woman stepped back, looked him up and down as he wiped the sweat from his face, then walked to her table.

The band took a break and I went into the toilet. A man was inside leaning against the sink, one hand clenched and raising a vein in his forearm and in the other a syringe. He looked up at me. 'You want some, brother?' he asked. 'No, thanks,' I said. 'Well, just to let you know you're welcome.'

When I went back out again I saw Junior Wells come into the bar alone, carrying his harmonicas in a leather case. He had on a broad-brimmed black hat, a camel's hair overcoat, a white silk scarf and a look of supreme disdain on his face. He stepped up to the bar and was given a cognac without having to ask. He acknowledged people with a faint passing of his hand. Everybody was waiting for him, but he was going to make them wait longer. He had another drink, received visitors. Someone took his coat away and he stepped onto the stage, his back to the audience as he opened his case, looked at all his harmonicas lying in their velvet beds and took one out. Years later, when black Chicago had in the main lost interest in the blues and the bluesmen had to play in music bars on the white North Side, I saw him and a large band in a place on Lincoln Avenue. 'How y'all tonight?' he called out and smiled, then jived his way through two long sets. Here in Theresa's he played just five songs, standing still as a pillar, the music dark, raw, breathtakingly artful and delivered with an imperiousness that declared that we shouldn't think he was playing for us, but rather for the music itself. I had heard, and would later hear, a lot of blues on record and in clubs in Europe and the United States, but nothing so intense, so coldly passionate and expressive as these five songs. Perhaps he thrived best among his constituents.

I went to the bar to get a beer. A man with shoulders like a heavyweight's sat on a stool next to where I stood, drinking alone. When my beer arrived he put a dollar down. 'I've got that,' he said to the barman. Then to me, 'White this, black that. It's boring, isn't it? We can get past that, don't you think?' He held out his hand. 'It's good to see you down here.'

A guitar player got up in front of the house band and began to play. I took another glass of whiskey from the flask of one of the ladies at our table, closed my eyes and tried to give myself to the music note by note. When I opened them I wrote out a few sentences in a poor hand on a serviette, the sentences still poorer, I would discover later. Then I watched the guitarist shaking his head at his licks, sprays of sweat flying through the beams of light as if from a boxer getting hit. People were dancing. I asked one of the girls in our company to come up with me, and she did. We shuffled around, loose from the drink. Out on the periphery a woman danced alone. She looked to me like she was somewhere in her forties. She wore a short black dress and a platinum blonde wig. Her hands hung loose from her wrists like drying clothes as she swayed and shivered to the music. Without my seeing how she got there she was suddenly before me. She bumped the girl I was with out of the way with a swing of her hip and began to dance, feet planted wide, lips parted, her hands running up along her sides, hips to breasts. The song ended with a bang on the drum. I made a move to sit down, but she stopped me and we waited together for the next song. It was slow and raw, another tale of the perfidy of women, runs of notes from the guitar framed by single drumbeats. She stepped towards me and put her arms around my neck. We moved around in a slow circle, the whole of her body pressed to mine, the music coming towards us in a slow pulse through the thick air. Then she stopped, one hand on the back of my neck, the other on my hip, and slid her knee slowly up the inside of my thigh, whispering into my ear, 'Now I'm going to teach you how the niggers dance, boy.' I held on tight to the end, then got back to my chair. Maybe it was the sex that white Chicago was afraid of, rather than the guns.

Thirty years later I drove again through the vanquished streets of the South Side. They had once been so populous that a new black quarter had to be created in Lawndale on the West Side. Now they looked as though they'd long been under aerial bombardment. 'Reminds me of a diseased jawbone,' wrote Henry Miller after passing through the South Side, 'some of it smashed and pulverized, some of it charred and ulcerated.' Tower blocks of flats rose up in clusters and there were houses here and there and apartment buildings, many with their windows boarded up; there were churches, including Louis Farrakhan's Nation of Islam national head-quarters, hair and nail shops, liquor stores, used-tyre dealers, a few middle-aged men sitting on wooden crates. But all in all, it seemed, there were more vacant lots than filled ones.

Many attempts have been made to cure the South Side and places like it. There have been community centres, black cooperatives, schools run by charities, incentives for business, new parks, religion, revolutionary politics, philanthropy and job-training programmes. The Kennedy administration thought that the inner cities presented the gravest domestic problem of all and put forward numerous programmes to cure it, including the idea of federally funding radical community leaders to agitate around issues of employment, education or housing in the hope of mobilising the disheartened into a political force that would revitalise the neighbourhoods. But there was no salvation. The stockyards moved to Oklahoma, steel mills automated and constricted and the little neighbourhood factories that used to be spread throughout the city shut down. Between 1972 and 1982 Chicago lost forty-seven per cent of its manufacturing jobs. This was the kind of work people had come up from Mississippi for, and now it was disappearing. All the government social programmes, in addition to the schools, the post office and the transport system, created thousands of jobs for black people, but as soon as they earned enough money they tended to leave for the suburbs. According to Nicholas Lemann's book *The Promised Land*, Woodlawn lost thirty-three per cent of its population in the 1960s and thirty-two per cent in the 1970s. Landlords set fire to their worthless buildings for the insurance money. When a group of South Side tenants demanded the presence of their landlord to make a number of complaints about maintenance, he appeared with his lawyer and said he would hand over the building to anyone who would give him a dollar. There are areas of the South Side where the per capita income is two per cent of what it is along certain streets just a few miles north on the Gold Coast. Meanwhile, in the 1970s alone, the black population of the Chicago suburbs grew by eighty per cent as black families entered the middle class. The city and the national government would appear to have given up on the South Side. I'd heard from more than one source that the notion now was to tear down the towers and decrepit apartment buildings, ship most of the remaining people out to the suburbs and build new developments for the upwardly mobile.

I headed north through the dereliction, railroad lines and entanglement of converging expressways, then came by chance upon the Prairie Avenue Historical District, a row of grand mansions from the time when the Near South Side housed some of the wealthiest families in the city. It was like finding opera glasses among the plastic ducks and cut-rate washing powder of a dollar store. Just along from there, at 21st Street and Michigan Avenue, is the Blues Heaven Foundation, once the Chess Records Studio, where Willy Dixon, Sonny Boy Williamson, Chuck Berry and Bo Diddley recorded. Muddy Waters made 'Mannish Boy' and 'I Just Want to Make Love to You' there, but when the Rolling Stones arrived at the Chess studio to record in 1964 they found him painting the walls for pay.

I went west and then north up through Little Italy and Greektown, nearly all of their homes and little shops ploughed under long ago to make way for roads and the Chicago Circle campus of the University of Illinois, its citizens and their descendants now in the suburbs. From there I drove west to Madison and California, where I had a job driving a truck for a food cooperative during the summer when I was twenty-one. They bought produce from farms and then sold it in a warehouse at below supermarket prices. Government-subsidised food programmes were also run out of there and my job was to deliver the food to suburbs where poor, mostly black people lived. Howlin' Wolf's regular weekend residency was in a bar two blocks away. This was another region of the city where it was said that you were unlikely to come out alive, worse still than the South Side. I'd have a break-fast of cornbread and home-made lemonade in a soul-food restaurant across from the warehouse, then go in and make my deliveries. Truckers who drove enormous articulated lorries would salute me with foghorns that rang out across the cornfields like ocean liners', as though I was one of the brotherhood.

I was asked by the committee who ran the cooperative if I would make a delivery for free on a Saturday morning for a community organisation. I said I would. When I got there I found out that the community organisation was the Black Panthers. A human chain was passing onions and collard greens and sweet potatoes into my truck and, when they finished, I drove the load and one of the Panthers over to their West Side headquarters. He was bespectacled, amiable and wore a buttoned-down shirt. He looked like he could be a student of accountancy. He told me that party philosophy had changed and that instead of militant revolution they were concentrating on what Huey P. Newton, inspired by Mao, called 'survival programmes' – food and clothing distribution, drug rehabilitation, an ambulance service, classes in politics, economics and self-defence and sickle-cell disease testing. Still, I couldn't but be aware of Panthers with guns, of shoot-outs with the police and that just three years earlier one of their Chicago leaders, Fred Hampton, had been killed during a police raid, and when a police car screeched to a halt just in front of me as we were pulling up to the Panther headquarters, I thought my heart would explode. A round black policeman got out of his squad car and bowled towards us at speed. He appeared at the window of the truck and asked, 'Do you need any help unloading?' Was this a joke? I never found out. 'No, thanks,' said my passenger, and the policeman went away.

Their office was a store front with the entire plate-glass front window filled with sandbags. Inside, in the shadows, three Panthers in black leather jackets, sunglasses and berets sat in silence around a desk. Another human chain appeared as if out of a fold in the air, we unloaded and I left. Four years earlier this region had been burned during the riots that followed the assassination of Martin Luther King. Large tracts of what remained had been, and would continue to be, torched by arsonists hired by landlords. A gang called the Vice Lords sold drugs, killed rivals and patrolled the projects. As an image of cool and power and possibility in this zone of deprivation and fatherlessness, the Panthers were, I thought, a compelling alternative to the gangs. J. Edgar Hoover thought so too and declared them 'the greatest threat to the internal security of the country'. They might, as Sinn Fein was to do later in Ireland, have generated a new kind of politics among those so far from the mainstream of American life that it was invisible to them, but the FBI and the metropolitan police forces planted spies and false evidence, coerced and cajoled, spread lies, turned black groups against each other through disinformation and at times resorted to assassination. Fred Hampton had been the most prominent of the Panthers in Chicago. He had studied law, worked with the NAACP and, after joining the Panthers, had brokered truces among the Chicago gangs and made political alliances with them and with radical student groups. On 7 December 1969 an FBI plant named William O'Neal cooked a meal loaded with seco-barbital for Hampton, his pregnant girlfriend and other Panthers at Hampton's apartment on Monroe near Western after Hampton had given a lecture at a church hall. Hampton passed out in mid-sentence while talking with his mother on the telephone. A police party representing every tier of govern-ment – city, county, state and national – broke in at 4 a.m. and shot Hampton and his bodyguard, both of whom were asleep. Hampton initially survived, but a policeman put two bullets into his head at point-blank range. The raiding party then fired on, beat and dragged the other Panthers into the street and arrested them for the attempted murder of police officers. Fred Hampton was twenty-one years old. 'He was a giant,' said Quentin Young, Studs Terkel's doctor and one of the country's leading advocates of national healthcare. 'This is a terrible way to put it, but the people who made it their business to kill the leaders of the black movement picked the right ones.'

I drifted northwards and eastwards, crossing the river on Chicago Avenue and then heading up Rush Street, the Strip, a zone of frivolity and decadence and tourist bars where Bill Glasson purchased the services of the man who broke the legs of his father's nemesis. It was too early in the day for the marks and the vultures. The Cabrini Green housing project, named for a nun who was the first American to be canonised, lay sullenly and obdurately just to the north of Rush Street, a canker in a prime real-estate zone. It was known as 'Little Hell' when Swedes lived in shanties beneath shooting flames and clouds of poisonous fumes from a gas refinery, and later as 'Little Sicily' for a subsequent wave of immigrants. The city built and in time came to ignore public-housing tower blocks, where twenty thousand people lived amid boarded-up windows, paved-over lawns, backed-up garbage in fifteen-storey chutes, burst pipes, cockroaches and rats, their balconies encased in steel mesh and their streets controlled by gangs. A friend of mine was driving through here one afternoon when the car in front of him suddenly pulled over and a tall shaven-headed man in a suit got out, trotted across wasteground to a basketball court and began playing with a group of boys. It was Michael Jordan, descended like Zeus from Olympus. The towers have come down now, new market-priced apartment developments and row houses are going up, with a small portion allocated for public-housing tenants, and two-thirds of the population has been dispersed. This is likely to be the destiny of much of the South and West Sides.

I met the south-west edge of Lincoln Park and then headed up Clark Street through zones that would later come alive with various forms of nightlife – gay, Irish, sports-mad, singles, bohemian. After that came old Swedish and German neighbourhoods and acres of store fronts and red-brick apartment buildings stretching all the way to Evanston. I'd once seen an innovative sign on it advertising Keim Furs. 'Save the Environment – Wear Furs! Non-Polluting, Biodegradable, Renewable Resource.' A friend of my father's used to strike a solemn pose and intone, 'I am Clark Street and Clark Street is me,' whenever he felt the need to explain himself.

Finally I got to Rogers Park up at the northern boundary of the city. I grew up here, first in a small apartment on Damen Avenue that my parents found after the war, then in a larger place a short distance to the west. Germans grew hay here and cucumbers for pickles after the Potawatami had been displaced. I left the car near my first home and walked over to the park named after this tribe. I played in a baseball league here and flattened pennies on the railroad tracks that ran along its eastern end. There was hardly a black person on the whole of the North Side when I was growing up, but Damen Avenue is now all black, or nearly so. We lived in an apartment block of three storeys wrapped around a concrete courtyard in a one-bedroom place where I slept in the hall. My closest friend was called Jimmy Hendricks. I nearly died there twice, once when I was four years old and a speeding car caught the tail of my shirt – but not me – as I ran past the front of it, and the other when I fell head-first from the top of a tree and was saved when my heel wedged between two low branches on the way down. Whispering Joe the janitor extracted me. One rainy summer night I went out into the courtyard to bring in my tricycle and saw the Virgin Mary in the sky, her arms opening to me. Or so my memory still persists in telling me.

We moved half a mile west to Claremont Avenue when I was five. This was, and is, a quiet and sedate neighbourhood of small apartment blocks and single-storey brick houses with well-tended lawns in front, the streets dense with trees, like most of Chicago. When we moved, the main road, Western Avenue, was like the mouth of a child losing teeth, with un-developed lots filled with weeds among the shops and bars. We dug holes and had wars in them and in the winter people sold Christmas trees. We lived on the top floor of a building with seven apartments, three on each side of the central stair-well and another in the basement. It had a big lawn along the side, with a cherry tree that exploded into pink in the spring.

There's another apartment building in that space now. Our landlord was Les Lear, agent and impresario, whose visitors included comics, singers, trick waterskiers, bathing beauties and Hollywood stars like Joe E. Brown of the rubberised mouth and the legendary Pat O'Brien who played cops and priests in movies and once at a party at Les Lear's house introduced me to his son, who was in the CIA. Mr Lear and his wife lived on the first floor, beside Laralu, who grew up to be the actress I stayed with in New York. Two elderly couples lived on the floor below us. I saw one of the women late one night running up and down the stairs in her nightdress, railing at invisible assailants. That was the first I ever saw of dementia. The coquettish Finnegan sisters, who were my age, lived in the basement, and next to us on the third floor were two beautiful teenage girls, one dark-haired and the other blonde, who babysat for me. One of them left a booklet of photographs of Elvis Presley on the landing for the janitor to take away. I opened it and saw that she had covered Elvis' face with blood-red imprints from her lips. I wondered which of them it was. That was the first I ever saw of sex, such as it was.

The local Catholic church, St Margaret Mary's, was a block away. Around it were distributed the priests' residence, convent, primary school and playground. That was my world. I only knew Catholics. I served Mass and was a member of the Future Priests' Club. We did the Stations of the Cross in Lent, crowned the Virgin in May and went to the church picnic on the Fourth of July. We played sports, gossiped and duelled on the school lot and sometimes sat on the school steps with girls, whose hands we might hold or whose cheeks we might kiss. When Monsignor Ferring, the pastor of the parish, heard of this, he instructed the school janitor to run a hose down from the bathroom, up the stairs, along the corridor and out the second-floor window where a brass pipe poured water continuously over the steps so that we would no longer sit there and indulge in these libidinous acts. New venues were found in bushes, passageways and, in one scandalous incident, the church choir loft.

Rogers Park was formed by Germans, developed by the Irish and later settled by Jews, but it grew slowly and peaceably into one of the most diverse districts in the country in all demographic senses – age, religion, race and level of income. Among the fathers of my friends were an electrician, a tailor, a brain surgeon, a policeman, a stockbroker, a factory hand, an academic, a barman, a manager of a printworks and a banker. The father of a girl I once kissed was a lift attendant in the building where my father had his dental practice. They were Swedes, Sicilians, Poles and Irish. No one had the sense that they lived differently from anyone else. Perhaps some occasionally went to restaurants, and others not. In the summertime we played baseball, sold lemonade on cardboard-box stands under the trees and followed Pete the Mailman on his rounds. Our mothers moved through the dappled light in their summer dresses. The men came home in their overalls or suits in the late afternoon. They had jobs for life. The American Dream, or a version of it.

I set out on a walk around the neighbourhood. There were more Korean and Filipino faces than there had been. The gaps along Western Avenue had all been filled in by buildings, but the butcher, the corner store owned by Chris the Greek and the small candy factory where Pete the Mailman worked part-time had gone. So had the taverns. A Sicilian couple who owned one of them had a son two years older than me. He had golden curls, a perpetual smile and, it was said, a mule-kick of a punch. He disappeared for a while, then came back one afternoon in a shark-skin suit and driving a convertible Mustang. People said he had a job collecting debts for the Mafia. Many years later I heard that he was found in the trunk of a car with a bullet in his head some time before he reached thirty. I passed an apartment building where there had once been a garden of corn, carrots and rhubarb kept by an old Irishman, then another building where the father of the prettiest girl in our class shot himself. You'd think, looking at it, that nothing could go awry here, but it had.

I'd delivered newspapers, shovelled snow, cut grass, ridden bicycles, been run over, debated, sulked, climbed roofs, ice skated, broken windows, grown three feet, fought and courted along these streets. I knew them grain by grain. There was hardly a square metre that didn't possess a story known to me. Yet somehow I began to migrate from them in my mind before I did in fact. The books I read, the music I listened to, the people I met lifted me out of them. They ceased to express me, nor could I express them. Each time I came back I'd take the same walk along them and hope that some arrangement of brick, a front step, a rose light from a church window or a shout in the playground would open a door and a full act of remembrance would flood in. But it never entirely happened, strive though I did. I couldn't get into alignment with it. It had its tragedies and glories and mysteries, I knew, but I couldn't see them. Like the buildings downtown it seemed too declarative, too much itself. It didn't imply. Walking there, I felt the affliction of not being able to feel.

I went back to my car and drove away. When I got to Lake Shore Drive I put on Van Morrison's *Astral Weeks* and listened to him say goodbye to Madame George. I took the bend at Oak Street beach, passed Lake Point Tower and Navy Pier and arrived at the downtown skyline, the city extending outwards in a galaxy of white lights twinkling prettily and, it seemed, elegiacally under a faint moon. Chicago is tenacious, plain-speaking and hospitable. It had found ways of absorbing its catastrophes and moving on. It was as handsome and well-turned-out a city as there was anywhere in America. 'I am Clark Street and Clark Street is me,' said my father's friend. Why couldn't I feel like that? Why couldn't I love, or even hate, it? 'Say goodbye, goodbye, goodbye,' sang Van Morrison.

I had a beer with Marcella when I got back, and then in the morning stood with her under the trees in front of her house. Much later I would learn that she knew I had watched the final desolating game of the Marlins–Cubs series with Pat and his girlfriend Barbara, because a detective engaged by her had been watching us. About this, she forgave me. She went on to work for a time in the same detective agency because its owner found her fascinating and she needed the money. Pat moved in with Barbara and he and Marcella made a financial agreement in the courts. Annie excelled at Macalester and travelled in England and Spain. But for the moment, as she stood beside my car saying goodbye, Marcella was still an open wound. I hadn't an idea of what to do for her. I found something in a book and read it out to her, but it was as nothing, for nothing could serve her apart from time and the will to survive.

I drove up through the city then and out, with reluctance.

Lakelands

In March 1973 I went west from Chicago in a high-finned 1960-model Oldsmobile 88. Robert Gregory, whose car it was, was driving. My friend Niki Gekas and a French girl named Marina, who had advertised for a lift on the university notice board, were in the back. We were going to San Francisco. It was my last American road trip before leaving for Ireland.

We got onto Interstate 80 near Joliet in the late afternoon and drove through the night into the vast American flatlands. In western Nebraska we heard on the radio about a blizzard that was running like an impregnable wall across the country from Montana all the way to New Mexico. We ran into it in Potter, a little town near the Nebraska border with Colorado, which once held the record for having the world's largest hailstone fall on it. This is an area of legendary, life-transforming weather, from tornadoes to drought. The snowfall that day was blinding. Trucks and cars lay in ditches like fish discarded from a catch. When I got out of the car to look at the scene, the wind blew me to the ground.

We crept along in the car over the snow to a gas station. A thin, worried-looking woman with lank hair that fell to her shoulders sat behind the till. She looked like a Dorothea Lange Dust Bowl photograph come to life. We asked her if she knew anywhere we could stay.

'The hotel's closed,' she said.

'Is there a church?' we asked. 'Maybe they'd let us sleep on the floor.'

'There's a church out the road there a few miles,' she

said. 'But I don't know if you'd find anybody in it. I'm sorry. It's terrible out. I wish I could help you.'

We went across the street into a large diner filled with farmers and people who'd been marooned by the snow. Their faces turned up to look at us, darkened, then reverted to their meals. Robert's hair looked like it was made of tiny black springs, mine was nearly as long as the woman's in the gas station. They didn't like us. We were of the odious Other America, as they were to us. We ordered food and put 'Okie from Muskogee' on the jukebox, Merle Haggard's paean to the American redneck, so that we could sing along to it. The tension increased a few more degrees. Would we stay here until the snow stopped, or until somebody punched one of us?

A pretty teenage girl came through the door and up to our table.

'Mama says you can stay at our house tonight,' she said. She was Becky Brake, daughter of the woman at the gas station.

They lived in a pale-green clapboard house set down on concrete blocks. Mr Brake was a railroad man who'd got polio and the family had drifted around America working at low-wage jobs and looking for deliverance. Nebraska was the sixteenth state they had lived in. Becky had a brother named Craig, who was eleven. Also present that night were an uncle and aunt. With us that made ten. The roof over the back part of the house where the bedrooms were had fallen in during the storm and we all had to sleep on sofas or chairs or the floor in the living room. Mrs Brake found pillows and blankets for everybody, gave us a shot of bourbon for warmth, lit the gas stove that was the only source of heat in the house and then sat down beside it to keep watch.

Outside after a while the wind dropped, the sky cleared and a full moon appeared, white and vast in the sky. People shifted and groaned in their sleep. I lay on my back and looked out the window at the moon. Mrs Brake was dozing by the stove. From behind me then I heard the soft strumming of a guitar and in a whisper the beginning of a song. I turned around and saw that it was Craig, the eleven-year-old boy. The moonlight was on his face and he was singing me a song about bad luck, hard travelling and an angry pistol shot fired in a bar.

'Did you like it?' he asked when he had finished.

'Yes,' I said. 'Thank you.'

'I wrote it,' he said.

'Really?'

'Yeah, and I've got a whole bunch more of them.'

'Where did you get the guitar?'

'My dad made it,' he said. 'You want to hear another song?'

'All right,' I said.

He sang about a double-crossing woman, his expression grave. In the last verse he set out on the road to a future of guitar playing in small-town bars, then finished with a flourish. The night settled in again.

'Where are you going when you leave Potter?' he asked.

'San Francisco.'

'Is that anywhere near Nashville?'

'No, it's a long way away.'

'And where are you going after that?'

'Back to Chicago.'

'Is that anywhere near Nashville?'

'It's nearer,' I said.

He went over to a chest of drawers and came back with two sheets of paper, which he handed to me. On them, written out in pencil, were the words of the songs he had sung to me. At the bottom of each he'd written © Craig Brake, 1973.

'Well, if you ever get to Nashville,' he said, 'you give those to Johnny Cash.'

We were in San Francisco for a week and when we came back through we looked for the Brakes, but the house was abandoned and no one we asked knew where they had gone. I kept Craig's songs for years in a wallet. Gradually they disintegrated, and finally I lost the wallet.

Thirty years later my destination as I left Chicago was again San Francisco. Previously, my way to the vast spaces, strange colours and spectacular shapes of the American west had always been the nearly nine hundred miles of flatland from Chicago to the foothills of the Rockies traversed by Interstate 80. Robert Gregory made the 2,300-mile drive back from San Francisco to Chicago unassisted in thirty-three hours that spring of 1973, one of the most amazing feats of endurance I've seen. Monotonous though it was, Interstate 80 was curiously rich in memories for me. I'd hitch-hiked over it, slept in strangers' houses and in a tent along it and nearly been killed when a mad bearded man who'd given me a lift decided during a frenzied monologue in Nebraska to drive into the support of a bridge and kill us both. I got the wheel out of his hands just in time. Earlier on that journey two couples from the hills of Tennessee stopped for me somewhere in the middle of Illinois. Beer cans filled the floor of the back seat, where both the man and woman were unconscious. I laid my backpack on the floor over the cans and got into the front seat, where a bag of dope sat on the dashboard. The driver let out a whoop and climbed to 115 miles per hour, which drew a state patrol car within ten minutes. As the driver pulled over he called out to the back seat, 'Jesse, I do believe I forgot my driver's licence.' The girl next to Jesse fished in his pocket, pulled out his wallet and handed his licence to the driver, who read it as he slowed, memorising the details for his coming impersonation, then said to his girlfriend, 'Better put that dope in the glove compartment.' When she opened it, the sunlight hit the barrel of an automatic pistol. I thought there wasn't the remotest chance I wouldn't spend the night in jail, but the driver, perhaps inspired by his various intoxicants, talked his way out of our predicament and we drove on. This time he didn't break ninety.

I thought of going that way again to see where those and other things had happened to me, but I had never been to the Dakotas before and I had a curiosity about Hibbing, Minnesota, Bob Dylan's childhood home, so I went north out of Chicago on 94. To the east were the North Shore suburbs, one of the greatest concentrations of wealth in America.

I passed acres of corporate headquarters looking out over the highway, their metallic walls and mirrored windows gleaming, their lawns being attended to by teams of Mexicans. This was a world I had never touched when growing up and I still knew little of it. What was it like in those buildings? In Chicago I'd heard one story about them from Dick Romano, a broker in his early seventies long descended from Sicily, who for two decades had handled some investments made by my parents and who also sat on various corporate boards. The story was about executive pay, with him as ingénue.

A publicly listed company on whose board he sat had appointed him to the management compensation committee, charged with deciding the salary, fees and perquisites of the CEO. 'We were presented with a package involving tax services, personal security, homes in Washington and New York and a combination of salary, bonuses, deferred payments and stock options with a value of around $10 million for the year,' he told me. 'I thought this merited a few questions and I asked them, but the other people there looked at me like I'd spoken out of turn. I got the impression that this was not done at these meetings and I stayed quiet. The chairman asked if there were any more questions, which there weren't, the package was approved and we moved on to the next item.

'I wondered how this system worked and what had gone on before this meeting. What I found out was this. The CEO hires a lawyer, at company expense, to protect his interests during negotiations. The company, under his direction, hires an ostensibly objective consultant to advise on the compensation package, based on what other CEOs in comparable companies get. These consultants' positions are very highly paid. The consultant is likely to want to please the executive so that he can get hired again the following year. The consultant, the lawyer and the CEO meet. The chairman of the compensation committee also meets with the CEO and his lawyer. When all these parties agree on the package – this doesn't take very long – it is presented to the committee, whose members generally have an allegiance to the CEO. This one person is in control of all the stages involved in determining his pay.'

They also control the redundancies, mergers, tailoring of benefits, union-restricting procedures and lobbying on labour law in Washington, which determines the pay of everyone else in the company. The result is that executive pay has risen by around seventeen per cent per year for the past fifteen years and is now four hundred times that of the average white-collar worker, while average wages of workers generally have declined since 1973. The retirement packages can be the most sensational of all. Lee Raymond, after twelve years at Exxon, was presented with a farewell gift of $400 million. John Walter was fired by AT&T after nine months in his job for what was described as a lack of intellectual leadership, but the company gave him $26 million anyway. Executives have become a kind of Brahmin caste, living in gated communities and serviced by yacht, private-jet and luxury-car manufacturers, Michelin-starred restaurants, five-star resorts, country clubs and domestic help.

'They're not in the least ashamed of these quantities of money,' said Dick. 'In fact they want everyone to know about them. It feeds their egos.'

I left 94, went west on 173 through Antioch to US 12, the road that passes by Ogden Dunes. I then went north on 12 over the border into Wisconsin. Due east was the lakeside city of Kenosha, where Orson Welles grew up, producing an annotated Shakespeare by the time he was nine. I passed Lake Geneva, then Elkhorn, a prototypical American town

that once had a jail in its central square where Baby Face
Nelson, a five-foot four-inch psychopath who worked for
both Al Capone and John Dillinger, was held. From there I
went through back roads past cornfields to Lauderdale, three
lakes surrounded by trees and holiday homes. One of them
was built by Bill Glasson's grandfather and now belongs to
him. My parents started coming here fifteen years before they
were married, and I was there every summer of my childhood from infancy on. Bill told me that an old man who had
worked with the lake association in the 1930s said that he'd
wondered if the house was a brothel, so wild were the parties,
with people dancing out on the pier in the middle of the
night and falling into the lake. I once saw a sequence of
entries made in the house logbook by my mother on New
Year's Eve 1932, ending at 7.22 a.m., her hand still steady,
describing my father walking barefoot in the snow under the
moonlight. She had just turned twenty-four. I went down to
the lake, then around the house, looking into the windows.

It was dark now. There was an old place nearby with
pine floors and walls that served pizzas and hamburgers on

a landing on the lake, but it was closed. I yearned for something similar, a roadhouse with a long wooden bar with farmers ranged along it, low lights, neon beer signs with pictures of pine trees and lakes, a white-haired bartender with an apron. Such places are a great comfort. I found one that looked likely on Route A at the edge of open farmland, wood-framed, warm light spilling from its windows. I parked in a lot among pickup trucks and went in.

At the door I was hit with a ferocious blast of loud rock. It was like being in a wind tunnel. Inside were bikers shaking their heads over imaginary guitars and a group of big women with 1960s hairstyles in tight dresses, playing darts. An enormous bearded man in a green baseball hat and a plaid shirt the size of a tent sat at the end of the bar scowling, still as a boulder. Any excuse would do him, I thought, and I went over to the dark side of the bar far away from him and ordered a beer.

I played a game of pool after a while with a wiry young man with a shaven head and a broken front tooth. He played left-handed in a sleeveless T-shirt, tattoos running up one arm. We played two games and split them, then sat down at the bar. His name was Kevin. He told me he was from Elkhorn.

'I know Elkhorn,' I said. 'I spent my summers around there when I was a child.'

'They had a Klan rally in Elkhorn a few years ago,' he said. 'I was in high school. No other town would let them in, but ours did. Our mayor said it was free speech. They came up from Indiana, Illinois, all around. I got the bright idea of going downtown that day with a few of my friends, who were minorities. We were exercising our free speech. We wanted to see what the Klansmen looked like. That was a mistake. They kicked hell out of us, and then a SWAT team beat us along the streets.'

The uproar in the bar was escalating. More people came through the door, some in leather, two in suits. I couldn't connect anyone I saw with the farmland outside.

'What happens around here?' I asked him.

'Industry's vanished,' he said. 'Two hundred thousand jobs have disappeared from southern Wisconsin. They used to make musical instruments, mostly brass. This was one of the main places in the country for that. It's nearly all gone now. My stepfather was in that business, but now he goes to China a few times a year to teach them how to make cases for tubas. We were the dairy state, remember that? Now California has more cows than us.

'I was at a dead end. There was nothing for me to do. So I joined the Army. Basic training down in Birmingham, Alabama. Ever been there? Man, those people. Some of them haven't crawled out of their holes in a hundred years. I went into a bar with some other recruits. They were minorities. I went up to play pool. This local guy says to me, "What are you doing sitting with them?" "Who?" I said. "Them niggers," he said. "That's none of your business," I said. He whacked me with a pool cue. He had friends with him. The guys from my table came up and held this one by the arms. I beat him to the ground. We took care of his friends too. The whole place was screaming. They thought the army boys were going to tear the bar to pieces. They called the cops, and the Military Police too. The MPs got there first. They were black. They asked us what happened and we told them. When the cops came, the MPs said, "We're handling this," and they took us back to the base, told us to say nothing. Birmingham, Alabama's the worst dump I've ever been in.'

'What are you doing now?'

'Security at a dog track,' he said. 'I'd be in Iraq now probably, but I dislocated my shoulder on a parachute jump. I had training in chemical and biological warfare. Sniping was my specialty. I was supposed to go to Russia for training in the snow and later to England for airborne work, but it never happened. I was also diagnosed as having Attention Deficit Disorder. They gave me Ritalin when I was a kid. You might think that's funny in a sniper. It is, I suppose. But sniping was my thing. I was good at it.'

The bikers began to dance. One of the girls got up on the bar, kicking her legs like a Rockette. The barman threw her over his shoulder and whirled around in a move that might have been called the Helicopter, had this been professional wrestling. Wisconsin has the highest incidence of obesity in the country. He put the girl down when the veins in his head looked like they could burst, then collapsed on the bar.

'That used to be easy once,' he said, gasping.

I ordered two beers.

'The Army taught me some things about guns,' said Kevin, 'but I already knew a lot. My stepfather had guns in the house – twenty-twenty, pump-action shotgun, .22, hand gun, air gun, dart gun. He had a laser-guided sight too. He showed me how to dismantle them, clean them, load them, shoot them. He had a 9mm Beretta. Ever seen one of those? One shot would take your cranium out.

'When I was sixteen my stepfather and my mother went away for a weekend. This was the first time I was left alone in the house. I was ready for everything. I had the guns, I had all the sight-lines figured out. I sat up in my room with the lights off and waited.

'After a while I heard a noise out in the yard. I saw the shape of a man moving around. I went and got the Beretta and loaded it. I watched him come to the kitchen door and try to open it. Then he tried the window next to it. He couldn't get in there, either. I sat at the top of the stairs watching him. I could have left his brains halfway down the block, but I decided not to just then. I called the cops. I wanted to cover myself. I told them who I was and where I lived and then I said, "I've got an intruder in the back yard. I've got guns, all licensed. I know how to use them. If he gets in I want you to know that I'm going to shoot him, and there's not a damned thing you can do about it." "Right," they said. "Okay. But just shoot to wound him, all right? Aim for his legs. We're coming right over."'

He had a way of dropping his head a little, grinning slightly and looking at me out of one eye, as though taking aim. He was doing this now, as if to say that the climax of this story was about to arrive.

'I knew I had time. The cops would be ten minutes. I went and got the other guns and laid them out on the floor of my bedroom. The guy in the yard didn't look like he was ready to go away just yet. I lined up a shot with each of the guns. I could have taken him out with any of them. He made a move to climb up the side of the house. There was a trellis there with a rose bush. He was going to try to climb up it and get in one of the bedroom windows. I went over to where I could get a clear line on him. I fixed the sight to the gun. He started to climb. I knew that if he kept climbing, the whole thing would fall away. He could break his back. I got his forehead in the sight.'

He stopped then to take a drink of his beer.

'And what did you do?' I asked.

'I pulled the trigger.'

'And what happened?' I asked.

'I hit him just above the nose.'

I saw the forehead collapse and its contents spill out, then a slow fall from the trellis, just as if I were there.

'You killed him!' I said.

'No.'

'What then?'

'I hit him with a paint ball.'

'A pain ball?'

'*Paint* ball. It was pretty funny. He was on his back in the grass with red paint running down his face. He was really pissed off.'

'Who was he?'

'He was my uncle.'

'Sorry?'

'My uncle. My mother's brother. He was mad at my mother because of some family property. He thought he deserved a share of it, but he didn't. My mother had stopped speaking to him. He knew she was going to be away that weekend and he was trying to get into the house to steal some papers.'

His mobile phone rang. I could hear that it was a girl. He crouched over the bar and into his conversation. I finished my beer and waved goodbye, but he stopped me.

'Where are you heading for?' he asked.

'I think I'll just go as far as Madison tonight.'

'Check out the Aloha Motel on Washington. They've got everything there except grass skirts.'

He went back to his phone and I took Route A over to Janeville, then Interstate 39 north towards Madison. He'd surprised me from the beginning. He had the hairstyle of a neo-Nazi, but was a racial egalitarian of a sort I seldom encountered – visceral rather than intellectual. He yearned to be a sniper, but his story about guns was one of gradual disarmament, beginning with an arsenal and an exploded cranium, de-escalating ballistically as he moved down through the firepower of his weapons, and ending with an irate uncle splayed on the grass with a red stain on his forehead. He'd led me up to a point just short of a bloodstained finale, then veered into comedy. He was smart, unschooled, witty, good-looking, lucid and doomed, I supposed, to a lifetime of low-wage jobs. But he had his diversions.

I woke up the next morning in the Aloha Motel, then went into Madison, praised by various journals and organisations as an American paradise on earth. The *Men's Journal* says Madison is the healthiest place to live in the country. *Forbes* says it has the highest concentration of PhDs and the lowest unemployment rate. It has six times the number of National Merit semi-finalists of comparable school districts. *Sports Illustrated* has called it the country's number-one sports town, and a guide to gay America declares it gay-friendly. *Money* said simply in 1996 that it was the best place to live in the United States.

It is beautifully set on a former swamp at the isthmus between Lakes Mendota and Monona, bought by a former judge called James Duane Doty. Doty persuaded legislators to choose Madison as the state capital while it was still just a diagram on paper. The University of Wisconsin came in 1848 and the city now has a student population of fifty thousand. Wisconsin filled with Germans and Scandinavians, and it seems wherever they go in the United States a liberal tradition gets established, even in Texas. In Madison this was personified by 'Fighting Bob' La Follette, variously a Congressman, senator, governor and presidential candidate in the first quarter of the twentieth century, whose Progressive Party campaigned for a minimum wage, open government, progressive taxation, free speech, child-labour laws, railroad regulation, direct election of senators and women's suffrage. He thought the university should develop reformist ideas and programmes and that legislators should listen to them, something that became known as the Wisconsin Idea and resulted in various policies that were eventually adopted at a national level. Madison still has an unusually high number of food and housing cooperatives and leftists in political office and is the national headquarters of the Freedom from Religion Foundation, a free-thought organisation co-run by a former evangelist turned atheist named Dan Barker.

I parked by the capitol building and walked along State Street. It was full of restaurants and coffee bars, but after nearly an hour of looking I couldn't find one that served breakfast, at least not one large enough to get me up to the shore of Lake Superior. Perhaps this is one of the factors that made the *Men's Journal* declare it exceptionally healthy. A Vietnam veteran with a long red beard and combat gear was parked in his wheelchair on a street corner offering to tell a joke in exchange for a donation to his amphetamine fund. I left Madison with a parking ticket, looking down at its lovely lakes where, in 1967, Otis Redding's plane crashed, killing him just three days after he recorded '(Sittin' on the) Dock of the Bay'. Kite fliers gather there now when the lakes freeze over in winter.

I found US 12 again and went north. I passed Baraboo,

once the winter headquarters of the Ringling Brothers Circus. A man with a tape recorder interviewed me for the radio there when I was nine. Signs began to appear promoting the Wisconsin Dells resort area, 'The Waterpark Capital of the World' where go-kart tracks, mini-golf courses, cabarets and motels are spread around the glacially formed sandstone gorges of the Wisconsin River. 'Lost Canyon Tours.' 'Monster Truck World.' 'Noah's Ark Waterpark', the world's largest. 'Ripley's Believe It or Not Museum.' You can ride over the rock formations and down into the river on decommissioned Second World War vehicles known as ducks. The 'Fall Polka Festival' was announced. There was a sign for the Tommy Bartlett water show, which I saw as a child and which was the foundation upon which the whole area was developed. My parents took me to the Dells. I remember an Indian show and bouncing on a trampoline. 'Join the Fun – The Lion's Club,' said another sign. This may not be fun as it is understood by a New Orleans transvestite, but three million visitors come to this town of two thousand each year, served by a vast workforce of young migrants who come from all over the world for the summer. At times it could get just as wild as New Orleans, I imagine. The Ojibwa hunted buffalo here and gave this narrow part of the river a name that means 'where the waters gather', phonetically rendered by the French as 'Ouisconsin' and later anglicised into the name of the entire river and the state itself.

Wisconsin has four million cows and fifteen thousand lakes and there are fewer people in it than in the greater metropolitan area of Chicago. I followed 12 north to Eau Claire, then got on US 53, passing green hills and rocky bluffs, red barns and silos. It was a gentle, pretty drive composed in the main of the bright-green and red colours associated with Christmas, soft music on the radio and a serene, well-husbanded landscape outside. Further south I'd been in a bar with screaming guitar music, big, hard-drinking women with beehive hairdos and a young man who'd grown up surrounded by weaponry, and in the capital I'd seen a veteran taking up a collection for his narcotics. That too was the Midwest. US 53 took me all the way to the border with Minnesota, over a high bridge and into Duluth, a solid city of brick built into lakeside bluffs.

At the beginning of the twentieth century Duluth's port handled more tonnage than New York's, with which, over 2,300 miles of waterways, it is directly linked. There are many remnants of its boom-time era. I found a brewery that had opened in 1857 in one such building and had a fine meal there in a restaurant called Bennett's, then slept in a tiny motel cabin on the shore of Lake Superior.

In the morning banks of mist drifted over the water and around the pine trees at the shore, the colours white, silver and a pale green. It was all so ill defined as to be almost abstract. I walked down to the shore and sat on a rock, the sun slowly burning away the mist. I was only a few miles from Duluth, but it looked prehistoric. The northern shore of Lake Superior is one of the places least touched by modern human life in the United States, billion-year-old boulders and dense forest with moose, black bear, caribou and wolf living in it, stretching into Canada and around to Michigan's Upper Peninsula.

There is evidence of human settlement here nine thousand years before the first Europeans came. The Ojibwa have a legend that when they were living through a plague on the Atlantic coast they received a message from the sky that directed them to move west, where they would find food growing on water. They travelled by canoe up the St Lawrence River and through the Great Lakes, portaging at the western tip of Lake Superior and stopping at what is now La Pointe, Wisconsin, where they found marshes filled with wild rice.

The 31,700 square miles of Lake Superior spread before me, the largest surface area of any freshwater lake in the world. It's so big that it has a three-inch tide. Kipling thought it an abomination. 'Lake Superior is all the same stuff that towns pay taxes for [meaning fresh water], but it engulfs and wrecks and drives ashore like a fully accredited ocean

– a hideous thing to find in the heart of a continent.' Together the Great Lakes comprise one-fifth of the surface freshwater in the world, and ninety-five per cent of the United States'. If they were emptied they would cover all of the forty-eight contiguous states in a lake ten feet deep.

Six hundred million years ago the area of the lakes was covered in a warm, equatorial saltwater sea full of coral, molluscs and other primeval life forms. Then came volcanoes, and after that ice. The first glacier began digging out the lakes 1.8 million years ago and the last only retreated to the north some time between 8000 and 5000 BC, leaving behind the St Mary's River, which connected Lake Superior to Lake Huron, giving all the lakes an outlet to the St Lawrence River. The deepest cut was made for Lake Superior, which reaches a depth of 1,332 feet.

After the Indians, French explorers and fur trappers came. They were superseded, as they were elsewhere, by the English. Beaver-pelt hats lost out in popularity to silk, trapping declined, and then loggers came and in a Gold Rush-style frenzy cleared forty million acres of trees in Michigan, Wisconsin and Minnesota by 1900. Farmers, fishermen and industrialists came after that. All of these visitors in their ways lived from the lakes, and many affected them, usually adversely. Asbestos, heavy metals, motor oil and numerous toxic chemicals were dumped into the lakes for years and, though much of this has been stopped, a poisonous brew still lies in the sediment. Disturbed, it can pollute the air through evaporation. Roads and buildings have paved over the wetlands that had filtered the lake water for millennia. Water levels have dropped, possibly due in part to increased evaporation from hot summers and warmer winters. Marinas and harbours have had to be dredged and freighters have had to reduce their tonnage, losing in consequence up to $100,000 per voyage in revenue. One of the most complex and pernicious problems facing the lakes has come from the more than 140 different species of alien animal and plant life, many of them destroying native species and distorting the lake's ecology. Yet the lakes, particularly Lake Erie, are more alive than they were thirty years ago.

Jonathan Carver, a New Englander who toured the lakes in 1766, later wrote about his time on Lake Superior, 'When the weather was calm and the sunshine bright, I would sit in my canoe and plainly see huge piles of stones beneath six fathoms [thirty-six feet] of water. My canoe seemed to be suspended in air. As I looked through this limpid medium, my head swam and my eyes could no longer behold the dazzling scene.' Most of Lake Superior is still as clear now as it was then.

I got onto Highway 61 back towards Duluth. Highway 61 goes all the way from Thunder Bay in Canada to New Orleans, first along the shore of Lake Superior, then picking up the Mississippi and switching back and forth across it until both arrive at the Gulf of Mexico. It has a history both tragic and miraculous. Martin Luther King was shot and Bessie Smith was killed in a car crash on it. Elvis grew up on it. T.S. Eliot and William Burroughs were born in St Louis, through which it passes. The television evangelist Jimmy Swaggart was caught by a rival preacher coming out of a Highway 61 motel with a prostitute. Many extraordinary events central to American mythology, history and culture happened in New Orleans, where Highway 61 ends, including Little Richard's spontaneous recording of 'Tutti Frutti'. It hasn't the legendary international status of Route 66, called the Mother Road by John Steinbeck, but it has more songs written about it. It moves through the bluesland of the Mississippi Delta and was the route taken by Howlin' Wolf, Bo Diddley and Muddy Waters, among many others, up to Memphis, where they got onto trains to Chicago. Son Thomas recorded 'Highway 61' and Mississippi Fred McDowell '61 Highway'. The intersection of 49 with 61 near Clarksdale, Mississippi is believed to be the crossroads where Robert Johnson went one night to sell his soul to the Devil in exchange for a supernatural capacity to play the guitar, or so his song 'Crossroads' suggests. Bob Dylan was born Robert Zimmerman on

Highway 61 and later wrote a song called 'Highway 61 Revisited'. His father Abraham moved the family from Duluth to Hibbing after contracting polio and went to work in an electrical goods store called Micha's, owned by him and his brothers. Highway 61 was the road to freedom for his son, leading south to the country and blues music he listened to at night on the airwaves. When he wanted to set out on it and into a career in music, his father told him he'd never get anywhere with that and should instead stay at home and work in the store with him and his uncles. In 'Highway 61 Revisited' Abraham is ordered by God to kill his son. The terrified prophet asks God where he should do it and is told 'out on Highway 61'. 'The town he lived in and the town I lived in weren't the same,' Dylan later said of his father.

I took 61 into Duluth, then got onto 53 going north towards the Mesabi Iron Range. I seemed to be moving into another kind of land, wilder, more wooded and isolated, the north country up near the borderline. I made my first direct move west since leaving Chicago when I got onto 37 by the US Hockey Hall of Fame, one of America's most obscurely placed museums. That led me into Hibbing.

Hibbing is the place where the Greyhound Bus Company began and Bob Dylan grew up. It's difficult to judge which had the greater effect on America. It was the latter in my case, for I was never on a Greyhound bus. But while the little visitor centre that I met on the outskirts of the town had information in its window about the bus company as well as the iron mines, I could see nothing about the singer.

I went up Howard Street, a main drag of brick buildings with 1940s signage hanging from them, the wind blowing up leaves and dust into whirlwinds. No one was out on this darkening October afternoon. Weak light spilled from the shops. I saw a place with guitars and horns in the window called Rupar Music and went in. Three men stood behind the counter attending this otherwise empty store.

'I'm going to ask you the town's most-often-asked question,' I said to them.

'WHERE DID BOB GROW UP?' they replied in a chorus.

They gave me an address on 7th Avenue East.

'He might still be here if the fools hadn't booed him and his band when he was in high school,' one said.

'Or at least he'd visit,' said another.

The owner told me he himself had been in a band, but had come here to open this shop. 'It's a good town,' he said. 'It's a strong union town because of the mines. We have the biggest open-pit mine in the world here. You won't see many foreign cars around Hibbing. They buy American. I'd like to do that too, but there are guitars coming in from China for $40. Workers in American instrument factories are getting $20 per hour. How can they compete?'

I went back down Howard and turned into the residential streets of Bob Dylan's old neighbourhood. I'd read the stories of his bar-mitzvah classes, ice-hockey games and courtships here. The town had a feeling of remoteness inconceivable in the east, locked in ice through the winter, with just small country roads leading in and out of it. It was innocent, he'd said, and occasionally exotic, as when the knife sharpeners came through or show wagons rolled down Howard Street with a gorilla in a cage or a mummy under glass. I passed the high school, institutional-looking but stately. It was financed, I heard later, by the mining companies. They'd put marble on the floors and modelled the 1,825-seat auditorium on a New York concert hall. There are six Belgian chandeliers hanging in it, each of them worth a quarter of a million dollars. That, I supposed, was the site of the insult thrown at Dylan and his rock-and-roll band by the town.

I'd first become aware of Bob Dylan when I arrived at my high-school parking lot in a friend's car and heard 'Like a Rolling Stone' on the radio four years after he'd recorded it. No living American could have been more alien to me then than him, with his polka-dot shirts and Cuban heels, his Warhol-like paleness, his viperous tongue and his surrealism. I wore the conservative clothes of the day, thought vaguely of studying to be a doctor. I aimed at a blameless life. But somehow I felt this song getting through to me in a way that nothing else ever had. I had no means of relating to a diplomat on a chrome horse. But there was in this song the intensity, the scorn, the shockingly vivid images, that 'wild, high mercury sound' he later talked about, the caustic passion with which he enunciated each stinging word. I listened to everything then, from 'The Ballad of Hollis Brown' and 'Tomorrow Is a Long Time' to 'Desolation Row' and 'I'll Be Your Baby Tonight'. How could one man do so many different things? Where had it all come from?

Outside Dylan's childhood house a man was raking leaves. I hesitated to approach him, but when I did he was disarmingly polite. His name was Gregg French. He had a young family and a job selling potato chips for Frito-Lay. He told me that Abraham Zimmerman had died of a heart attack in the house in 1968, but that Dylan's mother Beatty went on living there for many years before moving to Minneapolis. She left behind a lot of things in her neighbour's garage and, when Gregg French's first child was born, he was offered Bob Dylan's own childhood high chair for the baby. 'I couldn't take it,' he said. 'I was too embarrassed. Then I heard that a Norwegian bought it, along with an authentification certificate.' He took me to the back of the house and showed me the bedroom window that Dylan's girlfriend Echo Helstrom had had to crawl out of when his grandmother arrived home unexpectedly, then we went back around to his front yard, where he stood with his rake in his hand and his dog rolling around in the piled-up leaves telling me every story about Bob Dylan that he knew, including the one about being upset with the town for having booed him at his concert. In all I was there for nearly an hour. He was patient, courteous, modest and attentive, as many Americans are, but perhaps particularly those from the Midwest.

'How often does this happen?' I asked him.

'Well, I've been off work today so I've been around the house more than usual. You're the third today.'

'Three in a day! And it's not even summer. How do you stand it?'

He looked at me as though the question was very peculiar.

'Well, I don't look at it as a problem,' he said. 'I meet a lot of interesting people this way.'

I drove back over to Howard Street to Zimmy's Bar and Restaurant, a former streetcar terminus that is now the town's only visible homage I could find to Bob Dylan. In this, Hibbing is very different from Memphis or Liverpool, with their Elvis shops and Beatles tribute groups. I had a hamburger and a beer at the bar. A man came through the door like a count entering a grand hotel, his brow arching a little as he looked left and right, his step a long, cool glide that seemed not to touch the floor. He sat up at the bar beside me. He was around eighty, I thought. He had on a beret, nylon jacket and string tie, all of it in shades of grey and black. His shoes had a soft, pewter-like glow.

'You're in the Town That Moved,' he said to me. 'Did you know that?'

'I didn't,' I said.

'They discovered in 1919 that there was ore under where the original town stood and moved the whole thing two miles up here on trucks. A hotel fell off and broke up out on the road. They didn't move the last house until 1968.'

I told him I'd come up here to see Bob Dylan's home town.

'I was working in the high school and I had to console that poor boy when they gave him a hard time at a concert,' he said. 'He was always ahead of his time. The town couldn't understand him. Never came back. You know, I still see his uncle every day. We had a fine Jewish community here. They had the dry cleaners, electrical shops, movie theatres. Fine people.'

His name, he said, was Bud McKenzie. We had another beer together and he told me about his life in Hibbing, working for the government looking after public buildings. 'I lost my wife last year,' he said then. 'I don't know what to do with myself. I come out looking for people to talk to, but it's no use.'

We got up together to leave when the beers were finished.

'I've got fifteen jackets and twenty-six cowboy ties,' he said. 'Everything has to be coordinated. I could take two hours to get ready in the morning, then I might change six or seven times in the day. If I can give you one piece of advice, it's to never get into that. Once you start you can't stop.'

I drove west out of Hibbing on 169 past Kelly Lake, where Dylan used to come with his friends in the summer to swim. His traumatic concert seemed a turning point in the imagination of this economically fragile town, its iron-mine boomtime long past. Were it not for that, their most gifted son might still be there. But, as he later wrote, 'I always knew there was a bigger world out there.' The Greyhound bus could take him there, or Highway 61, of which he said, 'I'd started on it, always had been on it and could go anywhere from it, even down into the Deep Delta country.' Life was elsewhere, as it so often is in America. Above all, the way out was through music. Abe Zimmerman, who – when told his son was an artist – said, 'Don't they paint pictures?', unwittingly sent him on his way out of Hibbing when he fixed a radio antennae to the television aerial on the roof of his house, for it brought music, with its 'outlaw women, super thugs, rich peaty swamps, with landowners and oilmen, Stagger Lees, Pretty Pollys and John Henrys . . . It was so real, so more true to life than life itself.' Like Craig Brake from Potter, Nebraska who wanted me to transport his songs to Johnny Cash, Dylan was already in another world long before he'd left the one he'd been given.

I passed Grand Rapids, where Judy Garland was born, and picked up 200, which went through the Chippewa National Forest with its Leech Lake Indian Reservation, where the Mississippi River begins as a twelve-inch stream coming out of Lake Itasca. The word Itasca was assembled from syllables three, four and five of the Latin *veitas caput*, or 'true head', by Henry Rowe Schoolcraft, who was led to the source by a Chippewa. Bob Dylan grew up in a land of iron and water and wood, with roads on land and on river that lead down from the ice of the north through the heartland of the country's music to the semi-tropical swamps of the south and the Gulf of Mexico. 'The same road, full of the same contradictions, the same one-horse towns, the same spiritual ancestors,' he wrote. I drove along this dark country road, the trees a deeper shade of black than the moonless sky, buffeting wind and the movement of animals to either side of the road, the whitened-out eyes of deer caught in the headlights. Back roads at night raise your alertness, but it is an alertness only in the service of staying on them. Ahead after a while I saw a white light over the trees that grew in intensity, then came to a casino at Walker, one of four on this reservation. I went in, thinking to have a beer, but the spectacle of people pulling on slot machines like the factory hands in Fritz Lang's *Metropolis* was so bleak that I walked back out again and drove on, turning off 200 onto 34 past Akeley and Nevis to Park Rapids.

I went into a bar there with a tricycle and an aeroplane hanging from the ceiling. There was a goat at the controls of the plane. It was a big, open place with the bar at the front and pool tables at the back. A small group of people in their twenties slowly walked towards me as though I was a meteor that had just landed in the middle of the town.

'What are you doing in Park Rapids?' asked a girl named Sarah. It seemed a great wonder to her. She was pretty, languorous, glassy-eyed. She moved as though underwater.

I told them I was on my way west.

'But *Park Rapids*?' she said. They may have had their civic pride, but they couldn't understand why anyone else might want to be there.

We had a few games of pool together. Sarah told me she'd lived in Los Angeles for a while, but had come back. 'There were so many *people*,' she said. 'And it was really expensive. I might try the northern part some day. It's quieter there, I hear. More like Minnesota.' She drifted away with her cue to look at things hanging on the walls.

I played against a tall young man with a beard. There was a gap in his résumé when he told me about his time in school and the jobs he had done. I asked him about it.

'That's when I was in jail,' he said.

'Really? For what?'

'For a whole bunch of stupid things I did when I was eighteen.'

When I left they followed me all the way out to the door.

'But how did you *get* here?' asked Sarah.

US 34 hit 10 at Detroit Lakes and I took it into Moorhead, part of the vague sprawl of Fargo, North Dakota, and found the Star-Lite Motel, blue and white and with low lines and sharp angles like an old Chevrolet Impala with fins. I rang a bell on the desk. From the other side of a door I heard a groan, some deep bronchial hacking, fumbling in the sheets and a 'G'wan and answer the door'. An elderly man in a rumpled T-shirt and pyjama bottoms with his white hair sticking up appeared at the desk. This was Bill, of the Bill and Roza that a sign said were the owners.

'Smoking or non-smoking room?' he said.

'It doesn't matter,' I replied.

He banged his pen down and leaned over the desk in my direction.

'Well, it matters to me, and I'm not going to give away a non-smoking room if you're going to smoke in it.'

'I don't smoke.'

He took my payment, dropped a key in front of me and hobbled and creaked his way back to bed. Being an hotelier didn't seem the best profession for him.

I went to sleep on the edge of the Great Plains.

The Great Plains

In the morning, light poured through the window of my room. I looked out. The sun had blanched and reduced everything to an incorporeality. The land itself was nearly invisible. I had not seen a light this powerful and pervasive since arriving. I got up, went out to my car. I planned to get down to South Dakota and across to the Black Hills by night. Bill, a load of bedsheets under his arm, waved cheerily as I pulled out of the parking lot of his motel. Sleep had evidently improved him.

I skirted the Moorhead–Fargo conurbation to the south, passing railroad lines and warehouses and a graceless retail sprawl. Fargo, named for the founder of the Wells Fargo Bank, is in the Red River Valley, an alluvial plain that was once covered by the glacial Lake Agassiz, the sediments from which have made the valley among the richest agricultural land in the world. Fargo was the 'Divorce Capital of America' before being usurped by the state of Nevada. It is an isolated city, but an improving one, with a low crime rate, low unemployment and a rising population. I found Interstate 29 and headed south past some of the largest fields I had ever seen.

Some time in the night on the way west from Park Rapids I had left the green hills and the lakes behind. The land had flattened and grown paler. I was in a prologue to the Great Plains rather than the thing itself, an area that does not fall into the sub-twenty-inch-per-year rainfall limit that defines the plains. There wasn't a tree anywhere here. Just fields of wheat that seemed to have no end. Curvature of the Earth was unimaginable. The sun burned inexhaustibly in a cloudless sky like a lamp in a police interrogation room. The air was so clear and the view so unobstructed that you felt you could see a mouse stirring the wheatstalks a hundred miles away. It was so emphatically flat that it seemed more a state of mind than a landscape. You felt both exposed and microscopic.

I crossed the state line into South Dakota and the Lake Traverse Indian Reservation, though I might as well have been looking at it through the wrong end of a telescope as from an interstate. Even great wonders seem like stage sets from an interstate. I saw US 12 again as it headed towards the western horizon from a town called Summit. It was beginning to feel like an old friend, but I passed it by and got onto 212 going west at Watertown. Further on was an exhibition of relic American cars ranged out in a field, a statement in metal with nothing to distract from it.

I got to Gettysburg, a small town named after the place of Civil War carnage in Pennsylvania, and drove around looking for a place to get a cold drink. On a back street I found a Veterans of Foreign Wars club with a bar. Inside were a jaded barman and an ancient couple as shrivelled as forgotten fruit. The barman was better presented than anything else that was visible, hair slicked back, shirt starched. He told me he'd tried to live in Los Angeles, but – like Sarah in Park Rapids – had found it too crowded.

'What were you doing there?' I asked.

'Working in a doughnut shop,' he said.

His disappointment, not entirely concealed, had the look of being at the limit of his tolerance.

'What happens around here?' I asked him.

'It's almost all farming. Didn't you notice? Corn, wheat, sunflowers, soybeans, cattle. There's buffalo farms, too. You can get that old frontier kick of shooting one for three thousand bucks.'

Outside a plane passed high above us. There was no other noise to compete with it. The most many Americans ever see of this part of the country is from that height, looking down at the beige and green agricultural rectangles as they stir in their seats and breathe the reconditioned air.

He placed two bourbon bottles in a rack with a world-weariness that seemed to have been developed elsewhere.

'It's all right here,' he said. 'It's a nice place to visit. But you wouldn't want to live here.'

'Where do you live?' I asked him.

His eyes rose slowly to mine like bubbles through oil. 'I live here,' he said.

I wondered if he had been in Los Angeles hoping to be noticed by a Hollywood talent scout. He still had that groomed, cynical look of someone on the make, though there in Gettysburg there was nothing he could do with it. 'California is a tragic country,' wrote Christopher Isherwood, '– like Palestine, like every Promised Land. Its short history is a fever-chart of migrations – the land rush, the gold rush, the oil rush, the movie rush, the Okie fruit-picking rush, the wartime rush to the aircraft factories – followed, in each instance, by counter-migrations of the disappointed and unsuccessful, moving sorrowfully homeward.'

A little to the west of Gettysburg I crossed the Missouri River and everything changed again. The land began to roll. It was a pale green, as though touched by frost, and un-demarcated by fences. The American flags and gleaming four-wheel drives I had seen at every point up to here were suddenly absent. It looked empty and untouched, apart from a few houses of minimal fortification and the odd battered pickup raising dust, a dog or an armchair in the open back. It reminded me of a border crossing I'd made from Germany into Poland ten years earlier, the roads narrowing, the turbo-charged Mercedes giving way to tiny Fiats with the firepower of lawnmowers and the country manors displaced by little bungalows with fragile columns of coal smoke rising from them. This land seemed both wild and homey, and raised the spirit in a way that the geometric fields on the other side of the river did not. This was the Cheyenne River Indian Reservation and my point of entry to the Great Plains.

The Great Plains comprise a 2,500-mile-long and up to six-hundred-mile wide semi-arid and nearly treeless area that the explorer Zebulon Pike, having toured the plains' southern sandhills in 1806, compared to the deserts of Africa. There are various brown, fertile soils on the plains, but also sand and gravel and alkali flats, stretches of land with a sodium or potassium crust formed by rapid evaporation. The mineral whiteness, the sand, the treelessness and the lack of people made many early travellers and explorers refer to it as a desert, but it was also the case that it was in the commercial interest of some, such as the fur companies, to promote the idea that it was uninhabitable. It is a place of extreme temperatures, wild storms, benign isotherms that bend to the north as they move westwards and the startling warm mountain winds called chinooks, which can raise temperatures up to sixty degrees in a couple of hours, melting vast tracts of snow and turning ice-locked rivers into torrents. A chinook is described in a Federal Writers' Project document: 'There is a low moaning sound, as of a prolonged sigh; the air seems alive. Water drips from the eaves of houses, and icicles shatter on the walk below. When morning comes the snow, which a few short hours before had glittered with blinding light, is sodden, turning to rivulets before the eyes. Sometimes as suddenly as the temperature rose, it drops again, as the wind veers from the west to northeast. Then the melting of the snow is halted, and streets and sidewalks are covered with treacherously corrugated ice.'

The Great Plains stretch from the boreal pine forests of the north to the deserts of the south and from the Missouri River in the east to the Rocky Mountains in the west. Walt Whitman, in *Specimen Days*, declared them the great American landscape: 'While I know the standard claim is that Yosemite, Niagara Falls, the upper Yellowstone and the like, afford the greatest natural shows, I am not so sure but the Prairies and the plains, while less stunning at first sight, last longer, fill the aesthetic sense fuller, precede all the rest.' It took a long time for anyone to know how to settle the plains, but after discovering the summer fallow system, which conserved moisture, and strip-farming, which kept the topsoil from blowing away, and certain hardy strains of Russian wheat, Great Plains farmers now produce, among many other things, two-thirds of the world's wheat. They are helped by an aquifer the size of Lake Huron, which lies under the plains' surface. This was once thought to be a resource without end, but the pumps that draw its water sometimes now suck up air instead because in some areas, particularly the southern plains, the aquifer is being used at a rate of one hundred parts for every single part that is replenished by rainfall. Farmers have seeded and dynamited clouds, sent up hydrogen balloons and gone to church in an effort to bring down rain, but it rarely comes. Even if it did, there are parts of the plains where only a fraction of the rainwater will get down into the aquifer because there it is overlain with a nearly impregnable layer of caliche. At the time I was there the Great Plains were three years into a drought that some climate experts could not see the end of. The drought that scorched the earth and raised the duststorms of the 1930s lasted ten years. This one could last one hundred. If the aquifer disappears, agriculture as it is known on the Great Plains will end.

The Great Plains, for much of the nineteenth century, meant freedom – freedom to get away from poverty or oppression and the freedom to be whoever you wanted to be. Mennonites came from the Russian steppes, home-steaders from the sweatshops of the east. A group of former slaves constructed their own town at Nicodemus, Kansas. 350,000 people traversed the plains on the Oregon Trail on their way to the Pacific Ocean. Cowboys, rustlers, gunslingers, Indians, claim-stakers and whores lived by their own laws here, and on this vast stage some of the iconographic figures of America – Billy the Kid, Wyatt Earp, Doc Holliday, Lewis and Clark, Kit Carson, Buffalo Bill Cody, Teddy Roosevelt, Bonnie and Clyde, General Custer, Sitting Bull and Crazy Horse – lived out the dramas of their free-ranging lives. It was a place in which you could move rather than settle. You fought the elements and you made your life. The vastness and, eventually, the arability of the plains fed Americans' idea of their country – invincible, plenitudinous and free. Then the buffalo disappeared, the last fences went up and the Indians were all confined within the reservations, and what had been radiant with promise became commonplace. 'The Great Plains are like a sheet Americans screened their dreams on for a while,' wrote Ian Frazier, author of a wonderful book called *Great Plains*, 'and then largely forgot about.'

Four bands of Lakota Sioux live on the Cheyenne River reservation. Sioux once moved freely over a quarter of the land mass of the continental United States. An 1868 treaty ceded them sixty million acres, but twenty years later large parts of it were taken back, such as the sacred but also gold-rich Black Hills. The Cheyenne River part of the Sioux lands comprises 2.8 million acres, on which live just 8,470 people. Two-thirds of them live on less than one-third of the average American income. In Ziebach County, the poverty rate is 49.1 per cent, the highest at county level in the United States.

Because of the drought, water from the Cheyenne River was arriving at the reservation treatment plant brown with mud because of low levels in the river and was contaminated with mineral waste from the gold mines in the Black Hills, the likely cause of the high incidence on the reservation of arthritis, lupus and rare cancers. The fourteen thousand miles of pipes, too small and of inferior quality to begin with, are breaking up. There wasn't enough pressure to build a necessary new hospital or even a single new house without knocking down an existing one. They needed a federal allocation of nearly $400 million to get a water supply on the reservation equivalent to what the rest of America takes for granted.

I came upon Eagle Butte, the reservation's capital. At an intersection was a tree with yellow ribbons in it, each one for an Indian soldier away at war. Just one month after I was there one of the ribbons would be taken down after the funeral of Sheldon Hawk Eagle, a Lakota and descendant of Crazy Horse, who died when his Black Hawk helicopter crashed in Mosul in Iraq.

Everything seemed a little more improvised here, less finished and more like a home – even the gas station, where people stood around the cash register and talked as if at a barbecue. I'd been told by a citizen I'd met in an Indiana bar that on the reservations wrecked cars and the sleeping bodies of drunk Indians would make the roads nearly impassable, but all here were perfectly sober so far as I could see, and this would continue to be the case on all the reservations I passed through on my journey.

I went into a restaurant called the Diamond A Cattle Company and attempted to eat a steak that would have overfilled four Spaniards. It seemed inappropriate to be using anything so delicate as a knife and fork on it. Carol Morgan, owner of the Diamond A, had taken my order and then stood by the table to talk after she brought the food, and finally sat down when I asked her to join me. Her husband Harley came over, then two of her daughters, and all of them sat across from me. I'd read that Native Americans used to find the white man's practice of shaking hands so hilarious that they'd walk towards each other with their hands out and then fall to the ground helpless with laughter, but none of the family demurred when I extended mine.

'He went out shooting rattlesnakes this morning,' said Carol of her husband.

'Did you get any?' I asked him.

'Thirty-two,' he said. He looked as if he'd just awakened from a long sleep, still warm from the bed, his eyes like pools of dark honey. 'I got them from my pickup with a pistol.'

I noticed a row of ceramic figures on a shelf over the next table depicting warriors on horseback looking free and heroic.

'A cousin of mine makes them,' he said. 'Do you like them?'

'The horses look alive,' I said.

They had another daughter, Carol told me, who was

intending to study computer programming in Santa Barbara, California.

'We went with her to see the college. Very pretty place. There's nothing here. Almost no chance of work. It's difficult for young people particularly. The girls get very down, the boys sometimes fall into trouble. But at least here you're not always reminded of who you are. As soon as any of us leaves our lands, that's what we get. They don't want to cash your cheques. When you go into a store, they follow you around because they think you want to steal something. You can't relax.'

When I got up to leave, her husband took a horse and rider down from its shelf and handed it to me.

'Take it,' he said. 'I'm sick of looking at it.'

An Indian folk singer named Phil Lucas declared the Indians and the white man a perfect match because the one always wants to give and the other to take.

I got back onto 212 and then finally left it after around 350 miles to drop down into the Black Hills, which, had it been light enough to see, would have been my first relief from limitless horizons since waking up. They are a prologue to the Rocky Mountains as the eastern Dakotas are a

prologue to the Great Plains. I came upon Deadwood, a replica Wild West town in a gulch that owes its existence to General Custer and his army having camped here in 1874 during his campaign against the Sioux and some of his men having come upon gold in the creeks. There had been financial panic in the east and drought in the Midwest, and refugees from these blows from the heavens streamed west in a gold fever with prospectors and other hunters of fortune. A wagon train of liquor and prostitutes quickly followed. Wild Bill Hickok arrived with his ivory-handled pistols and, after shooting a man with them, paid for his funeral, a gesture General Custer found supremely noble. Calamity Jane, an alcoholic part-time prostitute enthralled by Wild Bill, arrived too and now both are buried in the town cemetery. It was 'hog-wild', said one resident. If not for the gold, the Sioux might still be in the Black Hills.

In Wild Bill's lifetime, before he was shot dead in a Deadwood card game, the Wild West was already show business. Buffalo Bill Cody brought him to New York to appear in a play, the opening scene of which had the two of them and another western legend sitting around a campfire taking slugs from a jug of hooch. Wild Bill shattered the fourth wall on the opening night when he spat out his first mouthful, announcing in disgust, 'Anyone would know that's cold tea.' This was the era of mass industrialisation and the mechanisation of agriculture, with the consequent expansion of cities and the concurrent explosion of spectator sports. Sedentary or factory-bound workers needed to witness valour, raw nerve and physical mastery in the microcosm of arenas. The circus and Buffalo Bill's Wild West Show, which toured the world, served the same need.

In 1879 Deadwood caught fire and then blew up when the flames reached a storeroom containing eight kegs of gunpowder. But it was rebuilt in brick and stone, with banks and splendid eating houses and hotels, supervised on two occasions by Jewish mayors. A genteel, Victorian high society of mountain picnics, sleigh rides, tennis matches and balls grew up next to the hog-wild depredations that this tiny town exhibited from its beginnings. Signs of both worlds remain, thanks to $170 million worth of restoration work.

I drove along the main street looking for a place to have a beer, but all I found were casions. Deadwood was the third location in the United States after Atlantic City, New Jersey and the state of Nevada to legalise gambling and now has twenty casinos, most of them lined up side by side like carnival booths. I went into one hoping to find a bar of some kind, a place serene and easy and softly lit where everyone was amiable and at peace and exactly where they wanted to be, but all I found was a grilled cashier booth and chrome machines with pitiless and garish flashing lights digesting their coins with electronic grunts. The afflicted sat by them in trainers and jogging clothes and with a jailhouse pallor to their skin and a look of disrepair. They looked up out of darkly ringed sockets whenever anyone came in, then went back to the machines. It was like a morgue coming fitfully to a half-life, then receding.

I fled Deadwood along twisting mountain roads to Lead, found a bar where I had a desultory beer next to a man who kept putting his case to me for a small loan, then went to sleep in an unmemorable hotel.

Mount Rushmore, the indelible American monument, was just along the road. It was a thing of wonder and awe to me when I was a child, seemingly impossible, like those Greek churches I saw years later built into cliff-faces as evidence of devotion, but on so much vaster a scale. I didn't know then how many conflicting American histories were present in it.

It was conceived by local historian Doane Robinson in the hope that it would bring tourists to his state and was sculpted by Gutzon Borglum, the son of a Danish Mormon bigamist who had married sisters. Borglum was a fractious and possessed man, who had met Rodin in Paris when young and grew relentlessly in ambition, believing he could add to the wonders of the world with his sculpture. Robinson had become aware of him through his engraving of Confederate heroes onto the side of Stone Mountain near Atlanta, Georgia, the largest piece of exposed granite in the world and a site sacred to the Ku Klux Klan, who had relaunched themselves there in 1915. Borglum was friendly with the Klan, but perhaps more for financial than ideological reasons, for he also sculpted Lincoln and Tom Paine. Robinson had suggested great figures of the West, such as Buffalo Bill and Sitting Bull, but this was too parochial for Borglum. He said it needed a national theme, one of Manifest Destiny, with Washington representing the founding of the country, Lincoln its reunification and Jefferson and Roosevelt its expansion through the Louisiana Purchase and the acquisition of the Panama Canal respectively. And it must be vast, the greatest undertaking in sculpture since the ancient Egyptians. If the figures were full-length rather than just faces, they would be 465 feet tall. You can stand in Jefferson's eyes. 'There's something in sheer volume that awes and terrifies, lifts us out of ourselves,' said Borglum. 'I must see, think, feel and draw in Thor's dimension.'

To many Lakota Sioux, the monument is a hideous scar on holy land of which they have been dispossessed. Some progressives thought during its making that, if the monument was a celebration of American expansion, this should include the expansion of human rights. In 1937 a bill was introduced into Congress to include among the figures Susan B. Anthony, a nineteenth-century feminist who sought to bring together the labour, black-rights and suffragette movements. More recently a proposal was put forward to place Ronald Reagan up there. So far, only Borglum has prevailed. 'Borglum is about to destroy another mountain,' an eastern newspaper declared when he first received the commission. 'Thank God it's in South Dakota where no one will ever see it.' Three million people per year, it is said, visit Rushmore.

I turned off 385 to have a look at this thing that uneasily brought together the local and the federal, the dissenting and the imperial and the white man and the Indian, with a cameo appearance by the Ku Klux Klan, then looped back and continued south. On open land I came upon the Indians' riposte to Borglum and his presidents – the Crazy Horse memorial.

Crazy Horse was born somewhere not far away along the eastern edge of the Black Hills, to a warrior and interpreter of visions also called Crazy Horse and Rattling Blanket Woman, who later hanged herself from a tree when she didn't conceive any more children after her first. Crazy Horse was raised by Rattling Blanket Woman's sister, They Are Afraid of Her, a name she was given after her husband attacked her and she beat the hell out of him. After watching federal troopers kill a Lakota leader named Conquering Bear and several braves with cannon, Crazy Horse had a vision in the company of his father by Sylvan Lake in which he was transported first to the land of the dead and then to the land of thunder beings, shown the lightning streak and hailstone markings for his face that would protect him in battle, and given by these spirits a sacred song that is still sung by the Sioux.

In 1866 he was a decoy in a battle at Fort Phil Kearny in Wyoming that inflicted on the US Army its worst defeat on the plains up to that point. In the company of Sitting Bull, he attacked troops at Arrow Creek and later led 1,500 Cheyenne and Lakota against Brigadier General George Cook at the Battle of the Rosebud. Eight days later he and his braves along with Hunkpapa warriors led by Chief Gall annihilated General Custer at the Battle of the Little Big Horn. He was thought to be invisible to the enemy. Flying bullets and arrows seemed to vanish in the air before they could reach him.

Crazy Horse managed to avoid capture for nearly a year during the intense military campaign that followed Custer's defeat, but was finally persuaded to go to a reservation. Up to that time, and until his death, he never slept in a boardinghouse bed, wore white men's clothes, was photographed, met a president, performed in a Wild West show or was injured or captured in battle. He tried to live as he had before, while not causing offence to anyone. But he had become by then, according to one historian of the plains, 'a kind of Sioux Christ'. Some Native Americans saw in him the possibility of deliverance, others were jealous and the military didn't trust him. Eventually a conspiracy evolved to either place him in a corral cell in the Dry Tortugas in the Gulf of Mexico or to murder him. Finally, in a chaos of suspicion, intrigue and mistranslation he was stabbed in the jailhouse at Fort Robinson, probably by a soldier from County Tyrone in Ireland, and died several hours later, lamented in a death wail by his father and thousands of other Native Americans. He was carried away to be buried in a place yet to be discovered.

The story of the Crazy Horse memorial began in 1939 when a Sioux chief named Henry Standing Bear wrote to an east-coast sculptor named Korczak Ziolkowski, whose bust of Ignacy Paderewski won a gold medal at the New York World's Fair, asking if he'd be interested in creating a monument to the Native Americans in the Black Hills. Mount Rushmore, where Ziolkowski had worked under Borglum, was not yet complete. Ziolkowski began digging away at Thunderhead Mountain in 1948 with a Bud compressor that repeatedly stopped running, and worked there without salary until he died in 1982. Seven of his ten children are working on it now. It will depict Crazy Horse mounted on a horse and pointing out ahead of him, imagined by Ziolkowski answering the derisive question of a white man after he had withdrawn to a reservation, 'Where are your lands now?', with the reply, 'My lands are where my dead lie buried.' Around the monument, according to Ziolkowski's plan, will be a university and medical school for Native Americans. It will by a long way be the largest sculpture in the world. All four of the Mount Rushmore presidents will be able to fit within the head and flowing hair of Crazy Horse. The head of his horse will be twenty-two storeys high.

Working in stone on this scale involves thought with a long arc. Borglum knew that Mount Rushmore stone eroded at a rate of one inch every hundred thousand years and left three inches on his presidents so that they would not begin to decay for another three hundred thousand years. When Ziolkowski died after thirty-four years of continuous work on the monument, the only visible sign of his sculpture was Crazy Horse's head and it was nowhere near complete. It might be finished by 2150, or it might not. On his deathbed he asked his wife to please carry on with the project, but not too fast. 'Don't forget your dreams,' he advised everyone else. Borglum's and Ziolkowski's monuments, just seventeen miles apart, depict two Americas, one static, grave, venerable and representative of the expansion of the nation's boundaries, the other full of movement and about boundarylessness.

I kept going on 395 south to Hot Springs, then went west on 18 through the Buffalo Gap National Grassland to Wyoming. It was dusk. The gold at the tips of the grazing grass was so fine and gauzy that it seemed to become a mist. Below the gold was a pale green, then the colour deepened further down the stalks. Telegraph wires and trees were black against the orange and mauve of the sky. Some grasses of the plains: threadleaf sedge, inland saltgrass, blue joint, Indian ricegrass, prairie sandreed, switchgrass, love grass. Bluestem can grow to eight feet if it gets sufficient water. Blue grama grass was what the buffalo ate when they filled the plains. I stopped for a moment at the side of the road beside one. He looked up at me like a truck driver interrupted at his lunch, then went back to grazing.

There were once seventy million buffalo on the plains. Indians hunted them by chasing them into dunes or over cliffs. When they got horses they killed them with lances or arrows. According to Ian Frazier, an Indian who killed a buffalo might 'cut it open on the spot and eat the warm liver seasoned with bile from the gallbladder. The women followed to do the butchering, and could slice the meat as thin as paper. When it was hung on racks, the plains wind and sun dried it and then it would last for months. The Comanche liked to kill young buffalo calves and eat the curdled, partially digested milk from the stomach. The Asiniboin made a dish of buffalo blood boiled with brains, rosebuds and hide scrapings. The Arikara retrieved from the Missouri drowned buffalo so putrefied they could be eaten with a spoon. With stone mallets, Indians crushed buffalo bones to get at the marrow. There were cuts of buffalo just as there are of beef; the Hidatsa had names for twenty-seven different cuts. The Sioux boiled buffalo meat with heated rocks in a buffalo paunch, then ate the paunch, too. Roasted fat hump ribs, boiled tongue, and coffee was a meal Indians dreamed about. Buffalo meat did not make you feel full. Some Indians could eat fifteen pounds of buffalo meat at a sitting.'

A missionary named John McDougall lived with the Blackfeet and wrote of the other uses they got from the buffalo: 'Moccasins, mittens, leggings, shirts and robes – all buffalo. With the sinews of the buffalo they stitched and sewed these. Their lariats, bridle, lines, stirrup-straps and saddles were manufactured out of buffalo hide. The women made scrapers out of the legbone for fleshing hides. The men fashioned knife handles out of the bones, and the children made toboggans out of the same. The horns served for spoons and powder flasks. In short, they lived and had their physical being in the buffalo.'

Generally, an Indian got his share of the buffalo whether or not he or anyone in his family was involved in the kill. The principle tended to be: from each according to his ability, to each according to his needs. There was a communality to life and chiefs were accorded respect, but not absolute authority. 'This wild man who first welcomed the newcomer is the only perfect socialist or communist in the world,' wrote a British explorer named Captain William F. Butler. 'He holds all things in common with his tribe – the land, the bison, the river, and the moose.'

At Mule Creek Junction I turned south on US 85 and

stayed on it through the darkness all the way to Brighton, Colorado, where I took 7 west across the northern suburbs of Denver to Boulder, set under soaring sandstone peaks known as the Flatirons, where the plains meet the Rocky Mountains. I'd been there a few times when I was a student. I arrived once at night after a thousand-mile drive from Chicago and went straight up into the foothills with William Blake's 'Marriage of Heaven and Hell' in my mind and a hope for visions, but nothing happened. I hadn't much experience of mountains then and expected too much of them, and of myself. Boulder was then – and still is – a prosperous, relaxed, politically liberal university town a little like Ithaca, New York or Madison, Wisconsin, but with the added spectacle of a mountain wilderness forming its western border. House prices are double the national average. IBM, Ball Aerospace, the National Institute of Technology, Tyco and Amgen are here, but so are meditation centres, experimental architecture and henna tattooists. A Tibetan named Chogyam Trungpa founded a Buddhist-inspired university called the Naropa Institute here, where Allen Ginsberg opened the Jack Kerouac School of Disembodied Poetics. Gay marriage licences were available in 1975. One of its sister cities is in Cuba and the other is Lhasa.

I found a bar with an exuberant band crowded onto a small stage. A man whose vastness spread onto the two stools beside him at the bar watched the musicians with a scowl like a bad guy in a professional wrestling show. Sometimes he took bites out of a beer mat and spit the pieces onto the floor. The lead singer turned out to be from Howth at the north end of Dublin Bay. He told me he'd got into music in order to write a book about it one day, but so far he hadn't started, nor did he know what such a book could ever be. He was the only person who spoke with me in that thronged bar. I had found, and would continue to find, that in the little bars in the little towns out on the American road, particularly those where the grooming is haphazard, the language coarse, the prospects bleak and where it is believed that disputes both international and personal are best solved by violence, you are unlikely to get from the door to your chair without being engaged in conversation, and very often offered a bed in someone's house for the night, but in cities and university towns, no matter how politically or spiritually open the prevailing ideology, you are likely to pass your evening in silence.

My cousin David lived in Buffalo in north central Wyoming and I headed there in the late morning with a short detour into the eastern Rockies. If I pushed it I might get to Buffalo that night.

David had come back from Vietnam in 1971, then went west. In Colorado he moved earth, tended a bar, installed fireplaces, managed a fly-fishing shop, cooked in a Mexican restaurant, ran wildlife expeditions, busted broncos in a rodeo, lived in a tepee, went on binges and courted waitresses. His sleep was troubled by war dreams and he went north into a deeper wilderness in search of solitude. When my father died in 1993 David called me from a place called Hungry Horse, Montana. He'd had to drive twenty-five miles to find a pay phone. He was living on the floor of a van with two drunks who went through a case of beer each per day. He went south to get away from them and lived in a converted chicken coop on a nineteenth-century homestead, where he tended livestock, chinked cabins and talked to the two cats who were his only regular company. I'd last seen him in 1996, when he was working as a maintenance man at a Holiday Inn in Bozeman, Montana. When I was a child he was heroic to me. He carried something with him, some marvellous magical ingredient that I could not understand or attain, a lightness and an edge that made people want to be around him. He had rakishness and wit and a laugh like no other I had heard, a guttural, staccato sound, the shoulders rotating slowly, the hands lifted palms upward, a laugh weighted with incredulity and a sense of the grotesque and the absurd. I studied his movements and gestures. There was something feline about his walk, smooth and slow and capable of sudden eruption into great speed.

When he was seventeen and I was eleven he was co-captain and quarterback of the St George High School football team. He was five feet six inches, weighed just over nine stone and could barely see over the backs of his offensive line. St George was a small Catholic school in Evanston, just north of Chicago, and yet they were undefeated that year and ranked the number-one high-school football team in Illinois. The *Chicago Tribune* featured an article about its tiny, miracle-working quarterback and, after winning a game in football-deranged Ohio, a group of kids ran after him clamouring for his chinstrap. I asked him how he could prevail in this game of the collision of great corporal mass. 'Football is a game of leverage and deception,' he said.

When he finished high school he went to Southern Illinois University to study biology and physical education and when he came out, in 1968, he was drafted. That in itself was bad luck, but it was just the first twist in a run that he later described to me as like a long, very bad night at a poker table, all the cards falling wrong. It was bad luck to be drafted, worse luck still to be sent to Vietnam. But to be white, middle-class, university-educated and over twenty-four and be assigned combat duty in the killing fields of Vietnam's central highlands was a malign statistical improbability like the contracting of a rare tropical disease.

He was trained in artillery-shell trajectory calculation and sent on combat assault missions with the 7th Air Cavalry Division, General Custer's old unit. They dropped thousand-pound bombs in bamboo thickets to create Landing Zones, from which they harassed the Ho Chi Minh Trail. They slept in holes and were plagued without cease by rats, jungle rot, ringworm, trenchfoot, claymores and artillery fire. One night eight enemy sappers got through the perimeter defence with satchel charges to destroy the command post. A Landing Zone is circular and you can only fire on attackers at point-blank range in case you might hit some of your own. This was a fight full of fire and blood in which the combatants could look into each other's eyes. All the Vietnamese were killed, and so were a few Americans. After the attack they had what they called a Mad Minute, in which all the base's weaponry – machine-guns, M16s, RPGs, mini-guns – were fired into the 360 degrees of the Landing Zone's perimeter into the jungle. Everything within a hundred yards would die. The commanding officer ordered that six of the enemy bodies be burned because it would look bad for him if so many had got through the defences. 'They talk about our MIAs,' said David. 'But what about theirs?' The jungle was burning. Conscientious objectors were burning the waste in the latrines. The sappers' bodies were burning. The American dead lay in the dirt, rifles and bayonets sticking up beside them. Then a priest asked David to assist him in the saying of a Mass. He replied, 'I don't know if God exists, but if He does He's shitting all over this place this very minute.'

When he got back he discovered he'd forgotten how to act. He hadn't bought anything or been out of uniform during his time in the jungle. He got into a taxi at the airport in Chicago and told the driver he'd just come back from Vietnam. 'So what?' said the driver. 'Where do you want to go?' He went to a Veterans' Career Conference, but found that instead of offering jobs they were trying to sell cheap merchandise for the veterans to sell door-to-door. Insurance companies were there trying to sell policies. A group of men just back from Vietnam went through the hall breaking up the booths in their fury. Most, like David, had initially had a belief in their mission, then found they were bringing only chaos and death to the people of Vietnam. It was a war in service of national delusion and the profits of weapons manu-facturers. Then they discovered that the best they could hope for from their fellow Americans was indifference. This is when he went west.

I took 119 out of Boulder through the foothills and then turned north on 72 at Nederland. I passed old mines and abandoned settlements. Peaks soared around me as I drove.

Mountains can both dazzle and oppress with their great age and their vastness, but these had about them a feeling of youth, the pale rockfaces above the treeline seeming to have the complexion of children. Ute Indians hunted here in the summers, but few people ever settled. It's the home of coyotes, mountain lions, moose and black bear. In 1882 Oscar Wilde came into these mountains further to the south at Leadville, where, in a green overcoat and a miner's hat, he was lowered in a bucket down the Matchless Mine's new shaft, named 'The Oscar' in his honour. He opened it with a silver drill, had a meal consisting of three courses of whiskey and read to the miners passages from the autobiography of Benvenuto Cellini, a silversmith. I drove on through dappled light so dazzling it seemed made of molten silver, then stopped for a cold drink at the Millstone Inn 9,700 feet up in Ward. I sat at the bar and listened to a woman drinking rum and beer talk about killer dogs, then got back in my car and drove on. The air cooled and rarefied the higher I went. Each summer three and a half million tourists pass through the Rocky Mountain National Park just to the north-west of where I was, but for miles I didn't see another car on this autumn Sunday afternoon. In the freshness of these mountains and the glory of the light moving over them, and in my anonymity as I passed through them, I felt a sudden delirious sense of freedom, a gift from the American road. Through two peaks at the end of a chasm I saw golden churning clouds and a little turn-off with an historical marker from which I could watch the sky for a moment. I pulled over and ran in my shirt through the icy air to the sign, where I read about Calvin Ward discovering one of the richest veins of gold in the Rockies in 1860. He called it Miser's Dream. It was too cold to look for long at the spectacle before me, and I went back to the car.

I found all four doors locked, the windows closed, the only set of keys I had in the ignition with the engine running and my coat lying across the back seat. Somehow I'd tripped the central locking system near the door handle when I got out of the car. How inviting it was inside there, and how far away.

I could have smashed one of the windows with a rock, but that seemed too violent. My mobile phone was in the pocket of my coat, but it would have been no help anyway for, apart from in Boulder and briefly near Cheyenne, I'd had no coverage since Hibbing, Minnesota. I stepped up to the edge of the road to ask for mercy. The cold entered my body as though through a drip-feed. For a while I saw nothing on the road, then a car came towards me from the north followed by a battered open-backed truck. I raised a timid hand and the car passed by. So did the truck, but then it stopped up the road and came back. The passenger door opened and a woman nearly too drunk for speech fell halfway through it, then righted herself. The floor was full of empty bottles and a cooler with around twenty bottles of Budweiser still to go. The driver leaned across.

'Sorry, didn't see you at first,' he said. 'Can we do something for you?'

I told them about the car.

'How much gas do you have?' he said.

'I just filled it at Nederland.'

'That's one good thing at least.'

He told me they knew someone who lived not far away who'd have a phone. We could try to find a solution there, he said. He was Tom, and his friend was Marie. He offered me a beer, but I told him I'd wait until later. We drove for miles back along the way I had come and then turned off onto a dirt trail in deep woodland.

'Where were you going when you stopped?' I asked.

'We were just driving along the trails.'

He told me he'd been a truck driver, but was giving himself a rest for a while. 'The companies run you ragged and then cheat on the log books. I was making the same money I was making twenty years ago.'

Finally we came to a wooden house set in trees beside a river. In it was an elderly woman named Mrs Henderson and the grandson she was looking after for the day. She made coffee and tea and sandwiches. Marie seemed to find some equilibrium, but her eyes were fluttering. Mrs Henderson said that the volunteer fire department would know how to open the car. 'I'll try Ed,' she said, but she couldn't locate him or anyone else. 'Sundays are difficult days to get anything done,' she said. One hoped that didn't include the putting out of fires. She also called the police, but they told her they were prevented for insurance reasons from opening people's cars. She tried gas stations, breakdown services and locksmiths and finally found someone in Lyons around an hour's drive away who was willing to come out.

'Stay here in the warmth until he comes,' she said. She took me on a tour of the house. At the back was an unfinished room of wood and glass with a pit dug into it for a swimming pool. 'My husband and I came out here from Kansas when he retired,' she said. 'This was going to be his dream house. He built nearly all of it himself, then just before he finished it he died.'

Tom and Marie took me back to my car. It was as I had left it over two hours earlier, still and humming like a cat in the last of the sun. A lanky man with red hair arrived after a while in a tow truck and, with a long bar jammed down beside the window, manoeuvred open the door. I paid him ninety-seven dollars and he drove off.

Tom and Marie stepped out of the truck to say goodbye.

'You've been very kind,' I said.

'Don't mention it. We weren't doing anything anyway.'

'I'd like to buy you a meal or something, but I only have fifteen dollars with me. Would you take that?'

'No, we're fine. Thanks.'

'You'd be doing me a favour.'

'Keep it. You might need it for gas.'

'Would you be able to buy something from me for Mrs Henderson?' I held out the crumpled bills.

'We'll look after her,' he said.

'Isn't there something I can do for you?' I knew the futility of this as I said it.

'No, we're fine, really,' he said. 'Have a good trip. I wish I was doing it.'

He waved goodbye and got into the truck. I saw Marie lift a bottle of beer to her mouth. Tom waved again as they pulled out onto the road. I stood watching them until they disappeared, then drove slowly northwards.

When I went to see David in 1996 he took me out from Bozeman and showed me rivers where he fished for trout and to Three Forks, the confluence of the Missouri, the Madison and the Gallatin rivers where Lewis and Clark had passed. He told me about Indians, homesteaders, the fur trade, buffalo, grizzly bears, elk, eagles, cattle herding and horses. He told me about these things because he thought I had come to Montana to write about them. His brother Jack arrived and we drove down to the northern boundary of Yellowstone Park and stayed in a cabin that backed onto a river that crashed through the ice, the snow hip-deep on the banks and heavy in the pine boughs above. When he came out west, this was the landscape he had been seeking. 'The only thing I was looking for was serenity,' he said. 'That's what any Vietnam veteran I know is looking for. You can find it on the shore of a lake, in religion, in the quiet of a mountain. That sixth sense you developed when you were trying to stay alive, you can wake it up in the wilderness. When you get into the true wilderness, you feel you are entering God's cathedral. Just to be there is enough, to know that it exists and that everything in it is doing well. If you're fishing you learn to understand it, to read the water. You think: If I were a fish, where would I want to be right now? You know the trout has a visual spectrum of thirty degrees. You look at all the elements and you try to think of how you can present the fly so that it looks natural to the fish as it comes into his field of vision. It's an art form, like cooking. It involves science, timing and presentation. There are so many stories along a river, and when you're there you try to figure them out. You sit down for half an hour. The squirrels stop scolding, the owls don't mess with you. You become absorbed into the day-to-day routine. You get things into perspective, how insignificant and fragile we are. Millionaires and paupers are the same to a grizzly bear. The past is gone, as is the future. There is only that moment. The unfortunate thing is that you have to leave it.'

On the first night we had Mexican food prepared in a lodge by a large Austrian whom David had known in Colorado. 'You have to make certain sacrifices to live in Montana,' said David. 'It's full of rednecks, skinheads, Vietnam veterans on disability pay, fanatics of all kinds. There are people in the wilderness who would slit your throat in a heartbeat. It's difficult to find a person who knows a word longer than two syllables. And all the women are five axe handles between the pockets.' An axe handle, I learned, is a unit of measurement for the span of a woman's hips. At the bar a man in a black cowboy hat with no teeth was declaiming in whistles and grunts. He wanted us to take a case of beer to his house. He had thirty Chinese assault rifles in his living room, he said, and he lived with two women. 'How many axe handles?' asked David.

In fact, I had come to write about him, but I had not found a way to tell him. When I travelled around the country with Teresa in 1977 we had gone to see him in Vail. He was as ever lithe and witty, but the edge he had was still edgier, the lightness had all but gone and there was little of that eye-rolling laughter that seemed to say: What behavioural atrocity will I be looking at next? Above all, he was nervous and introspective. There was a tenderness about him that was both painful and inspiring to behold. He seemed without protection. And he was angry. One day, he said, he would write about what had happened to him in Vietnam. But then in Vail, as was again the case in Bozeman, the subject of Vietnam would be closed as soon as it had been opened, like the snapping shut of a small metallic box. Nineteen years had passed and he had yet to write his testimony.

That night the three of us lay in our beds along the cabin wall. Jack fell asleep. I was as awake as if I'd been doused by a hose. I heard David stirring. 'So what did you come out here to talk about?' he asked. He had seen without great effort that the eagles and bears and the Lewis and Clark expedition were not what I was there for. 'I'd like to talk about you,' I said, knowing that there was nothing that granted me this right. He took in a breath, then let it out. 'Ask me anything,' he said. 'Anything at all. I'm an open book.'

The following day Jack went out cross-country skiing and David talked to me for five hours over the kitchen table about his time in Vietnam. When he got to the end, he said, 'The rejection when I got back hurt me to the quick. I had never faced rejection before. This has brought about a demise of a whole section of our population. I hear that more Vietnam veterans have died from suicide than in combat. Others barely live with it. I see them sometimes deep in the wilderness, looking for some peaceful place where no man has walked before. They recognise me and I recognise them. There's nothing in the so-called real world that is ever going to duplicate the intensity of combat experience and that hyper-awareness you had to cultivate to get through it. Nothing seems to mean anything – a job, people, your own existence. Everything is trivial compared to the intense struggle to survive on an hour-by-hour basis. You turn inward, you withdraw. Nobody seems to have a clue about anything because they haven't been through what you've been through. You say to yourself about almost anything, "Fuck it, it don't mean nothing." That's the mindset of a doctor with a good practice and a family who, twenty years down the line from Vietnam, puts a gun to his head and blows his brains out.

'I'd like to eliminate the war as a defining part of my life. But I can't. I know that it will never be forgotten. I'll die with it. I was asked to do something for my country and I did it as well as I could. But it was a fraud. I was deceived by my government and then rejected by my fellow countrymen. All this weighs very heavily on me.'

When I got back to London I wrote the story. I sent it by fax to the restaurant where the Austrian was a cook, then called David there a few days later. He felt deceived and angry with what had happened between us, and said so. 'I won't publish it if you don't want me to,' I said. 'Go ahead,' he said. 'It's all true.' The story appeared in *Esquire* a few months later. I had more reactions to it from people both known and unknown to me than from any other piece of journalism I'd ever written. I exonerated myself for having done it with the thought that I had told him I would be writing about him and had also offered to leave it unpublished, if that is what he wanted. And it was, I told myself, an act of familial affinity, a making of a testimony for him that he hadn't made for himself. But I couldn't entirely persuade myself of this. Who was I to invade the mind of this private man, a man with such an acute awareness of venality, exploitation, compromise and bad faith, all of which he'd learned about in the US Army? Who am I to be doing it yet again? I heard about him through the years that followed in one-line reports in Christmas cards from his brother Jack. He'd had a run of low-wage jobs, then been for a time in the care of the Veterans' Administration. Now he had his own house in Buffalo.

A little while after I left Tom and Marie I arrived at Estes Park. I watched a herd of deer walk daintily along the main street with their noses in the air, then disappear behind some apartment buildings. Stephen King stayed in an Edwardian hotel here and then made it the setting for his novel *The Shining*, instead of the amusement park he had been planning. I dropped back onto the plains and arrived at Loveland. It once had the biggest cherry orchard west of the Mississippi and is said, curiously, to have large populations of both evangelical Christians and sculptors, but all I could see were malls. I found a tiny, nearly deserted downtown section with buildings that looked as if they might be more than fifty years old and a few people standing around in the shadows and had a Mexican dinner in a restaurant heavy with paintings and statues. There was a waitress of great beauty and silence who spoke only to ask me what I wanted to eat and to tell me that Loveland was the place where people from all over America sent their Valentine cards to be reposted with heart stamps, the town's postmark and romantic verses composed by Loveland's citizens.

Before I left I called my cousin Jack and asked him for the best way to get in touch with David. He told me that David almost never answered the telephone, but he had a number for a friend of his named Liz who was in regular contact with him. Jack was a mild-mannered, law-abiding Midwestern citizen who'd quietly raised two children with his wife Bonnie. After decades of middle management in corporations he was now retired. I'd never so far as I could remember had a political discussion with him. I hadn't been very assiduous in collecting opinions from those whose opinions I didn't already know, so it occurred to me to ask him what he thought about the president. 'I wish you hadn't asked,' he said. 'I can hardly bear to think, let alone speak, of him. I have never been so disgusted by a holder of American office in all my life. He's disgraced us in front of the world. He's without question a criminal and he should be in jail. The same goes for his administration. Rumsfeld was at G.D. Searle when I was there. He was dangerous then and he's worse now. I don't know how we wound up with such people. And I don't have any friends who think differently about this than I do.'

I got onto Interstate 25, wondering if I had a chance to make the three hundred and some miles north to Buffalo. The night was still, the air full of Christian radio stations fulminating against the state, soothing about the afterlife and selling prayer cruises in the Caribbean. Near the border with Wyoming I passed pylons with explosions of white light popping around them like Spanish fireworks. I went around Cheyenne, home in the great days of gold and cattle in the nineteenth century to an opera house that printed its programmes in blue on perfumed white satin. An exit sign announced Happy Jack

Road. Due west of Chugwater was the Como Bluff dinosaur graveyard, where fossilised remains of Jurassic Age creatures were found in the clay in 1877 by a station agent for the Union Pacific railroad, who wrote to O.G. Marsh of Yale University about them. When the professor arrived, he found the tail weapon of a stegosaurus tied to a horse to keep him from wandering. He eventually brought back five hundred crates of bones, some of which came to be assembled into the brontosaurus at New Haven's Peabody Museum. There are remnants of the migratory past everywhere here. When the Federal Writers' Project anonymous recorder walked around in Wyoming he found 'crumbling stumps and logs of old fur presses, ruts worked deep by rumbling wagon wheels, arrow-strewn battlefields, tumbledown shafthouses and rotting sluice boxes, stone abutments of an old railroad trestle, broken aerial tramway cables that whine in the wind, early-day branding irons and roundup camp kettles, ox yokes and rusty beaver traps'. In this dark night with the tyres of the trucks whining like swarms of insects, I could only imagine it all. I found a secular radio station which spoke of a new type of party where for $700 each guest could eat sushi in their homes off the body of a naked model.

I pulled into a little town called Glendo and found a dimly lit bar with three men and a woman being served by a tiny grandmother. As I came through the door I heard:

'Scottie combs his hair with a brick.'

I took up a place along from the group. They variously said:

'The beer cans were flying.'

'It was a rodeo night.'

'Toby got mad at Joe Banana.'

'He fell asleep on the third card.'

'But he woke up mad.'

'He was hair-pulling, vein-popping mad.'

'Steam was pouring out of both his pants legs!'

'He was going to put that senior citizen's head right though the fish aquarium there.'

'A shoe came flying and caught him between the eyes. Laid him out.'

'He looks like he combs his hair with a spare tyre.'

Scottie, it would seem, was one of that long line of hard-drinking, but indestructible American savages who live at the other end of the compass from effeteness. One predecessor would be Old Dan Tucker, described in a song of the same name written in 1843 by Dan Emmett.

> Old Dan Tucker was a fine old man
> Washed his face with a fryin' pan
> Combed his hair with a wagon wheel
> And died with a toothache in his heel

> Get out the way, Old Dan Tucker
> You're too late to get your supper
> Get out the way, Old Dan Tucker
> You're too late to get your supper . . .

> Old Dan Tucker got drunk and fell
> In the fire and kicked up holy hell
> A red-hot coal got in his shoe
> And oh my Lord the ashes flew . . .

By such men was the West made.

At the far end of the bar was a man with a florid face under a cowboy hat, a body as taut as a middleweight's and with white bandages around his fingers. His name was Kenny.

'Me and Linda went up to Douglas on Saturday,' he said. 'Can anyone here tell me if there's a lower form of life than what they got up there in Douglas? We sat in the McDonald's watching them. They don't even notice if you're retarded there. They scratch their buttholes, pick their noses, walk around with their tongues hanging out.' He got up off his stool to act this out. I checked my map and saw that Douglas was the next town, just fifteen miles or so to the north. At this point he looked over and decided to include me. 'You dress pretty nice,' he said. 'You go up to Douglas and they'll make you mayor.'

He told me he was a skinner in a butchering plant for game that hunters bring in. 'I skin them, get them naked, make sure their crotches are clean. I'm like a pimp.' He held out his bandaged hands. 'You get a lot of cuts in that job.'

They began to talk about guns.

'Charlton Heston is our president,' said the grandmother. She gave me a collusive wink and showed me a hand gun hidden in a drawer under the bar. 'That's my personal one,' she said. I wondered how she could lift it. Then she showed me photographs of the local taxidermist's house. 'It's one of our most interesting features,' she said. All over the walls was an inert menagerie of birds of prey, fowl, various antlered game, wild boar and, at the top of the stairs, a grizzly bear up on his hind legs and with his mouth open in a silent roar.

'Where are you headed?' asked the man next to me.

'To Buffalo, then into Montana and on to the coast.'

'Half the lunatics in the United States are in Montana,' said one.

'It's like a resort for criminals,' said another.

'If they got rid of all the felons in Montana, there'd be no one left to feed the cattle,' said a third.

At this the grandmother laughed.

'I don't suppose there's a hotel here,' I said.

'You'll have to go to Douglas, unfortunately,' said Kenny. Not one of the people here had been born in Glendo or even in Wyoming, but they were as chauvinistically caustic about their immediate neighbours as Greeks sometimes are about the neighbouring island.

Kenny asked for a crate of beer to be put on his tab, then walked over to say goodbye.

'I've raced horses, driven trucks and built bridges,' he said. 'I've lived all over the country. I'm thirty-eight years old and I have no destination. I'm the biggest fuck-up you ever saw. I'm the lostest, most unsatisfied and unknown-to-himself soul I know.'

– 205 –

He put one arm around the beer and the other over his girlfriend's shoulder and ambled out. I could have listened to him for a week.

In a bar in Douglas half an hour later a man called out to me, 'Are you a Jehovah's Witness?' It seemed my black clothes were for him a sign. I had a beer, then found a $45 motel run by a couple from India and set in a brown field. Humbert Humbert was consoled by the neatness and anonymity of the American motel as he drove around with Lolita and noted the various stock proprietors – 'the reformed criminal, the retired teacher and the business flop, among the males; and the motherly, pseudo-ladylike and madamic variants among the females'. Were he making his trip now, he'd have added the 'woman in sari'.

In the morning I drove across grassland towards Buffalo. This was the land of the rancher and cowboy, created by three events that occurred around the same time in the nineteenth century. The first was the virtual extinction of the buffalo, brought about by, among other things, the coming of the railway and the discovery that buffalo hides made excellent belts for power machinery in eastern factories. Thousands of buffalo hunters with guns were unleashed onto the plains. The second was the removal of the Indians onto reservations. The third was the invention in 1874 by a DeKalb, Illinois farmer named Joseph Glidden of barbed wire. He called it Twisted Oval and manufactured it on a converted coffee mill. Later came Briggs' Obvious, Allis' Sawtooth, Scutt's Arrow Plate and Brinkerhoff's Riveted Splicter. For the first time in this treeless terrain cattle could be fenced in, which meant that breeding could be controlled and one well could serve an entire herd. It also allowed vast ranches to have a sudden *de facto* validity where once there had been open range owned by the government. Those with the largest private armies tended to create the largest cattle empires.

General James S. Brisbin wrote a book called *The Beef Bonanza; or, How to Get Rich on the Plains* in which he demonstrated that an investment in cattle could double in five years while paying a ten per cent annual dividend. Bankers, manufacturers and European aristocrats, among them Winston Churchill's aunt, came to the plains or sent their money there. By 1884 twenty million acres of the plains were owned by foreigners. One of them, the Marques de Morès, himself 'weary of civilisation', came to North Dakota with his wife, who had the foresight to bring her silver hairbrushes in sets of two to accommodate either a left-handed or right-handed maid. Also there were small ranchers and rustlers, all living in uneasy proximity in this vast place.

On the night of 9 January 1887, the temperature dropped forty degrees Fahrenheit in two hours. The wind rose and snow began to fall. By the end of the storm sixty per cent of the cattle in Montana had died and hundreds of thousands more elsewhere in the plains were lost. Fortunes that had been made quickly were destroyed in days. The bankers and aristocrats went back to the east and to Europe, including the Marques de Morès, who lost $1.5 million.

In the straitened circumstances after the storm the larger ranchers tried to take greater control of land and water, often using lynchings and shootings to intimidate smaller ranchers, declaring in this time of ambiguous ownership that they were rustlers. In what came to be called the Johnson County War an association of large ranchers known as the Wyoming Stock Growers' Association hired fifty Texan vigilantes to end the resistance of small ranchers to their expansion. They moved north from Caspar, cutting telegraph wires all the way to Buffalo, and killed four innocent men at the KC ranch, owned by Nate Champion, who with other small ranchers was organising a round-up of cattle. The vigilantes set fire to Champion's cabin and gunned him down when he ran out. The sheriff of Buffalo raised a posse of two hundred to apprehend the killers at a ranch on Crazy Woman Creek, but President Benjamin Harrison sent the Sixth Cavalry to rescue them. No charges were ever brought against the vigilantes, or against the Wyoming Stock Growers' Association. There are incidents in American history where the federal government defended the citizen against corporate power, but this is not one of them.

Woodrow Wilson's government saved ranchers by breaking up a Beef Trust that was fixing prices and black-balling any ranchers who objected. Thereafter, ranchers operated in a free and open market, and by 1970 the four leading meat-packing corporations were slaughtering only twenty-one per cent of the nation's cattle. All this was reversed under the deregulation that took place during Ronald Reagan's administration. The four leading meat-packers now slaughter eighty-four per cent of America's cattle. Secret deals are made with the largest suppliers and prices paid to smaller ranchers have been suppressed. These have seen their share of every dollar paid for beef fall by one-third. Of the 1.3 million ranchers in the United States twenty-five years ago, only 800,000 remain.

I got to Buffalo and waited in a bar for my cousin David with his friend Liz. She ordered a beer, but I told her it was too early for me to start. 'Here we get up early, start drinking early and go to bed early. Some people are drunk by six and in bed by seven.' David came in with his head cocked to the side, half in scrutiny, I thought, and half in anticipation of a joke, and ordered a Scotch. A woman named Deb appeared and she and Liz danced to either side of him while he sang a song called 'I Should've Been a Cowboy'.

'I call them the Bookends,' he said when he finished. 'They put me in the middle and try to wear down my moral fibre.'

It had been seven years since I'd last seen him in Montana. There, apart from the long afternoon in the cabin when he gave me the gift of his testimony, he was opaque, his jacket zipped to the neck, the collar turned up, a baseball hat low on his forehead, his spectacles tinted. He seemed to move as if wreathed in smoke. Here the company of the women seemed to lift and reveal him. I could see again his alacrity and rakishness, his feline, prowling gait, his look that seemed to say: You can't fool me, yet which nevertheless invited you in to the jest. He'd acquired a theme song and after another Scotch he sang it again, doing a little dance step and throwing an imaginary lasso. We all went to eat and he held the table with wild tales of the town, of jokes played on greenhorns and with memories of his catastrophic career as an altar boy when he mixed up the Latin responses and rang the bells at the wrong time. One morning a drunk came up for communion and, when David held the brass disc under his chin, the man thought it was a collection plate and dropped a quarter on it instead of receiving the host. Hanging over all this for me was what I had written about him and about which peace was yet to be made. A writer digs into, perhaps plunders the self and others in order to write. What is a matter of the right to work to him may seem like a treacherous invasion to the person written about. What mattered more here in this moment was that, since I was a child, he was a person whose approval I had sought and, about this, it seemed he felt I had acted in bad faith.

Deb said she had to leave because she had to be up early to open the office of the Tie-Dye shirt company she worked for. 'I'm fifty, so I'm the expendable one. I have to be on time,' she said. We all went out to our cars.

On the way back to his house I asked David what he thought about the war in Iraq. 'I think they got the initial strategy right,' he said, 'but then there was no follow-up, no forward thinking. Now they're mired in there and digging deeper. They're getting into a situation where they're calling up reservists and sending men with families into one-year tours of combat duty. It's a psychological disaster. It happened in Vietnam and they haven't learned from history or from those who came back from that war. People paid with their lives or limbs or minds, and now it's happening again.'

The house was a long, low wooden building set among trees high above the town. In the back was a yard and in the front was a porch looking down the hill with an enormous

American flag suspended over it. Few gained entrance here, I imagined. Inside it was homey, warm, neat and entirely fascinating to me. We sat down on a sofa across from a room he used for making flies for fishing. The last time I saw him he said something about my father's gravity, which made me think he believed it curbed my mother's *joie de vivre*, but now he proclaimed him a stylish, generous and gallant man who'd helped see his family through hard times after his own father had had a stroke.

'It's good to see you,' he said. He had the affliction – or maybe the gift – of appearing to be without protection. But I could not yet see the way to ask for his blessing.

He got blankets and pillows to set up a bed for me on the sofa, then brought out a framed photograph of the 1962 St George football team. He was there in the centre surrounded by giants with a smile unblemished by doubt. 'Life was sweet then,' he said. 'But I can't get it back.'

He stood up then to go to bed.

'That article you wrote, it wasn't what you said that upset me,' he said. 'It was that I exposed myself so much. When Jack got it he sent it to a Veterans' Administration doctor and he saw post-traumatic stress written all over it. He made the diagnosis and my benefits went up so much that I was able to buy this house and don't have to work any more. So it ended well.

'Sleep well,' he said. 'I'm glad you came.'

I watched him enter his bedroom, the door closing with a click.

The Rocky Mountains

In the late morning I left Buffalo going west on US 16 and passed through the lower reaches of the Big Horn Mountains, a spur of the Rockies that came up with the Laramide orogeny around seventy million years ago. In the longitudes ahead of me that lay between the inland and coastal plains were red mesa desert, geyser basins, America's highest peaks, lava flows, virgin forest and gigantic sand dunes, stretching between the borders with Canada and Mexico. It is a land of strange and colossal shapes and unimaginable emptiness. Some of the wildest people in America once came here in search of refuge or fortune, and still do. If the Midwest, with its husbandry and thrift, could be said to represent America's superego, the East its ego and California and the Deep South the light and dark shades of its id, then the West is in another category, more to do with Jung than Freud. Henry Miller wrote that it 'is nothing but enchantment, sorcery, illusionismus, phantasmagoria . . . Here nature has gone gaga and dada. Man is just an irruption, like a wart or a pimple.'

I passed Meadowlark Lake, the consequence of a dam made in 1934 by the Civil Construction Corps, which also made fire lookouts, ranger stations, camp grounds and trails as part of the New Deal. There are some Americans still furious about the New Deal, others still giving thanks. I went through a long valley of green and golden scrubland with beige and red rock faces to either side of the road glistening from a fine rain. There was a monument to Gilbert E. Leigh, a big-game hunter who fell to his death over a valley cliff here in 1886 while pursuing mountain sheep. This is the sort of information that could provoke someone into a novel if they were in the right mood. Over the gateway to the valley arced a huge rainbow.

Out on the plains again I passed Ten Sleep, so named because it was a rest stop ten sleeps, or nights, from Fort Laramie, Yellowstone and the Indian Agency at Stillwater. A long-simmering war between cattle and sheep ranchers in which ten thousand sheep and sixteen shepherds had already been killed culminated here in 1909, when a cattleman-turned-sheep-rancher named Joe Emge was attacked and cremated in his camp along with one of his shepherds. All five of the raiding party, some of them prominent ranchers, were caught and convicted, and the violence abated.

US 16 went north at Worland and then joined 14 and 20 to become a single road for a time heading west. On it, I passed Emblem, population ten. A radio station offered pamphlets on the question of whether Christians should participate in Halloween. I turned the dial and listened for a while to Paul Harvey, a nationally syndicated broadcaster I thought was an old man when I used to hear him as a teenager, but he was still on the air in the same voice. He reported that a woman had telephoned the emergency services in her town because a McDonald's had charged her for barbecue sauce. I went through the Big Horn Basin and entered the wide main street of Cody, Wyoming.

There were shops selling Western furniture, artefacts and clothes to either side of the road and a tumbleweed blowing up the centre. Tumbleweeds, also known as Russian thistle, prickly glasswort and wind witch, are likely to have been brought by German religious exiles who had been wandering in Europe since the Reformation. They picked up the tumble-weed seeds in the Russian steppes, their last stop before the American plains, a nearly identical terrain. The tumbleweed grows in loose, sandy soil and breaks free in the autumn, distributing up to one hundred thousand seeds each in whichever direction the wind blows them. The seeds have long lives. One consequence of America's offer of freedom to these religious exiles was the tumbleweed, a nuisance to farmers; another was the arrival of people skilled at growing wheat in a dry climate. I saw these tumbleweeds throughout the western meridians, bounding along like kangaroos until halted by fences.

Buffalo Bill, already becoming in part fictional, founded with some eastern investors in 1896 the town that bore his name. It had once been Crow land. Crow, who chopped off their fingers when in mourning and grew their hair up to eleven feet long, sometimes had sex in public and raped buffalo cows. When the buffalo vanished, they went north to their reservation in Montana. Buffalo Bill had been a trapper, prospector, Pony Express rider, Union soldier and so effective an Army scout during the Indian Wars that he was awarded a Congressional Medal of Honour in 1872. He got his name in a buffalo-killing contest in Kansas in 1868, taking it from Buffalo Bill Comstock with a total of sixty-nine buffaloes to Comstock's forty-eight. He came to be called 'the world's most famous man' by acting out the life he had lived and witnessed in his Wild West Show, a touring extravaganza with up to 1,200 performers, including gauchos, Mongols, Cossacks, Arabs, Sitting Bull and himself as General Custer re-enacting with Indians who had fought in it the Battle of the Little Big Horn. Queen Victoria watched the show during her Golden Jubilee and gave Bill a cherry-wood bar, which he installed in the Irma Hotel in Cody, named for his daughter. Posthumously, his fame waxed and waned according to the popularity of the Western dime novel or cowboy television series or films, but he became the object of a cult called Billism in 1950s Leopoldville, now Kinshasa, among young Congolese who wore cowboy shirts, neckerchiefs and jeans and organised their street gangs around Western themes.

Buffalo Bill earned his living from nostalgia, but was committed to the living West, investing in mining, ranching and irrigation. He was also a progressive. He had a brutal early lesson in reactionary politics when he saw his father stabbed by a pro-slavery mob after giving an abolitionist speech in Kansas. His father later died from the wounds. Though he killed both buffalo and Indians, he was an early advocate of nature and buffalo conservation and Native American rights. 'Every Indian outbreak I have known', he said, 'has resulted from broken promises and broken treaties by the government.' He also believed in equal civil rights and equal pay for women. He built his town in a state whose slogan is 'Equal Rights' and was the first to grant women the vote. Wyoming had the first woman court bailiff, justice of the peace, jury member and governor. Now the state votes Republican.

There is a rodeo every evening in Cody in July and August, but there were few people out on this cold, windblown autumn day. I had lunch in Buffalo Bill's Irma Hotel, then drove out of this town where Jackson Pollock was born and John 'Liver-Eating' Johnson was buried. Johnson was a mountain man born in New Jersey who moved west to become a trapper. He married an Indian who was killed by the Crow. Johnson spent twenty years tracking down as many Crow as he could, killing them, then eating their livers. He was kidnapped by Blackfeet, who planned to sell him to the Crow, but he ate through the leather straps that bound him, then knocked out and scalped his guard before cutting off the guard's leg. He used it as a weapon to batter Blackfeet trying to recapture him and ate it during a two-hundred-mile journey to the cabin of Del Gue, his partner in the fur trade. He later made peace with the Crow and became the town marshal of Red Lodge, Montana. Or so it is said. But as Macaulay wrote in his *History of England*, '[In stories of the highwaymen who] held aristocratic positions in the community of thieves, [anecdotes] of their ferocity and good nature, of their amours, of their miraculous escapes . . . there is doubtless a large mixture of fable; for it is both an authentic and an important fact that such fables, whether true or false, were heard by our ancestors with eagerness and faith.' This is truer of the West than of anywhere else in the United States, except perhaps the Deep South.

Just west of Cody I passed the Rattlesnake and Cedar Mountains on either side of a long canyon formed by the Shoshone River. This led to Yellowstone Park. Snow appeared on the rocks as I began to climb. At the park's east gate was a motionless horse whose black and white coat was like a Dalmatian's. Yellowstone, which in 1872 became the world's first national park, comprises 3,468 square miles of mountain, pine, wild animals and such hydrothermal phenomena as bubbling mud, fumaroles spewing steam and geysers blasting up to three hundred feet into the air. The first white man to see it was John Colter, a member of the Lewis and Clark expedition, but his testimony, along with those of various trappers and explorers over the subsequent half-century, was dismissed as infernal ravings. I crept along the road through the Sylvan Pass and came to the edge of Yellowstone Lake, which fills some of the vast caldera made by one of the three supervolcanic blasts that have happened at 600,000-year intervals. At this rate, another is now due. There was low cloud and a driving rain. You could have ridden a surfboard on the waves coming in over the lake. Steam rose and the mud sucked and gurgled on the shore. There was a rank smell of sulphur. What did those who first saw it think of this place? It must have seemed a vision. I went around the northern edge of the lake, the largest high-altitude body of water in the country, to West Thumb and on to the legendary geyser Old Faithful, quiet now. It was getting dark. I had grown accustomed to watching with sorrow the light grow dim. You miss the companionship of the landscape. The trucks become predatory in the night. There is tiredness and a mild sense of menace and no visual diversion. But here it was different. Yellowstone Park was entombed in an inhuman, prehistoric silence. Just the sound sometimes of the hissing and popping of this cauldron beneath the earth breaking through the mud. A mist wrapped itself around the car. I tried to get a radio station, but nothing came in. There was no one around, just this preternatural, untouched landscape. There were signs warning of falling rock. I passed through banks of steam that had come up out of the earth. Soon it was utterly black. There was no sign that electricity or people were in the world with me. You have to drive slowly in Yellowstone and I still had miles to go before I got out. Here were mountain lions, grizzly bears and wolf packs. The discs on the reflector poles seemed like yellow eyes and the car a frail vessel.

I made it over the Montana state line and out the north gate of the park intact, then went into a bar in Gardiner. It was an oddly unsettled place, lit in the main by coloured neon, vast, wild-looking bearded men talking with others in suits and with briefcases, people moving around from group to group with puzzled expressions like children looking for clues in a treasure hunt. I heard one of the men in a suit say, 'I've got to hit somebody. Anybody'll do.' In my experience, this usually then happens. A woman sat down beside me and in a forty-five-minute monologue as she drank beer and shots of vodka she told me of the death of her parents, that her brother was in a mental institution and that she was adopted and had had an abortion. You could work next to someone in Europe for twenty years and not hear any of that. Thus emptied, she weaved her way along the bar to someone else.

'What's that whistling?' an old man next to me said to the barmaid.

'That would be the coffee machine,' she said. She made no effort to disguise how tedious she found him.

'Maybe it's that you never wore those pants before,' he said, then cackled like a chimpanzee.

Outside of Gardiner is the twelve-thousand-acre Royal Teton Ranch, headquarters of Elizabeth Clare Prophet's Church Universal and Triumphant. Prophet was a religiously precocious child. At the age of five she began a survey of the Jewish and Catholic churches and all the Protestant denominations practising in her home town of Red Bank, New Jersey, before electing Christian Science, which she hoped would cure her epilepsy. Later, she became a

Theosophist, with certain Native American and Gnostic Christian beliefs added, and met Mark Prophet, who claimed to be a Messenger for the Ascended Masters, having lived through previous incarnations as Lancelot and Henry Wadsworth Longfellow. They married, and together they created a new church.

The Church Universal and Triumphant has a number of features that are both traditional in developing religions and appealing in the new West. It has dietary, clothing and moral prescriptions, forbidding processed foods, orange, chartreuse or fuchsia clothes and oral sex, this last on the grounds that it misaligns the chakras of the offending couple, placing the upper next to the lower. It offers physical salvation to the faithful, New Age iconography and communal ecstasy through chanting. It has stockpiled high-powered automatic weapons and railed against what it sees as 'a one-world capitalist-communist conspiracy' intended to destroy divinely inspired America. The Church moved from Washington to Virginia, California, Idaho and Colorado before settling in Gardiner in 1986. I was shown its perimeter fence in 1992, guards at the gate, members moving in the compound behind high fences listening to the high-pitched chanting of Mrs Prophet on Walkmans.

In the late 1980s Mrs Prophet became apocalyptic, declaring that the Soviet Union was going to launch an unprovoked nuclear strike against the United States. This would happen, she said, in April 1990. The faithful should build bunkers near the church so that they might survive the attack and emerge to inherit the Earth. Hundreds left their jobs, sold their cars and homes, spent to the maximum of their credit-card limits and borrowed everything they could to come to Montana and build bunkers. The Church itself constructed one for 750 people, which included communications equipment, an air-filtration system, generators and food for seven years. It cost $20 million. Members descended into the earth in March of 1990 to wait out the war. Around a month later they came out into the light, homeless, broke and facing debts they had no means of repaying. Several of the tanks holding the fuel for the Church's bunker ruptured and 32,500 gallons of fuel spilled out into the surrounding land, portions of it reaching the Yellowstone River and the park's ecosystem. Mrs Prophet had precedents in America, among them William Miller, who led a multitude of up to a million in the 1840s and whose miscalculation of Jesus' return to Earth on 22 October 1844 became known as the Great Disappointment. In the immediate aftermath his movement disappeared as if it had never been. Elizabeth Clare Prophet developed Alzheimer's disease and was placed in supervised care in Bozeman.

I went north from Gardiner on US 89 behind a car that had a bumper sticker declaring, 'Gun Control Means Using Both Hands.' I passed a town called Emigrant and another called Pray, before arriving at Interstate 90 at Livingston. When I was here in 1992 I stayed at the Murray Hotel, where Sam Peckinpah used to fire rounds at the ceiling from his pistol while lying in bed. In Livingston there is a town that you can see and beneath it its underground doppelgänger, built by the Chinese to house their favourite vices. I took 90 over to Bozeman, and stayed there for the night.

In the morning I had breakfast in a restaurant where soft, synthesised instrumental versions of pop songs played and where the walls were panelled in a material that bore the same relation to wood as prosthetic limbs bear to flesh. Waitresses in alpine uniforms padded along on thick carpet and stopped at tables to say, 'How are we doing?', 'Did you get started all right?', 'Are you going to do the puzzle on the placemat?' There is much to be said for American service. It is very often rapid, friendly and uncomplicated. An Irish friend of mine who went to live in San Francisco in the 1970s said he called one afternoon to order a telephone for his apartment and they said, 'I'm very sorry, sir, but we won't be able to install the phone until tomorrow. Do you still want to place the order?' He'd had to wait a year and a half for a phone in Dublin. But sometimes the service is so cloying that it seems they're trying to disable you. Breakfast that morning in Bozeman was like being a resident in an old people's home.

When I visited David here in 1996 he introduced me to a woman named Rena, who worked in the restaurant of the Holiday Inn where he was a maintenance man. He thought I should meet her because she'd lived for a time in England. One night she invited me for a drink at the house she shared with her two teenage children, and then we went out to a bar to listen to a band. She left her coat over her shoulders and danced with a delicacy I did not then know the source of. Then she told me her story.

Her life changed course one day when her mother took her to see the ballet in Washington, DC, where the family lived. 'I loved everything about it,' she said, 'the costumes, the forms of the dancers when they made their leaps, the expressions on their faces. It was like I could see my own self being acted out in front of me.' Her mother enrolled her in classes. Her interest and her skill grew. Then her mother had a catastrophic breakdown and had to be cared for in an institution. Rena and her numerous brothers and sisters were sent to relatives around the country. She wound up on a farm in Nebraska, far from any ballet school.

She served out this time like it was a jail sentence, and as soon as she could she went back to Washington and resumed her classes. One day as she was walking along the street in the rain, an umbrella appeared over her head. She turned and saw an elegant white-haired man in a cashmere suit. He handed her the umbrella and said, 'A beautiful woman should be protected from the rain.' Then he got into the back of a long black car and was driven away. She was eighteen and about to audition for the national ballet company.

He reappeared the next day and invited her to dinner. He was the Naval Attaché at the British embassy. He mesmerised her, she said. 'He looked like he owned the world and would give it all away in a tip.' She tried to resist him, but hadn't the strength. What was it that got to you? I asked her. She shrugged her shoulders. 'The way he smoked cigarettes,' she said. When he was called back to London he took her with him. She never went to her audition.

He was married, with children, and lived in a big house outside London. He got a flat for her in South Kensington and stayed with her during the week. He took her on diplomatic missions to Jamaica, Chile, the Far East. When his children were grown up, he divorced his wife and married Rena. They had the two children who were living with her in Bozeman. When he retired they moved to a house on the Isle of Wight. By this time she had grown to dislike him, but she stayed with him until he died.

When she was out walking on the beach early one morning she met a young American. He was a graduate student at the University of Montana at Bozeman. They saw each other through the summer and when it was time for him to go back she sold her house, gave up her widow's pension and took her children to Montana to live with him. Soon after they were married.

One day she checked the account where she kept the money from the sale of the house on the Isle of Wight and found that, though she had used none of it, more than half of it was gone. She called the bank to find out what happened. 'Ask your husband,' they told her. She knew he drank and took cocaine. She didn't know he was addicted to Keno machines and bingo. She told him to leave and filed for a divorce.

Mad winds, it seemed, had blown her to Nebraska, England and now Bozeman, Montana. She was in her mid-thirties, alone with two children, with little money and no job training or degree. She'd hardly done anything of her own volition. But there was one thing in her life that was only hers, and though it had long been ignored, it was still alive. So, she told me, three afternoons per week after her shifts at the Holiday Inn she gave ballet classes to children.

'I didn't make it as a dancer,' she said. 'I let myself get interrupted. But at least I have this.'

She wrote her telephone number on a piece of paper, but when I called seven years later the line had been disconnected. At a ballet school on Bozeman's main street, though, I was told that she was still in Bozeman and still giving classes to children. Her story, which I displaced to Rouen, Alsace-Lorraine and Turku in Finland, later appeared in a novel.

I got back on 90 and drove along part of the route taken by Lewis and Clark, then got off at Butte, birthplace of the stunt rider Evel Knievel, who had an early criminal career here. Of all the boomtowns of the West, Butte was perhaps the grandest. It had opera houses, world-class hotels, millionaires' mansions, a red-light district known as Venus Alley and, in the Dumas brothel, the longest-running such establishment in the United States, having been open for business from 1890 to 1982. It is now on the National Register of Historic Places. Underground tunnels leading to Venus Alley from various buildings in Butte allowed anonymity to customers. Charlie Chaplin, who played in vaudeville here, expressed admiration in his autobiography for the variety and beauty of its women.

Butte became known as 'The Richest Hill on Earth' because of the mineral wealth in its mountains. Blackfeet are thought to have dug mining pits using elk horns. The first white prospectors came in 1864. They panned for gold, saw outcroppings in the rock they thought interesting in colour and found from an assay company that the rocks contained silver, copper and other valuable metals apart from gold. An Irish immigrant from County Cavan named Marcus Daly started the Anaconda Mining Company as a silver mine in 1880 with money from George Hearst, the father of William Randolph. When electrolytic copper was needed for Edison's new light bulbs, demand soared and Daly turned his attention to copper mining. He sold the company to John D. Rockefeller's Standard Oil in 1899, the year before he died, and demand went up again in the First World War, when each rifle cartridge contained an ounce of copper. The other great Butte fortunes, those of William A. Clark and Augustus Heinz, were amassed by more circumventive means. Clark mined for gold and traded, but built his empire after becoming a banker who repossessed mines when owners defaulted on their loans. Heinz did it through the purchase of judges. At one point he had thirty of them in his pay. In one instance he bought a tiny plot in the midst of three larger claims, dug straight down and then tunnelled out to extract ore from all around him. When the owners of the surrounding claims sued, one of Heinz's judges disallowed the case. In its best years there were 85,000 people and two thousand miles of tunnels in Butte.

I drove through downtown, gaps in the street where buildings had been torn down, offices with broken signage and their windows opaque with dust, bars boarded up, the grand old hotels and theatres shut down or converted into low-income housing or nursing homes. There were museums of the mines, but the machinery up on the hill where the mines had been was still.

I found the town archives in an old fire station on Quartz Street and talked with Ellen Crain, the Archives Director.

'This was a highly sophisticated city in its best years,' she said. 'There were great restaurants, lots of nightlife, wide-open gambling. Five railroads operated here. 1890 to 1921 were its great years. But Butte, like many places, is susceptible to forces beyond its control. Demand for copper and magnesium, which is used to harden steel, fell off after World War I. There was competition from Africa and South America. The area is by no means mined out, but the population is just a third of what it once was. There were maybe as many as ten thousand miners working here, along with many others in ancillary industries. At the moment there are two hundred employed in the Continental pit, which just opened last month after being closed for two and a half years, and that's it.

'A lot of Irish came in the late nineteenth century. Even now Butte has the largest St Patrick's Day parade between

Chicago and San Francisco. Thirty thousand people come here for that. Marcus Daly brought them here originally. Many of them were highly skilled men who had mined tin in Allihies on the Beara Peninsula in west Cork. There were Harringtons, Sullivans, Murphys. There was a depressed market in Ireland at the time. Some of them went first to Cumbria in England to mine coal, then went to Pennsylvania. The Molly Maguires were a militant anti-landlord organisation in Ireland, which got transported to the Pennsylvania coal mines and took up workers' issues, sometimes with violence. These were among the men recruited by Daly. But Daly was good with the workers. He provided homes and amenities. Standard Oil was not like that at all.'

During the First World War miners worked twelve-hour shifts in hot, dark tunnels four thousand feet below ground for the same pay they had received in 1878, despite the price of copper having risen 150 per cent. An electrical fire at the Speculator mine just two months after the United States entered the war left 163 dead. The Metal Mineworkers' Union was formed to secure the right to union membership and better working conditions and, when it was ignored, twenty thousand miners walked out. The companies dismissed the strike as pro-German and therefore seditious. An International Workers of the World organiser named Frank Little arrived in 1917 to promote a single union for all the world's workers and worker control of the means of production, and to dissuade the miners from participating in a capitalist war. Two weeks later, six men arrived at his boarding house in the middle of the night, beat him, dragged him by rope from the back of a car and then hanged him from a railroad trestle. Federal troops arrived to break the strike, as they did three years later when company agents shot fifteen striking miners on the Anaconda Road.

Dashiell Hammett, working for the Pinkerton Detective Agency, came to Butte on behalf of the Anaconda Mining Company to help break strikes. He said he was hit on the head by a miner, was forced to shoot another standing guard over a keg of gunpowder and was offered $5,000 to murder Frank Little. He later created Sam Spade, a detective who sometimes found his employers more corrupt than those he had been engaged to chase. His novel *Red Harvest* used Butte as its setting. His strike-breaking activities were prominent among the influences that turned him to the left. In the 1950s he was brought before the House Un-American Activities Committee, where he was asked, 'Mr Hammett, if you were in our position, would you allow your books in our United States Information Service libraries?' Hammett replied, 'If I were you, Senator, I wouldn't allow any libraries at all.'

After telling me the story of Butte and showing me photographs and records of the town and oral testimony from miners, Ellen Crain asked me, 'Do you know the story of the Montana Power Company?'

'I don't,' I said.

'That's a company with a long history here,' she said. 'It was a regulated company that mined coal, ran the generators, dams and power lines, supplied gas. They ran basically everything to do with gas and electrical power in the state. They were a solid, blue-chip company, the only Fortune 500 company in Montana. Then during the time when deregulation became popular, the new president, Bob Gannon, listened to advisors at Goldman Sachs and started to lobby the state legislature to deregulate. They had eighteen lobbyists in Helena working on this. This was Bob Gannon's world, as he had come to the company as a young lobbyist himself in 1973. They studied what had been done in California by Enron and applied it here. The company wrote the legislation and the lobbyists got it through.

'Shortly after that they dismantled the company and sold it in pieces. Most of it went to Pennsylvania Power and Light. The Montana Power Company had a telecommunications division called Touch America, mainly involved in creating a fibre-optic network for the Internet and telephones. This was doing very well. It was what was of most interest to the executives. They thought it would make a fortune. They'd said before they got the legislation through that they had no intention of getting out of the power-supply business, but as soon as the takeover happened the Montana Power Company was gone and in its place was Touch America. Someone from management said that it was difficult for the executives to concentrate on two such different businesses.

'Montana Power Company employees had long been obliged to make their pension contributions in the form of the purchase of company stock. For every dollar they put in each month, the company put in fifty cents. The stock over the years was generally solid. It had grown in value and paid dividends. But what happened immediately after they took the company apart was that electricity prices went way up – customers were at times paying twenty times what they had been paying – and the boom around telecommunications reversed. Touch America stock, which was at one time trading at around $69 per share, is now worth six cents. They've filed for bankruptcy. The pensions no longer exist. My friend Judy David who works here with me, her husband was working for the company for twenty-three years and they've seen $135,000 in retirement benefits disappear. He still works surveying power lines and substations for Northwestern Energy, which was one of the companies that bought parts of the Montana Power Company, but those new companies have no obligations regarding the pensions. There are people who worked for thirty years and took early retirement because they'd accumulated more than $200,000 in benefits and now they're working at Wal-Mart because they have nothing. There are people too old to work who are in a worse position still. It's a bad picture. Companies have gone out of business because of the rise in power prices. It's been disastrous for the tax base of the state. Families have been put under a lot of pressure. And people who worked in good faith for years have come out with nothing.

'Mr Gannon is still around. They burned his effigy here in Butte. He and a few top executives came out of it all with millions of dollars in bonuses for the selling off of the company. I think it was between five and six million. And I heard that Goldman Sachs, who'd also advised Enron, took $20 million for their part in it.'

The plan worked out for Enron was replicated in other parts of the country as well. The Kansas utility company Western Resources brought in an advisor from Salomon Brothers named David Wittig to merge and acquire companies beyond the remit of state control. They had the idea of leaving the debt acquired in this process with Western Resources, where it would be carried by Kansas taxpayers, and freeing the new companies to pursue profit unencumbered. This supposedly free-market procedure has come to be known as 'socialise the risk, privatise the profits'. Wittig changed the company name to Westar, bought a fleet of private jets, spent $6.5 million redecorating the company offices, purged the board of dissenters, picked up millions of dollars in bonuses and, after the company's share price fell by seventy-three per cent and large numbers of employees were laid off, left the company, local papers said, with further compensation of $42.5 million. It would be difficult, treated thus, not to feel invincible, or at least lucky.

Above Butte is the Berkeley Pit, created when the tunnelling operations were abandoned in 1955 and open-pit mining was taken up. Between then and 1982, when the pit was closed, one billion tons of material was excavated from it, only around 0.75 per cent of it copper. After it shut down and the pumps were turned off, the pit filled with water a mile wide and nine hundred feet deep so heavy with minerals that the water itself has been mined and so contaminated with such chemicals as arsenic, cadmium, zinc and sulphuric acid that 342 migrating snow geese who landed on it died, their livers and kidneys bloated and their oesophaguses eroded. The owners of the pit said that it was due to their diet. A quantity of money known as the Superfund was created by Congress in 1980 to clean up abandoned toxic-waste sites where no liability can be ascertained. The money comes from a special tax on petroleum and chemical industries.

The Berkeley Pit was one of the main beneficiaries of the Superfund, but a Republican Congress chose not to renew the taxes and the administration of George W. Bush opposed their reimposition.

It was nearly dark when I left Ellen Crain. I drove back out through the town towards Interstate 90. I saw an old man going into a bar and a pickup truck pull into a gas station, but otherwise there was no one around. Artists have come here because of the low rents and Butte has received such boostering designations as 'All-American City' and was one of the National Trust for Historic Preservation's Dozen Distinctive Designations, but its fall from grace is everywhere evident. You wonder who is sticking voodoo pins into this place, and why. Or maybe it's just the play of the market.

I got onto 90 going west. The beige land in the afternoon light looked as soft as the pelt of a mountain cat. I passed a town called Opportunity, then from Garrison until it turned off at Missoula I found I was on US 12 again. It was the first time I'd seen it since eastern South Dakota. My lights fell on a plain bumper sticker that read 'UNITED WE STAND'. This means, 'Dissent is sedition.'

I passed the Sapphire Mountains and then entered Missoula, where I found a bar called Charley B's. Missoula, a pretty university town with huge sawmills on its perimeter, was called Hellgate by French trappers after they found bones and corpses of Flathead and Blackfeet who used to battle in a canyon there. It was headquarters to the Army's 25th Infantry Bicycle Corps, which began investigating the use of bicycles in warfare in 1896 by having its members cycle to St Louis, over a thousand miles away. They returned by train and the experiment was abandoned. The film-maker David Lynch was born here. So was Jeannette Rankin, a pacifist who was America's first Congresswoman, having been elected before women were granted the vote.

The streets were thronged, as was Charley B's. There was a single free stool at the bar and I took it. The man to my left, white-haired, paint-bespattered and beaming, violated what I had taken to be a principle of university towns that strangers are not spoken to by saying, 'You're carrying a heavy load,' which startled me at first until I realised he was only referring to my books. He was Jonno Larson, a house painter, leaf raker and tree pruner who'd come here to study at the university and stayed. 'I write poetry occasionally,' he said, 'and a little less occasionally it's published.'

I wouldn't be the first to write about Charley B's, I learned, because the writer James Crumley comes in often and bases some of his characters on the people he meets here. In his novel *Dancing Bear* the detective Milo Milodragonovitch, left bleeding out in wild country, was consoled by the thought that he would again be back in 'the town with the best bars in a state of great bars'. Above all of Missoula's bars, its author admires Charley B's. 'Mr Crumley was just here a few minutes ago,' said Jonno. 'He loaned me a cigarette.' On the walls were large portraits of customers. They ranged in age from students to those who walked with sticks. 'This is a place of freethinkers, free spirits,' said Jonno. 'There is a continuity to the generations. It's like a family. There are all ages, all types. There are people I've been speaking with here for the past fifteen years two or three times per week and I don't even know their last names, but they're closer to me than some people in my family.'

I asked him if he knew anything about Elizabeth Clare Prophet.

'I wrote a poem about her once,' he said. 'But Sherry here has a story about her.' He called over a woman with Pre-Raphaelite hair and asked her to tell me her Elizabeth Clare Prophet story. 'Well, it's not much,' she said. 'It's just that I sell teas. The people at her ranch ordered some and I brought it over. I sent invoices, but they never paid. I'm not very pushy. Sometimes I'd phone them and say, "You know that tea . . . ?" and they'd say, "We'll look into it." Eventually I called and said, "I really have to collect that money for the tea." There was a fire in a forest near the ranch at the time and the person said, "We can't do anything about that now

because the non-essential people are all chanting at the fire."
It seemed the non-essential people included the accounts
department. I never got the money.'

'They had armed guards over there until Mrs Prophet's
husband was arrested for trying to buy assault weapons illegally in Idaho,' said Jonno. 'Guns are popular out here.
There are people in the wilderness with arsenals in their
houses waiting for the black helicopters of the United Nations
to invade. There's no hope when people can't think. The
Republicans learn from the marketing people. They pick up
their votes by concentrating on single issues like gun control
or abortion and follow them down through a kind of logic
until it becomes mad. They make the irrational rational.
They've got working people voting against their own
economic interests because they've become hysterical about
some issue. Goebbels would be jubilant to find that someone
had taken up his ideas.'

I told him I'd just heard in Butte about the Montana Power
Company and asked him if he knew anything about it.

'We all know about it,' he said. 'Bob Gannon went to a
funeral here and sat down next to a little old woman. She
said to him, "Would you mind sitting somewhere else, Mr
Gannon? One day someone is going to take a shot at you
and I don't want to be in the way."'

I got back onto 90 and drove through the Lolo National
Forest, which is just to the south of the Flathead Indian
Reservation. I had never heard of the Lolo National Forest,
but it comprises two million acres and four wilderness areas,
with numerous spruce and firs along with western red cedar,
larch and whitebark pine. The cedars grow to eight feet in
diameter and up to two hundred feet high. Mountain goats,
grizzly bears, bighorn sheep, golden eagles and trumpeter
swan live here. I'd had no idea until I drove through the
western states how vast is the uninhabited land, national or
state park or forest and Indian territory in America. The
National Park Service alone administrates around 84.2 million
acres in the country, staffed in the main, it seemed to me,

by rangers both knowledgeable and impassioned about their work. Indian reservation land comprises 55.7 million acres. Driving in the West you spend much of your time in one or the other.

I crossed the border with Idaho, its meaningless name the invention of a mining lobbyist who was looking for something that sounded Indian. Shortly afterwards I pulled into Wallace, birthplace of Lana Turner. It was a pretty, well-presented town with brick buildings in Art Deco, Chicago School, Queen Anne and neoclassical styles, built after yet another town-destroying fire in the West. I saw two bars that seemed still to have signs of life and chose Sweets Lounge. Mining was the theme inside. There were old photographs of miners, mining equipment mounted on the walls, glass cases displaying ore. Gold was discovered here in 1833, then silver, lead and zinc. The silver mines were among the most productive in the world, producing their billionth ounce in 1985. They're called 'right-to-work' mines now, which means that the unions there have been broken.

As I crossed the crowded room a large man with a red moustache called out, 'Let's go shoot some niggers!' He picked up a smaller man from behind, whirled him around and screamed, 'LET'S GET OUR GUNS AND PLAY COWBOYS AND MEXICANS!' I sat at the bar and bent low over a book. He looked like he might be suffering from the same complaint as the man in Gardiner who needed to hit somebody. The barmaid took my order. 'Don't worry about them,' she said. 'It's a birthday party. They're all miners here. They're drunk, but they're harmless. They work hard and drink hard and at the weekends they play golf.'

'Are you from here?' I asked.

'So far I've lived in California, Missouri, Louisiana and Alabama. My ex-husband was in power-line construction.' She gave me a tour of the bar's exhibits from the mines, the photographs and implements hung with skeletons and jack-o'-lanterns and cobwebbing for Halloween.

'This was the regional centre for prostitution until 1979,'

she said. 'One of the brothels was preserved and is now a museum.'

Two women to my right were cutting small pieces out of a newspaper. 'We're making a ransom note,' the one nearest me said. 'Someone from the Metal Bar stole our Halloween witch, so we stole their clown.' She held up the note. 'iF U WanT 2 c the cLoWN aLIVE calL SaTurDAY,' it said.

I saw a shadow fall from my left and turned to see the last person I wanted to see that night, his face six inches from mine, his eyes bloodshot and his heavy breathing sending out waves of bourbon-saturated air from beneath his red moustache. 'So what's YOUR story, then?' he asked me.

I told him about my journey and what I was doing it for.

'Sounds interesting,' he said. 'I'll look out for the book.'

He squinted at me then and leaned even closer.

'I had sixty-two registered kills in Vietnam.' His arm swept the bar and knocked over an ashtray. When he went to pick it up, the change fell out of his pocket and he nearly went over too. 'I'm from right here in Wallace,' he said when he came back up. 'Worked in the silver mine here. It was good, but I could make more in Nevada mining for gold. I work a fourteen-day month because of long shifts and make $70,000 per year. After twenty-eight years I'm worth more than a million dollars. Not bad, is it? My wife works with me. That's her right there next to you. We came back because we're buying a house here. This is the best place in the world.'

His wife was the woman who'd showed me the ransom note.

'Where did you meet?' I asked her.

'In the military,' they said together.

'I hate the French,' he said. 'When we got to Baghdad we should have turned left and wiped out the French.'

'Don't pay any attention to him,' she said.

'You look like an old soldier,' he said.

I'd never heard that before.

'Do you think you'll get to Nevada?' he asked. 'I'll take you down the mine.'

He took out his wallet, opened it the wrong way up and his cards fell to the floor. When he came up again he had a photograph of a smiling young woman in military fatigues with a gun across her knees sitting on top of a tank.

'That's my daughter,' he said. The randomness seemed to have gone from his gestures. 'This picture was taken in Iraq. She's there now. I did everything I could to stop her enlisting. So did her mother. But that was all she ever wanted to do since she was a little girl. Maybe she'll come out healthy, mind and body. But maybe not. A lot that I know don't. I just don't want her carrying around the same mess in her mind that I've been carrying the last thirty years.'

He went to put the photograph away, then held it up again for me to see.

'Look at her,' he said. 'Isn't she beautiful?'

In the morning I drove west past Silverton and Smelterville. Ernest Hemingway came to Ketchum, at the southern end of this state, after leaving Cuba. Hunter Thompson came to Ketchum five years after Hemingway died because he wondered what had lured him to this place. He concluded that the writer had been there when times were good in the Thirties and Forties, having finished *For Whom the Bell Tolls* there and hunted with Gary Cooper; and, unlike Paris and Spain and Africa and Cuba, it hadn't changed so very much. He was a man indisposed to politics and to theory. 'Aside from the brute beauty of the mountains,' Thompson wrote, 'he must have recognized an atavistic distinctiveness in the people that piqued his sense of dramatic possibilities. It is a raw and peaceful little village . . . From such a vantage point a man tends to feel it is not so difficult, after all, to see the world clear and as a whole. Like many another writer, Hemingway did his best work when he felt he was standing on something solid – like an Idaho mountainside, or a sense of conviction. Perhaps he found what he came here for, but the odds are huge that he didn't. He was an old, sick and very troubled man.'

In his last year Hemingway was asked to write a single sentence for a commemorative volume for the newly inaugurated President Kennedy, but after labouring all day he couldn't get it and gave up. He was flown to the Mayo Clinic in Minnesota for treatment, and at a fuel stop he searched in the hangar and the glove compartments of parked cars for guns with which to shoot himself and then walked directly towards the whirling blades of a taxiing plane, which cut its engines before he got to it. Early on a Sunday morning just after he got back he took a double-barrelled shotgun that he used for pigeon shooting, pressed it to his forehead and pulled both triggers. I was only ten, but I remember the headline in the *Chicago Tribune*. It was of a size normally reserved for national emergencies.

Both his father and his granddaughter killed themselves. His son, an alcoholic doctor debarred from practising, was arrested in Florida half in drag and killed himself in his cell. Is there a gene? Or is it that the possibility of suicide as a solution makes itself manifest early in life and remains urgently present? All of them seemed to have been following a map to their doom.

Lewis and Clark said that Idaho was the most arduous part of their journey west. They arrived exhausted, hungry and with many in the expedition ill. The Nez Percé fed them and looked after their animals until they were ready to travel again and remained at peace with white people for the ensuing fifty years. The discovery of gold, as ever, put pressure on the land, and the government negotiated a treaty with a breakaway group of Nez Percé, which gave away three-quarters of their land. A majority under Chief Joseph would not recognise this treaty. There was a prolonged stalemate and then finally the government demanded compliance with the terms of the treaty within thirty days. The Nez Percé asked for more time to collect their animals, but the general in command refused; 250 warriors under Chief

Joseph and another five hundred old people, women and children retreated 1,700 miles over a period of four months, fighting thirteen rearguard battles against two thousand soldiers before they were finally trapped just thirty miles from the Canadian border. Chief Joseph surrendered with the words, 'Hear me, my chiefs, I am tired. My heart is sick and sad. From where the sun now stands, I will fight no more for ever.' The majority were sent to Oklahoma, where many died of malaria. How different history would be if gold were valueless.

Many Indians sensed the genocidal catastrophe to come. Black Elk had seen what the white soldiers could do when he was at Wounded Knee and walked past the heaped bodies of women and children dismembered by artillery. 'I saw a little boy trying to suck his mother,' he said, 'but she was bloody and dead.' Chief Seattle saw it as early as 1853, when he gave a speech to the governor of the Washington Territory. 'It matters little where we pass the remnant of our days,' he said. 'They will not be many. The Indians' night promises to be dark . . . A few more moons. A few more winters – and not one of the descendants of the mighty hosts that once moved over this land . . . will remain to mourn over the graves of a people – once more powerful and hopeful than yours. But why should I mourn at the untimely fate of my people. Tribe follows tribe, nation follows nation, like the waves of the sea. It is the order of nature, and regret is useless. Your time may be distant, but it will surely come, for even the white man whose God walked and talked with him as a friend, cannot be exempt from the common destiny. We may be brothers after all. We will see.'

I was already getting near to Idaho's border with Washington. To the north of 90 was Hayden Lake and to the south was Coeur d'Alene. Coeur d'Alene, set on a glacial lake, had a Bates Motel with no ghoulishly kitsch lettering, photographs of Anthony Perkins or any other indications of self-consciousness, and a five-star resort with a golf course, which looked as if it was tended by a team of a thousand with nail scissors. Resort guests are taken by a hand-crafted mahogany launch from the hotel to the practice range, where before hitting balls into the lake they are soothed by a complimentary golfers' massage. The fourteenth hole has a man-made island green with bunkers and geraniums, which can be towed in and out various distances from the tee and which cost $3 million to construct. How many multi-millionaires are there in the world, and how many of those would like to come to north-west Idaho to play golf?

Hayden Lake had been the headquarters of the Aryan Nations, an anti-Semitic, white supremacist group formed in the 1970s by Richard Girnt Butler, who believed that Europeans are descended from the ten tribes of Israel and are God's Chosen People and that the Jews are the product of Satan's seduction of Eve in the Garden of Eden. Conferences organised at the Hayden Lake twenty-acre compound brought together Ku Klux Klansmen, skinheads, gun fanatics, freelance racists, Norse-god-worshipping Odinists and Butler's own Aryan Nationists, all united in their hatred of Jews, immigrants, affirmative action, homosexuals and interracial marriage. His aim was to found a secessionist state based on white power out of the combined area of Wyoming, Montana, Idaho, Oregon and Washington. The Aryan Nationists believe they must go to war in a final battle against the New World Order, Jewish internationalists and the United Nations in order to establish Christ's National Socialist Aryan kingdom. Many in it were enraged at encroachments on white liberty and were heavily armed. A secret group within Aryan Nations, known as the Bruders Schweigen Strike Force, set off four bombs in Coeur d'Alene, including one at the home of a human-rights activist named Bill Wasmuth. In January 1999 a woman named Victoria Keenan and her son Jason pulled over in their car to the side of the road outside the Hayden Lake compound to retrieve a wallet that had fallen from the car window. Just then, another car backfired. Aryan Nations security guards believed they were under attack and opened fire on the car. When it drove off they pursued it, ran it into a ditch, where Jesse Warfield, an alleged methamphetamine user who had done time for assault with a deadly weapon, dragged Mrs Keenan by the hair from the car, put a gun to her head and ordered her to keep quiet about the attack. The Keenans sued and won $6.3 million, bankrupting Aryan Nations and its leader. The Keenans acquired the land at Hayden Lake, sold it to a philanthropist and he handed it over to a local college. What there was left of Aryan Nations moved to Pennsylvania, where its new leader August Kries tried to make an alliance with al-Qaeda, who have not responded.

I crossed into Washington and entered a vast, featureless steppe on one of the three hundred days of the year that the sun shines on this part of the state. Unaccountably, my phone came to life at the border for the first time since Cheyenne, Wyoming. Around Spokane I listened to the children's author Maurice Sendak being interviewed on National Public Radio, until I passed beyond the range of its signal and the sound descended via electronic squawks and whoops and static into a wilderness of country, heavy metal, Christian radio and a right-wing talkstorm. One of the milder Christian stations held for a while, the host of the programme delineating university courses available in 'Yoga Spectrum', 'Zen Meditation', 'The Ancient Life Force Secrets: Effortlessly Unlocking the Door to Personal Empowerment and to Manipulating the Chi Energy', 'The Kundalini Force: Finding the Cobra God Inside of You', 'Herbal Remedies: Make a Nourishing Soup that Helps Not Only Your Body But Also Your Soul' and finally 'Belly Dancing'. He let the grotesqueness of this settle over his audience, then asked, 'And where are the Christian classes?' Fifteen states, he said, have a ban on state subsidy for Christian theology classes, and a student who wanted to use a grant to attend a Christian college was denied it. There are some improbable victims in the United States, Christians being high among them, but victimhood is a bargaining chip and for this (and I suppose psychological reasons) it has a growing population. At this point I lost him and picked up programmes on cattle farming and weight reduction. For around eight miles I got a tirade against gays, intellectuals, lovers of protected species, terrorists, sophisticated coffees, foreign sports, welfare mothers, Hillary Clinton and anyone who might wish to limit military spending or the gas consumption of SUVs. 'San Francisco', the presenter concluded, 'should be towed out into the ocean, incinerated AND SUNK!'

The airwaves here are full of fear and rage. They go together, like insecurity and vanity. The cause of the fear is described, indignation about it is vented. Those who are the most visibly angry – television evangelists and right-wing media commentators – are among the least proximate to danger, whether financial or mortal. Yet they fulminate, denounce and spew contempt through their allotted slots. Very often the speaker appears to be at the limit of his patience, as if he has been listening far too long to bleeding heartisms and pernicious liberal vaguery with forbearance and is just at that moment reaching his threshold. Michael Moore has said of this, 'If we on the left had the White House, both parts of Congress, most of the press, Greenpeace and Amnesty instead of corporations writing the legislation, our own cable-news network and Mario Cuomo and Jesse Jackson on the Supreme Court, would we be angry? I don't think so.' This media anger is more a style, I suppose, than something deeply felt, but it exists because it connects with and stirs its audience.

The appeal of righteous indignation is not difficult to understand. It produces a feeling of certainty, and makes you feel stronger than you perhaps are. But only the chronically weak, the most neurotically attention-seeking, make an identity of it.

In Europe this is less evident as a style. Politicians, particularly nationalists, sometimes express it. But it is fairly rare in broadcasting. In Valencia, where I lived for twelve years, life spreads out before you from birth like an unrolling carpet. You can walk on it until you die if you wish. It is a way of life that has been refined over centuries. You can live in the city of your ancestors, you can go to the school of your parents, play with your cousins and the children of your parents' friends and perhaps marry one of them, work in the family business, go to a church that has been there since the Middle Ages, and eat the food and drink the wine that your family has been eating and drinking for generations. There are half a dozen opportunities per day to sit on a café terrace with people who all know the same codes and expressions and gestures as you do. Nothing need be unfamiliar. This can produce a lack of resilience and adventurousness, but also a sense of ease.

In the American West I had yet to meet anyone who was born in the place where they were living. This migratoriness is general in the United States. Ralph Waldo Emerson wrote of the 'seeker with no past at his back'. Americans very often live far from their families. There hasn't been time to elaborate familiar modes of behaviour, a subtle cuisine or complex manners of greeting and leaving. Psychologically, they haven't the protection of everyday rituals. Lacking the proximity of their families or childhood friends, they look to connect with strangers, which is perhaps why I had so many conversations in bars. For structure, people may look to the making of money, or to religion, or to both at the same time. It is increasingly in the United States a religion not based on prayer, contemplation and good works, with the central texts being the Sermon on the Mount and the parts of the Gospels that depict the Passion, but rather one that derives from the Old Testament and the Book of Revelations and sees a world full of threats and temptation soon to be destroyed by a righteous God. Only Christ's soldiers will survive. Perhaps religion is the template for the angry voices on the airwaves.

US 2 leads west out of Spokane and intersects at Wilbur with 174, which leads to the Grand Coulee Dam on the Columbia River, the grandest of the New Deal Projects and still the largest concrete structure in the United States. Three thousand people watched the opening ceremony on

16 July 1933 for this project, which would irrigate half a million acres of fertile but arid land of loess soils over vast deposits of basalt left by prehistoric floods. As the floods drained, they left a potholed, rippled landscape unique to Washington and given the unappealing name 'channelled scablands' by J. Harlen Bretz, the geologist who studied them in the 1920s. At the time it was built, electrical power was not thought necessary for the area, but war demands, particularly for aluminium to build planes, changed that and the dam now generates power for eleven states and parts of Canada. When it was finished it was five hundred feet high and a mile long.

'Cast your eyes on the greatest thing yet built by human hands,' sang Woody Guthrie of the dam. He had been commissioned by the Department of the Interior at the instigation of folk-music collector Alan Lomax to write songs about it, and eventually produced twenty-six.

Uncle Sam took up the challenge in the year of thirty-three,
For the farmer and the factory and all of you and me,

he sang. Hundreds of Dust Bowl refugees, chronic migrants and men of all classes sent out onto the road by the Depression built the dam. Guthrie knew this life of flophouses, freight cars, brawls and solidarity, for he had lived it.

I worked in your orchards of peaches and prunes
I slept on the ground in the light of the moon
On the edge of the city you'll see us and then
We come with the dust and we go with the wind . . .

Green pastures of plenty from dry desert ground
From the Grand Coulee Dam where the waters run down
Every state in the Union us migrants have been
We'll work in this fight and we'll fight till we win.

In his autobiography *Bound for Glory* he wrote, 'Things was starting to stack up in my head and I just felt like I was going out of my wits if I didn't find some way of saying what I was thinking.' It is a book about the formation of a consciousness in boom-and-bust Dust Bowl Texas and the seeking it produced as he went all around America finding camaraderie in song. He joined the IWW and, in answer to someone who asked permission to sing his songs, he sent a song book on which he had written, 'This song is copyrighted in the US, under seal of copyright #154085, for a period of 28 years, and anybody caught singin' it without our permission will be mighty good friends of ourn, cause we don't give a dern. Publish it. Write it. Sing it. Swing to it. Yodel it. We wrote it, that's all we wanted to do.' *Bound for Glory* sent others onto the road after him and seems to have given names to two organisations. One is a band – 'You an' yore letter, an' yore mangy curs! Boom town rats!' The other is a legendary American institution – 'The whole air was full of a funny, still feeling, like all of hell's angels was about to break loose.'

Bob Dylan, a disciple who went looking for Guthrie all the way from Minnesota to New York after reading *Bound for Glory*, later wrote a song about an 'idiot wind' blowing from the Grand Coulee Dam to the capital, two Washingtons from the two sides of the nation brought together in a malign current of addled air.

The dam, on the southern edge of the Colville Indian Reservation where the great Nez Percé guerrilla fighter and tribal leader Chief Joseph died, created a lake that backs up nearly to the Canadian border and thereby destroyed the river where Indians had been fishing salmon for thousands of years. Another dam, also damaging to salmon, was named for him, but he was dead before he could demur. The federal government eventually paid the Colville Reservation Indians $52 million in compensation. Set on open land and extending a mile across, the dam looks curiously unimposing.

Interstate 155 leads south from the dam along the Columbia River to 17, 28 and finally 283, which meets Interstate 90 at George, having passed through Ephrata. I saw a town named Othello to the south-east of George and wondered how it got its name. At Ellensburg I had a sandwich in a health-food place. The Yakima River and Interstate 82 link Ellensburg with Yakima through the Yakima Valley. The Japanese Army, lacking the space at home, does artillery training here. This valley produces more apples than anywhere else in the United States. Hops, melons, peaches and, with a soil similar to that in parts of France, grapes for wine are also grown here. The writer Raymond Carver and William O. Douglas, the longest-ever-serving Supreme Court Justice, grew up in Yakima. Douglas studied economics and literature, but then attended Columbia Law School along with Paul Robeson. 'I worked among the very poor, the migrant labourers, the Chicanos and the IWWs who I saw being shot at by police. I saw cruelty and hardness, and my impulse was to be a force in other developments in the law,' he later said. Roosevelt appointed him to the Supreme Court, where he served for thirty-six years, surviving three impeachment attempts brought by the right. One of them, promoted by then House minority leader Gerald Ford, included the charge that he'd once written enthusiastically about folk music, '[praising] the lusty, lurid and risqué along with the social protest of left-wing folk singers'. Ford was also disturbed by an article by Douglas that had been published in the avantgarde literary magazine *Evergreen Review*, which had also at times published photographs of unclothed women. When Republican Congressmen refused to give copies of the magazine to Democrats, Representative Wayne Morris called out, 'Has anybody read the article, or is everybody over there who has a magazine just looking at the pictures?' Among the many things Douglas said were, 'As night-fall does not come at once, neither does oppression . . . It is in such twilight that we all must be aware of change in the air – however slight – lest we become victims of the darkness'; 'It is our attitude towards free thought and free expression that will determine our fate. There must be no limit on the range of temperate discussion, no limits on thought. No subject must be taboo.

No censor must preside at our assemblies'; and, in 1952, 'These days I see America identified more and more with material things, less and less with spiritual standards. These days I see America acting abroad as an arrogant, selfish, greedy nation interested only in guns and dollars, not in people or their hopes and aspirations. We need a faith that dedicates us to something bigger and more important than ourselves.'

I crossed the Cascade Mountains on Interstate 90, passed Mount Rainier with its thirty glaciers and then dropped down onto a narrow coastal plain. Ahead of me, in Puget Sound, was Seattle, with the Olympic Mountains and the Pacific Ocean beyond.

The Pacific Northwest

It was Halloween in Seattle. 'Wage Peace' and Howard Dean posters were propped on front porches amid cobwebs and phosphorescent skeletons. The staff of the Whole Foods supermarket wore witches' costumes and had bullet holes painted on their foreheads. A man at a driving range dressed as a gorilla hit a bucket of golf balls.

I had arrived from the east and driven north through wooded hills. There was water everywhere. Seattle once had such an abundance of animals and fish in its forests and waterways that it could support one of the world's only non-migratory hunter-gatherer societies. This complexity of hills and water and forest ceaselessly interrupts the city's crawl over the land.

Seattle lived through five distinct booms, each of them followed if not by a bust, then by a straitening. The first was the timber boom, which gave to the world the term Skid Row, where the economically vanquished gather. Skid Road in Seattle was where logs slid down Yesler Way to Henry Yesler's sawmill. Woody Guthrie sang of getting there too late for a boom-time job and hitting 'the skids on the old Skid Road'. Then came the Klondike Gold Rush, when Seattle was the centre of transport for Alaska and the Yukon, and after that ship building. Later, a boat builder named Bill Boeing generated Seattle's fourth boom by manufacturing war planes. Seventy thousand lost their jobs immediately afterwards, but the company came to life again with the demand for passenger jets. The most recent of the booms had its tentative beginnings in 1979, when Bill Gates and Paul

Allen brought their company Microsoft to their home town from Albuquerque, New Mexico. In 1985, its sales amounted to $140 million. In 1990, they had risen to $1.8 billion. By 1995 Bill Gates had become the world's richest individual and Microsoft its most profitable corporation. Thousands of Microsoft staff had become millionaires. All the booms except the last brought about the organisation of workers – printers in 1886, cigar makers in 1887, brewers and musicians in 1890 and newsboys in 1892. The IWW organised America's first general strike in Seattle in 1919. Like Vancouver, San Francisco and Los Angeles, Seattle has long ceased to measure itself by the older east-coast and Midwestern cities. It looks to itself, its region and out towards the Pacific and to Asia for its resources, its ambience, its markets and its future.

It has a small but significant history of unconventional, iconographic entertainers, with the lives of a disproportionate amount of them circumscribed by tragedy. Gypsy Rose Lee, America's most beloved stripper, was born and grew up in Seattle with a star-struck and rapacious mother who threw her children into show business and pressed and fretted over them thereafter. Gypsy later wrote about her mother in *Gypsy*, which became a film and stage musical. She also wrote a novel, the *G-String Murders*. She made her way to New York, where she lived in an apartment surrounded by paintings by Chagal, Miró, Max Ernst, Picasso and Dorothea Tanning, still in receipt of regular demands for money from her mother, who by then ran a boarding house for lesbians. The mad, alcoholic and brilliant actress Frances Farmer is also from Seattle, where she was already being accused of being a communist when she was still a schoolgirl. In and out of asylums, possibly lobotomised, she was both undone and vaulted to greater heights by her inner voices and her anguish. Courtney Love wore a dress of Farmer's for her wedding to fellow Seattleite Kurt Cobain, who wrote a song called 'Frances Farmer Will Have Her Revenge on Seattle'. Kurt Cobain shot himself in a room above his garage on Lake Washington Boulevard East. Jimi Hendrix grew up in the city's Central District, saw Elvis at Sick's Stadium, strummed a broom until he knocked all the straw out of it and finally got a guitar with a single string. He passed all his classes at school except music.

I arrived in Cowan Park near the university, a serene and leafy district of pretty and unpretentious houses, with well-tended lawns, good schools, a near-wilderness of a park, rivers, lakes, ocean and mountains not far away and a citizenry of neighbourly, tolerant, civic-minded people who kept their sidewalks swept and saluted you when you passed. There was a lack of guard dogs, 'Armed Response' signs and perimeter fencing. The houses seemed almost to extend themselves outward in greeting, the windows uncurtained, the doors ajar. Central Connecticut University declared Seattle 'the Most Literate City in America', and *Men's Fitness* has judged it the fittest. Joggers with their dogs stir the breezes around you, and through the windows you can see living-room walls laden with books. Out in the surrounding high streets are cafés, restaurants, bookshops, bars with live music, almost no franchises, but instead the kinds of traditional businesses and shops that were once distributed around the central squares of America's small towns. I went into the Whole Foods supermarket, an emporium built around the celebration of food (much of it organic) such as I had never seen before, full of colour and surprises and with a staff more knowledgeable, enthusiastic and, I heard, better paid than any other I had been in. Many companies restrict the working week for many of their employees to less than the minimum hours required for the payment of healthcare benefits; Whole Foods staff begin to receive benefits with only a twenty-hour working week. Employees vote every three years on the company's benefits package, which includes disability, retirement and eye and dental care, as well as health insurance. Of *Fortune* magazine's '100 Best Companies to Work For', they are one of only sixteen that pay one hundred per cent of healthcare premiums. Ask a question of the young man at the cheese counter and you will receive, if you wish, a passionate and learned oration on all the flavours and textures that are available for you to experience, along with information about the composition of the cheeses and how they are made. Food becomes a wonderland.

Seattle is temperate and calm, being protected from Pacific storms by the Olympic Mountains and from Arctic winds by the Cascades. It has a reputation for wetness, but in fact receives less rainfall than Atlanta, Houston or New York. The wild and angry men on the radio hate it for its liberalism, but I've yet to meet anyone who has lived in it who doesn't have a feeling of affection for this city. It is open, prosperous, at ease with itself, an American Dream of the small town projected large on a dramatic water- and landscape. It is one hundred and fifty years old and has survived several economic lifetimes, but retains a feeling of youth, with everything still ahead of it. The mayor's office has plans to accommodate 350,000 more people by 2040.

I was to stay for two nights with my friend Martin Hayes, a fiddler from Feakle, County Clare in the west of Ireland, and Liz Roth, a former mime artist who'd crossed the country from Connecticut and was for a time Martin's agent. I first saw him in a bar on the north-west side of Chicago in 1990. It was summer. Televisions up on the walls screened baseball games. The air conditioner groaned and dripped. Men in T-shirts splattered with mortar and sweat-drenched faces called for drinks, abused the players on the television, told jokes, entered oblivion and attempted to present their cases to women, but never turned around to see a three-man band called Midnight Court, an electric guitar player on one side, a Japanese bassist on the other, a drum machine vibrating on a pool table behind them and Martin Hayes in the centre playing a white electric violin, hair flying, foot stomping to the raging tune, his being seemingly submerged in the music. A semicircle of people who had gathered in front of the band watched entranced, but beyond them virtuosity was met with indifference.

He'd been a boy wonder, winning six all-Ireland championships by the time he was eighteen. His father and his uncle played the fiddle. Other players came from all over Ireland and elsewhere in the world to the farmhouse where he grew up. Tommy Potts, one of the great fiddlers of his time, came sometimes from Dublin. 'He recorded an album and when they handed him a cheque he nearly got sick,' Martin told me. 'He couldn't conceive of being paid to play music. It would be like selling prayers.'

The music had been all around him, but his relationship with it lacked ease. Its worth was evident, but what to do with it? Was it just a relic of something that he was alone in valuing? Who would listen? Martin left school, started and then abandoned some small businesses, looked around for deliverance but couldn't find it, then packed up and flew to America, where he played to the uncomprehending at less than full strength in bars where Irishness was a kitsch pastime. 'This music has great power,' he said to me in Chicago. 'It shouldn't be devolved into a sequence of small entertainments that arrive ready-made and wrapped up. It's not just for making you feel you're having a nice time. It takes profoundly felt emotions of grief or sadness or joy or love and expresses them with a sense of wonder and of beauty.' For this he had the knowledge and the passion, but lacked the vehicle. One day he left for Seattle.

I saw him rarely then, but it happened that we were in New York once at the same time and I saw him play with an authority and grandeur I had not seen before. It was elegant, witty, worldly, moving, simple, concise and passionate and had the capacity to reveal and transform.

'How do you do that?' I asked him.

'Each phrase has a certain number of basic notes, which make it what it is,' he said. 'Most players don't think they're really playing if they just use those notes. They think you have to decorate it. I used to be the same myself. You'd be afraid people would think you're not equal to it. You wouldn't think you would be allowed to just play the tune simply. Maybe it's like a writer with adjectives. They might think that

– 247 –

a simple sentence without adjectives doesn't count. You can have a fear of simplicity. But now I just play those basic notes, and the feeling emerges.'

I had dinner with Martin and Liz in a Sicilian restaurant called Brad's Swingside Café where the owners sat with us, then drove back to their house through Fremont. Martin pulled over at a corner so that I could look at a sixteen-foot-high statue of Vladimir Lenin in bronze, flames and symbols of war around him, his chin jutting out purposefully. It had been jointly commissioned by the Soviet and Czechoslovak governments and placed in Poprod, in what is now Slovakia, in 1988. Its life there was brief, for it was turned over the following year during demonstrations celebrating the collapse of the Soviet Union. A schoolteacher with an opportunistic eye named Lewis Carpenter from Issaquah, Washington was in Poprod at the time. He thought its scrap-metal value could be high and shipped the abandoned figure home at a cost of $41,000. Shortly after he got back he was killed in a car accident, leaving his family with a house and a statue of Lenin in its back yard. They sought a buyer, but none was forthcoming. A local foundry hauled the statue away and placed it in Fremont. There the Prince of the Revolution is sometimes honoured with a red star, sometimes with Christmas lights. During the Solstice Parade he is refashioned as John Lennon and during Gay Pride Week is given lipstick and a dress. It's still for sale. When I saw the statue I thought it an assertion from Seattle's left, but it was a case of capitalism unrequited.

In the morning Martin made us fried eggs with apple chilli sauce and vegetarian baloney on an English muffin, a breakfast uncommon in Feakle when he was growing up. His fiddle lay in its box beside a wall.

'For years I played one that my father brought down out of the attic,' he said. 'But I was looking for a warmer, smoother sound and had one made with a bigger body to produce that effect. But we went too far. I'm happy with the one I have now. It has the same dimensions in its body as those they arrived at three hundred years ago. You can't adjust the science of the instrument, it seems. The optimum was found long ago.

'My father went through a lot of fiddles. I picked one up for him in a pawn shop in Chicago. They had the attitude that one was as good as another. There were regional styles and an individual might have his own sound, but they didn't dwell on technique. They really didn't dwell much on themselves, either. If ever they thought they might have something, some talent, they'd assume it would go forever unrecognised. They felt absolute, genuine humility. But they could have moments of greatness, moments that were magnificent in their transmission of pure feeling. Very often it was sadness, the final articulate rendering of their own misunderstood position in the world. But they'd feel the wonder of expressing it. They'd be lost for a moment in their own ecstasy. They'd become the piece of music, the expression of the idea or passion behind it. They'd gone beyond themselves. You don't really have to be able to play well to get there, and nor are years spent in a conservatory a guarantee that you will ever get it. If the person is feeling the music with sincerity, his every gesture is revealing it. And if the feeling is, say, sadness, then the player has dealt with it in the expression. There is a glory and a righteousness in experiencing that fully. Very often, I would say, it was their humility which allowed this to happen. The people around mightn't see it because it was hidden behind poor instruments and poor technique. But it occurred to me when I was witnessing these moments that I was in the midst of something magnificent. I'd watch them and try to piece together their interior world. I began to realise that it was not about the music that people play, it's about the soul of the people who play it, the sincerity of gesture in expressing that soul. That's what endows the music with the quality it needs in order to be understood and felt. They cease to think of not playing badly or of making an impression, and play without discomfort or tension or even without any objective. Then the phrases of the music fall where they should.

'Then I was on a mission to preserve what I had seen. The music was pulling me into the peasantry and at the same time my education was trying to lift me out of it. It's a terrible thing to face an educational system that is constantly degrading where you come from, that is reaching out to you to relieve you of the ignorance of your forefathers. This tension made me something of a misfit. I felt socially uneasy, and internally I had more angst than I'll ever have of any feeling again. But I could deal with this in the playing. I played loud, cathartic music. It wasn't about sweetness or tenderness. Even as a kid, before I played I'd go into a room, close my eyes and fantasise the performance, the tones, the quality of the sounds, a broad, expansive way of playing, where the feelings didn't get used or dissipated in the process of making their way to the instrument, but instead flowered out in the playing. There was great freedom in this, when I could make it happen.

'When I got to America I knew the value of this music. But I didn't know who could be interested in receiving it. I thought it was something I had to put away, to preserve. I'd put it into a box like old photographs, and maybe I could open it when I was seventy and its worth would be seen. I wasn't in the best circumstances. Business projects had gone bad. I seemed to have no trouble of finding ways to sabotage myself. I began to lose my natural reference points. I looked at the music around me in America and thought I had to go that way somehow. I saw that rock and roll establishes immediate communication. It's loud and it bombards people into submission. I thought my future, if there was to be one, lay in some rock or jazz fusion. I could be cynical about the music I'd grown up around. I could think it was just something sentimental, see no point in it. I went down, really. I was lost.

'The time came when I thought, "I have this language in my possession. Why don't I have the courage to use it? What am I running from?" I was able to get back to it then, having banished a lot of the uncertainties that would have plagued me had I not taken some detours. I can hear the influence of some of them now when I play. I imagine Keith Jarrett's purity of expression, Miles Davis' sour note, John McLaughlin's intense interaction with people. I don't play their music, but they help me to imagine my music, and play it. It's a fusion, but not on the instrument. I got those things here in America.

'You play for the music itself rather than projecting yourself forward towards some effect. You have to stay in it, live with the ambiguity of it. Music gives you that. You want to have as few steps as possible between you and the people you're trying to talk to with the music. You sing the tune to them through the fiddle. My hands are developed to respond to the instrument in the way that my tongue is developed to form words. And though you don't want to get ahead of yourself in an effort to produce an effect, you do have to understand clearly what the music can say. If you don't have a clear point to make, you will fill the tune with unnecessary decoration. You become ruthless in stripping out anything that is distracting. If there is a single note on which the tune turns, you don't want anyone missing it.

'The whole of the day is leading to the performance.

Tonight has to be the night you've been waiting for all your life. I know what true musical genius is and what I have is insignificant compared to that, but I also know what it feels like to be on the way to what music can do. You close in on the feeling, the beauty and magic of becoming its expression. You feel free in this. You're on the way. Everyone is invited to come along, but you're going there anyway.'

We went out then into the bright day. The other thing, apart from the statue of Vladimir Lenin in Fremont, that Martin thought I might be interested in seeing in Seattle was the grave of Jimi Hendrix. We drove south through the hills to the Greenwood Memorial Park in Renton. Nuns at my school used to cite the genetic catastrophe of Beethoven's family as an argument against abortions performed to avoid deformity, for you might get genius instead. Jimi Hendrix could have been another. His father Al was born with six fingers on each hand. Al's mother cut off the extra ones, but they grew back. A brother of Jimi's named Joseph was born with a club foot, a cleft palate and two sets of teeth. His sister was born blind sixteen weeks premature. Lucille, Jimi's mother, died of cirrhosis of the liver when he was still in school. He wrote of the fragility of this structure that was around him in 'Castles Made of Sand', of how they slip into the sea, eventually, as he did himself in a London flat, aged twenty-seven, on 18 September 1970, having evidently choked on his own vomit.

One night a year or two before that, I was watching a talkshow on television with my father when Jimi Hendrix came on, played a song with his band and then sat down to be interviewed in a purple satin shirt with Regency ruff, a headband and rings and bangles festooning his fingers and wrists, his eyes half closed and his body arranged in a slouch as though he'd been taken there in a rickshaw from an opium den. He spoke about being in the Army, playing the blues, touring with Little Richard and then moving on into a musical world of his own invention. I parted my hair, wore shirts with buttoned-down collars, knew nothing of drugs and played on my high-school golf team, but I nevertheless felt some generational responsibility for the impression that Jimi Hendrix might make on my father. He watched intently, then turned to me when it was finished and said, 'What an exceptionally interesting man!'

Someone who stayed in the same house with him one time later said what fine company Hendrix was, how genial and self-effacing, and that whenever he went into the kitchen or toilet or sat on the sofa and talked, he played his guitar. The sound he made from it, he said, was made of 'earth', which came from blues, funk or jazz, and 'space', a high-pitched, whining, psychedelic overlay that he said he first heard from wind whistling through parachute shrouds when on jumps with the 101st Airborne. I heard it said that when Jeff Beck and Eric Clapton first heard Hendrix at a concert in London, they felt they should retire.

He'd been reinterred the previous year and was now with his father, stepmother, grandmother and various siblings by a sundial around a kind of polished grey stone gazebo, under the dome of which was due to be placed a bronze statue of him playing the guitar. A long white hearse was in the cemetery driveway. A tall, broad man in a plaid suit stood beside it, beaming at any who passed. This, it seemed, was a funeral director. His had the look of a face for all occasions, bonhomie or empathy ready-made. 'If I was looking for consolation,' said Martin, 'I wouldn't look there.'

In the morning Martin gave me a tofu scramble with mushrooms, soya and garlic, and I headed south. In two days I was to fly home from San Francisco. Had I the time, I would have made my way over to the mountains and rainforests of the Olympic Peninsula, found US 101 and made a grand finale of this first part of my trip along the wilderness dunes and beaches of Washington and Oregon, but fed myself instead to the brutalising monotony of Interstate 5. Somewhere in southern Seattle I pulled off for petrol, took a wrong turn and found myself next to the perimeter fence of an airfield belonging to Boeing. Martin told me that Boeing wastes no opportunity to use their position as the state's largest employer to press for increasing tax and subsidy advantages under the threat that they will move elsewhere if not satisfied. Investigators for the European Union, acting in support of Boeing's competitor Airbus, claim that Boeing has received $23 billion in federal government subsidies since 1992, in contravention of World Trade Organisation agreements. From the beginning a large part of Boeing's income was from government contracts. They began to manufacture military and post-office planes in 1916. Their B-29 dropped the atomic bomb.

The ability to manipulate governments is in itself a prized executive skill. ConAgra threatened to move out of Nebraska unless the state changed its tax legislation. They rewrote the tax codes themselves and got them pushed through the legislature. IBP received subsidies of between $13,000 and $23,000 for each new job they created in Nebraska, paid no corporate tax for a decade, then moved to South Dakota, which was offering them zero corporate tax and zero personal income tax.

Government subsidy to private industry has taken many forms and has a long history. There have been bail-outs, give-aways, tax loopholes, debt cancellations, loan guarantees and discounted insurance. The United States doesn't have large nationalised industries, and it has been the salvation and strength of its economy that the government has provided much of the transport, power and communications infrastructure, has improved through subsidy the competitive position of American companies in the world market, has trained workers for industry in the military and has provided research and development through defence and subsidised university projects. But you might wonder which person sitting at which desk decided to allocate $300,000 to the Walt Disney Corporation to perfect its fireworks displays, or $2 million to McDonald's to market Chicken McNuggets in the Third World. Though fast-food executives have publicly proclaimed their wish to develop equipment to the point where no training whatsoever would be necessary to use it, the government offers them through the Work Opportunity Tax Credit programme tax credits of up to $2,400 per new worker hired, in compensation for the training the companies provide. Most of the workers in this minimum-wage economy have no intention of staying in it and the turnover rate is three to four hundred per cent. The companies can then collect on the replacements. Government loans have been used by the fast-food industry to set up new franchises in risky areas or to overwhelm competition, 'thereby turning a federal agency that was created to help independent, small business into one that eliminates them', according to Eric Schlosser in *Fast Food Nation*. He also reports that a hamburger-making company named GFI America, Inc. recruited migrant workers in Texas for its plant in Minnesota with the promise of steady work and housing, brought them north by bus and then dumped them at a county-subsidised homeless shelter. Yet it is welfare mothers that appear to be the most prominent in the consciousnesses of many as scroungers of taxpayers' money and blights on the American concept of the free market. Are the subsidies worth it? It would appear that some have been necessary, as competing industries from other countries have subsidy and tax advantages from their own governments, but according to Stephen Moore of the Cato Institute, 'The government has never been good at picking winners and losers. The Commerce Department and Congress are influenced by lobbying more than the market. That makes for a certain corruption in the market. And this in the long run is bad for the national economy.'

I got out from behind the Boeing airfield and back on Interstate 5, moving south and then west along Puget Sound to Olympia, where Lushootseed-speaking Indians gathered shellfish in the tideflats and fished for salmon in the streams for thousands of years. Olympia, the state capital, has been the home of numerous cartoonists, including *Simpsons* creator Matt Groening, musicians and professional baseball players. Groening grew up in Portland, then attended Evergreen State College in Olympia, which he described as 'a hippie college, with no grades or required classes, that drew every creative weirdo in the Northwest'.

Rachel Corrie, who as a student at Evergreen joined the International Solidarity Movement, travelled to the Gaza Strip from Olympia in January 2003 shortly after graduating. Three months later she and seven other activists went to Rafah by Israel's border with Egypt to prevent Israeli bulldozers from destroying Palestinian farmland and houses. She stood in front of one of them wearing an orange fluorescent jacket. The machine kept moving towards her, picking her up in its shovel and throwing both her and the earth upwards until she was face to face with the driver. She slipped down the pile of earth, fell under the blade and the bulldozer drove over her. Other activists ran forward, waving at the driver and shouting at him through a megaphone. Rachel was still alive beneath the machine. The driver paused, then reversed back over her, crushing her under the sand. She was taken by ambulance to the hospital in Rafah, where she died. The Israeli military placed all the blame for the incident on the protesters for having been in a place where they shouldn't have been. At a memorial service in Rafah a few days later a tank appeared and sprayed the mourners with tear gas, then armoured personnel carriers and bulldozers fired bullets and percussion bombs at them.

To the south of Olympia is Centralia. A Missourian named J.B. Cochran arrived here in 1850 with his slave, George Washington, and staked a claim. He then freed George Washington, adopted him and sold him the claim for $6,000. Washington built his home there and divided his property into lots, which he sold for ten dollars each, with an extra lot free for anyone who built a house. Lumber companies came to dominate the town and the IWW, known as the Wobblies, arrived to organise. The companies portrayed the union as hostile to the war effort, conspiratorial and communist. Patriotic sentiment, as it often curiously does, conflated with the interests of capital. The Wobblies were pushed out of two union halls by citizens and the third was attacked by American Legionnaires in 1918. The Wobblies prepared defences for the Armistice celebration the following year and when the Legionnaires broke from the parade and moved on the hall, the men inside opened fire, killing four. Several Wobblies were captured, among them Wesley Everest. The sheriff released Everest from the jail into the hands of a mob, who smashed his teeth with a rifle butt, castrated him, strung him up in three locations and then shot him several times. The coroner proclaimed the cause of death as suicide.

I stopped for a meal in Eugene, Oregon. Jogging was imported into the United States here from New Zealand by an athletics coach named Bill Bowerman, who invented the waffle running shoe and started Nike with Phil Knight, a graduate from the Eugene campus of the University of Oregon. I asked one of the waiters if he knew anything about Ken Kesey, who'd lived for decades near Eugene and had been buried there just two years previously, and he spoke admiringly of him and his family for their farming activities in Pleasant Hill, just outside the town. 'His widow still lives out there on the farm,' he said.

When I was a student I fell sideways for a time into a 'death of the novel' cult, the central belief of which was that all a novelist could do was to look up from his desk in despair at the exhaustion of the form and then resume mocking and jibing and parodying. I thought that if I could find a way, I would do that too one day. I was saved by the fresh, detoxifying and finally liberating breezes blown by two books beginning with the word 'One' – *One Hundred Years of Solitude* and *One Flew Over the Cuckoo's Nest*. Ken Kesey was an outstanding student and champion wrestler in Eugene. At his high school he was voted 'most likely to succeed'. He worked in a hospital psychiatric ward, volunteered for a research programme testing the effects of LSD and eloped with his high-school girlfriend, Faye Haxby. 'If American literature ever had a favourite son, distilled from the native grain, it was Kesey,' wrote Robert Stone. 'In a way, he personally embodied the winning side in every historical struggle that was nineteen-sixties America ... I imagine that Fitzgerald endowed Jay Gatsby with a similar charisma – enigmatic and elusive, exciting the dreams, envy and frustration of those drawn to him ... Kesey felt that the world was his own creature.'

After his second novel, *Sometimes a Great Notion*, was published, he said he was finished with writing. 'I'd rather be the lightning than the lightning rod,' he said. He entered a psychedelically decorated period of living theatre in a 1939 International Harvester school bus with a band of revellers called the Merry Pranksters, fuelled by hallucinogens and with a script from a superhero comic, all paid for with his movie rights sales. The bus became the most famous vehicle of its kind in the world. His third novel appeared twenty-eight years after the second. I saw him read from it around that time in Chicago. He was wearing a high top hat with a 'Legalise Marijuana' badge stuck to it. So formidable had he seemed to me from what I'd read about and by him that I was taken aback by his gentleness. 'I've run a farm, written several books and raised a family, all at least moderately well,' he said. 'And I've smoked pot every single day.' I wondered were the effects as negligible as he supposed? Could a man that intimate with language, that beset by vast, animating ideas and that competitive willingly turn away from writing? I'd long thought marijuana the most innocuous of diversionary intoxicants, but then had watched energy and ambition drained as if by leeches from people I knew who, like him, smoked it every day. At a trial for a drugs charge a judge called Kesey a 'tarnished Galahad', and while in Mexico he wrote a song with the verse:

What people once called a promising talent
What used to be known as an upstanding lad
Now hounded by the laws of two countries
And judged to be only a Tarnished Galahad.

Perhaps there were times when he really saw himself thus, or perhaps – like the photographer Charlie Cendrars with whom I'd had lunch in a little town in New York state, who had given it all up in an instant – expression sold in the marketplace seemed all vanity, an impediment to living. Perhaps books were too like the closed systems Kesey had striven to transcend. 'The answer is never the answer,' he'd said. 'What's really interesting is the mystery. If you seek the mystery instead of the answer, you'll always be seeking.'

I found his address in a telephone directory and drove in a deluge to Ridgeway Road in Pleasant Hill. I sat in the car then and looked at the pitched-roof wooden barn-like house where he had lived and worked. To the side was an outbuilding, in which was the bus that had traversed the country in 1964 with Neal Cassady at the wheel, the single word 'Further' on its windscreen. Through a huge window I could see Kesey's widow Faye moving around alone in the house. What were the books he read? At which table did he write? I wasn't going to find out that night, and after a while I got back onto Interstate 5 heading south.

Less than an hour away to my right was what some people told me was the most pristine and beautiful coast-line in America. There are cliffs, beaches, sea stacks and patches of forest erupting from dunes. To my left was the 1,900-foot-deep Crater Lake, the caldera of a volcano forty-two times more powerful than the explosion at Mount St Helens. In its midst is Wizard Island, a cone of cinder that is still rising. Instead of any of that, I had franchise signs on long poles and the low growl of traffic. It would be difficult to find an answer here, but more difficult still to find mystery.

I arrived in Medford. Lumber mills once dominated here, but no longer. Some blame the campaign to save the Northern

Spotted Owl, the *reductio ad absurdum* of the environmental movement from the point of view of those who oppose it. Only five per cent of Oregon's forests have been closed to logging for environmental reasons, however. Of Medford the Federal Writers' Project reports, 'Poor indeed is the home that has neither apple nor pear trees in its yard. In the last two decades Medford has made rapid growth . . . but in spite of this it is a well-planned city. Native trees . . . give a park-like effect to the town.' Something catastrophic appeared to have happened in the intervening years. All I could see were long strips of low-grade fast-food franchises, pornography shops, tattoo parlours and flophouse motels without any trees to be seen and with a faintly sinister air. Rusting cars were sinking into the ground on the outskirts and there were dead, mangled animals on the side of the road – dogs, rodents, deer. I drove all around its grid looking for a bar, but found nothing. It was the most unrelentingly ugly place I'd seen since leaving New York, what a friend of mine refers to as a 'five-mile-long truck stop'. I thought of a song I'd heard back along the road:

I been here a month or more, stuck in this old city,
People that have to call it home, they're the ones I pity.

I thought I'd have to give up on the bottle of beer. I'd tried Grants Pass further back along the road, but all I'd found was a strip-lit place where an exhausted-looking girl eating doughnuts offered soft drinks and an old man seemed hooked into the Keno machine before which he sat as though it was an iron lung. Southern Oregon seemed like a dry county in Texas. Finally there in Medford I passed a corner place with some exterior lights, a few cars parked outside, frosted windows and an open door. There was the form of a woman etched onto a panel on one of the windows. I walked past a doorman, down a corridor and up to a bar, where the two people serving made it immediately apparent how indifferent they were towards their work. Three or four customers standing around the bar wore the same look. It seemed like a require-ment there. Behind me was a small, round spotlit stage, a chrome pole and five audience members in chairs, astride one of whom a topless woman slithered and writhed, one breast half an inch from his nose. I will not pretend now that I was astonished by this. I had thought it could have been such a place, or perhaps a disco. But it was the only place I could find within thirty miles where I could have a beer.

I sat at the bar and read the book section of the *New York Times*. Behind me dancers came and went from the stage. There were more of them than there were customers. One of them sat down two stools away from me at the bar, looking in my direction. I didn't flinch. She went up to dance again, then came back.

'How are you doing?' she said.

She was tall, with long dark hair and a strong frame. In another context, and in different clothes, she might have been a college basketball player.

'I'm fine,' I said. 'And you?'

We passed through a minimal sequence of questions and answers, then she asked, 'Would you like a private dance?'

'I'm just here for a beer,' I said. 'You shouldn't waste your time.'

'It's all right,' she said. 'I don't have anything else to do.'

She told me she'd studied landscape gardening, but that she'd been lap dancing for six years, since she was twenty-one, driving around the country in a van looking for lucra-tive clubs. 'In Nebraska they pay you a fee,' she said. 'But everywhere else I've been, we have to pay the club.'

'How much can you make?'

'One night I made fifteen hundred dollars. The next night I made four. You never know.'

'This is the ugliest town I've seen in 6,500 miles of driving,' I said.

'Yeah,' she said. 'I know what you mean. But Ashland's nice. That's where we live, in an RV camp on Emigrant Lake. It's the next town to the south.'

She lived in a trailer there with her two-year-old daughter and the child's father, a mechanic.

'You've been reading since you came in,' she said. 'Do you read a lot?'

'I can hardly be alone without doing so. Do you?'

'Some,' she said.

'What, for instance?'

'Self-help books. And I read books about children to try and figure out my daughter.'

She took a turn on the dance floor for an audience of two. I couldn't watch her. She came back to the bar and approached a man in his thirties wearing a leather jacket. She talked, he shrugged, then he followed her into a passageway. I had another beer. A little later the route to the bathroom took me past the room they'd entered. It had a wide doorless entryway and looked like an airport waiting area. He was in a chair, his legs splayed, and she was kneeling before him, moving as if to a slow, light tune played on the piano. I don't know what degree of virtuality or actuality her movements had, but after a while the man came out looking as if he'd eaten something disagreeable and was confused by it. He paused at the bar, then walked out.

I slept that night in a $40 hotel for the lost and drifting and broke. Weekly rates were available. It had the feel of a dog pound.

In the morning I drove past vineyards to Ashland. She was right. It was set in gentle hills, prettily arranged and mani-cured, with galleries, whole-food shops, bed and breakfasts, fine houses up in the hills and its own Shakespeare festival. The Ashland peach won first prize at the 1893 World's Fair in Chicago. Around fifteen years later lithia water was discovered in Ashland. This curative mineral is used in high-performance alloys, microwaves, batteries, heat-transfer applications and as a treatment for manic depression. Lithia Park, intended at first to be a spa, is now the site for the staging of Shakespeare's plays during the festival. I had a fine breakfast in Ashland. It cost fifteen dollars, a record up to that point of the journey.

There was snow on the fir trees. I began to climb into the Klamath and Siskiyou Mountains in the border area with California. I was utterly in the clouds, the snow whirling in cones. Then I descended into California and sunshine, the road under the wheels sizzling like oil in a pan. The most diverse conifer forests in the world are here. This is where the redwoods begin to appear and carnivorous cobra lilies grow in bogland on the forest floor. A change in the movement of tectonic plates meant that I was moving from an area of volcanoes to one of earthquakes.

It was early enough, I thought, to get to San Francisco that night without the interstate. I got onto 96, which began just over the border and then followed the Klamath River through national forest to the coast.

The Klamath National Forest comprises 1,726,000 acres, of which only one-tenth is old-growth. Here are Douglas, red and white fir, Jeffrey pine, ponderosa pine, the bark of which smells like vanilla, and incense cedar, the preferred prime material for pencils. As I turned onto 96, a truck laden with massive logs groaned up an incline. When it passed, I saw a sign that said I was to be on this twisting, mountainous road for 192 miles, the first stretch of my last American drive until I would return the following year.

The day was bright. There were old houses with American flags on the porches, pickup trucks and farm vehicles around wooden barns, cattle on the river valley floor. I passed Horse Creek, Seiad Valley and Happy Camp, home of the Karuk tribe. The further I went, the more desperate were the signs of human life. There were trailers in among the trees with battered sides and plastic in the windows, rusting cars mounted on stones like pieces of sculpture, misshapen, improvised shacks with smoke coming out of chimney stacks. Who lived in such places? What catastrophes had driven them here? The river meandered or rushed or plunged over falls or gathered in pools beside me, firs rising up the white stone cliffs. A river traversing land such as this has so many ways to move. A career aptitude test I took when I was in high school produced the result that I was best suited to be a forest ranger, so disposed to solitude I must have seemed to the computer that performed the assessment. Had I followed its advice I might have come to work in a place such as this. The sunlight fell softly on pines and rocks and river. It was pristine, thrilling, glorious.

I came upon a small gathering of wooden buildings in a clearing among tall pines. One was a restaurant, and I went in for a cup of tea. Across from me was a family that included a boy of around fourteen who was eating a pizza, his fat spreading over the chair arms and the table in front of him as though it was oozing out of him. In the categories of fatness determined by Body Mass Index, he might have been among the six million Americans categorised as 'super-obese'. The rate of obesity among children has doubled since the 1970s. More than half of America's adults are now over-weight or obese. The Centers for Disease Control and Prevention studied the issue and one of their scientists remarked, 'Rarely do chronic conditions such as obesity spread with the speed and dispersion characteristic of a communicable disease epidemic.' 280,000 Americans per year die from causes directly related to obesity, says this insti-tute, with healthcare costs from the treatment of obesity-related diseases amounting to $240 billion per year.

Twenty years earlier I'd seen a parade of fat people wheezing and rolling out of supermarket doors and had asked my mother how this had happened. The answer, according to Eric Schlosser, is fast food, together with a more seden-tary lifestyle. Americans, he says, spend more on fast food than they do on education. They also spend more on it than they do on movies, magazines, newspapers, videos, recorded music and books, combined. In 1970, they spent $6 billion on it. In 2001, they surpassed $110 billion. Cheaper commod-ities have allowed the fast-food chains to offer French fries triple and soft drinks quadruple the size of what they were in the 1950s. Like the Jesuits, they go after their prey early. They use playgrounds, psychological testing, toys, advertisements, mascots and joint promotions with sports and entertainment corporations to get into the consciousnesses of children and stay there. Schlosser's *Fast Food Nation* was the most important and revealing of all the state-of-the-American-nation books I read during the time of working on this book. Addressing himself solely to the topic of fast food, he extends his investigations through issues of health, worker and executive pay, job safety, marketing, land use, lobbying, corporate subsidy and globalisation to make a devastating picture about the application of power in America. One of the most depressing of his revelations concerns the arrival of fast food in education. School districts suffering from high enrolment and tax cuts have allowed fast-food companies not only to serve students fast food in their cafeterias, but also to advertise on their school buses, rooftops, educational television channels and on the radio stations playing in the corridors. In Evans, Georgia, 1,200 students were brought together in red and white clothes in the school parking lot to form huge letters spelling out COKE for visiting Coca-Cola executives. They were hoping to earn their school a $500 prize. Some companies go after those not yet able to speak. Soft-drinks manufacturers formed a partnership with Munchkin Bottling, Inc. to encourage parents through labelling to give their drinks to babies in bottles normally intended to contain milk. 'Discover your own river of revenue at the schoolhouse gates,' said a brochure displayed at a Kids Power Marketing Conference. 'Whether it's first graders learning to read or teenagers shopping for their first car, we can guarantee an introduction of your product and your company to these students in the traditional setting of the classroom.' Desperate schools have even turned to corporations to provide them with textbooks and teaching aids, such as the Exxon Educational Foundation material, which advises students that fossil fuels are only minimally harmful to the environment and that alternative sources of energy are too expensive. Companies that provide this material can then deduct the cost of it from their taxes. 'Schoolchildren', writes Schlosser, 'are becoming a captive audience for marketers, compelled by law to attend school and then forced to look at ads to pay for their own education.'

The pizza that the boy across the aisle from me was eating could have fed my family. He accompanied it with a Coca-Cola drunk from a container nearly the size of a bucket and then had a bowl of ice cream drenched in a vibrantly red, almost luminous syrup. He had predecessors, it seems. The English actress Fanny Kemble wrote about her 1832 American tour, 'My only trial here was one which I have to encounter in whatever direction I travel in America – I allude to the ignorant and fatal practice of the women of the stuffing of their children from morning till night with every species of trash which comes to hand.'

As I was leaving a postman came in. I told him I'd driven from the junction with Interstate 5 and had wondered who lived in this forest. He was a serious, compact, tidy man with a bald head. He looked at me for a moment, perhaps wondering whether it was wise or even legal for a postman to reveal such information, then proceeded cautiously.

'There are people working for the government – on roads or in the forestry service, for example,' he said. 'There are people who come only at the weekends, people who work from home via the Internet, service workers in the travel and leisure business, loggers, Indians.' He looked up at the ceiling, having run out of categories.

'Some of the homes have a very temporary look about them,' I said.

'Well, there are some people here in the forest with a regrettable . . . um . . . unfortunate . . . *disadvantageous* relationship with the law,' he said.

'What about the shacks along the river?'

'Those are usually inhabited by single men.' He said this with a certain delicacy and respect, but still managed to enshroud it in darkness.

I crossed the Humboldt County Line and entered Six Rivers National Forest, every twist in the road presenting a new spectacle of rock and water and trees. One of the rivers is the Mad and another is the Eel. I was in Yurok tribal land. A gas station with Art Deco pumps had an advertisement in the window promoting a woman running for the tribal council, declaring her to be modern and independent, but also traditional. There was a sign with a drawing of a hand holding a gun pointed at the viewer, with a warning printed below: 'If you are found here tonight, you will be found here tomorrow.'

I entered the Hoopa Valley Indian Reservation, home of the third and last of the tribes along state highway 96. Its main town had a cemetery heavily festooned with tributes to the dead, a football field, a fire department and a substantial school, but the homes seemed barely able to maintain their shapes. Debris was scattered in the yards as if it had fallen there after an explosion. It was difficult to imagine how a living could be made here. Eighty per cent of the neighbouring tribe were below the poverty line, I read, and three-quarters hadn't telephones. Just beyond the reservation I saw two white men with long beards, shredded clothes and packs on their backs walking with blazing eyes and purposeful strides along the shoulder of the road into the wild. In another time they might have been whiskey traders or wolf hunters, but who could say where they had come from or where they were going? Perhaps the postman.

I began to climb the final section of the mountains I had first entered in South Dakota, long shadows now falling from the peaks and the land beneath them seeming to settle in for the night. I then descended along 299 through Korbal to Arcata and the Pacific Ocean. Here were palm trees and calmness, everything – even the air itself – a pastel colour. Arcata, where, I was told, even the babies and the grandmothers look like hippies, is the capital of the Humboldt County marijuana industry and part of the Emerald Triangle, which also comprises Mendocino and Trinity counties. It was the first place in the country to elect a Green Party majority to its town council. They have since limited franchise restaurants, banned genetically modified foods, called for the impeachment of the president, made it an offence to co-operate voluntarily with the Patriot Act and established Arcata Marsh on an old dump, an experiment in natural sewage treatment that has drawn the attention of scientists and won awards from the Ford Foundation and Harvard. 'Bicycle Bill' Burton started the Bike Library here, a loaning service that offers refurbished bicycles as an alternative to cars.

I turned south on US 101 and passed through Eureka, named for Archimedes' shout in the street, to which he'd run naked after discovering buoyancy in his bath. Ken Kesey, hoping to avoid jail after a drug conviction, faked his suicide here, leaving his truck at the edge of a cliff with a note inside declaring, 'Ocean, Ocean, I'll beat you in the end.' There was a tangled mess of metal where once there was a building, there were the Lost Coast Brewery, the Broadway Cinema, Kerr's Clothing. The town strung out southwards in cube cinderblock structures set down in the middle of parking lots. Who could ever have thought that this was a good method to build a town? The Wiyot Indians lived here until the Gold Rush began to disperse them. To the prospectors were added farmers, ranchers and loggers. On the morning of 25 February 1860, following a Wiyot Renewal ceremony on Indian Island the day before, a group of white men from Eureka arrived with hatchets, clubs and knives and slaughtered up to two hundred Wiyot. Bret Harte, then working for a local newspaper, went out to the island afterwards. 'Old women wrinkled and decrepit lay weltering in blood, their brains dashed out and dabbled with their long gray hair. Infants scarcely a span long, with their faces cloven with hatchets and their bodies ghastly with wounds,' he wrote. The *Humboldt Times*, on the other hand, applauded what the men had done.

I turned inland then and below Redcrest entered the Avenue of the Giants, a thirty-two-mile road passing through an old-growth redwood forest beside the Eel River. These trees, the tallest living things in the world, can live for up to two thousand years and reach a height of more than 350 feet. The bark alone can be a foot thick. 'The redwoods, once seen, leave a mark or create a vision that stays with you always,' wrote John Steinbeck in *Travels with Charley*. 'The vainest, most slap-happy and irreverent of men, in the presence of redwoods, goes under a spell of wonder and respect.' Walt Whitman, in 'Song of the Redwood Tree', imagined the ancient, elegiac voice of one of them as it was being felled in sacrifice to the expansion of the country. I parked the car and got out. It was windless and silent, the day's light leaking slowly away. I walked underneath one of the redwoods and looked up. Here was an overwhelming experience of volume, great age, power and verticality, the borders of the tree tapering in infinitesimal decrements as it rose into the sky. It seemed a kind of god.

Logging companies prize redwoods because of their beauty, their light weight and their resistance to decay, termites, water damage and fire, and of course their yield. The chief engineer of the San Francisco Fire Department gave credit to the redwood used on the exteriors of buildings for containing the damage from the fires that broke out after the earthquake of 1906. Its fire resistance is due to its lack of resin. In Scotia I had passed the Pacific Lumber Company, the main loggers in the area. Scotia became, and remains for the time being, a company town, with Pacific Lumber owning the homes, the movie theatre and the school. In 1999, the same year that they created a three-acre buffer zone around a six-hundred-year-old redwood named Luna, in exchange for an environmental activist named Julia Butterfly Hill leaving the tree she was living in, they signed a habitat conservation plan called the Headwaters Agreement. According to the Environmental Protection Information Center of Garberville, however, the company committed 325 violations in the five years after signing the agreement. The battle between the environmentalists and the company has been unrelenting, with the company losing territory and direction. In January 2007 they filed for bankruptcy. If they are not rescued, Scotia, it would seem, will become a ghost town.

I passed Garberville, once called Dogtown, but later renamed for himself by town postmaster Jacob C. Garber, and went south in the darkness through America's most important wine-growing region without seeing a single vine. In a little while I saw the Golden Gate Bridge glowing red and gold in the night. Beyond was the soft pulse of the city lights.

On 19 March of that year an Iraqi-American real-estate agent and father of two young children climbed onto an outer beam of the bridge and lashed himself to a railing to try to draw the attention of the world to the innocent women, children and elderly who would die in the war that the United States was launching that day. His name was Paul Alarab. A Highway Patrolman recognised him as the same man who, fifteen years earlier, had suspended himself in a rubbish bin at the end of a nylon cord attached to the bridge so that people would listen when he spoke about how badly treated were the handicapped and the elderly. The cord snapped and he crashed into the bay at around eighty miles per hour, breaking his ankles and three of his ribs and collapsing his lungs. On this second occasion he told those watching that he would climb back onto the bridge to safety once he'd had the opportunity to read out his statement to CNN. When, forty-five minutes later, they had yet to appear, he unwound the cord from his wrist and either fell from the bridge or jumped. On this occasion the impact killed him. If he jumped, he would be one of the two that on average kill themselves each week by jumping from the Golden Gate Bridge, the leading site for suicides in the world. 'Jumpers are drawn to the Golden Gate because they believe it's a gateway to another place,' Dr Lanny Berman, executive director of the American Association of Suicidology, has said.

*   *   *

In May 1992 I sat one evening in the Cinna Bar in the San Francisco Tenderloin, drinking a beer and watching a basketball game on television. Two Latin Americans were shooting pool, a group of Koreans were playing a game of dice. A man walked in off the street and fell on his face, unconscious. The walls and lights were red, the faces radiating a Hadean glow. Women in mini-skirts came and went, their hands shaking a little as they drank their wine coolers.

I was in San Francisco to make a radio programme for the BBC about the Californian writer William T. Vollman, at the time thirty-two years old and the author of eleven published books, one of which was nine hundred pages long. He had another ten in preparation. He had been working sixteen-hour days at his computer for so long that, like a stripper he knew who was required to masturbate all day on stage, he had developed Repetitive Strain Syndrome. In 2004 his seven-volume, 3,300-page study of violence, *Rising Up and Rising Down*, was published.

He'd gone to a tiny college called Deep Springs, which was founded in 1917 by the inventor of the oscilloscope and takes just twelve students per year, and then to Cornell. He spoke several languages, taught differential equations as a hobby and manufactured special editions of his books decorated with butterfly wings and pubic hair purchased from prostitutes. When he was twenty-two and had seen *Lawrence of Arabia* he flew to Pakistan, crossed the mountains of the North-West Frontier and travelled with the Mujahideen during their war against the Soviets. At the time I was with him in San Francisco he was having a bullet-proof vest made in preparation for a trip to Yugoslavia.

When he was nine and in charge of his younger sister he became so engrossed in a book he was reading that he could not hear her cries as she was drowning in a pond behind their house. 'I felt like a murderer,' he said. 'An outcast. At times I felt that I was an extra-terrestrial. I couldn't be like people who were leading ordinary, happy lives. I became interested in failure.' Writing was perhaps the only cure. 'If

I couldn't get out of the world of my books, at least I could bring other people in to visit me.' He sought out transvestites, retarded people, skinheads, prostitutes, prisoners serving life, and made them his subjects.

His idea for the radio programme was to build it around his research for a story he wanted to write called 'The Queen of the Whores'. 'I see an underground place in a city with trash piled up around the entrance and catacombs inside. You go down through there and come into a big room with fires burning in trash cans and a queen holding court over a multitude of crackheads, pushers, pimps, alcoholics, all the forsaken. She might be a beautiful runaway or she might be blind, but I think she's a prostitute.' He liked to work from life. He'd rented a room in a Tenderloin dive where he was to pay prostitutes forty dollars to improvise their version of the underground queen. A photographer friend of his named Ken Miller, whom he called Code Six, was to bring the prostitutes from the street, and the BBC producer was to hide in the closet of the room. I was to bring the wine coolers and then wait in the Cinna Bar.

When the basketball game I'd been watching was over, I went back to the hotel. 'Transients Welcome' it said on its sign. The stairwell was full of political slogans, drawings of marijuana plants and mandalas decorated the doorways to the rooms of transients who'd stayed on. The door to Vollman's room was open. He was lying on the bed wearing a baseball hat and military fatigues, taking notes. A white-haired Chinese woman in blue pyjamas and workmen's gloves was beside him with her hand on his crotch, murmuring like a person praying. I heard later that her daughter had been raped and murdered and that since then she had been insensible.

Code Six was sitting on a shelf up near the ceiling. The BBC producer was on the floor with earphones on and with the wheels of his tape recorder turning. A frail girl with purple rouge named Cookie was looking through a pile of Code Six's photographs of street prostitutes. 'OD'd.' 'In jail.' 'In a clinic,' she said as she went through the pictures. 'Oh, no. Lucy. Her pimp killed her with a high-heeled shoe.' She began to cry.

In a chair facing the bed was a heavy black woman named Angel in a red mini-skirt, finishing her testimony. 'I be your queen,' she said. 'I be your queen because no one in the Tenderloin can make you feel so good as Angel. I give the best head this side of the Mississippi. I can suck a baseball through fifty feet of garden hose.' She swaggered out, her cannonball hips flattening me against the door.

A good-looking blonde with large eyes named Domino came in. Vollman thought he and Code Six should be alone with her, so the rest of us left. The next day he showed me his notes. 'Long white lines of a motorcycle accident. The white band of a bullet wound . . . Lying naked on the bed, playing with a gold chain across her breasts, chewing gum . . . The orange glow of the pipe against her cheek. She exhales the crack into my mouth. Taste of bubblegum breath. Lips numb, tongue numb, the heart racing, the famous head rush . . .'

San Francisco can be lived in with an easeful pleasure rare in the world. It's temperate, beautifully set, low-built, compact, prosperous, diverse, smoothly paced, sophisticated, tolerant, tasteful. The franchise shopping and food places are rare enough that you have to make an effort to find them. You can be who you want to be here without fear of censure, and each morning when you wake up this city of small, beautifully conceived modern houses and Victorian terraces looks as though it has been freshly cleaned and painted overnight. But the true descendant of its original settlement is the Tenderloin, where Bill Vollman conducted his research, for in the beginning it was named the Barbary Coast, in honour of the Arab pirates of the waters of north Africa. It came into existence because of the 1848 Gold Rush, in the year after which the population of this city grew twenty-five times. 'The Barbary Coast is the haunt of the low and vile of every kind,' wrote Benjamin Estelle Lloyd in 1876. 'The petty thief, the house burglar, the tramp, the whoremonger, lewd women, cutthroats, murderers, all are found here. Dance-halls and concert saloons, where blear-eyed men and women drink vile liquor, smoke offensive tobacco, engage in vulgar conduct, sing obscene songs and say and do everything to heap upon themselves more depredations, are numerous. Low gambling houses, thronged with riot-loving rowdies, in all stages of intoxication, are there. Opium dens, where heathen Chinese and God-forsaken men and women are sprawled in miscellaneous confusion, disgustingly drowsy or completely overcome, are there. Licentiousness, debauchery, pollution, loathsome disease, insanity from dissipation, misery, poverty, wealth, profanity, blasphemy and death, are there.'

The pressure to conform can be constrictive in the east, the Midwest, the south and the plains. Those who can't or won't succumb to it often head west, to places like Montana, Wyoming, Idaho and the Pacific Northwest, where there's more room. Great masses of such people went to California, and still do. An Englishman named Joshua Norton arrived in San Francisco with $40,000 during the Gold Rush and built it into a fortune of a quarter of a million, which he lost. Afterwards he patrolled the city in a military uniform and sword and with two dogs, declaring himself to be Emperor of the United States and Protector of Mexico and collecting taxes on the street and writing cheques for small amounts, which the banks always honoured. One of his proposals was for a bridge over the bay. I'd seen and met (and heard stories about) many who couldn't accept what they had been born into as I made my way west, the commune members, criminals, arms stockpilers, war veterans, marijuana growers, survivalists, the single men in shacks along the Klamath River, people like Kenny the animal skinner in the bar in Glendo, Wyoming, who told me he had no idea who he was, but was clearly looking. I'd come in from Marin County and over the Golden Gate Bridge and had then driven around North Beach, downtown, on and around Market Street, and saw many more moving in the shadows with their belongings on their backs, blown out here to the coast and having run out of land and with no way back.

When I came here after the drive from Chicago in Robert Gregory's car in 1973 I saw one evening in the typing room of the main library at Grove and Laramie a wild-looking man in an orange mechanic's jumpsuit and with his white hair standing on end, alternately dozing off over his books about outer-space travel and the Mayan Indians and getting up to shadow-box around the room to wake himself up. I was typing letters, he was working out some riddle of the universe. I wanted to talk with him, to know who he was, but he left before I found the nerve. I had a second chance, though, for when I went into a cafeteria on Market Street a half-hour later he was there. I got some food and asked if I could sit with him. He pulled out a chair for me. We ate our meals and then walked the streets for hours, getting moved on by police who believed us to be vagrants from public benches and the Greyhound Bus terminal, with him asking me questions, repairing my broken boot and telling me how he had been an Iowa state official in the department dealing with drivers' licences until his wife and child were killed by a nuclear test in Nevada. After that, he started walking. At the time I spoke with him he was living in a cardboard box in Golden Gate Park. He was kind, curious, lucid and powerful, and he seemed to bear these qualities easily. Before we parted he ran across a street to an all-night restaurant and brought back two packets of salt, which he handed to me. 'Friends should exchange salt upon parting,' he said, then walked into the night. 'Here are the roughs and beards and space and ruggedness and nonchalance that the soul loves,' wrote Walt Whitman. No one I had yet met had made me feel so bourgeois.

I drove west then along Geary to the Plough and the Stars, an Irish bar that Martin Hayes had suggested I visit. There is music here most nights, but when I arrived there was just a barman, a customer in his early thirties with a baseball hat and a long beard that might have had as an antecedent either a biblical patriarch's or an Irish folksinger's, and a large empty space full of unfulfilled promise. I sat down and the barman started talking to me as though we were resuming our conversation of the previous night. The bearded man joined in. He was Irish American, his father a publican. I learned that he had been working as a defence attorney for three years in the tribal legal system on the Pine Ridge Sioux reservation in South Dakota.

'Is the system different there from how it is elsewhere in the United States?' I asked him.

'First of all they only have jurisdiction up to misdemeanour level. The maximum sentence is a year, and it is served in really gruesome prisons on reservation land. The judges don't generally like to convict. Many cases are settled by the returning of things stolen, some form of reparation or a face-to-face apology. One of the main differences in the process has to do with the rules of evidence. American courts are full of objections during testimony. A hearing becomes a game with each side manipulating court procedures. The objective is a victory, rather than establishing what actually happened. The Indian judges don't like that. They prefer to hear the whole statement. They let the person talk.

'I'll miss it. I had a good time there. They looked after me. They thought that a single male, living alone, would feel lonely or wouldn't eat well enough. Family is very important, hospitality is very important. There's a culture of visiting. They'd come over with food or beer. If you stood on your porch talking to them, they'd understand that they weren't supposed to come in, so they'd talk for a while and then leave. If you waved them in, they could stay all night. That was the etiquette, very simple, very pleasant.'

Crazy Horse had been born close to the Pine Ridge reservation. I asked the bearded man what the feeling on the reservation was about Korczak Ziolkowski's monument.

'To many of them Mount Rushmore was an act of violence. To go in and beat up a holy mountain, to dynamite and gouge something held precious was a terrible act of defilement. The Crazy Horse memorial is thought of in the same way by some Indians. Black Elk's great-granddaughter Charlotte thinks the face on the monument is Ziolkowski's and that the whole thing is a stupendous act of egotism. Some others are in favour of it. I would say that in the end they'll have their hospital and university that are planned there, because in my experience when the Indians say they will do something, they may move slowly, but they usually get there.'

The following evening I left my beige Chevrolet in the airport parking lot, aged by nearly six weeks and 7,182 miles since I picked it up behind Louis' Lunch in New Haven, and flew back to Spain.

Interlude

Through the winter and spring I was in Valencia. One night in a bar an American asked me, 'Do they hate us?' A waiter in another place, he told me, had taken everyone else's order before his, and this is how he interpreted it. He asked the question not with indignation or curiosity, but rather as though he'd been discovered in a transgression. In thirty years of living in Europe I hadn't been asked such a question before. 'It's not that I'd blame them,' he said.

On another night, in the same city, one of a group of American students on a tour of Europe had gone back to his hotel early, too depressed to continue his night out with friends. 'We passed a group of Spaniards,' one of them told me. 'One made some kind of aggressive gesture towards us. It might have been aimed at somebody else, or it might have been a joke. But he thought it was because we were Americans. He thinks they despise us.'

Since I had been in Europe I had heard Europeans judge Americans to be bombastic, materialistic, naïve, poorly educated, excessively patriotic and lacking history, cuisine and culture. But they also watched America's movies, listened to its music, wore its clothes, attended its universities, sought its counsel, admired its landscapes and its cities, yearned for its freedom and accepted its military protection and its cash. In the main they had an amused, paternalistic affection for the United States. And while the United States had overthrown governments elsewhere in the world, with Europe they had made treaties, set up cultural exchanges and study programmes, rebuilt infrastructure with Marshall Aid and other forms of assistance, celebrated common values, venerated Europe's age and its beauty and despatched some of the best of its minds as advisors and diplomats. And they bore European mockery with good humour.

One of the gifts bestowed by the United States on many of its people has been an ease of manner, a confidence, even an insouciance at times, born out of the country's wealth, power and progress and the desire of so many of the world's people to come to it. But for this to be sustained the reception has to be hospitable. Such a sensibility curdles rapidly in the acid of others' contempt. Confidence can turn into paranoia.

This seemed to begin to happen around the year 2003. As Europeans began to replace their amused affection with a view of America as an ungainly bully stumbling around with no agenda other than its own compulsion to dominate, many Americans felt first misunderstood, then unloved, then fearful, then outraged. Epithets of abuse about a cowardly and derelict Europe came from the American media and politicians. The little American consulate in Valencia began to feel it needed a police guard. Crash barriers, cameras and armed guards appeared around the embassy in London. America suddenly looked alone and defiant. Europe, and much of the rest of the world, was turning away from it, economically, politically, culturally, the relation between the two continents circumscribed by feelings of shame, fear and bewilderment. 'What has happened to America?' people asked.

Isolationism, rather than war, has been popular in American electoral politics, at least until wars start. When George Bush was running for president in 2000 and was asked about anti-Americanism in the world, he said, 'It really depends on how our nation conducts itself in foreign policy. If we're an arrogant nation, they'll resent us. If we're a humble nation, but strong, they'll welcome us.' The United States had in particular to be humble in their relations with 'nations that are figuring out for themselves how to chart their course'. He wanted American troops out of Bosnia and Kosovo and said that it was not the job of the military to transform countries into stable democracies.

But within months of becoming president he withdrew the United States from the Kyoto Protocol on global warming, sent anti-abortionists rather than medical experts to the World Health Assembly, cancelled negotiations with North Korea, alienated through his selection of aggressive delegates the UN Commission on Human Rights, withdrew from the START II treaty negotiations about the reduction of nuclear weapons, refused to participate in a global initiative on land mines, ceased working with the Organisation for Economic Cooperation and Development in their efforts to control offshore banks and their money-laundering operations, withdrew from the Comprehensive Test Ban Treaty, the Small Arms Control Treaty and the Biological Weapons Convention, and began from his first meetings with Tony Blair to push the idea of an invasion of Iraq.

In *The Grand Chessboard*, published in 1997, Jimmy Carter's former National Security Advisor Zbigniew Brzezinski pointed out that the territory from the eastern border of Germany to China, known as Eurasia, contains seventy-five per cent of the world's population, sixty per cent of its GNP and seventy-five per cent of its energy resources. It was imperative, he believed, that the United States rather than China or Russia control these resources. This would require a massive military build-up, an extension of influence across the globe and the perception that the United States possessed obliterating, unanswerable force. This policy, he further believed, would be difficult to implement 'except in the circumstances of a truly massive and widely perceived direct external threat'.

A group of men including Dick Cheney, Donald Rumsfeld, Richard Perle and Paul Wolfowitz believed similarly. They were participants in the Project for the New American Century, an independent group that advocated a massive increase in military spending, the control of all energy resources, a building of alliances with the like-minded and a vanquishing through first-strike attacks of anyone who stood in the way and an extension of global dominance through total war. I saw on CNN a former CIA man describe the plan as 'the American *Mein Kampf*'.

In the distance were China and Russia; in the foreground was the Middle East. In order to protect Israel and facilitate American control over oil and gas, and with American bases in Saudi Arabia in jeopardy in the event of an Islamist regime taking over there, a complete remaking by America of the Middle East had to be undertaken. Iraq was the country selected for invasion. Colossal American firepower could be demonstrated, a regime neutral to Israel could be installed, the Saudi bases could be transferred and the world's second-largest oil reserve would come under American control. The removal of its dictator, Saddam Hussein, was not of primary importance, according to the Project's authors, but he could provide the pretext for the invasion. In order to mobilise public opinion, however, something more was needed – 'some cataclysmic and catalysing event – like a new Pearl Harbor'. This plan was presented to President Clinton, who rejected it. Bush took it on in its totality, and a group of men set on American global domination through war came to be in charge of American foreign policy, unopposed.

After the 11 September attacks, President Bush began to speak of 'pre-emptive war' and an 'Axis of Evil', comprising Iran, Iraq and, to many people's surprise, North Korea. According to *The Right Man*, a book by a speechwriter of Bush's named David Frum, North Korea was added because it was felt that a list of three has a greater rhetorical power than one of just two. Afghanistan, where Union Oil of California had been frustrated by the Taliban in their plan to build a pipeline from Turkmenistan through Afghanistan and Pakistan to the port of Karachi, was invaded. After the Taliban had been deposed, two former Union Oil employees, John J. Maresca and Hamid Karzai, became, respectively, US envoy and president, and the pipeline project was approved.

Attention turned to Iraq. Colin Powell addressed the United Nations with a list of chemical and biological weapons believed to be in the possession of Iraq, neglecting to add that it had been supplied by a defected Iraqi defence minister who also said that these weapons had been destroyed, under his supervision, after the First Gulf War. Iraq, which had neither invaded nor threatened anyone and which was hostile to al-Qaeda and other forms of Islamic fundamentalism, was invaded. Syria and Iran were threatened. The president then derided the movement for détente between North and South Korea and said of North Korea's leader, 'I loathe him . . . I want to topple him.' Prisoners taken by United States forces in the Middle East were humiliated and tortured, brought to holding centres outside American jurisdiction and held without charge. Rights long held by Americans were abrogated under the Patriot Act. The United States exempted itself from any war-crimes charges that could be heard by the International Court of Justice. The balance of powers became distorted through an increasing concentration in the executive branch. 'We're going to push and push and push until some larger force makes up stop,' declared David Addington, the vice president's chief of staff. The military budget soared. A seemingly endless war against a nebulous enemy was declared, justifying a constant state of alert, huge spending, the revocation of rights and the unleashing of weapons against civilians. 'All this talk about first we are going to do Afghanistan, then we will do Iraq, this is entirely the wrong way to go about it,' said Richard Perle to the journalist John Pilger. 'If we just let our vision of the world go forth, and we embrace it entirely and we don't try to piece together clever diplomacy, but just wage a total war . . . our children will sing great songs about us years from now.' This is a policy without a mandate.

Concerning 11 September, the world in general responded with indignation towards the attackers and sympathy for the United States. From all over the Middle East, including Iran and Syria, came messages of support. 'We are all Americans now,' declared *Le Monde*. The choice of Perle's 'total war' as a response brought about the most rapid reversal in America's relations with the rest of the world in my lifetime. Public opinion in Europe against the invasion was eighty per cent. In Spain the figure was ninety-two per cent. Three million people demonstrated in Madrid. In Valencia the figure was 750,000, equivalent to the entire population of the city. The Valencian demonstration looked like Fallas, the city's springtime saturnalia, with students, punks, farmers, civil servants, factory workers, professionals, mothers with children, dowagers in furs, the young and the fashionable all together in the streets. The demonstration in London was the largest in British history. The leaders of both Spain and Britain nevertheless committed themselves to America's war. It was widely assumed that they'd either been bribed or coerced and that it was through one of these methods that the United States now conducted its foreign policy.

Henry David Thoreau, writing of an Indian who called himself 'Lieutenant Anthony' and showed up in Massachusetts demanding payment for lands appropriated from the Indians by the Pilgrims, said, 'Who knows but a Lieutenant Anthony may be knocking at the door of the White House some day? At any rate, I know that if you hold a thing unjustly, there will surely be the devil to pay at last.'

You grow up in America with a sense of its invincibility. I imagined that, when riled, our military machine would knock out anyone foolish enough to provoke us. America's political leaders predicate their geopolitical decisions on this idea. But the American military machine has tended not to prevail in its wars of the last half-century. It is now difficult to imagine how a young man from a small Midwestern town with no employment prospects would impose his will on an ex-Mujahideen in the mountains of Afghanistan. Walter Bagehot wrote in 1861: 'The fact is, the Americans are *a wholly untried people* ... They have neve been *tested* by any great difficulty, any great danger, any great calamity; they have never been called upon for any sustained effort, any serious sacrifices, any prolonged endurance. They do not know, therefore, – nor do we – the possible reach of their virtues and their powers, nor the possible range of their vices and their weaknesses. They have never yet faced a truly formidable foe . . . They have gained their ends hitherto not by fighting but by bullying . . . and their success in this sort of warfare has not only enormously enhanced their own conceptions of their military prowess, but has entirely blinded them to the flimsy and *unproved* foundation upon which these conceptions rest.' The century and a half that has passed since has perhaps not fundamentally altered this peculiarly American predicament.

At the end of the Cold War, George Kennan, the principal architect of American foreign policy in the post-war years, said that he believed the battle for universal democracy was futile, that the most the United States could ask of other countries was for 'minimum standards of civilised diplomatic intercourse', and that there was no need for an American military presence anywhere in the world outside its boundaries, except perhaps in Asia, because of treaties with Japan. He asked why, in 1992, was the United States giving military assistance to forty-three African countries and twenty-two of a total of twenty-four Latin American countries. There are, at the time of writing, American bases in 132 of the 192 member-states of the United Nations, housing around 325,000 military personnel. Military spending, including war costs and the budgets of non-Pentagon agencies, was estimated to be more than the defence budgets of the rest of the world combined. The State Department has spent $23 billion in subsidies to encourage foreign countries to buy American weapons. The annual interest charges on the part of the national debt attributable to military spending have been estimated at $138.7 billion and the Star Wars project, which has been demonstrated to be unworkable, will cost $1.2 trillion by 2015. 'Against whom are these weapons conceivably to be deployed?' asked Kennan.

When Dwight Eisenhower was leaving office in January 1961 he said, 'The conjunction of an immense Military Establishment and a large arms industry is new in the American experience. The total influence – economic, political, even spiritual – is felt in every city, every statehouse, every office of the Federal Government ... In the councils of government we must guard against the acquisition of unwarranted influence, whether sought or unsought, by the military industrial complex. The potential for the disastrous rise of misplaced power exists and will persist.'

The American arms industry was in fact at that moment on the precipice of a boom. A shrinking balance-of-payments surplus during Kennedy's administration led to an increase in arms sales as a solution. This was vastly accelerated by the oil crisis of the early 1970s, when arms sales went from $1.6 billion in 1972 to $10 billion in 1975, with the Middle East rather than NATO countries being the principal market. Large clandestine supplies of weapons went to Iraq during its war with Iran, and in 1987 alone $634 million in arms went to the Mujahideen in Afghanistan. Between 1990 and 1997 the United States supplied $42 billion worth of weapons to the Gulf Cooperation Council, composed of Bahrain, Kuwait, Oman, Qatar, Saudi Arabia and the United Arab Emirates. An area fraught with religious factionalism had become what Kevin Phillips described as 'an Islamic Dodge City'.

Military operations were privatised through the creation of Private Military Corporations by Dick Cheney in 1992 when he was Defence Secretary. These companies took over numerous building, logistic, training and other security functions, including the provision of mercenaries, from the military. They could go where the military could not without technically violating neutrality or being subject to public or congressional scrutiny. New companies came into being that fed off the escalating military budget and won their contracts by employing former politicians and advisors. A merchant bank known as the Carlyle Group invested in military industry companies such as United Defence, BDM, Vinnell, US Investigations Services and Vought Aircraft, among many others, hired George Bush, Sr and James Baker, among several other cabinet and regulatory agency officers, and delivered profit increases of thirty to forty per cent per year. Richard Perle was with Trimene Partners Ltd, which invested in various companies involved in preparation for war in the Middle East. Cheney became CEO of Halliburton, which was awarded contracts to rebuild Iraq following the bombing that he had supervised as Defence Secretary during the First Gulf War. Halliburton, with Cheney having become vice president in 2001, was able to repeat the procedure for the second Gulf War. The Homeland Security budget increased the proliferation of security companies and the lobbying in Washington for contracts, with companies with connections to Perle, ex-CIA director James Woolsey, Iraq administrator L. Paul Bremer III and the president's brother Marvin among the beneficiaries. Oil interests, arms manufacturers, security companies, clandestine operations, lobbyists, the military and both serving and ex-politicians were entangled to a degree that Eisenhower could never have foreseen. 'Wars and panic on the stock exchange,' wrote John Dos Passos in 1919 of the banker J.P. Morgan:

machine gun fire and arson,
bankruptcies, war loans,
starvation, lice, cholera and typhus:
good growing weather for the House of Morgan.

James Madison wrote in the first years of the American Republic, 'Of all the enemies to public liberty, war is, perhaps, the most to be dreaded because it compromises and develops the germ of every other. As the parent of armies, war encourages debts and taxes, the known instruments for bringing the many under the dominion of the few. In war, too, the discretionary power of the executive is extended . . . and all the means of seducing the minds, are added to those of subduing the force, of the people.' For a hundred years foreign wars were in the main avoided, so that in 1884 Henry Adams could write, comparing Europe to America: 'Endless wars withdrew many hundred thousand men from production, and changed them into agents of waste; huge debts, the evidence of past wars and bad government, created interests to support the system and fix its burdens on the labouring class; courts, with habits of extravagance that shamed common-sense, helped to consume private economics. All this might have been borne; but behind this stood aristocracies, sucking their nourishment from industry, producing nothing themselves, employing little or no active capital or intelligent labour, but pressing on the energies and ambitions of society with the weight of an incubus.' The United States, by contrast, offered wealth as a reward for labour, and with the infrastructure and machinery that this would produce, and without the distraction, wastage and debt creation of foreign wars, would soon surpass Europe. As in fact it did.

The roles, tragically for the United States, have reversed. Total war has driven national debt towards the eternally unrepayable and drawn tax revenue away from investment, diplomacy and social programmes, the beneficiaries being an aristocracy-like corporate management class that lives extravagantly from the public purse. Executive power has extended, minds have been seduced and the force of the people has been subdued.

Had the United States pursued a policy of non-intervention beginning in the 1960s, 'there would', William Pfaff has written, 'have been no American war in Indochina . . . The United States would never have been defeated, its army demoralized, or its students radicalized.' There would have been no Khmer Rouge genocide, no intervention in the internal problems of Iran and no war in Iraq. He thinks such a policy should appeal to an American public that believes in the autonomy of the market, is hostile to ideology and supports concepts of constitutional order, pragmatism and compromise. International relations would be pursued through the avenues of diplomacy and analytical intelligence, with particular attention being paid to history. 'The current crises in Afghanistan, Iraq, Lebanon, Palestine–Israel, and Iran', he writes, 'are all colonial or post-colonial in nature, which is generally ignored in American political and press discussion.' The more eager emperors are to increase their domains, it has been said, the less attention they pay to historians.

With a policy of non-intervention the United States could spend its tax revenue on the well-being of its citizens and on opening markets and improving relations with the rest of the world. Instead of arms and war, it could export pharmaceuticals, new technology, food, business acumen, new means of clean energy, training methods, machinery, sport, art, design. Its universities are the best in the world, and it could become better known for education and research than for smart bombs and regime changes. And with the released revenue, it might draw back into the diplomatic and intelligence services the sort of bright and ambitious people the American government lost to banking and new technology. Perhaps with the attitude of humility advocated by George Bush during his first presidential campaign, the distribution of rights and resources might be more equitable in the world, poverty could be alleviated and Americans could feel well received when they travel. 'Why can this President not seem to see that America's true power lies not in its will to intimidate,' asked the eighty-five-year-old Senator Robert Byrd on the eve of the invasion of Iraq, 'but in its ability to inspire?'

All this could be thought naïve, but so, experience has shown, are the hubristic, imperial delusions of the advocates of total war and world domination, who have followed the paths of emperors through the ages in growing more arrogant with their defeats. The United States was beaten in Vietnam. It cannot control either Iraq or Afghanistan. If a heavyweight boxer was repeatedly defeated by flyweights, which boxing authority would issue him a licence? Yet still threats are directed towards North Korea, Syria and Iran, each of which knows that America's debts are rising, its military manpower is limited and that to launch more invasions would require conscription, likely to divide the country as the Vietnam War did and lead to mass resistance. Who will fear the United States now?

Detroit and California

The following June I flew into Detroit. I picked up a car at the airport, checked into a hotel in Royal Oak and drove downtown. 'Don't forget the Motor City,' sang Martha and the Vandellas in that celebratory, pan-American song of spontaneous happiness, 'Dancing in the Streets'.

Known in the late nineteenth century as the Paris of the West, Detroit became by the 1980s a world icon of post-industrial despoliation. I drove for miles on Woodward from Royal Oak all the way to the Detroit River, a strait that connects Lake St Clair and Lake Erie and forms a border with Canada. Louis Hennepin, a Flemish friar who sailed with the French explorer La Salle on the *Griffin*, passed here in 1679 and wrote, 'Those who will one day have the happiness to possess this fertile and pleasant strait, will be very much obliged to those who have shown them the way.' All around were meadows and forests with wild grapes, berries and nuts and so many deer, elk and buffalo that the crew were able to get enough meat for the whole of the rest of their journey from a single hunting trip.

Woodward took me right through the heart of the downtown business district. I passed a cluster of glittering, Golden Era skyscrapers and two theatres with vintage marquees, a kind of theme park of urban Americana with only two pedestrians visible on this weekday afternoon. Further on were an opera house, football stadium, a conference centre and the six towers of General Motors' Renaissance Center, built after riots in 1967 that destroyed 1,300 buildings. This area too was eerily silent. Such expenditure and such effort by both business and the local government to brighten the look of the city were heart-rending in the face of its aborted economy. Detroit is one of the world's strongest cities for music – the Four Tops, Aretha Franklin, Alice Cooper, John Lee Hooker, Iggy Pop, Marvin Gaye, Eminem, Kid Rock, Yusef Lateef, Milt Jackson, Smokey Robinson, Dinah Washington, Stevie Wonder, the White Stripes, Madonna and techno were all either born in or lived in Detroit – but its reliance on a single industry long in crisis has given it, in parts, the feel of a ghost town, as though life had suddenly been radiated out of it, *Twilight Zone*-style.

Henry Ford built his first car in a rented workshop here in 1896. General Motors began in Flint in 1908 and Chrysler opened production in 1925. These three companies made Detroit long unrivalled in vehicle manufacture throughout the world. Ford had a private army of 3,500 and recruited both Klansmen and blacks in the south to deter union organisation. The *New York Times* called him 'an industrial fascist – the Mussolini of Detroit'. But he paid well. When he was paying five dollars per day and other tycoons berated him for it, he said, 'If I didn't pay them well, how else could they buy my cars?' This was a philosophy that extended in influence throughout the United States, so that by the 1960s the economic strata had moved closer together and the economy in general was prospering with the growth in purchasing power at all levels. This process began to reverse in the early 1970s and the reversal was greatly accelerated by Ronald Reagan's 'trickle-down' policies of tax cuts for the wealthy designed to 'liberate' money at the top. Ford was eventually forced to negotiate with the United Auto Workers in 1943, when only thirty-four of his 78,000 workers voted against joining a union. Walter Reuther, an anti-racist and one-time socialist who was the head of the UAW, played the three companies off against one another to gain for his workers not only high wages and paid vacations, but also employer-funded pensions, medical insurance and unemployment benefits. The industry could afford this because it benefited from government subsidies, price supports, guarantees and protection from foreign competition.

The automobile industry in Detroit was hit by oil crises, competition from Japan, the weight of its obligations to both its serving and its retired employees and by its own complacency. General Motors, long regarded as the index of the health of America's economy, has $300 billion of long-term debt. It saw its share value halve in 2005 alone. The health benefits it provides to 1.1 million people account for $1,500 of every car it produces. It is extremely difficult for its manufacturing operations to make a profit under these conditions in a time of intense global competition. General Motors is in a virtual state of bankruptcy that may become real, but so were Chrysler and Nissan at different points, and both survived.

I turned left in the heart of downtown onto Jefferson. Within half a mile I came upon something I'd never seen before, a brief prelude of abandoned apartment buildings and boarded-up shops leading to a vast open area gone wild with high grasses and brush, within minutes of the financial centre of the city. If Louis Hennepin were to sail back into Lake St Clair and focus on just this spot, he might have thought that little had changed in three and a quarter centuries. Job losses, heroin, crack and arson sprees on Devil's Night on the eve of Halloween had obliterated this place where once there was a neighbourhood. I learned that such phenomena are called 'urban prairies'. Detroit has several of them, where trees grow up through houses, packs of wild dogs roam, pigeons and raccoons live in apartment blocks and high streets change into meadows. Trees of Heaven, also known as ghetto palms, were imported from China in 1789 and now burst into life in the middle of roads and on rooftops. Pheasants, opposums, wild turkeys and foxes have come back into the inner city. As I drove on, this urban prairie returned to a wasteland of parking lots, abandoned businesses and apartment buildings and then suddenly, as if you've passed through a door in a video game, there were the mansions of Grosse Point with their initialled iron gates and vast grounds that appeared to have been tended by manicurists. All of this on Jefferson Avenue, possibly the most Third World of American roads.

That night I had dinner in a Mexican restaurant and watched the final game of the National Basketball Championship. The Detroit Pistons won and people poured from restaurants, bars and their homes into the streets of Royal Oak. They danced, sang, toasted and embraced each other. It was buoyant, with a slight edge from the alcohol, but with no evidence that it would turn to rapine. Then police with batons on horseback and on foot moved up the main street like a storm cloud, shoving and shouting and prodding as they went. They looked furious. It was difficult to see what could have made them feel this way. People gradually went back into the bars like children despatched to their rooms.

The next day I drove to the airport, whence I was to fly to San Francisco to resume my journey. I'd bought a ticket by telephone for a Northwest Airlines flight from Detroit to San Francisco from a Mr John Triantafilou of American Travel in north London. It cost £259. Before I left Valencia I noticed that I had twice been debited for the price of the ticket. Mr Triantafilou assured me that the money would be restored to my account.

At the airport the queue for the check-in was inert. Nearly half an hour went by without any movement at all. An overweight businessman turned red over his buttoned-down collar. An Hassidic Jew began to quake. A college student danced to a tune only he could hear. A woman with a child called out for mercy. By the time I arrived at the desk there were only thirty-five minutes to go before take-off.

After a lot of typing the woman behind the desk told me there was no record in their system of me having a place on the flight to San Francisco. I showed her the receipt I'd got from American Travel.

'That's nothing to do with us,' she said.

'What can I do then?' I asked.

'You can buy a ticket.'

'How much is that?'

She went back to her keyboard, typed rapidly, squinted at the screen and said, '$1,553.19.' She pronounced the nineteen cents at the end with a precision that seemed pure malevolence. The amount in total was, more or less, my hotel budget for the journey from California to the east coast.

At no point during my appeal to a Northwest manager at the airport, my paying of the $1,553.19, my run to the plane, my conversation with two women beside me who had paid $116 each for their tickets, my call the following day to Mr Triantafilou or my appeals by letter to Northwest Airlines did I really think I would lose all this money. But that is what happened. Mr Triantafilou was a fraud. Northwest informed me that they had behaved correctly. At the beginning of my journey I'd been molested by a policeman. This time it was the travel industry.

On a bright June day I crossed the Golden Gate Bridge going north, gulls turning through the girders below me and the water of the bay sparkling in the sun. There was a cold bank of fog wrapped around Fort Point at the foot of the bridge that extended like a spectral arm along the shoreline, but the bay and the city were bright. In San Francisco, different weathers in different parts of the city are visible concurrently from bridges and hills. I could see Telegraph Hill, Alcatraz, Angel and Treasure Islands, the wooded hills to the north and a headland further on called Tiburon, 'Shark' in Spanish for its snub-nosed shape. Simone de Beauvoir crossed this bridge in 1947 and later wrote, 'The city is all white and golden in the setting sun. It's heart-stopping. Something so new in America – a city whose form is visible, a city that hasn't just capriciously risen from the ground but that has been built and whose architecture is part of a great natural design.'

The bridge, which at the time of its completion in 1937 was the longest suspension bridge in the world, took only four years to build. Joseph Strauss, the chief engineer, said at the inauguration ceremony, 'What nature rent asunder long ago man has joined today,' then read an ode he had written for the occasion:

> As harps for the winds of heaven,
> My web-like cables are spun;
> I offer my span for the traffic of man,
> At the gate of the setting sun.

Just over the bridge is Sausalito, a former fishing village built up from the bay into the hills that has retained, implausibly it would seem, a hominess and sense of proportion in the face of what must long have been intense and heavily financed demands for property in such a serene and exquisite place so close to the city. I was on my way to see Michael Murphy, a man I first became aware of twenty-five years earlier when I went into a second-hand bookshop in north London and found a copy of his book *Golf in the Kingdom*. It had an inaccurately drawn pair of hands at the top of a backswing on its cover and cost sixty pence. A small biography of its author said that he had co-founded the Esalen Institute in Big Sur, a centre dedicated to the study of esoteric practices of medicine, psychotherapy, Eastern religion and physics. I bought it, took it home and read with a growing sense of wonder this story of a round of golf in Scotland played by a tall, bearded professional named Shivas Irons, a pupil of Irons' named MacIvor and a young American on his way to India whom Murphy named after himself. Under Irons' otherworldly but trenchant tutelage, Murphy's game disintegrates to the point where he can barely hit the ball, but then magically reconstitutes itself before the end. It is a story of a journey down into the darkness and up again into the light, with breakdown and liberation between, and by the end Murphy sees with an acuity he had never known before and is in a sense reborn. Afterwards there is a dinner at which the guests have convened, as in Plato's *Symposium*, to discuss love, specifically their love of golf. They drink whisky, dance reels and then Irons and Murphy run out into the night, meet a seer in the dunes and play a par three in a heavy wind with a pair of featheries and a shillelagh. Irons has a hole in one.

There wasn't, I supposed, a Scottish teaching pro living or dead named Shivas Irons, but somehow, such was the particularity and the conviction of this book, that it felt as though it had truly happened. In fact, it seemed unimaginable to me that it hadn't happened. I hadn't experienced this sensation in reading before. If it had only happened in Murphy's head, what power gave it such an unavoidable feeling of fact? There was something about it of the word being made flesh. How had Murphy done this? Who was he?

He was already finished with his salad when I arrived, so long had it taken me to traverse the city from its far south end beyond the Castro where I was staying. He was seventy-two, athletic-looking, rich in stories, with luminous eyes under heavy black brows. I asked him about *Golf in the Kingdom*.

'I was nearly forty when I started it,' he said. 'Up to then I had mostly been meditating and reading. My father told me I had to get a job, so I worked as a busboy and a gardener. Then we started Esalen in 1962 and I began looking further into the question of human transcendence. I'd long had the intuition that sport can be a vehicle for that, golf in particular. So I started writing. It was the easiest, most joyous experience. Norman Mailer has said that God gives every true writer a free book. If I'm a true writer, that was mine.

'All this began for me when I was a student in pre-medicine at Stanford and by mistake walked into a class being conducted by Frederic Spiegelberg on the points at which Eastern and Western thought come together. It turned my life around by giving me an intellectual framework for some of the things I was experiencing. I was led to the works

of Sri Aurobindo, a staggeringly great figure – a nationalist, a political figure of the first rank, a neo-Hegelian mystic, a poet and intellectual. He studied at Cambridge and received the highest marks in Greek. He's too intellectual for the New Age. Unlike a lot of other gurus, he believed in engaging with rather than withdrawing from the world. It's as if Jefferson had the contemplative capacities of St John of the Cross. I finished at Stanford, went into the Army for two years, then spent eighteen months in the Sri Aurobindo ashram in Pondicherry.'

When he came back to the United States he moved into a centre in San Francisco run by a disciple of Sri Aurobindo and meditated for eight hours per day. He met Dick Price, whose journey of the consciousness had led him to be hospitalised in a psychiatric ward, and together they began Esalen on land owned by Murphy's grandmother in Big Sur. It had a hot spring and had been leased out as a resort for bohemians and gay men from San Francisco. Hunter Thompson was the security guard. Murphy found him there one day running around the grounds discharging automatic weapons. Price was interested in a form of gestalt psychotherapy that would allow the patient to make his journey in company and with protection, rather than being characterised as ill; Murphy was interested in transcendence, the divination of humanity that Sri Aurobindo had searched for. B.F. Skinner, Timothy Leary and Alan Watts came and spoke. Esalen pre-dated the counter-culture and was also exploratory rather than prescriptive, unlike many New Age cults that came later. 'The interior world is the last frontier,' Murphy told Jackie Krentzman in an interview for *Stanford* magazine. 'We know about exploring outer space, but the human race is not fully acquainted with the stupendous nature of this inner frontier. Where we are now in relation to the possibility for the advancement of human nature is analogous to where natural science was in the early seventeenth century.'

After lunch we walked up a hill towards his small apartment. At the door were photographs of Ben Hogan, Bobby Jones and Babe Ruth. Inside the floors were wooden and on the shelves were books by Hegel, Schopenhauer and Pythagoras. A little terrace looked out onto the glimmering bay. 'Upper-level monastic', he called his home. He told me about his encounters with Henry Miller and John Steinbeck, whom his grandfather, a doctor, had delivered. I read later that Steinbeck was supposed to have based the characters Aaron and Cal in *East of Eden* on Michael and his younger brother Dennis. We watched the US Open golf tournament, which was taking place that summer across the country at Shinnecock Hills on Long Island. It was a bad year for Tiger Woods, then in the midst of a swing reconstruction from which he would emerge late that autumn to renewed dominance. 'He set out on a quest with an impossible goal,' said Murphy. 'He's faltering now, but through the desert you have to go on the journey towards any mastery. It's like a Tolkien story.'

I walked back down the hill with two of his books – *The Kingdom of Shivas Irons*, a sequel to his first book, and *The Future of the Body*, a long work on the subject of human potential, on which he had spent seven and a half years. I had also read and been drawn to the work of Sri Aurobindo at around the same age as he had. I thought of going to Pondicherry, but didn't. Murphy had a life-transforming revelation beside a lake in California on the day after I was born. I carried *Golf in the Kingdom* around for years from house to house, country to country, talking about it with anyone whose interest in golf and books coincided, and have it still. When I was writing a book called *On Golf*, it was Murphy's book that guided me to the end. He appears in the last chapter as a guest at the dinner in Scotland that he himself had invented. A novel of mine, *Light*, had its genesis in a conference on physics that took place at the Esalen Institute, elaborated in a book called *The Dancing Wu Li Masters* by Gary Zukav. I wondered at these synchronicities, and wondered still more at the unaccountable elation I felt as I walked in the afternoon sun along the waterfront after I had left him, an elation so thorough it seemed to be taking place at the molecular level.

I called my daughter Aoife, whose twenty-third birthday it was, then drove back to the city.

Big Sur glowed green and copper in the morning light. The scale of the great surges of rock and earth that seemed to have been heaved up by the sea silences you, but the colour gives it delicacy. It looked innocent in this low-lying light with no one around. In a country of profit seekers and libertarians, Big Sur has been allowed to remain itself. The Monterey county council allows no advertising on Highway 1 and permission to build is almost impossible to get.

Big Sur became a place into which to flee, and then discover yourself. The New Carmelite Hermitage, a Catholic monastery, and a Buddhist centre called Tassajara were established here, as well as Esalen. The evangelist Aimee Semple McPherson, who preached to crowds of thirty thousand, vanished one day in mid-May 1926 from Ocean Park Beach in Los Angeles wearing her swimming costume and reappeared thirty-five days later in her street clothes at the edge of a Mexican desert claiming she'd been kidnapped, drugged, tortured and nearly sold into white slavery, but she'd been seen during this time in a Carmel hotel with Kenneth Ormiston, a married engineer at the radio station where she preached. Artists driven out of San Francisco by the 1906 earthquake also gathered in Carmel, where many remained for the rest of their lives. Jack London wrote about them in *The Valley of the Moon*. The poet Robinson Jeffers, with a scandal at his back, came to Big Sur with the wife of a Los Angeles lawyer and built Tor House and Hawk's Tower himself out of granite. He thought the grandeur and beauty of Big Sur so great that it 'cried out for tragedy' and wrote some himself in a manner that recalled the Greek dramas he'd first encountered as a prodigy. Elizabeth Smart waited at a bus stop for the English poet George Barker, whom she hadn't met, but was already in love with through reading his poems, and then went along the coast with him and his wife. 'The Pacific in blue spasms reaches all its superlatives,' she wrote in *By Grand Central Station I Sat Down and Wept*. After his journey of horror around America, recorded in *The Air-Conditioned Nightmare*, Henry Miller found refuge in Big Sur and stayed for nearly twenty years. Jack Kerouac, on the run from fame, delirium tremens and drunks vomiting in his house on Long Island, came to Lawrence Ferlinghetti's tiny cabin here in order to cure himself, without lasting success. He went down to the shoreline and tried to transfer to the page the sound of the surf arriving on the rocks. The Beats, in the American manner, had high ambitions for what could be done with language. William Burroughs thought that if he could get the right combination of sounds on the page he could, through a biochemical reaction among his readers, commit genocide.

Ohlone, Esselen and Salinan tribes of nomadic hunter-gatherers lived here, grinding acorns to make flour and collecting abalone and mussels from the sea. The Spanish passed first in 1542, but didn't land until two hundred years later, so hostile to life did the area seem. There was some limestone processing, gold mining and lumbering of redwoods, but all travel had to be done by sea as there were no roads. Few lived in this wilderness, and among those who did only two households in the 1920s had electricity. US Highway 1, the Big Sur section of which is thought by many to provide the world's most beautiful drive, was built with labourers from prisons and New Deal money. It opened in 1937. 'Before the convict workers put in the road,' wrote Elizabeth Smart, 'loneliness drove women to jump into the sea.'

I turned off Highway 1 below Carmel into Colorado Canyon. Here were redwoods, dappled light, the smells of pine and of the sea. Wooden houses lined the road under the deep shade of the trees, many with small American flags. One of the flags was made of flashing lights. The Manson Family lived here for a time. I stopped at a restaurant at Nepenthe, where a man in a broad hat and skirt was entertaining the elderly with folk songs, and then went down the road a short distance to the Henry Miller Memorial Library, a bookshop, music venue and shrine to the writer George Orwell called 'the only prose writer of the slightest value who has appeared among the English-speaking races for some years past . . . a sort of Whitman among the corpses'. Like the French with Rimbaud and Baudelaire, Americans form cults around writers who consume their lives in the pursuit of extremity – Miller, Kerouac, Charles Bukowski, Hunter Thompson. They seem to see in them a purity, even a saintliness.

I drove on through spectacles of grandeur until the landscape began to relent in its drama some time before the Hearst castle at San Simeon, its façade based on a sixteenth-century Spanish cathedral, its walls, ceilings and floors torn from European churches and palaces and its rooms filled with tapestries and other treasures. Americans had been engorging themselves on the art of Europe since the Gilded Age of the last quarter of the nineteenth century, none more so than J.P. Morgan, who began with a manuscript by Thackeray and went on to bronzes, jewellery, enamels, paintings and whole libraries. 'Today,' says Robert Hughes, 'you cannot study the Italian Renaissance without going to America.' Orson Welles parodied this in *Citizen Kane*, turning San Simeon into Xanadu. Welles and Rita Hayworth bought a house up the road at Nepenthe, but never spent a night in it.

On the radio there was a report about a woman named Judith Scruggs, a fifty-two-year-old divorcee from Connecticut. Her son Daniel had an IQ of 139, but had trouble reading and had become an habitual truant. When he went to school he wore mismatched clothes that smelled of urine. At twelve he weighed four and a half stone. Children abused him up and down the school hallways and beat him up in the yard. When the school put him into a special programme, he raised his rate of truancy. He was moving at increasing speed away from the rest of the world. In a single summer both his grandparents died. One morning after he had missed seventy-four of the previous seventy-eight school days he went into his closet and hanged himself with a necktie. His mother had two jobs and didn't find him until she got home in the evening.

Judith Scruggs launched a case against the city of Meriden, Connecticut for its school system's failure to protect her son from bullying. Four months later the police called her. She thought it had something to do with her case. Instead they counter-charged her with being responsible for the death of her son on the basis that she allowed him to keep knives in his room and that the house was a mess. The defence presented evidence of the chronic bullying and pointed out that he had died from hanging, not knives. The jury convicted. Four of the six jury members later said it was because of the knives. One said he had taken into account the case she was taking against the city.

After the trial, Wal-Mart fired her because of bad publicity from the case. She quit her job at a school to avoid being fired by them. She was evicted from the apartment she'd been in for a decade because she could no longer pay the rent. Her car was wrecked in a crash and, when she borrowed an unregistered one to get to her new night job at a Stop and Shop, the police arrested her.

Had the city of Meriden, Connecticut decided to brutalise one of the most hard-pressed of its citizens in order to ward off a case against itself? Was there anywhere the law demurred to go? It seemed at times like floodwater, cruel, remorseless, insinuating itself into every corner and crevice.

There are now a million lawyers in the United States, one for every 280 people. How had this happened? Could all of them make a living? What effect were they having? I asked three different legal historians, the first of them Robert Gordon, who had been a reporter in Rio de Janeiro and a public prosecutor in Massachusetts and was at the time I spoke with him on the faculty of the Yale Law School.

Why, I asked him, are there so many lawyers in the United States?

'There has been an explosion of law in all forms – legislation, regulation, litigation, legal transactions – and with it of lawyers and legal services. This has happened over a period of time and was provoked by specific developments in politics and the world of business. The number of lawyers relative to the population remained fairly stable until the New Deal. At this point the state began to tax, spend and regulate in a way that it hadn't before. It built dams and highways and other public works on a grand scale. It became the biggest buyer of goods and services. All of this required laws and regulation and, in consequence, lawyers. Previously the principal form of government income came from tariffs. Then with the Internal Revenue Act of 1939 there was a whole new branch of tax law. Each new regulation brought about a new branch of legal activity.

'Civil-rights legislation in the 1960s and social regulation to do with worker safety and the environment generated more legal activity as people used the courts to enforce these new laws, and law firms specialising in them began to appear. Public-interest groups, first from the left and later from the right, began to challenge the government, requiring it to engage more lawyers. The government had a few hundred lawyers in the 1930s, five thousand by 1940 and now around twenty thousand. Mass tort class-action suits exploded in the 1970s. There were cases against tobacco companies, property developers who'd used asbestos, doctors, pharmaceutical companies, the makers of Agent Orange and breast implants and all kinds of vehicle manufacturers and operators. Claims of this sort have numbered in the millions. There has undoubtedly been a rise in claims consciousness in the United States. Where before people might have regarded bad things that happened to them as accidents of fortune, now they want redress. Most societies would use government for this, but in its absence they turn to the law. Further on came globalisation and corporate mergers. Multinational deals require more lawyers because of different jurisdictions, different laws. There has been a large expansion in consequence at the top in the large law firms. In 1960 around seventy per cent of American lawyers operated alone or with one or two others. Now these little practices account for only around thirty per cent. Legal firms with over a thousand lawyers are not at all uncommon now. They can offer a wide range of specialised services to corporate clients, a kind of one-stop shopping place, like a supermarket. Due to all this growth, the number of lawyers relative to the population has doubled since the 1970s.'

He subsided into calm at the other side of the desk.

'You should speak to Lawrence Friedman,' he said. 'He's the most knowledgeable legal historian in the United States. He's at Stanford. You're going to California, aren't you? He has interesting things to say on how the legal system is perceived, and what is behind this perception.'

The day before I drove through Big Sur on the way to Los Angeles I stopped at Stanford University and went up to a small room heavy with books in the law school and met Lawrence Friedman, a scholarly and somewhat rabbinical figure already in semi-retirement. I asked him about the million lawyers and America's mania for litigation.

'Do you think society is so litigious? Why? Do you know many people who have initiated lawsuits? I don't. Who benefits from the impression that Americans are wantonly suing one another? Litigation often disturbs powerful interests. Businesses don't like to be sued because they haven't provided ramps for disabled people or if they've treated someone badly because of race or sex. Doctors or drug companies or vehicle manufacturers don't like to be sued if they make errors that harm people. The insurance companies have been in a prolonged war against lawyers, running campaigns to get legislators to limit recovery amounts or to put other restrictions on what lawyers can do. There has undoubtedly been an increase in rights consciousness. But is this necessarily a bad thing? Should we be discouraging this? Is it better to have a society where people are passive in the face of the transgression of their rights?'

In Chicago I spoke with John Heinz, who with two other academics produced a paper based generally on national legal trends and specifically on surveys of Chicago's law firms made in 1975 and 1995. In those years nationally the number of lawyers more than doubled, while the quantity of money spent on legal services more than tripled, a rate of increase twice that of the gross national product and exceeding even the rise in spending on health services. Most of this was due to corporate work. As for the pestilence of ambulance-chasing lawyers and their personal injury claims, the survey showed that in 1975 and 1995 personal injury claims accounted for six per cent of legal activity *in both years*. There had been no rise in proportion whatsoever. What had changed was public perception of the law. Part of this was due to advertising and public-relations campaigns about the 'litigation explosion' paid for by insurance companies and aimed specifically at creating pressure on legislators to institute tort reform

– that is, a limit to class-action suits and the amount that could be paid out in them. The widespread awareness of the case taken against McDonald's by the woman who spilled coffee on her lap, and the joke about the lawyers at the bottom of the sea and others like it, represented the triumph of this campaign. I had been among those thus conquered until I spoke with these legal historians.

'There are many people here who feel aggrieved by their experience of lawyers and the law,' Robert Gordon had told me. 'It's very expensive, beyond the reach of most. A competent lawyer costs between $200 and $800 per hour. There has never been much of a legal-aid system here, and what there was the conservatives have cut back. The talent in law is intensely concentrated at the top, and through the rest of the legal system there are many examples of poor service, malpractice and overcharging. The quality of trial lawyers is generally high, but those of state-level judges, where the majority of cases are heard, extremely low. Very often a judge-ship is a reward from a party machine. The law seems arbitrary to many people who've had direct experience of it. It's complicated, confusing, terrifying. And for each of the steps in the expansion of the law there's been a backlash. There was, and still is, a backlash against the New Deal, particularly its labour provisions. The backlash against the civil-rights legislation and social regulation acts of the 1960s and 1970s formed conservatism as it is now known – libertarian, anti-tax, anti-regulation, financed by business, but with popular support because people believe that their taxes go to the undeserving. Airlines, telecommunications, trucking, power and banking have been deregulated on the wave of this back-lash. Many of these services have become more dangerous and more expensive as a result. Savings and loan institutions were deregulated and then collapsed. This cost the taxpayers nearly a trillion dollars.

'But of all the forms of authority – charismatic, trad-itional and rational-legal – it is the last of these that seems now to be in the ascendant. Law, in the form of bureaucratic, court-enforced rules, seems to be a growing form of governance. It's full of errors and frustrations and the incomprehensible, and it's very expensive, but it offers the only possible solution for many problems.'

After I left Standford I went by Silicon Valley, the capital of America's high-technology industry, then got onto 101 once again until I turned off north of Salinas. I passed broccoli, cabbage, carrot, spinach, watermelon, strawberry and above all lettuce fields. General John C. Frémont planted a California flag with a bear on it to antagonise the authorities when this was still Mexican territory. John Steinbeck found old cannon-balls and bayonets from the Mexican wars when he was a child here. He climbed Fremont's Peak during the journey he made for his book *Travels with Charley* and looked down on Mount Toro, Salinas, Monterey Bay and the farm where he grew up and realised he could never come home again. 'I felt and smelled and heard the wind blow up from the long valley. It smelled of the brown hills of wild oats,' he wrote.

Seventeen Mile Drive on Monterey peninsula passes several of America's finest golf courses, including Cypress Point, Pebble Beach and Spyglass Hill, and is the main route around the largest gated community I have ever seen. You have to pay a toll to enter it. I had an appointment to play Spyglass Hill, named in honour of Robert Louis Stevenson, who walked this coast and foresaw that Mexican influence here would be despatched by 'the millionaire vulgarians of the Big Bonanza'. He was speaking of the Gold Rush, of which Thoreau had written, 'The gold of California is a touch-stone which has betrayed the rottenness, the baseness, of mankind. Satan from one of his elevations showed mankind the kingdom of California, and they entered into a compact with him at once . . . The hog that *roots* his own living, and so makes manure, would be ashamed of such company.'

When I got to the first tee the starter asked me if I'd like to play with two 'employees'. One was a big man in his forties lounging in a buggy and the other was a woman who was a chef in one of the hotels. She was just about to hit.

'I see this is a Robert Trent Jones, Sr course,' I said to the man. 'I've just played one of those.'

'Oh yeah? Which one?'

'Oakland Hills.'

'I know it,' he said. 'I played in the US Amateur there.'

I looked out at the fairway and there in the centre, around 315 yards from the tee, was a tiny white speck, his ball. Golf is an unremitting lesson in humility. Why hadn't I learned it?

He was a single libertine from Kentucky who dealt in private planes and flew around the country playing in amateur golf tournaments. He was thinking of turning pro when he was fifty in order to play the seniors' tour. 'I can handle most of those guys,' he said. The next day I saw him in his convertible red sports car in Big Sur when we both stopped for gas in the same place. He loved Big Sur, he'd said when we were playing golf.

'If I could have anything at all in the world right now, I'd take a house made of wood in Big Sur, a bottle of Margaux, an open fire . . .'

'. . . and a hooker,' said the little lady chef.

'How did you know?' he asked.

American states generally derive their names from prominent men, European cities and Indian names for natural phenomena. California is different. It was named after an imaginary island in a sixteenth-century Spanish novel. The novel is *The Exploits of Esplandia* by Garcia Ordóñez de Montalvo and it describes a paradise overseen by Queen Califia and called California, which was inhabited by griffins and athletic black women and whose only metal was gold. Since then California has been an El Dorado, the Promised Land, Dream Factory and Land of Eternal Youth. Like all Edenic places, it is thought of as a haven of imperturbability where all time is ceaselessly the present. Its state flower is the California poppy, a mild opiate when smoked, and its motto is 'Eureka!'

No other state functions this way in the minds of Americans, the mythic and the illusory crowding out the facts. Los Angeles, its major city, is the epitome of this. 'Los Angeles did not just happen or arise like so many other American cities out of existing circumstances – a harbour, a river, a railroad terminus,' wrote the historian Kevin Starr. 'Indeed, for a long time it had none of these. Los Angeles envisioned itself, then externalized that vision through sheer force of will, springing from a Platonic conception of itself, the Great Gatsby of American cities.'

Seafaring Tongva and Chumash Indians lived here for thousands of years, fashioning their boats from planks of wood and caulking and coating them with pine pitch or tar that washed up from underwater oil leaks. Mexicans turned it into a ranch, and later both oil and aeronautics industries flourished here, but it was property developers who were behind the expansion of the city. They sold the idea of all-white planned communities with palm trees, verdant lawns, bungalows, two-car garages and modern appliances, expanding to a thousand square miles, linked by freeways and enjoying a perpetual summer. Los Angeles is a confection imposed on a desert, predicated upon the necessity to be what it is not. When Thomas Mann came here he was suspicious of the violet and grape colours of the flowers, which he thought looked like they were made of paper.

Henry Miller wrote of it: 'Los Angeles gives one the feeling of the future more strongly than any city I know of. A bad future, too ... Eurythmic dancing, ball room dancing, tap dancing, artistic photography, ordinary photography, lousy photography, electro-fever treatment, internal douche treatment, ultra-violet ray treatment, elocution lessons, psychic readings, institutes of religion, astrological demonstrations, hands read, feet manicured, elbows massaged, faces lifted, warts removed, fat reduced, insteps raised, corsets fitted, busts vibrated, corns removed, hair dyed, glasses fitted, soda jerked, hangovers cured, headaches driven away, flatulence dissipated, business improved, limousines rented, the future made clear . . . From the car window it's like a strip teaser doing the St Vitus dance – a corny one.' Another New Yorker, Neil Simon, expressed it differently. 'In New York, when it's one hundred degrees, in Los Angeles it's seventy-two. When it's twelve degrees in New York, it's seventy-two in Los Angeles. There are six million interesting people in New York; in Los Angeles, seventy-two.'

The illusion is contingent upon getting water to twenty million people living in a desert that has sufficient supplies for only around one per cent of that amount. Between 1905 and 1913, a former miner and ditch digger from Belfast named William Mulholland oversaw the construction of a 233-mile aqueduct involving two thousand workers, 164 tunnels and coercion and bribery that drained Owens Lake in the centre of the state in fifteen years and began to turn the Owens Valley, known as 'the Switzerland of California', into a desert. In 1928 Mulholland's St Francis Dam collapsed and sent a ten-storey wall of water down the Santa Clara riverbed to the sea at Ventura, leaving around 450 dead, including forty-two schoolchildren. Los Angeles has since taken water from reservoirs, underground sources and the Colorado River, but long-term drought and expansion have resulted in severe water restrictions in this city where thirty-five per cent of the water supply is used for landscaping. Los Angeles too could become a Petra, or a city one one-hundredth its current size, where the oleanders seen by Thomas Mann will bloom no more.

In the early evening after coming in from Big Sur I entered the Los Angeles freeway system, average speed, according to the LA 2000 report, seventeen miles per hour. A friend of mine who lives in Valencia told me that he was once on a Los Angeles freeway that had two lanes reserved for the forthcoming exit, two for the exit that followed and around six lanes for traffic continuing straight ahead, and not a single car was moving in any one of them. There are people in Los Angeles who commute by air on scheduled flights from one part of the city to another.

I had been in Los Angeles twice before, but hadn't entirely felt as though I had. 'There's no "there" there,' it has been famously said. The first time I stayed in Century City, a pristine arrangement of office blocks, apartment complexes and hotels where no one was visible on the streets. Walking there, I felt like a misplaced figure on an architect's model. I got to a mall. The shoppers looked like extras. All was virtual. In my room one afternoon I turned on the television and watched a promotional programme for the hotel that was on a loop. On it, among the stars, was Richard Nixon. He said, 'The celebratory dinner for the astronauts who made the moon landing took place in the Century City Plaza. I still hear from statesmen from all over the world how wonderful it was. The president and the first lady were there, of course, and that made it special. And then there were the astronauts. But what made it most special of all was the graciousness and efficiency of the hotel staff.' Then that slightly twisted smile, as if the muscles around the mouth were not in harmony.

The second time was for a reading I was to do at a bookshop. It was Oscars night, and one person showed up. That was Barbara Williams, an actress and singer I had met a few years earlier in Belfast with her husband, the political activist Tom Hayden. We left the bookshop, with me never having opened my book, and went to their house, where she consulted me about the dress she was to wear that night to the Vanity Fair party while we waited for her husband.

I first saw Tom Hayden when he spoke at my university during a Disorientation Week for new students organised by radicals. He was on trial in Chicago on conspiracy charges connected with the demonstrations at the 1968 Democratic Convention. I saw him again later that autumn in a park, his face lit up by a bonfire as he addressed a squad of around twenty young men and women standing in ranks approximately at attention, wearing motorcycle helmets and carrying what looked like spears. This was during the 'Days of Rage', when a crowd of around six hundred intent on 'bringing the war home' stormed through the city breaking the windows of cars and buildings.

Tom Hayden wrote the Port Huron statement in 1962, a manifesto on civil rights and participatory democracy that became a – or perhaps the – central document of political protest of that decade. Since then he has involved himself in poverty, environmental, employment, anti-war and race issues, among many others. In 1972 he went to Vietnam with Jane Fonda, whom he married. When the war ended he felt that organising a political movement outside the party political system was impossible and became a California state senator as a Democrat.

I phoned ahead from Valencia to ask if I could see them and they invited me to stay in their house in Brentwood. We went out that night to Santa Monica and Venice. At one point we were in the bar of a $1,300-per-night hotel on the beach, with softly gleaming wooden floors and waiters in blue suits who looked like models in a grooming magazine. 'This is all for free,' said Tom. 'People who stay in places like this deduct the cost of hotels, planes, cars, clothes, meals, maybe even their therapists and their golf-club memberships – everything that keeps this lifestyle afloat – from their taxes. They're here compliments of the taxpayer. I could do it myself if I was at a certain income level and was so inclined.'

I tried to keep the night going, but it was difficult to find a place with any life in it. Simone de Beauvoir had the same problem. 'At midnight when the bars close,' she wrote, 'Hollywood seems like a Puritan village, not a huge, noisy, glamorous city.' There are drinkers, but there exists a powerful ethic against the practice. A friend of mine from Dublin spent some time with a Hollywood actress who drank carrot juice and attended a gym twice daily and thought the average Irish drinking of my friend so apocalyptic that she begged him to see a therapist. The Puritanism extends into other areas. David Reiff, author of *Los Angeles: Capital of the Third World*, said that his fellow New Yorkers who had spent time in Los Angeles tended to view it as 'a smog-smeared, lobotomized universe of fast food, endless car trips and airheads of both genders and every known sexual orientation, most especially, I was told, chastity'.

The next morning I met Alex Sanchez, a thirty-three-year-old member of the Mara Salvatrucha Stoners street gang and co-founder of the Los Angeles branch of the Homies Unidos community action group, on the upper floor of an office building on Olympic Boulevard in Koreatown, which was barely hanging on to the underside of seriousness. Tom Hayden, who had been working with and writing about Los Angeles gangs for fifteen years, knew him and suggested I meet him.

I had driven through Brentwood, Beverly Hills and Wilshire, past teams of Latin American gardeners leaping from pickup trucks to cut lawns and prune flowers, child minders with pushchairs and uniformed maids polishing door knockers, into a region where many of these maintainers of the Los Angeles New Eden lived, sharing rooms, raising families, shopping at discount stores, attending churches, getting high and dodging the immigration police. They are in the main unseen and unrecorded, yet a great deal of noise is raised about them – about their illegal immigration status and their involvement in gangs. Rhetoric about the latter increases police budgets and leads to the building of more jails. Rhetoric about the former resonates with a public made to feel it is under siege, though generally little is done to mass-deport those who are in the United States illegally. Who would cut the grass or clean the floors? Who would work for a minimum wage in a non-organised, low-technology industry? Edward Soja, a professor of urban planning at UCLA, described Los Angeles' passage through an economic cycle during which unionised heavy industries closed one after the other and were replaced by high-technology industries with highly skilled and highly paid workers and also low-technology factories where immigrants work for low pay. It has been in the interest of politicians to appear to be tough on immigration, and in the interest of business and middle-class and above home owners that little is done to implement an anti-immigration policy.

The Bracero Program, established in 1942 through an agreement between the Mexican and United States governments, was meant to permit the immigration to Stockton, California of a few thousand Mexican agricultural workers to assist in the sugar-beet harvest at a time when many Americans were away at war. It was ended in 1964, by which time there had been four and a half million border crossings from Mexico into the United States, changing for ever the demographics of the two countries and the expectations of their citizens with regard to the labour market. A new initiative by the Republican Congress in 2000, called the Agricultural Opportunities Act, again invited Latin American workers north to work across the range of American agricultural, industrial and service sectors, thereby creating a buyer's market among employees, depressing wages and enfeebling unions. The new guest workers would have to return to their home countries each year to apply for re-entry and would not be considered for citizenship. They would effectively be serfs.

Alex Sanchez was born in San Salvador and grew up in a time of civil war when up to forty per cent of the population was driven from the land and squads of killers connected to the military were executing a thousand people per month. Salvadoreans fled north in vast numbers. Between 1980 and 1984 their population in the United States quadrupled. The largest amount were in the Pico-Union area of Los Angeles. Alex's parents went first, when he was three, then he and his brother followed five years later, having been left until then in the care of neighbours.

'I was scared when I came here,' he said. 'We travelled by train, bus and then in a van over the border with people I didn't know. The first white person I ever saw was an immigration officer. When I met my parents I didn't know who they were. I had photographs, but they didn't look like that any more. We drove to Koreatown, where they lived, down Olympic Boulevard, this long straight road without any bumps. Everything looked different.

'I went to Hobart Annexe Elementary School, then got sent out to the Valley. I didn't speak a word of English, and the Spanish I heard wasn't like the Spanish I spoke. Especially the swearing. We were shifted around, never made any good friends. My father had two jobs, glass-blowing and delivering the *LA Times*, and a lot of the time he was out. He was into the party scene. My mother had become a Jehovah's Witness. She was trying to push that on me all the time. I got my first taste of violence when I was in the fourth grade, and what I learned was that violence could help me. I was playing with a paper aeroplane and this Mexican kid, the biggest bully in the school, got hold of it, crushed it in his hand right in front of me and threw it in my face. I knocked his tooth out. There was blood all over the place. I got a reputation from that.

'By the time I was in sixth grade I was hanging around with rough kids, isolated kids like me. They had tattoos. We used to drink their parents' alcohol. Some of their parents were active in gangs themselves. This was a shelter for me because I didn't have any connection with anywhere else – school, the community, home. Finally I chose the streets. I lived in abandoned buildings and on rooftops with a little group of seven runaways, all of us looking after each other. We stole from supermarkets to get food.

'I got into *la vida loca*, a life lived at the speed of light-ning, a life with no meaning, no sense of consequences, free from religion, free from people telling me what to do. We were stoners, into heavy metal. I loved Metallica. I was initi-ated into the Mara Salvatrucha Stoners in a ceremony that involved a thirteen-second beating and went further into violence, drugs and alcohol. It was the first time in my life I felt like I belonged somewhere.

'The violence stepped up in 1985 when a friend of mine named Rocky was killed by a gun when he was coming out of school. Before that, the worst of the fighting was with chains or knives. Now we looked for the biggest guns we could find. I became more violent. I went looking for enemies. I got arrested for things like car theft and possession of weapons and went to prison three times. I got shot in both legs after leaving jail one time. That didn't stop me. It made me proud that I'd been in a war, that I had my stripes. I went deeper into violence, deeper into drugs. There were over one hundred killed in a war between us and the 18th Street gang. I got depressed. I tried to commit suicide once. Finally I got deported.'

He was one of four thousand Salvadoreans deported from the United States between 1993 and 1997. By the late 1990s forty thousand were being sent back each year to Mexico and Central America. Many had nowhere to live, no chance of employment, no family. They re-formed their gangs, with their sign language and their tattoos, in their own countries, committed crimes for survival and profit and perhaps, above all, out of habit, and were preyed upon by squads of vigilantes with names like Death Shadow, who executed them with the approval of the public. Tom Hayden called it 'globalising the gang culture'.

In El Salvador, Alex thought about his life. He was tired of going to jail, tired of being chased by the police, tired of *la vida loca*. After all the slaughter between MS and 18th Street in the early 1990s he'd taken fifteen members of his gang to a meeting in Los Angeles with one thousand Mexicans, where a truce was worked out. This was the way forward, he believed. His parents were getting old and he realised he'd never had any kind of relationship with either of them. He'd become father to a boy, who was living with his mother in Los Angeles. He wanted to watch him grow, be a father to him in a way that his own father hadn't been to him. Gang members often meticulously plan their own funerals and have a desperation to have children because they believe they will die young and want somehow to be remembered. Alex's child made him want to live. He crossed the border surreptitiously at Brownsville, Texas in 1995 and disappeared into Los Angeles, getting a job in a sweatshop and looking after his son.

In El Salvador, Homies Unidos, a self-help organisation that had been brought into being by deportees, had conducted a survey of gang members there that showed that while the vast majority could read and write, most were no longer in school, did not work and did not live with their families. The majority had been hospitalised and had someone close to them killed. They had got into gangs primarily because of family problems and the sense of community that the gangs provided. Homies Unidos petitioned the American government to give visas to gang members trying to broker truces and giving advice about jobs and education, and requested that deportees be given access to Homies Unidos representatives and that small loans be provided to ex-deportees to start businesses.

Alex emerged from his underground life to help set up a Homies Unidos office in Los Angeles and immediately drew the attention of the police, who declared that Homies Unidos was just a front for the gangs. They picked him up various times, drove him in a squad car through a rival gang area to give the impression that he was a police stooge and raided a surprise birthday party he had organised for a woman who had just come off drugs and been cured. Special unit CRASH officers attended a Homies Unidos meeting in a church and afterwards pushed gang members up against the walls and threatened them. An immigration officer named Hung Nguyen identified Alex as having been deported and, on the strength of this, he was arrested by a CRASH officer named Jesus Amezcua, who told Alex that he was going to take everyone in Homies Unidos down 'one by one'.

In detention, Alex became the focal point of a battle between the immigration service and the police on one hand and activists and the nascent Homies Unidos on the other. Tom Hayden was among those organising Alex's defence. During protests at the 2000 Democratic National Convention marchers carried a huge puppet with Alex's face on it and 'Free Alex' placards to the Rampart police station in Pico-Union. At a hearing involving clergymen, the police chief of San Salvador and three anthropologists, Alex was granted political asylum and freed.

'When there is a truce between two countries,' he said, 'what do you do? You bring assistance – resources, funds, materials – to keep that peace and develop it. A great opportunity was lost in this part of Los Angeles after the 1993 truce between the gangs. The police looked at us and said, "Once a gang member, always a gang member," and the politicians just talked about extending the anti-gang laws. Proposition 21 was brought in so that fourteen-year-olds could be convicted like adults. A sixteen-year-old could go to a maximum-security prison. When they're released, they're put into a halfway house with a bunch of addicts. They might have gone in for drug offences, and the first thing they see in the facility is someone smoking crack. How is he going to function? How is he going to get away from that life?

'Prisons are a business and there's a lot of money to be made from them. Since they've been privatised the idea has been, "the more prisoners, the more profit". The corporations who run them want kids in there. The younger they start, the longer they'll be in there. They finance politicians, who then step up the laws, like this three-strikes law which says that if you're convicted of a third felony, you can be put away for twenty-five years to life. In the last twenty-five years there have been twenty-one prisons built in California and one university. You've got some correctional officers making $150,000 per year with their overtime. Teachers can make less than a quarter of that. They took the Black Panthers down fast, but not the gangs. They want them there. They're not a threat because they're just killing each other, and they keep the flow going into the prisons. If the gangs started organising, of course, they'd come down on them like they did on Saddam Hussein. That's why they didn't like the truce and why they don't like Homies Unidos.

'Why should a kid stand on a street corner with a beer bottle in his hand knowing that the cops are going to mess with him because of the way he acts or dresses, or that someone from another neighbourhood is going to come along and shoot him? Why choose that over an education? Why choose to go to jail instead of being at home and being loved by your parents? Why choose death over life? The reason is that there's nothing out there for us. The parents aren't around. They're working extra jobs because no one wants to pay them a living wage. The kid goes out into the street or the alley and there's people sitting in the corner taking drugs. What is there for him? He goes to school and sees the teacher doesn't care about him. She tells him to shut up, sit down, go to sleep if he wants. The school is a battlefield. Instead of learning, he's got to prepare himself to go to war. The only politician who ever stuck up for kids like that was Tom Hayden and they attacked him for being soft on crime. After that he lost the election. Why should that kid care? Why should he give a damn about tomorrow or what his parents or society thinks of him? If they don't give a damn about him, why should he give a damn about them? That's the attitude. Everywhere he looks he sees people against him – all except the people in his gang. He knows they accept him for who he is. He knows they'll go all the way for him if he's in trouble. I never see the police coming into the neighbourhood trying to get to know anybody. They just want to arrest or beat or handcuff somebody, or keep him in a car for an hour dehumanising him in front of his neighbours. They look at youth as a plague, the enemy, instead of thinking, "How can we help him get out of this life he's in?"

'That's the life I lived. My parents weren't around. I preferred to go to prison than to school because I got more respect that way. I was competing with my home boy to see who would get to prison first. He made it by a week. When I saw him at a reception centre I said, "You beat me, man." I've got two children now and I just have to feel my way

through it. No one ever taught me how to do it. My dad never hugged or kissed me or told me he loved me. I had to apologise to my kids one day. I said, "I'm sorry, I don't know how to be a dad. But I love you and I'm trying."

'I'm still in my gang. I'm in constant contact with them. They look at me differently now. I'm not the one who tells them how to gangbang or how to make money. I'm the one who helps them get a job, a chance, a start. They got confused at first. When I was in prison they'd say, "Look at the home boy, man, I hope he beats his case." They'd see me in the neighbourhood not doing this negative stuff any more, but instead coming out and being positive, and they'd say, "Why is he doing that?" And someone might say, "Just let him do it. He's playing them." But they know that I'm with them like before, that I'm not two-faced. I don't tell them to leave the gang. That's something personal. The gang is what created the support system they have lived by, that gave them a sense of belonging and friendship. People have been shot to defend it. That's not something you can take away from somebody by saying, "Now you've got to leave that family you created." Instead I say, "You're getting old, man. What about your kids? *La vida loca* is temporary. You don't have to live in the violence, you don't have to do drugs all the time to make you feel better. We can give you the tools." Our biggest enemy is the way we downplay ourselves, the way we accept the stereotype the society puts on us. We think, "We can't be good." When these guys show up here, we look at that. We start talking. They relate to me because I've been there. They see me and they say, "If he did it, I can do it too."'

Tom and Barbara's house is entered from a suburban street and backs onto a wilderness, the terrace overlooking a slope of Mandeville Canyon in the Santa Monica Mountains. The light through the trees splattered the terrace with flitting beads of gold. On the canyon slopes in these mountains are chaparral and sage brush and further down are live oak, willows, sycamore and California bay laurel. The fire-resistant and acorn-producing live oak, used by the Chumash Indians for bow-making, dye, fuel, medicine, food and shelter, has been losing out to the blue-gum eucalyptus, imported from Australia in the nineteenth century and so explosively combustible that firefighters call them 'gasoline trees'. Eighteen species of snakes, including the Pacific rattlesnake, and eight species of lizards live here. Birds include the American goldfinch, dark-eyed junco, mourning dove, crow, oak titmouse, Nuttall's woodpecker, cedar waxwing, bushtit, ruby-crowned kinglet, hooded oriole, Nashville and calliope hummingbirds, Canadian goose, green parrot, various hawks and owls, the peregrine falcon and the golden eagle. The names, as with fish, are wonders. 'Calliope hummingbird' could have been invented by Whitman. There are mule deer, bobcats, a few mountain lions and many coyote. Simone de Beauvoir stayed near here with a French friend who raised ducks in her back yard until a coyote climbed up the canyon wall and ate them. 'One feels that the most sophisticated city in the world is surrounded by indomitable nature,' she wrote. 'If human pressure were relaxed for even a moment, the wild animals and the giant grasses would soon reclaim possession of their domain.'

I sat out on this terrace in the rich light and birdsong of my last day in Los Angeles. It smelled like Andalusia and had in the air that dreamy comfortableness that draws people to the Mediterranean coast. Barbara came out and began talking about her life on Vancouver Island, where she had been born to an Indian logger father who pretended to be white and a blonde-haired, blue-eyed mother who ran away from a foster home where she'd been abused. She was in the foster home because her mother had killed herself. Barbara's father was often away at logging camps and her mother was often pregnant. One night in the middle of winter she took her fifth and final child from the house, saying she was going to the hospital, and didn't return for a year and a half. 'I couldn't handle it any more,' she later said. The children fended for themselves, their father came and went and when Barbara was old enough, she made her way to Vancouver for theatre school, then to Toronto and finally to Los Angeles. She was cast in the lead of a film shortly after arriving, but was then effectively blacklisted after she sued the film's producer, Don Simpson, devotee of plastic surgery, sadomasochism and enough drugs to cost him $60,000 per month, for making her work uncontracted hours and for using a body double without her consent. The pay is good in Hollywood, but the price would seem to be obedience. 'The paternalist is a sentimentalist at heart,' wrote Christopher Isherwood in 1947, when he was in Hollywood writing scripts, 'and the sentimentalist is always potentially cruel. When the studio operatives ceased to rely upon their bosses' benevolence and organised themselves into unions, the tycoon became an injured papa, hurt and enraged by their ingratitude.'

Barbara went into the house and came back with a picture of her father, looking spectacularly handsome, which a photograph can convey, and imposingly tall, which it cannot.

'He had no barriers,' she said. 'He went wherever he wanted to go and had no sense of owning anything. He gave away Tom's ties to people in bars. He lived in a truck for a while. He'd get up with the dawn and drive. I was behind him one time and saw a box I recognised with clothes we had given him, blowing along the freeway. These were Indian characteristics, but the sadness in our family had a lot to do with him not embracing who he was. Instead he hid it.'

'Did you stay in contact with him after you left home?' I asked her.

'I'd been so far from all of them for years, but then I went on a long odyssey with Tom to find them. Also to find out what it meant to have an Indian for a father. I hadn't any idea about that. My father was sick. He was told he had terminal cancer.

'We met Charlotte Black Elk on that journey. She was a lawyer, a mother, a thinker, and a Republican Catholic – Republican, she said, because Nixon had allocated more funds to the Indians than other presidents. She was formidable. She could remember everything she ever heard. She asked my father if he wanted to attend a Sundance, but as he was too sick to go, she then invited me. It was at Devil's Tower in Wyoming. We were driven through lightning across a field with wild horses in it. We were going to get a tall pine tree for the ceremony. A knife from the fifteenth century was symbolically used. Everybody stood around to catch it when they were chopping it down, to prevent it from hitting the ground. They drove it in a flatbed truck to Devil's Tower and then I went to sleep in a tepee with Charlotte. The feeling looking up at the sky through the top of the tepee was like looking through the window to the heavens in the dome of the Pantheon in Rome. When I was at the airport in Los Angeles I saw that O.J. Simpson was being chased in a car, and I ran out that night from the tepee to a gas station to see what had happened to him. I was still in that other world. Then in the morning the Sundance started.'

'Do you remember it?'

'I would never forget that.'

'Can you describe it?'

'I think so. It happened on this field of flattened grass. There were twelve dancers and thirty observers. The tree we'd brought was put in a hole in the ground and every-body attached ribbons to it for their wishes. There were red ribbons for the east, which meant new beginnings, and yellow ribbons for the earth. I was there for my father and my wishes were for him. They started a fire to cook buffalo meat. The dancers would eat nothing for the whole four days. They only swish their mouths with a herbal concoction. The food was for the observers. There were elders and children sitting around. There were drums and chanting. The dancers moved clockwise in a circle around the tree. After a round, one of them pierced the flesh of his back with a shard of buffalo bone which has six buffalo skulls attached to it. If the flesh doesn't tear, the children sit on the skulls. All the dancers did this once. Then a pipe of sweetgrass was passed. The observers had a meal at the end of each day and went into sweat lodges, which are low tents over a pit. Heated rocks were put into the pit and covered with water. On the fourth day shards were placed in the dancers' chests attached by lines to the tree. They leaned back, suspending themselves until the flesh tore. Observers could also give a flesh offering. I did eight – one for everyone in my family plus Tom. You wrap the flesh in a cloth and place it by the tree, then the wound is covered with sage leaves, which are both analgesic and antiseptic. I never felt any pain. I was right into what was happening all the time. When it was over we drove to the airport. I cried when we flew over Devil's Tower. I'd cried in the sweat lodge as well.

'After I got back, my father went to Tom's doctor. There

was no sign of the cancer. He lived another four years, the final eight months on a boat I bought him. He invited over a friend of his from Brixton in London, a postman named Red. Finally he said, "Time to catch the boxcar." I was with him for the last six hours. He was seventy-one.'

I put my bags in the car and drove out the Pacific Highway to Malibu, the homes of billionaires to the right and left. The rich arrived early here, or at least one did – Fred H. Ridge from Massachusetts, who bought a 16,350-acre ranch in 1892 in the hope of creating a new Riviera. He died in 1905, leaving the estate to his wife Mary and their three children. Mary fought developers, railway companies and the state for thirty years in an effort to keep the property in the pristine state in which she had inherited it. According to the Federal Writers' Project, 'She hired armed, mounted guards to patrol her boundaries, built high wire fences with barred and chained gates, plowed county-built highways under, turned droves of hogs upon cuts for new roads or planted them with alfalfa; and during 1915–17, when her gates were systematically

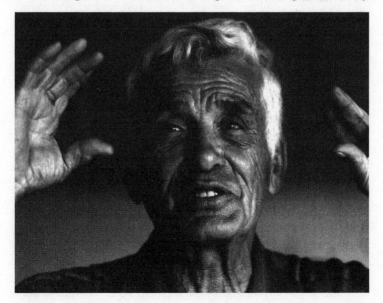

smashed and her guards overpowered every week by crowds of farmers and travellers trying to get through to Santa Monica, she dynamited her roads.' Her son sued her to stop her from continuing to diminish the estate by $1 million per year. In the end it was handed to a trustee, who sold off its beach front in lots. Had she won, Malibu might have had something of the feel of Big Sur. As it is, the feel is of great wealth and carefully managed comfort.

From Point Dune I turned east for the first time in my journey. My nights in Brentwood were to be my last in a home until Alabama. I crossed Los Angeles and entered a desert that stretches nearly halfway across America.

The Southwest

Around a quarter of a million people were blown out of the Dust Bowl in the 1930s and came west to California. 'Crazy world these days,' Woody Guthrie was told by a woman in Arizona who gave him a meal. 'Everybody's cutting loose and hitting the road.' Most of them came on Route 66, 'the main migrant road' John Steinbeck called it, among other things, in *The Grapes of Wrath* – 'the long concrete path across the country, waving gently up and down the map, from the Mississippi to Bakersfield – over the red lands and the gray lands, twisting up into the mountains, crossing the Divide and down into the bright and terrible desert . . .'

Route 66 starts at Buckingham Fountain in downtown Chicago and finishes in Santa Monica, just short of the ocean. The Dust Bowl agricultural migrants came west on it, then those looking for work in the Los Angeles weapons and plane factories and finally tourists, for whom were spawned America's original fast-food drive-ins, motels in the shape of tepees and reptile farms in gas stations. The champion of its construction in the 1920s was Cyrus Avery from Oklahoma, who gave it its number, thinking it had a symmetrical and melodious ring and would be easy to remember. 'Get your kicks on Route 66,' wrote jazzman Bobby Troup at the suggestion of his wife in 1946, having driven to Los Angeles on it with her. Nat King Cole, Chuck Berry and Van Morrison later sang his song.

Steinbeck wrote biblically about Route 66 – 'the path of a people in flight, refugees from dust and shrinking land . . . from the desert's slow northward invasion, from the twisting winds that howl up out of Texas, from the floods that bring no richness . . . 66 is the mother road, the road of flight.' With this at their backs, the Joad family entered the desert, 'where the distance shimmers'. 'At last,' he writes, 'there's Barstow.'

I arrived at Barstow from the west in the early evening. Henry Miller passed through on a hot day and wrote, 'It was sizzling outdoors. The street was just a fried banana flaming with rum and creosote.' I checked into the Route 66 Motel, which had its own transport museum in the parking lot and office – cars ranging in age and status from a Model T up to a yellow Cadillac Sedan DeVille, with gas pumps, bicycles, stop signs, licence plates, motorcycles, wagon wheels and railway memorabilia parked, stacked up or hanging from walls.

Barstow, an old gas and railroad stop, is on the list of the ten poorest cities in California. Forty per cent of its population is on welfare. Houses in the dust seemed to be breaking down in the heat. Casinos, I read, were planned. Nearby are two Marine bases. I went out to Ruby's nightclub and watched men and women in cowboy hats doing line dancing. Most, I gathered from the conversations I heard, were in the military. I was within the borders of California, but appeared already to have arrived in Texas. A tiny disc jockey with no teeth put on country records and then hopped down from

his station onto the floor to dance. I don't think he missed a single one in the time I was there. The men were more flamboyant as they danced, the women more rhythmical. Around one-third were black. Racial integration is perhaps more advanced and more solidly grounded in the military than anywhere else in America. The Marines in particular have a colour-blind loyalty among them more intense than that of a religious congregation. 'If I meet a group of Marines anywhere in the world, they're already my friends,' a black ex-Marine in Valencia told me. 'It's instantaneous, and it never fails. They're my people in a way that no one else can ever be.'

My room at the Route 66 Motel was in its own concrete cube built in the manner of an old adobe house, vintage cars parked to either side and a Route 66 sign hung on the back wall above one of the cars. Inside was a circular bed.

I went into the office to pay my bill in the morning. There was the smell of dal and chilli peppers drifting in from the kitchen of Miss Mridu Shandil, the owner, a tiny woman in a straw hat who had emigrated to Barstow from India. Amid the junk-stall detail on the walls of licence plates and old 45 rpm records were photographs of the town from 1910. 'Barstow is beautiful!' Miss Shandil said. She told me that an Elvis impersonator had come into town one day, and the club where he was performing booked him into the town's Day's Inn, a large and impersonal franchise hotel.

'That wasn't the place for him,' she said. 'He was sad there. He used to come by to look at the old cars, so I gave him a free room. Then he was happy. People like my place. It's more funky.'

I drove out into increasing desiccation and fierce heat. Daggett, Yarmo, the Twenty-Nine Palms Marine Corps Air Ground Combat Center, Bagdad, Amboy. A deserted house sat out on the desert floor like ash that had fallen from a cigarette. Further on, a broken shack with rust-pitted frames of trucks and cars sinking into the sand had a hand-painted 'For Sale' sign hanging from a fence post.

I turned north into the Mojave National Preserve, with its

vast dunes of aeolian, or wind-blown sand. The sand sings in a low-frequency hum if you slide down it. I stopped at Kelso, a ghost town named for a railway worker who won a contest with that honour as its prize. During the Second World War there was an iron mine, a railway station built in the 1920s in a Spanish style and a population of two thousand people. Iron was brought in from the desert mines to Kelso to be shipped by rail to the Kaiser Corporation's Pacific mill, where they had reduced the time needed to construct Liberty ships from 244 days to just forty-six. Now there is no one in Kelso. It's cold here in the winter and rains then can create spectacular displays of aster, blazing star, mariposa lily and primrose on the desert floor, but when I got out of the car, the force of the heat nearly dropped me to my knees. I walked around looking at the abandoned houses, roofless and with gaps between the planks like the ribcages of dead animals. Pitted and blistered coffee and soup cans eroded to the fineness of paper lay in little drifts of sand. Such places have a quiet allure, suggestive of the life that was lived in them, but leaving them mysterious. I drove on past sagebrush, creosote and Joshua trees, named by the Mormons, who were reminded by them of Joshua petitioning God with hands upraised to the sky. Creosote can be dangerous – it is thought to have caused cancer of the scrotum in chimney-sweeps – but Indians, and others since, have used it as an analgesic and to cure fevers, nausea, arthritis, skin cancer and premenstrual syndrome.

I met Interstate 15 and drove over the Nevada state line into Las Vegas. When I was in school and had been assigned an essay about the place I would most like to go, I chose this one. It seemed from a distance to embody danger, the transcendence of law and convention, glamour and suave rakishness. All that Puritan America would forbid – gambling, alcohol, divorce, prostitution – was available here around the clock. As Simone de Beauvoir said, noting that it had neither commerce nor industry and had been set down on land that produced nothing: 'No bourgeoisie, no bourgeois morality.'

Las Vegas means 'The Meadows' in Spanish. It was a grassland on the Old Spanish Trail created by artesian wells. It was terrorised by a gang in 1879 composed of Mysterious Dave, Pawnee Bill, Hoodoo Brown, Pancake Billy, Jimmy the Duck, Doubleout Sam, Wink the Barber, Flyspeck Sam, Web-Fingered Billy and Tommy the Poet, among many others, until the gang was decimated by repeated hangings from a windmill in the town square. The city began its long and still-continuing boom in the early 1930s with the construction of the Hoover Dam, just twenty miles away, later accelerated by the presence of military bases. Government money made possible America's fastest-growing city, where the dollar is worshipped as nowhere else. In 1900 its population was thirty. Now it is a million, having tripled in a little more than twenty years. The Federal Writers' Project observer could write in the 1930s, 'No cheap and easily parodied slogans have been adapted to publicize the city, no attempt has been made to introduce pseudo-romantic architectural themes, or to give artificial glamour and gaiety. Las Vegas is itself – natural and therefore very appealing to people with a wide variety of interests.' Did the city have some grudge against Roosevelt and his New Deal projects, that it set out to systematically disprove everything the Federal Writers' Project delegate said? More recently Eric Schlosser wrote, 'Las Vegas is now so contrived and artificial that it has become something authentic, a place unlike any other.'

I had been fascinated by professional gamblers since I first encountered them as a caddy in Chicago. One of them was the legendary Marty Stanovitch, a short, round man with a roundhouse golf swing and a garage-sale set of clubs, who trawled resorts looking for victims in pancake make-up to disguise his tan. I was fifteen when I saw him, and had I not known who he was, I would have thought from the way he looked on the first tee that I could have beaten him. I watched him come in with a sixty-nine, which disappointed him. Afterwards he went back out onto the open road with his clubs in the back of his car, improvising as he went, using his imagination, looking always for a finely calibrated edge of advantage, entertaining himself and others as he preyed on human greed with his feats of skill and illusion. Once, I heard he'd had his fingers broken on the West Coast by an enraged victim, then went back to work when he was healed. It seemed to me a life of nonchalance, mischief and wit, with money – the subject of such anxiety and grave thought in the world outside – just a plaything to him.

Years later in London I met a few professional poker players. One, Donnchadha O'Dea, a former Olympic swimmer for Ireland and the son of two actors, had played often in the world championships in Las Vegas. He spoke to me of the camaraderie of the night, the badinage and warmth among a group he thought of as 'the last of the buccaneers'. They were probably somewhere in Las Vegas when I was there, but I didn't see them. I walked the Strip past a legion of men and women in pressed shorts and T-shirts and with cameras around their necks, moving as if on a belt until they were driven by the 104-degree heat into the air-conditioned casinos. In this way the desert assists in the generation of the casinos' profits. These evocations of the South Seas, medieval England, ancient Egypt and Rome and contemporary New York were more earnest than amusingly kitsch or louche. Bad taste could be thought of as its reverse in Las Vegas, but it wasn't bad enough. Families abounded. It could have been Disneyland. Inside, thousands sat before slot machines gambling industrially. It looked the most lonely and dehumanised of pastimes. In the 1960s, seventy-five per cent of the casinos' profits came from table games such as baccarat, roulette and blackjack. Now two-thirds of the profits come from video poker and slot machines, machines programmed to deliver profits of up to twenty per cent, or four times that of roulette. In these palaces of fortune, nothing is left to chance. 'It is the ultimate consumer technology,' Eric Schlosser has written, 'designed to manufacture not a tangible product, but something much more elusive: a brief sense of hope. That is what Las Vegas really sells, the most brilliant illusion of all, a loss that feels like winning.' An English friend of mine lived here for a time and had as his neighbours a retired couple from Florida. One day bailiffs arrived to take away their furniture and repossess their home. The man was bewildered. 'But I don't have any debts,' he said to them. He then found out that his wife had put the million dollars they'd saved into slot machines. They had to move to Iowa to live with their daughter.

Thirty million people arrive in Las Vegas each year, taking rooms in, among other places, fourteen of the fifteen largest hotels in the world and then feed billions of dollars of coins into machines. Among the arrivals would be some of 'the last of the buccaneers' who choose casinos for their poker games because of the secure environment they provide, but none would be playing the casino games. 'I hate casinos,' a professional race and sports better named Harry Findlay told me. 'I hate the décor, the noises, the uniforms. Why would anyone want to go to a place for gaming where knowledge and skill mean nothing and, statistically, you are guaranteed a loss?' If Manhattan has America's densest concentration of intellect, Las Vegas contains the most foolishness. In retrospect, I preferred Medford, Oregon.

I got onto 93 and crossed into Arizona at the Hoover

Dam, which blocks the powerful Colorado River as it passes through a mountain chasm. Full of cables, turbines and other devices, it looks like a vast, infernal laboratory. It was completed in 1935, two years ahead of schedule. Union Carbide was contracted to infiltrate the dam with refrigerated water to counteract heat generated by chemical reactions in the cement, which, if left alone, would have prevented the dam from setting for 125 years. As it is, the dam is still setting, and getting stronger by the day.

I got to Kingman, then drove east over open land in the dusk to Flagstaff. Only fifteen per cent of Arizona is privately owned, the rest of it being made up, in the main, of national or state parks, military artillery ranges and Indian reservations. 'The West is archetypically the place where Big Government is distrusted, the land of independent man going it alone,' Robert Hughes has written. 'Yet much of it – states like Arizona, for instance – has depended, not marginally or occasionally but always and totally, on Federal money for its economic existence. The Southwestern states would never have been settled at their present human density without immense expenditures of government funds on water engineering. They are less the John Wayne than the Welfare Queen of American development.'

Flagstaff is beside the largest contiguous ponderosa-pine forest in the continental United States. A Lieutenant Beale, part of an Army survey team, ordered that the trunk of one of the pines be set into the earth and have a flag run up it on 4 July 1876 in honour of the country's centennial. From this pole, which became a landmark, the town derived its name. Pluto was discovered here in the Lowell Observatory, brought to Flagstaff because of its clear skies. Wonders are all around – the red sandstone mesas and buttes of Oak Creek Canyon to the south, the multicoloured Sunset Crater and the Wupatki National Monument with its ancient dwellings to the north and Walnut Canyon, with its Sinagua cliff dwellings, to the east. Beyond Oak Creek Canyon is Sedona, home of the retired and those devoted to the New Age, the two conditions often combining in the same person. New Age pilgrims began to come here in large numbers after the popular American psychic Paige Bryant said Sedona was 'the heart chakra of the planet'. The German painter Max Ernst preceded them in the 1940s, incorporating this 'gaga and dada land' as described by Henry Miller into his surrealist paintings. Immediately outside of Flagstaff are the San Francisco Peaks, the highest in Arizona. They are sacred to the Navajo, the Hopi and other Southwest tribes, who have been trying since the 1980s to stop the owners of the White Vulcan mine there from gouging out any more of the mountain in their search for pumice with which to stonewash jeans.

I checked into the Monte Vista Hotel, opened in 1926 after a public subscription drive led by the Western novelist Zane Grey. I walked the corridors, reading the names on door plaques of the illustrious who stayed here, a mixture of Golden Age Hollywood – Gary Cooper, Clark Gable, Barbara Stanwyck, Jane Russell – and 1970s and '80s musicians – Freddie Mercury, Bon Jovi, Michael Stipe, Siouxsie Sue (of the Banshees) and Linda Ronstadt. More than one hundred Westerns were made around Oak Creek Canyon, and a scene from *Casablanca* was shot in one of the rooms of the hotel. The musical sector was a mystery to me, however. Two spectral prostitutes are said to live in the hotel too, murder victims who haunt benignly.

Down in the bar, percolating gently with young people perhaps one-third of the way into their night's drinking, a man in his late twenties with a miniature ski slope of a beard grabbed me by the shoulders and told me I had the fortune to be in one of the three best towns in America, the others being Ashville, North Carolina and Austin, Texas.

'Why do you say that?' I asked.

'You have mountains, deserts, forests. There are all kinds of outdoor sports you can do just outside of town. The rock climbing is fantastic. The weather's great and the air is clean. It's full of young, cool people.'

'You've made an exhaustive search?'

'This is reliable testimony,' he said. 'I've been around.'

The Men's Journal, as it happened, agreed with him, placing Flagstaff second on their Best Places to Live list.

I went into the streets, music spilling from the bars on this Saturday night. There was too the whistle from a train coming in from the east. Up to a hundred a day pass through, the click of wheel on track setting a beat. The town is an agreeable enclosure amidst monumental landscapes of green, slate and red. I went into the Weatherford Hotel, which had live Irish music on its first floor and a sardonic, lugubrious ballad singer at street level. I watched the red-faced and breathless dancers upstairs for a while, then chose the singer, who was playing at a rhythm closer to mine after the drive from Barstow. Next to me at the bar two men and a woman in their twenties were drinking with method and drive in the direction of oblivion. The man nearest me was the most purposeful in this, mixing Red Bull with a liqueur and rum in a pint glass, his eyes just out of focus. He had a ponytail running down his back and matching it in front was a beard sculpted into the shape of a duck's bill and reaching to his chest. He saw me watching him mix his concoction.

'I know it's a little unconventional,' he said. 'But it gets me drunk in a way I like.'

He was from West Virginia, where he'd trained as an electrical engineer. His father was in the military.

'I said to my father, "The first thing they did when they got into Iraq was to secure the oil fields." "Of course they did," he said, as though that was what they were supposed to do. Next to him I felt like I'd grown up on another planet. I got into trouble with drugs and had to get out of there. I thought I'd like some wide open space in the west, so I closed my eyes and let my finger fall on a map. It hit Flagstaff, and I came here. I got a job cutting timber for fire prevention and making trails in the forest.'

He took a shot of vodka on its own.

'I only do this Friday and Saturday nights,' he said. 'Usually.'

'Are you being interviewed, Jimmy?' asked the woman who was with them.

'Yeah.'

'So, what's your American Dream?' she asked.

He held up his glass.

'It's right in here,' he said.

'I'd say the American Dream has been run over by a truck,' he said to me. 'People are asleep now, but one day – maybe it'll be fifty years from now – they'll wake up and tear the place to pieces. There's another outrage every day, worse than the one before.'

The next day I stood on the South Rim of the Grand Canyon, looking out. Two billion years of the Earth's history are exposed in its layers of sediment. The remains of ancient warm seas, swamps and giant desert dunes are visible in its walls. Its depth was increased when the Colorado Plateau was heaved upwards sixty-five million years ago during the Laramide orogeny up to two miles above where it had been, steepening the gradient of the Colorado River and increasing its power to cut through rock. This was accentuated when Ice Age run-off was added to the river's volume. The canyon is now 277 miles long and up to a mile deep. You pass through different weather systems as you descend.

If you move a step, the canyon changes. New columns of layered rock come into view, others vanish, the shadows alter. If you focus on a single spot, the rest blanks out, turns to nothing. It is beige, grey, yellow, rose, ochre. If you hold still and try to take in its immensity, it seems to dissolve in a blue and lavender mist. Or so it happened to me that day. Henry Miller felt when he saw it 'as though Nature were breaking out in supplication . . . It's mad, completely mad, and at the same time so grandiose, so sublime, so illusory, that when you come upon it for the first time you break down and weep with joy.' I couldn't apprehend it, try repeatedly though I did. It was as though my eyes sent a message and my brain couldn't receive it.

I walked back through several hundred people and past tour buses to my car, then drove east. The canyon flickered through the tree trunks. I came upon the Desert View Watchtower on the canyon's edge, which offered views from its upper floors of the river below. It was designed and built in 1932 by Mary Colter, an employee of tour operator Fred Harvey, to resemble a Pueblo tower. Harvey called his journey by chauffered car through the deserts and Indian villages of the Southwest 'Detourism'. Clients stopped at Harvey Houses, which were staffed by Harvey Girls.

I came out of the trees of the Kaibab National Forest along the Little Colorado River into the vast openness of the Painted Desert. It was like coming out of a tunnelled chute into the sky. This is a desert without scrub or cactus, just canyons and solidified, striated dunes in greys, roses and beiges, which deepen in the low evening light into red, violet and gold. It is huge, silent, pared to the skeletal, timeless and delicate. Human or animal life here seemed unimaginable to me, yet this is the Navajo Nation, where 175,000 of a total of 300,000 Navajo live on what is the country's largest reservation, bigger in area than ten of the fifty states. On this mineral land, many ranch and farm, the land being held in common ownership by the tribe. 'Navajo' probably derives from a word meaning 'thieves' given to them by the Tewa Pueblo Indians and taken up by whites. To themselves, they are the Dineh, or 'the people'.

They were driven out of their territory and into eastern New Mexico by an expeditionary force led by Kit Carson in 1864 in what became known as the Long Walk, but then, in an unusual reversal by the government, were allowed to return within a few years. Within their newly created reservation were their predecessors here, the cliff-dwelling Hopi, who grow blue corn, squash, beans, peppers, melons, apricots and peaches on tiny plots fed by rainwater gathered in the spring. The Hopi's two and a half million acres suddenly collapsed to half a million and they have been fighting the Navajo in the federal court system for the return of their lands – 'those who settled first seeking judgement from those who came later through laws of those who arrived last', as William Least Heat-Moon described it in *Blue Highways*.

The Navajo language was used as a code in the Second World War. A section was established at Camp Pendleton in California to develop Navajo words for military terms, with four hundred Navajo being trained as 'code talkers', who eventually developed the capacity to encode, transmit and decode a three-line English message in twenty seconds, a job that took a machine of the time half an hour. 'Were it not for the Navajos,' said Marine signals officer Major Howard Connor, 'the Marines would never have taken Iwo Jima.' Navajo, unlike most languages, is remarkably impervious to foreign terms. There are more than two hundred purely Navajo words for automobile parts.

I drove north-east through the light-flooded air of the desert. The tortured Marsden Hartley, a painter from Maine who came to the Southwest in 1919, wrote of it, 'It is the only place in America where true colour exists. It is not a country of light *on things* – it is a country of things *in light*.' I passed little wooden stalls where Navajo women sitting under canopies sold their jewellery of silver and blue stone, Bob Dylan's 'Tangled Up in Blue' playing on the car's sound system, a road song of love and loss that takes in work on a fishing boat in Louisiana, a car abandoned in the west and 1960s bohemian New York. I went through Tuba City and passed the Elephant's Feet, two beige sandstone columns widening at the base and looking leathery in texture like the appendages their name describes. This was just north of the Hopi enclave, with its three sacred mesas extending down into the heart of their territory. I had a meal in an Indian diner in Kayenta served by teenaged sisters with perpetual smiles speaking in Navajo and gliding across the floor to a tune on the radio. I went north then on 163 to Monument Valley, holy ground to the Navajo.

It was evening, the low-lying light turning the desert floor and the air just above it into bands of red and blue. The russet sandstone buttes and pinnacles of Monument Valley rose to heights of up to a thousand feet from rounded earth plinths. I turned into a dirt road. There was a booth selling entrance tickets and three cars in the parking lot. Two Navajo, laughing, were in the booth. They were about to close, but they let me through. There were no tour buses, guard rails, rangers or security systems. Everything was proximate. I drove the seventeen-mile rutted red dirt road past the enormous and unfathomable formations rising all around me, the colours becoming richer, more luminous as the sun dropped. I pulled over into the shadow of a butte and got out. It had rained here in the afternoon, the stone, earth and plants on the desert floor newly washed. There were silver beads of rainwater among the tiny green leaves, and blue and red pools in the road and among the rocks reflecting the sky and the buttes. Currents of cool air moved lightly through the heat and the smell of fresh earth rose in waves, as though the ground was breathing. The only sounds were of these light, wafting breezes and birdsong. As the air moved, so, it seemed, did I. Everything around was fresh and alive and ripe and intimate, the air and colours and bird-song delicate in this light, which was growing richer before it would fade. This was all that was happening. For a time I could let it in. Then it went and I got back into my car.

I checked into a hotel overlooking the San Juan River twenty miles up the road in Mexican Hat, Utah and went out to Swingin' Steaks, where the meat is cooked in iron hammock-like beds that pass back and forth in a pendulum over an open fire. I ate a meal difficult enough for the waitress to carry, let alone for me to eat. People in the west eat in quantities I've read about in nineteenth-century novels, but have never otherwise seen. Afterwards I had a beer with the owner and her son-in-law Clint.

'We had a gold frenzy here once and then not so long ago there was uranium,' said Clint. 'It's all shot now. We got up to twelve hundred people here. Now there's thirty-five.'

'How did you wind up here?' I asked the owner.

'I'm a native,' she said. 'That's rare. My father's family

were Texas outlaws who went on the run here to Mexican Hat and changed their name to Wilson. The part about being on the run is not so rare out here. But my husband's family – that's him over there in the cowboy hat cooking steaks – I'd say they're pretty unusual. His mother's father was a Sicilian who was executed in jail. His mother became an orphan in Chicago and went out to the streets. Then she made her way west and became an opera singer. That's where she met my husband's father. I don't know what it was, the Sicilian blood or what, but they had a very stormy relationship. Break up, get back together, break up. All in all, they divorced and remarried eleven times.'

I thought I'd misheard the number, but she repeated it.

'We're a little off the main track here,' said Clint. 'We get people, but not so many. We tend to notice them. We had a guy in here the other day, long hair, tie-dye shirt. He was expressing some opinions that weren't very popular here in the bar, and we let him know it. Then a Mercedes pulled up in front and another guy with long hair came in. The first one thought he had an ally and he starts telling him what a bunch of fascists we are here in Mexican Hat. The second one stops him right away. "Look here," he says, pointing up at his head. "The only thing this long hair is doing is covering up my red neck."'

'What did the first guy do?' I asked.

'He left,' said Clint. 'No one to talk to.'

'What do you do here?'

'Apart from sitting in this bar?'

'Work, I mean.'

'Not a lot. I've got a few oil wells. I was in the construction business, but I got sick of all the regulations. I lived in Indiana, Montana, Texas, San Francisco. South Texas, that's the sweetest spot I know. Most of the wells you see around here are mine. It's more like a hobby. I just produce a couple of truckloads a month. It's a crime to be blowing this stuff out of the back of cars. It's the most flagrant waste of a precious resource that I know. Oil is something necessary for plastics and pharmaceuticals, not cars. But you know why nothing changes? Because big oil and car-manufacturing corporations are paying them in Washington not to change it. There's not a person of integrity inside the Beltway. A friend of mine wanted to get into politics and go there. I begged him not to do it. No one comes out of there with their soul.'

The young man with the long hair and the tie-dye shirt no doubt feels the same. Generally Americans, right or left, are united in their loathing of corporations, lawyers and Washington. Washington is the Central Market for the Venal. It's a place in the public mind of moral infection, rather than where 'the first among equals' gather to combine their skills and steer the country with rectitude and, where necessary, imagination and courage. Politicians entirely embedded in it have to pretend to be outside it to win elections. George Bush is a third-generation Washingtonian, but strove to present himself as a Texas rancher. What are the consequences to citizenship when a country is united in its abhorrence of its own capital?

Above Mexican Hat is another phantasmagorical gallery of rock, the Valley of the Gods, from just above which you descend precipitously back towards Mexican Hat on a dirt road known as the Moki Dugway through extreme twists high above the valley floor. I watched bicyclists take the turns with admirable ease. Further on, just beside Mexican Hat, the San Juan River, its banks verdant in this beige and grey land, loops around striated rock formations in the Goosenecks State Preserve. The bicycles were the only other vehicles I met on the Moki Dugway.

I had breakfast back at my hotel. Two Native American girls, smiling and laughing, waited on the tables. The owner pointed out to them that a tableful of men had yet to place their orders. The girls hurried over, still laughing. Indians seem perpetually in on a joke that everyone else is missing. A man in a sleeveless T-shirt sitting with the owner pointed at the girls and assembled his face into an expression of mental retardation. This was a step up, I thought, from the sneer he had been wearing before.

I drove east out of Mexican Hat, past the sombrero-shaped rock formation from which this little gathering of buildings gets its name, then followed 163 in a gentle arc past Bluff and Montezuma Creek. I turned onto the minuscule 262 and took it through Aneth over the Colorado line to 160, which felt like an autobahn in comparison. I passed Cortez and Durango, the oranges, pale greys and beiges of Utah giving way to the slate and pine green of the San Juan Mountains of Colorado. The stretch of 350 out of Durango into the old mountain mining towns to the north is known as the Million Dollar Highway because the gravel it was built with was laden with gold. I stayed east on 160 to Pagosa Springs, then dropped down on 84 into New Mexico, with Ute and Apache reservations just to my right.

I passed Los Ojos ('Eyes'), Brazos ('Arms') and Tierra Amarilla ('Yellow Earth'). Further back was Dulce ('Sweet'). The Spanish first passed through this region in 1536. A detachment from the settlement established in Mexico by Cortés pushed north to look for Indians to enslave and met by chance three Spaniards, an African slave called Esteban and six hundred Indians straggling across the desert. Their leader was an Andalusian named Álvar Núñez Cabeza de Vaca, who had been part of the Spanish expeditionary force routed by Indians at Tallahassee in Florida. He escaped the slaughter and headed west with other survivors until they were captured by Indians near what is now Galveston, Texas. Cabeza de Vaca ('Head of a Cow') convinced his captors that he was a medicine man and was able to set out again, trailed by devotees and gathering more along the way. He was intending to get to Mexico City, but eventually reached the Pacific after two years of walking, just under 250 years before Lewis and Clark made their coast-to-coast journey.

Cabeza de Vaca and Esteban told the Spaniards they met in the desert that they had seen evidence of a wealthy civilisation on their travels. Cortés, eager for more treasure, sent Esteban back with a Franciscan friar, Marcos de Niza, who returned with tales of seven cities made of gold. A full-scale expedition was despatched, but they found nothing. It was perhaps the sun that the friar had seen reflecting on the mud walls of the Pueblo settlements. Willa Cather, in *Death Comes for the Archbishop*, wrote of how she imagined this landscape looked to early European visitors: 'This mesa plain had the appearance of great antiquity, and of incompleteness, as if, with all the materials for world-making assembled, the Creator had desisted, gone away and left everything on the point of being brought together, on the eve of being arranged into mountain, plain, plateau. The country was still waiting to be made into a landscape.' Despite their disappointment at not finding the cities of gold, and despite New Mexico's aridity and punitive heat, the Spaniards came back in 1598 in search of silver and souls and, with their missions and purges by their army, broke the Indian resistance and assumed control.

I went east on 64 through the Carson National Forest. This was a landscape that conveyed sweetness rather than the grandeur of the Colorado Rockies or the concentrated, pitiless severity of the desert. It had cream-coloured rock and trickling streams. Deer walked among the pines. At the eastern edge of the national forest was Tres Piedras ('Three Stones'), a place of rusting cars, trailers that looked like they'd been pelted with bricks, houses set up on blocks. Thick windows of yellowing plastic were taped where they'd ripped or had shopping bags stuffed into holes. Small oil wells bobbed up and down like pigeons on the town's outskirts. I stopped at a gas station. A four-wheel drive with a fender falling off pulled up beside me. A small man, swaying a little, got out of the passenger side and put his face in my window. His teeth were like a mule's. Hair grew all over his face and neck. The driver was similar. Predatory, half-naked and drunk, they seemed to have regressed thousands of years through the evolutionary chain. In front of me at the till was a line of white, Hispanic and Indian loggers and ranch workers with packs of beer under their arms. Some looked indifferent, others as though they harboured bad intentions. The pair from the four-wheel drive came in. Anything could happen here, I thought. It seemed I was among wolves. I paid the cashier and got out.

I was headed for Taos, which a friend had told me had seen the worst and the best of the Sixties – communalism, ecology, spiritual growth and experimental art on the one hand and mind-shattering drug-taking on the other. There were remnants at least of the more salutary. Just outside Taos I saw a house built into a pit and covered with logs and mud, like the ancient Basketmakers' houses of the Pueblo Indians from two thousand years ago. A man standing at the entrance said that all their power is solar-generated and that whatever water they use comes from the sky. All grey water is recycled. He had an ideological purity, but only about what he could see and touch in his daily life, like a Shaker. This ecological and civic-mindedness with regard to the specifically domestic and local is there to see all across America, particularly in leftist gathering places like Ithaca, Seattle or Acoma. It is the analogue of the view of Washington as corrupted beyond redemption. In Ithaca they even have their own secessionist money.

Artists began to come to Taos early in the twentieth century in search of the mythic and the primitive. Robert Hughes called it 'America's internal Tahiti'. Modernism arrived in 1919 with the heiress and arts patron Mabel Dodge and her third husband, the painter Maurice Sterne. She had lived in Florence, where she survived two suicide attempts, one by laudanum and the other by eating figs laden with glass, and New York, where she held leftist salons in her Fifth Avenue apartment. But she found some kind of peace in Taos and remained there for her final forty-three years. A Tiwa Indian named Tony Luhan persuaded her to buy a twelve-acre property. She extended an existing two-hundred-year-old house and there she entertained D.H. Lawrence, Carl Jung, Willa Cather and Georgia O'Keeffe, among many others. Lawrence made paintings on the bathroom window so that he wouldn't have to look at the naked Mabel Dodge. Tony Luhan lived in a tepee on the grounds and drummed every night to get Mabel to come to him. Eventually she did, and he became her fourth and final husband.

To some Taos was a cursed place from its dark and violent suppression of the Indians and its later excesses. Dennis Hopper could have accounted for 'the worst of the Sixties' aspect of it on his own with his colossal intake of drugs at Mabel Dodge's house after the shooting of *Easy Rider*. But it was miraculously transformative to many who came to it in its art-colony years. 'If you ever go to New Mexico,' said Georgia O'Keeffe, 'it will itch you for the rest of your life.' Lawrence wrote, 'In the magnificent fierce morning of New Mexico one sprang awake, a new part of the soul woke up suddenly, and the old world gave way to the new.' It was the desert, with its evocation of biblical prophecy, and the ancientness and inscrutability of the Pueblo Indians that produced this. Mabel Dodge's beautiful house, its rooms named for artists who stayed there, is now an inn. D.H. Lawrence's glass paintings are still there on the bathroom window. I tried to get a room, but there was a conference on weaving going on and the weavers had taken all the rooms. I found a clean, unmemorable place up on the main road, checked in, then walked to the plaza, all its buildings finished in rounded adobe. Ethnic jewellery and bright paintings abounded. Simone de Beauvoir passed through here on her way east and wrote, 'The Indians have remained rather impervious to the influence of whites, but the whites who live here have been profoundly susceptible to the Indian influence. They've adapted the taste for vivid colours, for hand weaving, for the long past.' I had a beer in the La Fonda Hotel, which fully embodies this cultural transference and has a few erotic paintings by Lawrence hanging in its lobby. I walked then through the little streets to the north of the square. A young woman crouched in a doorway was weeping because her friend hadn't returned from a rock concert. I thought I'd be able to calm her down, but couldn't. Later, in a smoky bar with Mexican food and rollicking piano music, a couple in their twenties described to me their journey by car from Washington state to Taos along a nearly identical route to the one I had taken. 'We haven't eaten fast food or slept in a chain hotel yet,' said the woman. They were travelling to Willie Nelson's annual Fourth of July picnic in Dallas. From there, he would fly back to his job in Washington and she would drive to New York, where she would begin attending fashion school. They'd been together in high school, broken up and got back together. They'd been living together for two years in Washington, and now they were on a long, elegiac drive to look at America together before parting. 'It's a two-and-a-half-thousand-mile goodbye,' he said.

The next day I dropped down out of the Cimarron Range, the easternmost part of the Rockies in the Southwest, and again entered the Great Plains, the land settling into low plateaus and river cuts and at times arriving at the flatness of a lake on a calm day. I went south to another Las Vegas, east through what seemed a single vast ranch, the cattle up on a mesa with the spring grass, and then down to Fort Sumner to visit the grave of Billy the Kid. Born Henry McCarty on the Lower East Side of Manhattan in 1859, he came west to Silver City, New Mexico with his stepfather and mother and lived a blameless schoolboy life until he was arrested with some stolen clothes taken in a prank on a Chinese laundryman. He escaped up the jailhouse chimney and became a fugitive. In Lincoln County he got a job as a cattle guard in the employ of a lawyer named McSween, who at the time was involved in a range war with a former Army officer named Murphy. Murphy and a group of soldiers set the McSween house on fire while waiting outside with rifles and a twelve-pound cannon. Billy played the piano as the walls burned, then escaped after killing one of the besiegers. He was later captured by a former buffalo hunter turned sheriff named Pat Garrett and brought to Garrett's office on the second floor of the courthouse in Lincoln after being sentenced to hang. Held in shackles, he was shown a double-barrelled shotgun by deputy Robert Ollinger with which he would be shot, he was told, if he tried to escape. When Ollinger went across the street to a hotel for a meal, Billy got out of his irons, grabbed a gun from guard J.W. Bell and shot him dead. He stepped onto a balcony and when Ollinger, who had heard the shot, came running into the street, Billy called out, 'Hello, Bob!' and shot him with both barrels of the shotgun. He did a little dance on the balcony, then escaped on a horse, singing. Two days later the horse was returned.

Garrett eventually tracked Billy down to the house of his friend Pete Maxwell, whose sister Paulita, it is said, Billy intended to marry. Billy entered a room where Garrett and Maxwell sat talking in the darkness and, after whispering 'Quien es? Quien es?', was shot over the heart by Garrett. He was buried in the Fort Sumner military cemetery with his friends Charlie Bowdre and Tom O'Folliard. Above their names is carved the word 'Pals'. The tombstone has been stolen and recovered three times and is now in a steel cage. Simone de Beauvoir paid a visit to a house in Santa Fe that Billy was said to have lived in and was mystified by a country that could be sentimental about a man said to have killed twenty-one people, one for each year he had lived. Billy wore a sugar-loaf sombrero with a wide green band and, in his one surviving photograph, looks a little like Oscar Wilde. Garrett himself established the myth of Billy by writing a biography called *The Authentic Life of Billy, the Kid*. Others who wrote about him include Michael Ondaatje and Jorge Luis Borges. King Vidor, Howard Hughes, Marlon Brando, Gore Vidal and Sam Peckinpah made films about him. Aaron Copland staged an opera and Billy Joel, Tom Petty, Bob Dylan and the German heavy-metal group Running Wild all recorded songs about him. He was the singing escapee who defied the law, lived free and died young. His grave was my last encounter with the Wild West, having entered the vast stage on which its spectacles were enacted far to the north in the Black Hills.

I went north-east through small state roads past House, McAlister and Ragland, narrowly missing my near-namesake Grady, to Tucumcari, named for the agonised lament of an

Indian chief whose beautiful daughter Kari killed herself, after a duel between a suitor she despised and another she loved was won by the former. There at a public phone by the side of the road I called home and got my five-year-old daughter Beatriz. 'Are you wearing a black T-shirt and white trousers?' she said. That was the first time she'd ever asked me such a question. I looked down and discovered she'd got it exactly right. Further on, at Glenrio, I entered the Texas Panhandle.

During the First World War, with Europe in a state of devastation and Russian wheat being blockaded at the Dardanelles by the Turks, the demands for American wheat grew. Farmers borrowed and bought machines, grazing land was put into wheat production and profits rose until the war ended. Then the prices collapsed. Farmers planted more wheat in a race to keep up payments on their debts. In 1932, as Ian Frazier wrote in *The Great Plains*, 'Much of the native sod of grasses and roots which had held the soil in place since the last Ice Age was gone.' Then in 1934 the wind began to blow, raising a dust cloud in Colorado that came south through Kansas and into Oklahoma and Texas. 'The wind grew stronger,' wrote John Steinbeck in *The Grapes of Wrath*, 'whisked under stones, carried up straws and old leaves . . . the air and the sky darkened and through them the sun shone redly, and there was a raw sting in the air. During a night the wind ran faster over the land, dug cunningly among the rootlets of the corn, and the corn fought the wind with its weakened leaves until the roots were freed by the prying wind . . . The dawn came, but no day. In the gray sky a red sun appeared, a dim red circle that gave a little light, like dusk; and as the day advanced the dusk slipped back toward darkness, and the wind cried and whimpered over the fallen corn.'

A dust storm in May of that year blew a black cloud eastwards, dumping an estimated twelve tons of topsoil on Chicago, blacking out New York and sprinkling dust from the plains on the White House and on ships three hundred miles out in the Atlantic. A horrific storm in April of the following year came down into the Texas Panhandle and hit

Pampas, where Woody Guthrie was living. '"This dust, blowin' so thick ya cain't breathe, cain't see th' sky, that's th' scourge over th' face of th' earth!"' a neighbour screamed at him. '"Men too greedy for land an' for money an' for the power to make slaves out of his feller men! Man has cursed th' very land itself!"'

'There isn't a healthier country than West Texas when it wants to be,' wrote Guthrie in *Bound for Glory*, 'but when the dust kept whistling down the line blacker and more of it, there was plenty of everything sick, and mad, and mean, and worried.'

The dust storms of the Great Plains were the most cata-strophic natural disaster of the century up to that point. It was an event that came to be acted out in retrospect for the public in Steinbeck's great novel, the songs of Guthrie and the photo-graphs of Dorothea Lange. Franklin Roosevelt's government replanted sections of the plains as grasslands, provided relief and bought emaciated cattle from ruined farmers. Still, people were displaced in the hundreds of thousands, perhaps millions. Many starved in the great migration to the west. There wasn't another natural disaster on this scale in the United States until Hurricane Katrina hit New Orleans in August 2005.

Among those who set out from the southern plains was Woody Guthrie, leaving Pampa in a windstorm with his sign-painting brushes rolled up in a shirt. He passed his first night on the road to California in Amarillo ('Yellow') and spent all the money he had in the world on a cinema ticket, a bag of popcorn, some tobacco and a room in a boarding house. I arrived from the west into this city, 'Helium Capitol of the World', passing a town on the way called Bushland. Amarillo was once called Oneida, but was changed either for the wild flowers that appear in the spring or for the colour of the earth on the banks of its creek. An early promoter of Amarillo hoping to draw buffalo hunters had all the city's buildings painted yellow. Plainsmen could identify if a dust storm had originated in the Texas Panhandle if the cloud was a dirty yellow. Amarillo packages a quarter of America's beef and at Pantex has the only nuclear-weapons assembly and dis-assembly plant in the country. A state prison completes this industrial triumvirate. There's a museum here with the world's largest collection of barbed wire. In Bob Dylan and Sam Shepherd's song 'Brownsville Girl', Amarillo is called 'the land of the living dead'.

I'd heard of an Amarillo lawyer named Jim Wood who'd been involved in injury cases against the big meat packers and arranged to meet him at a chain place called Chilli's, a cuboid in a parking lot under Interstate 40. He came in wearing jeans, a string tie and a Stetson and told me he was one of the few Democrats still left in the Panhandle. 'Texas was founded by populists and had a wonderful constitution which placed limits on corporations,' he said. 'It was long a one-party Democratic state, but the Republicans assumed control of the gun and abortion issues and have convinced even the poorest people that if they don't vote Republican they're not American and they're not Christian.'

He told me that the meat-packing business, once centred in Chicago, where the work was unionised and wages were high, had dispersed decades ago into rural areas, where the conditions and the wages are poorer. 'IBP, which is owned by Tyson, employs three thousand people here in Amarillo,' he said. 'They bring people in from all over the world – many Hispanics, but there are also Laotians, Burmese and Vietnamese. In Chicago they'd slaughter around fifty cattle per hour. Here it's three hundred. They're working under extreme pressure with knives. There are bound to be injuries.'

Most states require companies to carry insurance against injuries on all their workers. Texas has a workers' compensation scheme, but companies can opt out of it. IBP elected to opt out and in its place operate something called a Workplace Injury Settlement Programme, whereby if an employee is injured, he's asked to sign a document waiving his right to sue before he's given access to medical treatment provided by the company.

'They'll do anything to get you to sign that document,'

he said. 'They'll even threaten the person that he'll lose his job if he doesn't, which would be illegal. But a lot of these people are immigrants who have little English and who are easy to scare. They don't know their rights.'

He took a case for an IBP manager named Steve Klumpe, whose stepson Chris Escamilla lost three fingers using a hock-cutter on the slaughterhouse floor. Klumpe said that a plant supervisor instructed him to get his stepson to sign a waiver document and told him that if he didn't do it, he'd be fired. 'Steve Klumpe knew exactly how the company operated in cases like this and what was at stake here. He'd operated the policy himself,' said Wood. 'So he advised his stepson not to sign, and that's what happened.' IBP's response was not only to fire Klumpe, as promised, but to sue him for having removed from the plant documents that the company said contained 'trade secrets', but which Klumpe claimed his own lawyer had told him to get as they were important in the case he was going to bring over his dismissal.

'Our case against IBP was about the company trying to involve Steve Klumpe in a fraud by getting him to try to obtain a signature on a document that was deceptive. We had a jury, I would say, entirely composed of conservative Republicans and they unanimously agreed with us by awarding $10.8 million against IBP. $10 million of this was punitive damages, which indicated how the jury felt generally about IBP's dealings with its employees. The judge, whose name was Mary Lou Robinson, then took the unusual step of overturning the jury's decision, using the only legal basis she had to do so – which was that no group of reasonable people could possibly have arrived at such a decision. Then she ordered Steve Klumpe to pay IBP's costs.'

IBP lost their first hearing in their case about the documents, but won on appeal. Jim Wood appealed Judge Robinson's decision, but lost. A Judge Keith P. Ellison in a dissenting opinion wrote, 'If judges are willing to set aside jury verdicts as readily as was done in this case, the entire rationale for the civil jury system is sharply attenuated.'

'Judge Robinson is by no means the worst around here,' said Wood. 'But the corporations are enormously powerful. A federal jury in Alabama awarded $1 billion against IBP in an anti-trust suit taken by cattle farmers over price-fixing, but the judge there overturned it too. In both cases the judges were appointed.'

Steve Klumpe, upon whom all this was visited because of his refusal to conspire with his employer against his own stepson, filed for bankruptcy.

'Do you know what happened to him after that?' I asked.

'The last time I spoke with him he was mowing people's lawns,' Wood said.

I went south-east out of Amarillo on US 287, which runs down through Wichita Falls to Dallas–Fort Worth. There, on the following morning, I was to meet my friend Steve Pyke, the English photographer with whom I'd once produced a book. We'd been out on the road together often, in England, Ireland and the United States, and he wanted to come out onto it again to get away from the grief he was in from his wife having just left him after twenty-four years.

I passed Claude and Goodnight, Texas, then stopped in Clarendon for gas. A woman behind me in the queue for the till said, 'Where did you get those shoes?'

I told her I'd bought them in Spain.

'Well, I didn't think you'd bought them in Wal-Mart.'

Further on, US 83 crossed 287 at Childress. Around twenty-five miles up 83, at a bridge just north of Wellington, the outlaws Bonnie and Clyde veered off the road and plunged into the Red River. In the car with them were Buck Barrow, Clyde's brother, their white pet rabbit and Clyde's saxophone. By then they'd been driving around for about a year, robbing banks, stores and gas stations in small towns and shooting policemen. When the local sheriff and police chief arrived at the Red River bridge, the four-foot-ten-inch, eighty-five-pound, poetry-writing Bonnie Parker, the inside of her thigh tattooed with two hearts and the names Bonnie and Roy, disarmed the policemen, who were then driven over the Oklahoma border and tied to a tree with barbed wire. Bonnie and Clyde and their gang stayed on the run for another year, until 23 May 1934, when they were killed at Bienville Parish, Louisiana in an ambush involving 130 rounds of ammunition, led by a former Texas Ranger named Frank Hamer.

I'd spent the morning at an auction in the Amarillo stockyards. Cattle ran into a pen in a small amphitheatre, spurred on by flicks from a drover's switch, while an auctioneer gabbled stridently into a microphone up in a booth. There was a heavy, inert smell there – more of death, I thought, than life, though that could have been from my sense of foreboding about these doomed, nervous animals running skittishly around the ring. Or it could have been the stacks of meat in the restaurant along the corridor waiting to be eaten for lunch by the ranchers at the auction. They sat in the raked gallery in their boots, jeans and Stetsons bidding with single, upraised, laconic fingers. They were otherwise as still as lizards. There is a look I saw often in Texas, and these men had it. They were primarily of a Scots-Ulster Low Church background. These were people who had been transported from Scotland to the north-east of Ireland in the seventeenth century to subjugate Catholics and hold the Union for Britain. They then went to Appalachia, where they wiped out the Cherokee. From there they entered the Deep South. Church-going, country music, laissez-faire government, large steaks, anti-intellectualism, personal freedom, executions, creationism, the military, county fairs and barn dancing are popular here. Environmentalism, government regulations, taxes, homosexuality and feminism are not. There is an idea of masculinity here connected with stoicism, unfetteredness, plain speech, pitilessness when necessary, and unshakeable belief. Sophistication is girlish, doubt a weakness. When I was growing up, the cowboy was a political neutral and the archetypal conservative was a cautious banker prudent with figures but unskilled at enjoying himself. But now Texas, home of Enron, execution capital of America, vanguard of Christian pre-millenarian fundamentalism and with its nostalgia for the Confederacy, has become definitive of American conservatism. There are other Texases, of course, as there are many other Americas, but often now when the outside world thinks it is looking at America, it is really only seeing this Texas.

I drove on, passing a place called Wisdom, then another called Electra, and got into Wichita Falls in the early evening. The roads of America, I'd noticed, are full of shattered tyres and dead animals. I drove around looking for something to focus on in this place of bail bondsmen and pawnshops and abandonment, but couldn't find where the city was supposed to be. I stopped the car, ran into a bar and asked a waitress where I could find the centre of Wichita Falls. She looked at me as though there was some kind of trick to this question, then said, 'I think of that as the mall,' and turned away. I passed the Rock Inn and the High Chaparral, which looked like they might be strip places, then entered a grid of empty brick buildings and finally found an agreeable-looking Irish bar. I went in for a beer. Two tables away, amidst a group of fellow cynics, a young man tried out a spontaneous song. 'Psychopaths and desert rats . . .' he started, then stopped. '. . . Broken-down cars and boarded-up bars . . .' That went nowhere, either. I finished my beer and as I walked past his table he took this last opportunity to add to his audience by singing out at full voice, his fingers drumming on the table:

Vietnam vets and mutant pets,
No jobs, just a town full of slobs,
Don't come to Wichita Falls if you're a tourist . . .

Then his whole table sang together,

Unless you want the Wichita Falls blues,

just for me.

I drove south on 281 to Jacksboro and checked into a small motel run by an Asian with a mild stutter. His daughter drove in circles on her bicycle in the parking lot singing a pop song in an American accent. Jacksboro, I discovered, is in a dry county. The small government activists on the religious right generate a lot of *in loco parentis* legislation. Their source is the Book of Leviticus. I stayed in my room, where I read the following sentence on the subject of democracy by Aristotle: 'To take no part in the running of the community's affairs is to be either a beast or a god.'

The next day around noon Steve Pyke came down from his room in the Holiday Inn Select near the Dallas–Fort Worth airport, having arrived the night before. He'd been as thin as a scalpel since I'd known him, but was more gaunt still from his suffering, the skin drawn over his skull like a surgical glove.

'How was the night?' I asked him.

'Great. I sat in the bar for an hour listening to a drunk pilot talking about strangling a dog. He was really into the detail.'

'At least you could get a drink,' I said.

The Deep South

We drove south on the western flank of Interstate 35 along the Balcones Fault, an escarpment that divides the rocky hill country of west Texas from the alluvial, wooded, black-earth, cotton-producing flatlands of the east. The former belongs to the Great Plains, the latter to the Deep South.

The flatlands were settled by plantation owners and their slaves, the hill country by Mexicans, emancipated blacks, German, Scandinavian and Czech small farmers and artisans, many of them freethinkers, progressives, nonconformists. Some of the Germans were idealists turned refugees from the political upheavals of 1848. The political, cultural and social distinctions between these two Texases were severe enough for the western progressives to propose after the Civil War that the state (larger than France) be divided into several smaller states, lest the defeated anti-emancipationists succeed in establishing a new *de facto* Confederacy. The state constitution still makes at least symbolic provision for the two sides, reserving the rights of Texas both to secede from the Union and to subdivide itself into up to five new states. Had Texas been partitioned, the Texas political commentator Michael Lind has written, 'One or more states formed from west Texas – Lincoln was one suggested name – would have joined the progressive prairie states like Kansas and Nebraska, and the South would have ended in the vicinity of Austin.'

We drove in a throng of four-wheel drives and pickup trucks that was like a herd of migrating wildebeests, jostling and surging and grunting in a single, organic mass. The flags over company headquarters, police stations and pizza parlours were at half-mast, in mourning for Ronald Reagan, who had died just over three weeks earlier. Roadkills and these flags were to be Steve's sole photographic subjects during our week together. His shattered marriage was moving through him like a poison, and these were the pictures that expressed it, I supposed. All the way to Austin and into the night he excoriated, lamented, extolled and speculated. 'If I were to do X, do you think she would do Y?' was the form of much of it. He desperately wanted her back. He was a vanquished and anxious Utopian, yearning and plotting and dreaming about a return to the Promised Land.

We passed Waco, which drew the attention of the world on 19 April 1993 when, after a fifty-three-day siege, government forces in tanks stormed the compound of David Koresh's Branch Davidians, following the cult's killing in February of US Bureau of Alcohol, Tobacco and Firearms agents who had been trying to confiscate their illegally held guns. A fire broke out during the attack and eighty-one Branch Davidians, including several children, died. To the far right, including some in the Republican Party, the Branch Davidians became martyr-heroes. Timothy McVeigh cited what happened that day as his justification for blowing up the Murrow Federal Building in Oklahoma City on the second anniversary of the attack. How do believers in Jesus, personal freedom and, allegedly, democracy come to champion a blasphemous, self-proclaimed messiah whose followers forsake citizenship and the law for disciplehood? Somehow anger about large and powerful government moving against the marginal, the weak and the lost, along with the issue of the right to bear arms, transcended any revulsion at cults. Being a victim of the government is a stirring theme in the United States. Politicians invoke it with regularity. When the segregationist Alabama governor George Wallace was running for president he said, 'The common man has had enough. He's been pushed around *too long*. He's had to settle for second class in his job, in the schools his kids attend, in the hospitals he's payin' for and he's the one payin' the taxes. It's them in Washington that's been ripping the little man off, and it's them big city socialists like the Rockefellers who ride around in big black limousines because of what they're takin' outta *you*.' It might be thought surprising that Wallace would raise these issues when Alabama had no minimum wage, had the lowest workers' compensation rates and money spent per pupil in America, its hospitals were described by a federal judge as 'barbaric' and both its taxes and its poverty rate rose faster than anywhere else in the country while in his charge. You might also wonder when the Rockefellers became socialists. What is stranger still, I think, is this appeal to the sense of being abused, fed up, being ever on the losing side, in this country so focused on and celebratory of winning. America is often so successful in bestowing a sense of confidence in its citizens. Why is an appeal to them as 'little' so resonant? Perhaps this only works when the force doing the knocking around is Washington, the national nemesis.

Texas is the land of the cowboy, but not exclusively so. A US Department of Agriculture inspector named Dustin whom I met in Valencia told me that Texas has vast citrus, vegetable and grain industries, produces more cotton than any other state and harvests more timber than Oregon. The logging industry in particular, says Dustin, faces a threat that could destroy it. 'The Asian longhorn beetle, the emerald ash borer and the wood wasp pose greater environmental threats than road building, industry, logging and air pollution, in my opinion,' he said. 'The Asian longhorn beetle killed fifty per cent of the trees in Central Park and in Australia eighty per cent of their loblolly pine plantation. I think the environmental movement is behind the times in much of what they do. The presence of these insects is a consequence of globalisation. Most of them come in with packing materials. This stuff is supposed to be fumigated or treated with heat, but you can find the insects on palettes stamped as having been treated. I've seen larvae crawling out of the stamp itself.'

Waco, where Wichita Indians once grew corn, pumpkins

and melons, became the capital of Texas' cotton industry at a time when America led the world in cotton production. It is southern rather than western, having produced six generals and raised seventeen companies for the Confederacy. During Reconstruction, a black ward of an army lieutenant dealing with the welfare of freed slaves was kidnapped and castrated by two of Waco's physicians. Some years later, in 1916, a black seventeen-year-old named Jesse Washington who had been convicted of murdering his boss's wife was seized by a mob, taken to a fire on the courthouse lawn, covered with oil and cooked alive. The mayor and chief of police were in the celebrating crowd. Waco now has entire museums devoted to the soft drink Dr Pepper, invented in Waco in 1885, and the Texas Rangers, and is the site of Baylor, the largest Baptist university in the world. Baylor has produced many evangelical Christians, along with Thomas Harris, author of *The Silence of the Lambs*, and Willie Nelson.

Two of America's great iconoclasts, one a satirist and the other a sociologist, also lived in or were from Waco. William Cooper Brann came to Waco from Illinois and opened a journal that attained a circulation of 120,000. Many of its pages were devoted to attacks on Baylor University. After he wrote of the rape and impregnating of a thirteen-year-old Brazilian girl by the son-in-law of the university president, students surrounded Brann's house, harassed and threatened his wife and eventually kidnapped him and beat him nearly to death. On he went with his journal, until 2 April 1898, when a Baylor supporter named Tom Davis shot him in the back. Brann wheeled around and killed Davis with a pistol shot, but died later at home. H.L. Menken was an admirer.

The other was C. Wright Mills, born in Waco in 1916. From the late 1940s and into the Sixties, when he died aged only forty-five, he wrote of the robotisation and alienation of workers, of the co-opting of labour leaders and, in *The Power Elite*, of the concentration of political, economic and military power in a single class, with its various members interchangeable and all of them dedicated to creating, as he put it, a 'permanent war economy'. He fathered the New Left. Tom Hayden wrote his Masters thesis on Mills, and the Port Huron Statement, issued in the year of Mills' death, is full of Mills in ideas, aspiration and even style. Mills disdained theory and the practice of intellectuals maintaining a remoteness from the world in universities. He believed that sociologists should find their themes in individual lives, including their own. 'Mills' writing was charged – seared – by a keen awareness of human energy and disappointment, a passionate feeling for the human adventure and a commitment to dignity,' wrote Todd Gitlin, a sociologist and political writer who was one of the founders of the Students for a Democratic Society in the 1960s. 'In a vigorous, instantly recognisable prose, he hammered home again and again the notion that people lived lives that were not only bounded by social circumstance but deeply shaped by social forces not of their own making, and that this irreducible fact had two consequences: it lent most human life a tragic aspect with a social root, and also created the potential – if only people saw a way forward – of improving life in a big way by concerted action.' Mills believed that only intellectuals could apply reason to power and start the historical processes that would make these improvements possible. They could locate society's dilemmas in the lives around them, examine them openly and scientifically and, animated by an empathetic passion, bring solutions out into the world to be taken up by democratic movements. To be an intellectual was to be an activist.

It would be difficult now to think of anything less frightening to concentrated power in the United States than an intellectual. Anti-intellectualism is a never-failing rallying point and source of amusement with a president boasting of his C grades, and those who might once have aspired to be activist-intellectuals having retreated deep into the academy decades ago, like bears entering their caves for a long winter sleep. Americans spent, thought, agitated, wrote and sang their way out of both the Depression and segregation in the south. Demonstrations against the Vietnam War, at which intellectuals were prominent, broke Lyndon Johnson, ended the war and led to a generation thinking differently about the nature of power. It was not so long ago that Gore Vidal and Norman Mailer ran for office in New York, and James Baldwin, at the time enjoying a European bohemianism, decided to return home to participate in the civil-rights movement. Both Roosevelt and Kennedy opened the White House doors to radical thinkers to present solutions to the problems of poverty. An embrace of theory and a withdrawal to the universities by the intellectual left began to take place some time in the late 1970s after the end of the Vietnam War seemed to lead to an end of radicalism. Professors who might still call themselves Marxists entered a fogbank of post-structuralism in which society was seen to be a construct of encoded repressions and language a useless tool to combat them. The idea of class action was replaced by complaint and theorising about race, gender and sexuality, in particular about repressive language associated with these issues. This was a phenomenon that constantly supplied its own absurdities, such as the University of California administrator who campaigned for an end to the use of the phrases 'a nip in the air' and 'a chink in one's armour', as they could be offensive to Asians. This was a radicalism, puritanical in style, that never left the theoretical. Its main characteristics were inactivity, ineffectuality and a prissy censoriousness. The right grew more scornful while the intellectual left, such as it is, concentrated on justifying its own failure. As the Texas style became more dominant in culture and politics, the left receded to near invisibility. 'We squandered the politics,' wrote Todd Gitlin of fellow 1960s radicals, 'but won the text-books.' I've heard it said by those working in American universities that a reaction against theory has set in and that in fields such as sociology there is a movement towards what can be practically applied in the world. Epoch-making action led by intellectuals, however, looks far away.

We got into Austin, one of the finest places in America

according to the young man I met in Flagstaff, and checked into the Hotel San Jose on South Congress. This was once one of the first motor court hotels, opened in 1936, and has since evolved into an open, airy, pastel-coloured minimalist sanctuary for the hip, the elegant, the easy of manner. Outside in the street were galleries, boutiques, clubs and retro diners. No Stetsons or cowboy boots, just cool beats and flowing linen. My accommodation intermittently, and briefly, rose in quality while I was with Steve. We stepped across the street to the Continental Bar, one of the best music venues in one of America's music capitals. We leaned on the bar and listened first to rhythm and blues and then to a folk singer. A girl came up and handed us each a laminated card with a group of people holding little Ø signs on it under the declaration 'Stop Mad Cowboy Disease' and the address of an anti-Bush website, www.SeeYaGeorge.com.

'Isn't he your boy down here?' I asked.

'He should be in jail,' said the girl. 'He makes me feel ashamed to be American.'

In the morning I played nine holes in brutal heat at the Pedernales Golf Club in Spicewood, which is to the west of Austin. Its owner is Willie Nelson. On the wall of the pro shop were gold records in frames, Nelson family pictures and a signed photograph of Alan Shepard hitting his six-iron on the moon. Next door was a recording studio and a tour bus was being hosed down in the parking lot. The course was sequestered by the government when its owner was having trouble with the tax authorities, but a wealthy benefactor purchased it and restored it to him. On the back of the scorecard are listed various local rules: 'When another player is shooting no player should talk, whistle, hum, click coins or pass gas'; 'No more than twelve in your foursome'; 'Excessive displays of affection are discouraged.' They believe that a lost ball should not incur a penalty as it is not actually lost, but will in fact be found by someone and can then be deemed to have been stolen.

'Who wrote these rules?' I asked the man in the pro shop.

'Willie,' he sighed.

This is the Texas Hill Country. A German aristocrat named Ottfried Hans Freiherr von Meusebach arrived here in 1845 and immediately divested himself of his title, taking the name John O. Meusebach. He founded Fredericksburg as a free, pluralist microcosm, began to amass a large library and on 1 March 1847 convened a meeting by the San Saba River with several hundred Comanche under the leadership of Chiefs Buffalo Hump, Santa Ana and Old Owl. He and his fellow delegates openly discharged their weapons into the air until they were empty to demonstrate their peaceful intentions, and then brokered a treaty. Meusebach declared through his interpreter his hopes for racial harmony, brotherhood and eventually inter-marriage. The treaty held. He died fifty years later in his cottage surrounded by books and a garden containing pears, peaches, apples, plums, grapes, sixty varieties of roses and other flowers from three continents. While, just to the south in San Antonio, large crowds amass to celebrate the Battle of the Alamo, Fredericksburg has an Easter Fires ceremony commemorating Meusebach's treaty.

A little to the south of Fredericksburg are Boerne, named for a radical Jewish German journalist of the nineteenth century, Ludwig Boerne, and Bettina, named for the German feminist and friend of Meusebach, Bettina von Arnim. A group of exiled German academics turned farmers held weekly meetings at which only Latin was spoken. 'It sometimes occurred at these meetings that Comanches stood listening at the open door, while one of the Latin farmers was lecturing on the socialistic theories of St Simon or Fourier,' wrote the historian Maritz Tiling.

Dustin, the agricultural inspector, grew up well to the south of here on a 64,000-acre ranch near Sonora, beyond the reach of the German Latinists or the genteel influence of Austin. 'Out there it's six-packs and gun racks,' he told me. 'They place bets on how far a chicken will walk before he defecates. They go out hunting wild pigs with pit bulls and mastiffs. It's the redneck sport from hell, four teeth among twenty of them, all or most of them drunk, setting dogs on the pigs or chasing them down in their Broncos, jumping out to catch a small pig and then running like hell from the sow. A sow is worse than a wolf, it'll just tear you to pieces.' There are a few small black towns in that part of Texas, he told me, their inhabitants the descendants of freedmen. 'I used to see some of them on horseback riding the trail past my house, black cowboys in Stetsons and spurs,' he said.

We turned back to the east, passing Austin and then Bastrop. There is an annual festival in Bastrop devoted to the lumber industry, which features a man known as Loblolly Lou dressed as a pine. We met state highway 21 and went north-east for a while. Highway 21 was laid out first by migrating buffalo, was then developed by Indians trying to hunt them and then the Spanish made it part of their *Camino Real* linking Florida with Mexico via San Antonio. I wanted to see Dime Box, for its name, but also because it marked a moment of literary transcendence in William Least Heat-Moon's *Blue Highways*. Somewhere to the east of Dime Box he stopped to look at the remains of an Indian village and realised that his ceaseless attempts to comprehend everything were removing him from the experience of his journey. 'To insist that diligent thought would bring an understanding of change was to limit the comprehensible,' he wrote. Lightning streaked the sky, there was booming thunder and he got back into his van and drove to Dime Box, where he went into Ovcarik's Café and recorded the observations of a man who didn't know what day it was, a woman and her half-blind caterwauling mother, a general conversation involving the best means of killing fire ants, and one man's story of an uncle of his who fed ants on molasses, fattened them up, put them on buttered bread and ate them – 'Claimed molasses gave them ants real flavour,' he said. Least Heat-Moon had his hair cut in a barbershop set at a tilt by a sycamore pushing it upwards from the back. He'd acted quickly on his revelation at the Indian mound, for this recording of the revealingly inconsequential is a prolonged, vivid and very funny example of what can happen when a person excises 'diligent thought' and allows a landscape, the hitting of a ball, the playing of musical notes, an event or a person simply to happen to them.

We turned off 21 onto Farm Road 141, passing the churches and small white houses of Dime Box with gardens in pink and blue and white, people out on their porches in the low afternoon light. An elderly black lady dressed all in white waved to us. This is a town one-third German, one-third Czech and one-third black. We stopped at a general store. Steve bought a beer and sat on a bench under the shade of a tree, smoking a cigarette and trying to conjure some sense from the dust at his feet. I went for a walk around the three streets of downtown Dime Box, population 313. It used to be called Brown's Mill, but the postal service kept getting it confused with Brownsville and it was renamed after a box where people left their letters to Giddings, which is twelve miles away, depositing a dime for postage. I looked at the café where Least Heat-Moon heard about the man who ate molasses-flavoured ants and the barbershop where his hair was cut. Both were closed, but the sycamore hadn't yet tipped over the latter. It was now called Ronnie's Barber Shop and opened Tuesdays and Wednesdays only, 1.30 p.m. to 5.00 p.m. In the window was a fading photocopy of an article from the *Weekly World News* under the headline 'Man's Head Explodes in Barber Chair'. This short walk had the feel of a literary pilgrimage, like rowing out to the Lake Isle of Innisfree in Sligo.

I headed back to the store. I saw Steve, inert on the bench beneath the trees, dragonflies passing through the beams of sunlight above him. Two young black men stepped down through the door of the store. One got into a car and the other walked up to Steve. He leaned over him from behind and whispered something to him. One hand hovered over Steve's back, but stopped short of touch, and the other held out a bottle of beer in a paper bag, a little plume of steam rising from its contact with the hot air. Steve took the bottle without surprise. 'Thank you,' he said, and took a drink from it. The young man nodded, backed up a few feet and got into the car where his friend was waiting. How had he known? I wondered.

The Deep South would have been contiguous culturally from the Georgia coast to the Balcones Fault, were it not for the arrival of French Catholics from Nova Scotia into southern Louisiana in 1755. They'd been farming, fishing and hunting there for more than a hundred years, but when the British took over and the Acadians, as they were known, wouldn't forswear Catholicism or give their allegiance to the English king, the British drove them out and they migrated from a cold maritime place to Louisiana swampland. Almost no one noticed they were there until the 1940s, when large roads made incursions following the discovery of oil. As you travel east, names like Hank and Chet, snub-nosed Anglo-Saxon names, give way to Achilles, Perpetuée, Lastie, Télémaques, Titi, Bos and Noonoon. It's a land of foetid water, live oaks and cypresses, baroque, graven images, gumbo, craw-daddies, hot boudin, accordions, fiddles, non-stop dancing and the cry 'Laissez les bons temps rouler!' – each of these, bar the trees and the water, an anguish to the evangelical teetotallers around them. Spanish moss, related to the pineapple, hangs like ectoplasm from the trees, a boon to Louisiana's upholstery industry. 'None bar the Chinese can ever hope to paint this moss,' Henry Miller was told while visiting New Iberia. 'It has a baffling secret of line and mass which has never been approached.'

We crossed into Louisiana after passing Bon Wier, already Cajun in name, I thought, until I read that it came from B.F. Bonner, sawmill manager, and R.W. Wier, town surgeon. Perhaps it was natural to think of the two professions together.

Through De Ridder and along state highway 26 past forest and waterland unruffled by a breeze, we were still in Anglo-Saxon Louisiana. We got to Oberlin, just north of the Coushatta Indian Reservation. The Coushatta's devastating encounters with white people began in 1540 when a party of explorers under Hernando de Soto, who later had a car named after him, kidnapped the chief and threatened to burn the tribe's villages if they were not given whatever they wanted. The Coushatta were driven off lands from Georgia to Texas through the centuries that followed, each government treaty further reducing what they had. They were part of the Creek Confederacy that lost twenty-two million acres after the wars of 1813–14. A chief named Red Shoes led a small band into Louisiana. They eventually bought a thousand acres of farmland, swamp and forest near Oberlin, obtained federal recognition as a tribe in 1973, began farming rice and crawfish, obtained an exemption from state tax and then, in 1992, made a management agreement with Grand Casinos, Inc. for a gaming complex on US Highway 165.

We found a hot-dog stand appended to a hotel and sat under the shade of a tree. Wet heat billowed up from the soft earth. The owner came over and sat with us. He was an economic refugee from Rhode Island, where he'd been bankrupted, and most of what he'd built up since then, he said, he'd lost in a divorce from a woman he only referred to as the plaintiff. He was wiry, dissatisfied, agitated, his small, pale hands flitting in the air.

'You want to see how these crackers down here treat the Indians,' he said. 'The casino has brought in a lot of money for them, so they wanted to make a gesture to the parish. They gave a cheque for $2,000 to each schoolteacher and $250,000 to the local government. When they politely enquired what had been done with the money, they were told it was none of their business. There was a farmer owned a little strip of land the Indians wanted for their complex down there. Do you know how much he stuck them for? $3 million plus five per cent of net profits from the casino.

The parish needs the Indians more than the Indians need it. The median income here is half the national average.'

We crossed the Bayou Nezpique River then and went through north Cajun country to Baton Rouge, the road uninspiring most of the way, but passing through a region of beautiful names – Opelousas, Bayou Queue de Tortue, Shadows on the Teche, Butte La Rose, Plaquemine. Huey Long, the Kingfish, ruled Louisiana from Baton Rouge from the late 1920s and into the Depression. 'I used to get things done by saying please,' he once said. 'Now I dynamite them out of my path.' He repealed the poll tax and thereby hugely increased the voters' rolls, increased by a factor of seven the state's roads, extended the public-school system, adult education and the state university, infuriated the oil companies with tax legislation and harassed Roosevelt from the left with his Share Our Wealth programme, which proposed a limit to personal fortunes and inheritances to $5 million and annual incomes to $1 million and a guarantee to every family of a house and a minimum income. He was shot dead in the capitol building in 1935, aged forty-two.

From Baton Rouge we crossed the swamp beside Lake Pontchartrain and arrived in New Orleans, where we rented a high-ceilinged apartment with wooden floors, a fireplace, four-poster beds and a Jacuzzi above the R-Bar in Faubourg Marigny and went out into the night. We walked the arcaded and shaded streets, a hush under the broad leaves of the trees. We had rice and shrimp in a Creole restaurant and a drink in Napoleon House amid ivory candles, Beethoven and a density of two-hundred-year-old elegant detail held just above the point of collapse, then entered the illuminated raucousness of Bourbon Street, the volume fully up. Professor Longhair tapdanced for tips here. 'When I get to New Orleans,' he later sang with his band the Shuffling Hungarians, 'I want to see the Zulu King!' We went into a large, thronged bar where a Cajun band was playing. Steve, in a red Hawaiian shirt, propped himself by his elbows on the bar like a dressed pheasant hung from a butcher's hook. A group of women down from the north for bacchanalian tourism took him out onto the dance floor and seemed sad to leave him when they went out to continue their debauch. We walked along Bourbon Street then, rock, jazz, hip-hop, blues and zydeco pouring from the bars. I don't know how long it would take to find poor to mediocre music in New Orleans. Perhaps you never would.

The French Quarter is disdained by many New Orleans residents and aficionados as supine before mass tourism, with everything faked from Virgin worship to music to witchcraft and even to its own renowned sweet gaiety, its streets clogged with conventioneers, braying fraternity boys and stampeding hordes of drunks. I, however, have been seduced on each of the three occasions I have been there. It's unlike anywhere else in America, or even the world, as I've experienced it. Its seductiveness is in its racial mixtures, its tropical courtyards, its chankety-chank zydeco, its inclination to refinement, Gothicness, emotional breakdown, ribaldry, euphoria. Men replete with arcane knowledge and wearing white suits with boutonnières, hand-made shoes and carrying silver-topped canes stroll the avenues and take lunch for five hours. I met one in 1992 who studied ancient Greek, Byzantine theology and rare psychological diseases and travelled the world with his piece of string measuring the girths of trees. 'A true eccentric', said his daughter, 'cannot tell you the origin or the objectives of his obsessions.' Death is as present as *joie de vivre*. Buried bodies gurgle upwards through the saturated earth. Headless ghosts stalk the corridors of town houses. But death occasions a party, as love occasions heartbreak, and a man can be called Fox and a woman George. It's camp, debauched, corrupt, emotionally extravagant, baroque. It's the one place in America without a trace of Puritanism.

We got back to the R-Bar around 4 a.m. There were still another two hours to go there. We played a couple of games of pool and were then challenged to a doubles game. We won that and the succeeding eight. I was drinking beer and our various opponents were trying to disequilibriate Steve with vodka and tonics. His walk became increasingly unsteady, but when he crouched over the table he was a perfectly repetitive machine.

When we got upstairs to our apartment I sat down in a chair in the living room and he went back to the bar, where he'd forgotten his cigarettes. I fell asleep. He, I discovered later, found the bar closed and then walked around the neighbourhood looking for a place to buy cigarettes. Nothing was yet open. When he got back he found that he didn't have the keys to the downstairs entrance. There was no bell connected to the apartment. He called out to me from the street, but I couldn't hear him. An hour later, after finding the owner of the hotel, he got back in to the apartment. He walked past me and got into bed, a bed so high you had to climb up steps to get into it. It was like a pyre. Some time after that I woke up in the chair. I didn't immediately know where I was. I looked around and saw him stretched out on his bed, the bedside light on, his whole body convulsed with sobs.

The Quarter is said to be at its best in the milky light of the morning. The heat is not yet oppressive. There is the smell of beignets and coffee flavoured with chicory in the air. Residents stretch and step slowly into the day, shop doors open and let in a breeze, those among the vast band of visiting revellers who endured the longest shuffle towards their hotels with red eyes. The American full-on partying male, his features unnuanced, his gestures staccato, his voice a hoarse, perpetual shout, is in his bed unconscious and still drunk after twenty-five cherry bombs or tequila sunrises. A Federal Writers' Project observer woke to the call of '"R-R-R-R-R-Romanay! R-r-r-ramonez la chiminée du haut en bas!" . . . You rub your eyes and stare at the extraordinary creature who is emitting these blood-curdling noises. He is a tall, unbelievably black Negro with crooked toes peeping out of shuffling shoes, non-descript trousers, a venerable frockcoat carrying the dirt of ages in its frayed threads, and cocked over one eye a stupendous top hat with most of the crown bashed in. He carries an unwieldy bundle containing a rope, a sheaf of broom straw, and several bunches of palmetto. Look at him closely. He is the last of his guild, a chimney-sweeper; and it may be a long time before you see him again, for he and his *compère*, the coal peddler, who calls "Mah mule is white, mah face is black; Ah sells mah coal two bits a sack!", are rapidly being forced to retreat before the increasing popularity of gas heat. *Adieu ramoneur*!' The writer then steps out into the day, nearly gets hit in the head by a bucket lowered by a Creole woman from a balcony for the collection of her morning coffee from the grocery man below, and watches a 'spasm band' made up of children on the corner of Royal and St Peter Streets, its beat frenetic and its instruments made from household dry goods. It seems like a scene from a medieval French village.

Steve and I didn't see the morning. We sat out on our terrace for a while watching people move around in the Faubourg Marigny and then went at 3 p.m. to the Clover Grill on Bourbon and Dumaine, motto 'We love to fry and it shows!' A huge black man calling everyone 'Baby' as he counted money by the till directed us to one of the four tables by the window. You can get some form of breakfast in the Clover Grill all day and several people were having it. Casualties of the night need never feel alone here. Steve chose an omelette that the menu declared had been de-veloped in 'a trailer park in Chalmette, Louisiana'. The menu also stated various house rules: 'Keep your hands on the table', 'No talking to yourself' and 'Dancing in the aisles only'. And finally, 'We don't sleep in your bed, please don't sleep on our tables.' It announced, 'Select members of our staff available for private parties.' A couple of these listed their hobbies as 'dressing up in drag', and of another it was said, 'He loves hanging out with his wife and his boyfriend.' That the Clover Grill had this strain did not mean that the menu included exotic yoghurt creations or bread flavoured with black olives or had opera playing on its sound system. This was an All-American short-order grill in a 1930s style with a long counter and a menu of hamburgers, chilli ('Our chilli speaks for itself . . . sooner or later'), pancakes, waffles and eggs. Men wearing hard hats and others with masscaraed eyes sat side by side at the counter chewing their way through the fried food. 'We're here to serve people and make them feel prettier than they are,' a sign said.

We went our own ways then for what remained of the afternoon, Steve to drift through the Quarter, me to an Internet café. I read on a screen there that Marlon Brando had just died. Tennessee Williams had said of him, 'There was no point in discovering him, it was so obvious. I never saw such raw talent in an individual . . . [He] was a gentle, lovely guy, a man of extraordinary beauty. He was very natural and helpful. He repaired the plumbing when it was on the whack, and he repaired the lights that had gone off. And then he just sat calmly down and began to read.' Brando learned the drums and applied for patents for his inventions. He suspended acting for a time so that he could devote himself to the civil-rights movement. He weighed more than three hundred pounds, according to the newspaper notice I was reading. Of acting he said, 'If they'd pay me the same for sweeping the studio floor as for acting, I'd sweep the floor.' Barbara Williams met him at a lunch in Los Angeles. He spent most of it admiring Liam, then two years old. 'He's so very beautiful,' he said. When she started to speak with him about what he'd done in a particular performance, he interrupted her. 'When I think of acting, I want to vomit,' he said. That said, he was probably the most authentic, original and influential performer of his century.

I walked along the leafy streets, an aura of anticipation for the night already in the air. When in Albuquerque, Simone de Beauvoir wrote, 'We feel rather lost; there must be places where the whiskey tastes of the desert and the music would give us the keys to this land with its rich past – but how to find them?' This is the daily longing of the random traveller.

I'd felt it sometimes as I drove around a town or city looking for somewhere where something might happen. She wouldn't have had a problem in New Orleans. If the place you enter isn't right, there's likely to be another next door that is.

I hadn't washed any clothes since Los Angeles and was running out. I went into a small clothing shop, found two shirts and a pair of jeans and went to the till to pay someone who looked like a Hell's Angel. In front of me a black man in his fifties, tall, slender and seemingly nonchalant, had laid out some articles on the counter and was taking out his money. A large woman was in a collapsible chair next to the counter, fanning herself and waiting for the man. The shop-keeper held up a pair of checked boxer shorts, looking for the price tag, and then a pair of Y-fronts. The customer winced at the indecency of this exposure. He turned to me.

'You see, I'm not sure which ones to get.'

There was a pause while the shopkeeper continued his examination.

'There was a time when I used to buy silk,' the man in front of me said then, to the room generally.

The woman in the chair closed her eyes, fanned herself a little faster and said, 'Shi-i-i-i-ny and pressed.'

'That's right, Mrs B,' he said. 'Shiny and pressed!'

The fan stopped in mid-stroke.

'That was back in the Seventies, wasn't it?' she said.

The man looked suddenly like a flattened tyre.

'That's correct, Mrs B.'

Then he turned to me.

'Too much information, right?' he said.

The previous winter I'd met a group of New Orleans rappers called Da Rangaz at a private concert in Hackney, east London. Their names were DJ Chicken, Snoop and B. It was their first time out of the southern United States. They'd been brought there by the writer Nik Cohn, then nearly sixty years old, who was their improbable producer. 'Look us up,' the rappers said when I told them I was going to be in New Orleans that summer. 'We'll take you out.'

Steve was out on the terrace reading a book in the sun when I got back to the apartment with my new clothes.

'What did you do?' I asked him.

'Walked around, had a beer. I also went into a voodoo shop. And listen to this. As soon as I walked in, the woman at the counter said to me, "Are you looking for something for grief?"'

'Without you saying anything?'

'Yeah. She just picked it up. She told me to look for rosemary and lavender. I'm supposed to keep it in my pocket and next to my bed at night.'

'How much was it?'

'She said there was no point in her selling it to me. I could pick it up anywhere.'

'Are you going to do it?'

'Wouldn't you?' he said.

He was to be a temporary addition to the fifteen per cent of New Orleans residents who follow voodoo.

I told him about the rappers.

'Call them,' he said.

I called Snoop, who'd been born with the name Kent Wilkins. He told me to meet him in the Daiquiri Shop in the Seventh Ward on Elysian Fields Avenue in half an hour. He lived in the Ninth Ward, where Fats Domino grew up. It was named variously 'The Mighty Nine', 'Cross the Canal' and, with the same initials, 'Cut Throat City'. But he had grown up with B in the Seventh near Hunter's Fields, and they had both gone to John F. Kennedy High School there. His father was a house painter and his mother a special-needs teacher. He had degrees in sociology and criminal justice and worked as a juvenile parole officer.

In *Triksta*, the book Nik Cohn wrote about his experiences as a New Orleans rap producer, he quotes Snoop as saying: 'We're a black city, and black leaders keep pounding their people every day. Why? Because they feel threatened. They think, "I can't show that brother how to rise, he might take my spot." So they crush 'em. They've got their nice houses and nice suits, and all these white folks telling them, "I like you. You're not like them, those other animals. I can work with you, but those others, they ain't shit." And the black businessman lets them say it. He doesn't tell them, "What do you mean, *animals*. Those are my brothers down there. They ain't shit, they just misguided" . . . *No corruption, no crime.* That's the ticket the city's running on, trying to show big business it's able to come here. So how they do, they'll catch a kid with a nickel bag, slam him in the system. Then he has a record. All he can do the rest of his life is menial work. One nickel bag, and they got 'em a virtual slave . . . Send out the message loud and clear: "If you want to be stealin' in this town, you better think in millions. Steal you a million, two million, you can sit down with us to dinner. Steal you a few hundred bucks, we'll nail your ass to the jailhouse door."'

Snoop was already in the Daiquiri Shop when we got there, sitting at a table with B, also known as Shorty Brown Hustle, but born with the name Brandon McGee. His shaved head gleamed in the light. Three of their friends, Eric, Jamal and Terrence, were at another table next to it. They bought us a pitcher of beer. 'Welcome,' they all said.

The day before, said Snoop, he and Terrence had rapped into a camera for two and a half hours straight. I don't think I could improvise rhyme for fifteen seconds.

'How do you do it?' I asked him.

'It's there,' he said. 'You just have to open your mouth. The mind is infinite.'

'You see him?' said B. 'Intellectual, detached, so cool sitting back there in his chair. He's like Chuck D out of Public Enemy.'

'No rapper I knew was deeper seated in street lore than Snoop or had a sharper view of what was really happening to this town,' wrote Nik Cohn. 'You could throw any word in the air, and he'd riff for ten minutes without catching breath. Born to freestyle, that was Snoop.'

'New Orleans is more musical than other places,' he said. 'Brass bands, jazz. You had Louis Armstrong, Fats Domino, Mahalia Jackson. Jelly Roll Morton was from right here in the Seventh Ward. It's more instrumental than other cities, not so hard. Hip hop came in the late Eighties. Rap was big. Dave Bartholomew, the band leader, I grew up right next to him. Music is everywhere. I like R and B, but I can't sing. So I rap.'

'We do it for the fun,' said B. 'We're party people. Our whole life's a party. That's what we embrace.'

'We got some social conscience,' said Snoop. 'We do that. But music isn't made to depress, it's made to uplift.'

'Look at that girl up at the bar, man,' said B. 'Check her out. Look at the body. Why anyone want to talk about shooting somebody?'

Da Rangaz rap bloodlessly, non-violently. Gangsta is backward, cheap, they think. 'Every rapper in New Orleans keeps saying the same shit,' Snoop told Nik Cohn. *I'ma shoot you, I'ma kill you, I'ma blow out ya brains*, that's the only way they can sell down here. We've been desensitized so far, we can't see we're doing the white man's dirty work. Black people are losing. We're dying out here, and who gives a fuck? Get a deal, get the gold. Make a million-dollar video for BET and tell the world how they shot all these niggas, left their mamas crying. Then they put their name on a foundation, the Big Ass Fund, and throw a little spare change to the ghetto. And meanwhile they're wearing a forty-thousand-dollar bracelet. How can they live with themselves? Don't they know what they are? *106 & Park*, that's a minstrel show. All these rappers, they're nothing but Sambos.'

'How was it in England?' I asked them.

'Oh, man, we've got to get back there,' said B.

'Got to get back to that club in London, China White's,' said Snoop. 'We were dancing on the sofas, taking our clothes off. They opened up their arms to us.'

'We want the full rock-star life,' said B.

'We want the cocaine even if we don't use it,' said Snoop.

'You ever have any problems with one another?' I asked.

'I hate that motherfucker,' said Snoop. 'I hate B. I hate that bitch.'

Eric leaned over from the other table.

'You don't want B to like you,' he said. 'The more he likes you, the more he talks about you.'

'This fucker would tell nasty jokes about nuns,' said Snoop.

'He stole his own car,' said Jamal.

'He was so drunk once that his mother put rosary beads around him and a pill up his ass,' said Snoop.

'Can you make a living from the music?' I asked.

'Are you serious?' said B. 'We got to Florida once. But that was it, apart from London. We don't care about money, anyway. We'd do it for free. Me, I work in the Charity Hospital. It's like a fucked-up project with doctors – blood, piss, shit, missing fingers. But it's the best. Jamal got hit with a shot from an AK-47 coming home from work. Got caught in a crossfire. He came in like a piece of driftwood you'd find in a lake. Next thing, he's shaking hands with everybody. Charity Hospital saved him. I work in the laundry room. I'm on the bus at five, at work at seven.'

'He's the best mediator,' said Snoop. 'He makes every-body laugh until they realise how stupid they are. Everybody's got their craft. That's his.'

'I've got to laugh to stop myself from crying sometimes,' said B. 'You can shoot yourself in the head or you can laugh at yourself. A sense of humour is the best thing to be born with. There's just nothing you can do to piss me off. One time it wasn't like that. I was scared of grass, red Kool-Aid, the letter D. No more. My mama came back and gave me love. That's the cure. That's where the music comes from. My day is comfortable if everybody gets along. I'm not scared of anything now. I'm not scared of that girl up there at the bar, for instance. And you know what? Ever since I got this bald head, my pussy rate went right up.'

'You don't want to look inside that head,' said Jamal.

'That's a twenty-six-day story,' said Eric.

'You'd never get to New York,' said Snoop.

When Nik Cohn had grown despondent about his role as a rap producer, it was B, he said, who saved him. 'Nobody else could have said the things he did without getting killed,' he wrote. 'He walked up to cripples, and mongols and chemo patients, threw their infirmities in their faces, and somehow they took it from him, embraced it even, for there was greatness in his heart, they knew it on sight. He never bragged on himself, yet according to Snoop, who'd known him all their lives, he shared everything he possessed . . . One night, leaving the house, he said casually across his shoulder, "All we've got is skin and our souls."'

Just over a year after I was there, B stayed home while a million people were fleeing New Orleans in anticipation of Hurricane Katrina. He went over to see his cousin in New Orleans East after his mother called to tell him to get out. When the storm hit, the roof blew off and the water began to rise. They grabbed a passing boat and B got an elderly woman in a wheelchair named Miss Beulah, three children and a woman with a baby into it. They paddled with their hands past corpses and debris in the toxic water until they reached a freeway overpass, where they camped with hundreds of others for two nights, getting some food from an abandoned grocery store. Hot, saturated air rank with the smell of sewage and decomposition lay over them like a blanket. They were moved by a Coast Guard launch to higher ground and ate spoiled fish from a seafood restaurant called Capt. Sal's. Miss Beulah was confused, in pain and incontinent. Five loose pit bulls attacked them in the night. Police and National Guardsmen drove by without stopping. Finally, four days after the levee broke they were moved to the city's Convention Center, which was taking the overspill from the Superdome, the original 'shelter of last resort'.

B thought they'd be all right there. There was bound to be medicine, food, nappies, clothing, showers for the people he was with. They drove past abandoned cars and refugees, with eighty per cent of the city underwater. When they got to the Convention Center it was too crowded to find a place inside, so they stayed out on the sidewalk. When B tried to get into a bathroom, he found the door blocked by bodies. He slept for only minutes at a time. People urinated and defecated where they could. B thought he might crack. Finally, eight days after the hurricane hit, they were evacuated, first to a place in Texas and then, through a stroke of fortune when a white man in a minibus offered help, to a church, where they got food, clean clothes and showers. They'd all survived.

Ken, my black ex-US Marine friend in Valencia, told me he'd always been quick to defend the United States when Europeans attacked it, even doing so with a certain pleasure, until Katrina. 'How can you leave people in those circumstances for eight days? A country that can repeatedly launch invasions can surely save its own people from drowning and starvation quicker than that. This wasn't a logistical problem, this was a statement: We don't care about you. I don't say this was because the majority of the people stranded were black. I believe it was because they were poor.'

Nik Cohn, who'd lived intermittently in New Orleans for thirty years, went back to look at it after Katrina, finding submerged cars, children's toys up in trees, mementoes of lives covered in muck scattered in yards, ripped buildings, an upended barge thrown a hundred yards inland. Some people told him they thought the downtown levees had been blown deliberately to spare the Quarter and the wealthy areas uptown. This happened in 1927 when city leaders ordered the dynamiting of downtown levees so they could keep themselves dry. It is also thought by some that the poor black neighbourhoods are not being restored because the overall plan for the city is a remaking of its racial composition, with a vast dispersal of blacks out into the south and New Orleans' conversion into, as Nik Cohn calls it, 'a boutique city', a tourist destination with more pedigree than Las Vegas, suburban developments and golf courses in the once-black neighbourhoods, and a new army of servers made up of Hispanics without residency permits living in tent cities. This might sound paranoid, but then before writing this book I wouldn't easily have accepted that lobbyists were writing the nation's legislation, that people had been denied the vote on the basis of their colour, that insurance corporations were spending fortunes to discredit the legal profession, weren't paying bills to the medical personnel who worked for them and conspired in the mistreatment and even deaths of their own clients, or that the invasions of Afghanistan and Iraq were first steps in a geopolitical plan aimed at world domination. It could be that a 'paranoid', as William Burroughs once said, 'is someone in full possession of the facts.'

It was the Fourth of July and we were moving out. Before we left, though, we drove over to Julia Street to see a painter, gallery owner and bandleader named George Schmidt, whom I'd met when in New Orleans twelve years earlier. He showed us around his gallery and then brought us into a back room for a cool drink, where he played us a couple of tracks from an album by his band, the New Leviathan Oriental Foxtrot Orchestra.

'This city is forty-nine per cent under sea level,' he said. 'This has affected the city's history and its consciousness. When they buried bodies under the ground, coffins would float up through the wet earth and pop out. They couldn't keep them down. That's why the Creoles buried their dead above ground. The side of this house here was a running sewer. Damp came up through the bricks. The whole city was a yellow-fever nest. They thought at first that inhalation of vapours coming up from the ground caused it. People weren't dying at home in their beds, but suddenly, in shops or out in the streets. The treatment was immersion in ice-water. Creoles had immunity, so it was mostly immigrants who got it. A lot of Irish got it. The Irish were the servants here. They were cheaper than black slaves. Five thousand Irish died, incidentally, digging the Basin Canal here, since filled in. That wasn't considered a disaster. Every civilisation has a dark underbelly. There's an optimum number of deaths it will tolerate in order to make money.'

'What are you going to do for the Fourth of July?' I asked him.

'The Fourth of July? I hadn't actually noticed. My New Orleans isn't America. Mardi Gras has been the thing here, of course. Everyone knows that, but they don't know how it looked from the inside. You just lived for it. Carnival was a true manifestation of place. The cultural war here was between French Catholics and newly arrived Americans. These Puritan Americans thought the Catholics were barbaric. They banned the Creole Carnival. The Carnival would suggest what England was like before the Puritan revolution. The people here could be very emotional. They could look at a painting and say, "I can't breathe." Carnival, though, is play. My parents were crazy for costumes. They dressed me up as Toulouse-Lautrec. The kind of play that Carnival is is hierarchical. It's not America. It's a thing of tableaux, balls, masques, a king and queen. You'd see somebody getting out of a taxi cab dressed as a Pharaoh. No movie star had the same status in New Orleans as the King of Carnival. It's not ruled by the Constitution. When you celebrate it you feel like a real human being. It's pre-Enlightenment. It couldn't happen elsewhere. People knew that and fought like hell to preserve it. I mounted a picket against making a talkshow host the King of Carnival. I had a bumper sticker that read, "Carnival Is Ours, America Go Home." But it's being killed by tourism, government, egalitarian social engineering, and the city's going with it. We had an old and beautiful place and they've taken a ball-peen hammer to it. I have to put a sleeping mask on when I come in from the airport so I won't see the suburbs. It's like watching your mother die.'

We went back through the swamps by Lake Pontchartrain, black, limbless trees in the still water. Water is everywhere here like blood in a body, rivening the land into fragments in this vast emptying of the Mississippi. The land to the south has the look on a map of shrapnel at the moment of an explosion. A friend of mine from Flint, Michigan was down in this land- and waterscape of petroleum and shrimp to help someone open a bookshop and saw in a Thibodaux newspaper called *The Alligator* the exclamation 'FREE BOOBS!' in an advertisement for a local bar. Each Wednesday, he discovered, the bar conducted a raffle and the winner got breast implants.

We went around Baton Rouge and once again I was on Highway 61, this time going north. I'd last seen it in Minnesota. The road took a bend at St Francisville. I stayed here in 1994 and visited Rosedown, a preserved nineteenth-century cotton plantation, once comprising 3,455 acres and owned by Daniel and Martha Barrow Turnbull. A woman in a frilly, peach-coloured period dress replicated in rayon guided a group of us around the house and grounds, lingering over porcelain, silverware, the ornamental garden and the imported chairs. She pointed out the slave quarters, but mentioned nothing of the institution, which supplied the Turnbulls with 450 free labourers. 'In America . . .' wrote Henry Miller, 'the great houses followed the great crops: in Virginia tobacco, in South Carolina rice, in Mississippi cotton, in Louisiana sugar. Supporting it all, a living foundation, like a great column of blood, was the labour of the slaves.'

We were headed into the Delta, an alluvial plain misnamed as it begins at Memphis and ends well to the north of where the Mississippi begins to fragment before emptying into the Gulf of Mexico. 'That Delta. Five thousand square miles, without any hills save the bumps of dirt the Indians made to stand on when the river overflowed,' wrote William Faulkner in *Sanctuary*. At the beginning of the twentieth century it was a wilderness of cypress and gum trees inhabited by panthers and bears, but the rich soil and the institution of slavery turned it into a cotton empire. It is America's Sicily, a place of hierarchies and dark secrets and with a long history of anguish, its cruelties overlaid with silence. We crossed the Mississippi state line and took a turn through leafy Woodville, outside of which the façade and barbed wire of a new prison sparkled in the sun like a marzipan, glitter-strewn birthday cake. Woodville was once known as 'Little Jerusalem' because of the presence of Jews here, one of whom, Charles Louis Levin, was wounded in a duel for which he had as his second Jefferson Davis, later the president of the Confederacy. For most of the Jewish merchants who came here it was a pause in a journey that ended in New Orleans. We drove into Natchez, the Mississippi seeming to whisper and exhale as it flowed past the grassy banks. It is the oldest permanent settlement on the river. Sun-worshipping Indians lived here, as did the French, Spanish and British before it became a showcase of Greek Revival mansions. Below, at the landing stage on the river, is Natchez-Under-the-Hill, once, in the days of heavy riverboat traffic, a centre of debauchery called the 'Sodom of the Mississippi'.

Before the Civil War, Natchez had the most millionaries per capita in the United States, living the pre-Enlightenment life George Schmidt talked about. Many had their plantations on the other side of the river in the flatlands of Louisiana and built their houses on the hills of Natchez. Of them and others like them, the historian Raimondo Luraghi wrote: 'However different the external conditions, both Americas, from French Canada down to Spanish South America, showed striking structural similarities. The exceptions were New England and the so-called Middle Colonies (New York, New Jersey, Pennsylvania), which were bourgeois and capitalist. Everywhere the foundation of society was agriculture, mainly based on large-scale land property; every-where a distinctive single-crop or single-staple economy prevailed (furs in French Canada; tobacco, rice and indigo in southern English colonies; sugar in the Caribbean and Brazil). Everywhere . . . slavery was the dominant labour system; everywhere the social body was ruled by a partic-ular class, agricultural, paternalistic, more similar in its social connotations to European nobility than to the bourgeoisie, with whom, indeed, it had nothing in common.' Michael Lind in *Made in Texas* compares the landowners to European knights, as opposed to the bourgeoisie, who tended to concentrate on trade, thrift, long-term investment and a consequent willingness to experiment. 'The knights', he writes, 'often commanded vast territories, but seldom ventured beyond them, unless on a Crusade or an expedition of conquest. The merchants, from their tiny walled cities, sent forth, and sometimes led, trading expeditions to the edges of the known world. The knights disdained labour; the burghers prized it. The knights spent their wealth recklessly; the burghers accumulated it. The knights, on encountering foreigners, sought to subjugate them; the burghers wanted to barter. The knights disdained profit and treasured honour; the burghers, although they were not insensible to honour, valued profit more.' The burghers feared the arbitrary powers of bishops, kings and tyrants and thought constitutional democracy the best protector of their assets; the knights thought the law a decorative triviality to be dispensed with whenever it stood in the way. The one was progressive, the other reactionary.

A visitor to Natchez named Joseph Ingram was taken to a slave market there in 1835 by a planter, who paused before a young man named George and said, '"Let me see your teeth – your tongue – open your hands – roll up your sleeves – have you a good appetite? are you good tempered?" "Me get mad sometime," replied George to the last query, "but neber wid my horses."'

The plantation society was one of play and conspicuous display, of outsized emotions and of cruelty and darkness. The opportunities for comedy and tragedy were present everywhere, and anyone with an inclination to write began with an advantage if born in the south. There are blood feuds, dynasties, breakdowns, gargantuan characters that could have been invented by Dostoevsky or Gogol, a language of ripeness, eccentric idiom and wonderfully purposeless flight. Compelling plots are at hand on any given street. One wonders if America could be considered to have a literature without southerners or Jews.

But there was a price, in waste, stagnation, parochialism and legally enforced inequality. The attempts to remake the south after the Civil War were abandoned, allowing the plantation owners to live as they had done, with the sharecropper system replacing slavery. When Simone de Beauvoir witnessed it in the 1940s she wrote, 'There is no European country where agricultural workers constitute such a vast and wretched herd; you could only find such conditions in their colonies. Here, the colony is within the United States itself.' Sharecropping was dismantled by mechanisation, legal separation of the races was abolished by civil-rights legislation and the old southern aristocracy faded away and was replaced by agribusiness. But the ethos of an unregulated, low-tax, low-wage society remained. 'What might be called Southernomics is based, like pre-industrial agrarian economics, on extensive development, not intensive development,' wrote Michael Lind. 'Running out of oil and gas? Don't make engines more efficient, or power vehicles with hydrogen or electric batteries; drill in wildlife preserves and conquer oil-producing countries in the Middle East, installing pro-American puppet regimes. Is there a tight labour market? Don't invest in machines that permit one worker to do the work of three; hire illegal aliens, while lobbying the government for guest worker programmes and increased immigration quotas. The pre-modern mind can conceive of economic expansion only in terms of applying traditional techniques to one resource.' The knight, he believes, lives on in other forms in the stories of Enron and WorldCom, one headquartered in Texas and the other in Mississippi, both typically southern in their strategy for growth based on 'good-old-boy politics [combined] with bluffing and swindling on a heroic scale'.

Steve, with an instinct developed from years of expense-account travelling, found the best restaurant in Natchez. As we waited to be seated, a northern couple who had emigrated to the south spoke of how happy they were to be there. A friend of theirs walked in and we were introduced. He was just back from London, he said, which he had enjoyed, as always, very much. He had an apartment there.

'What do you do?' I asked him.

'Building projects mostly,' he said.

'Such as?'

'Did you come through Woodville?'

'We did.'

'Did you see the prison?'

'That would be difficult to miss.'

'I built that,' he said. 'It's for lifers. If you're going on up north from here you'll see another new one just outside of Clarksdale.'

'What brought you to London?' I asked.

'That was just a stop-off on the way back from Basra. We're doing some work over there too.'

He had hit upon two of America's most rapidly growing markets – the criminal-justice system and war – both wholly paid for by the government.

After dinner we kept going on 61 until Port Gibson and then turned onto the Natchez Trace Parkway, an Indian trail that the Chicksaw called the 'Path of Peace' and which now links Natchez, Mississippi with Nashville. It became a trade route along which itinerant preachers and bandits roamed. Meriwether Lewis, who had opened up the west with William Clark, had stopped for a rest on it at Grinder's Stand in Tennessee, deeply depressed, it is said, at the state of his finances. He bought some gunpowder, and hours later in the night two shots were heard. He'd taken one to the chest and one to the head. The cause of his death remains in dispute, though it is said he'd tried to jump into the Mississippi shortly before arriving at Grinder's Stand.

To the west of Jackson we got onto US 49, going north. We crossed the Big Black River just before Bentonia, and then entered the Hillside Nature Wildlife Reserve, a 15,572-acre strip of land originally purchased by the Corps of

Engineers to entrap sediment and silt running off the surrounding loess hills and thereby prevent it entering the Yazoo and Mississippi Rivers. It was dark by the time we got to Yazoo City, originally known as Jannan's Bluff, then Manchester. It got its present name in 1839. Yazoo is an Indian term meaning 'River of Death'.

We found a place called the Horseshoe Tavern. They wanted $6 for entry to a karaoke night, a large sum, we thought, for what was on offer – a music-producing machine, an autocue, two singers and a single customer sitting up at the bar, a man of about sixty in a baseball cap drinking shots. He stopped us like a toll-taker as we passed.

'Where y'all from?' he asked.

Steve mentioned England.

'I been in England,' he said. 'I work in the sawmill now, but when I was in the military I was stationed there. King's Lynn. Good place.'

'What did you like about it?' asked Steve.

'Weren't no niggers there,' he said, then the rat-a-tat-tat of his laughter. He'd staked a claim on the small space on which Steve and I stood, but we moved out of it and up towards the stage. A young woman with black eyes sang Jimmy Webb's 'Galveston' with disarming beauty and feeling.

US 49 split at Yazoo City, and in the morning we took the east fork up through Eden and on to Greenwood, named for the Choctaw chief Greenwood Leflore, who – with his signature in 1830 on the Treaty of Dancing Rabbit Creek – ceded eleven million acres of Indian land in Mississippi in exchange for fifteen million in Oklahoma. Their journey there on foot became known as the 'Trail of Tears'. Remembering this, they sent money a few years later to Ireland when they heard people were starving in a famine. The Yalobusha and Tallahatchie Rivers meet here to form the Yazoo.

Greenwood, the largest cotton exchange in America after Memphis, is a place of grand mansions and shacks. We went looking for Lusco's, an Italian/Cajun restaurant on the poor side of town where the cotton magnates came to drink moonshine in private booths lined with chintz curtains during Prohibition, but we found it closed. A man with dreadlocks sat under the brutalising sun on a bench by the railroad tracks, a traditional borderline separating the races in the south. We went into the Riverfront Liquor Store and bought cool water. The owner said he had grown up on a hundred-acre cotton farm, but told us such places no longer existed, having long ago been swept up with many others and amalgamated by out-of-state corporations. He had the liquor store, was a part-time constable and his wife taught at a school that was seventy per cent black.

'I've seen changes,' he said. 'The neighbourhood where I live is integrated. There was a black wedding at the white Baptist church. That caused a stink, but it died down. Every time something like that happens another step is made. But this is still the south. I don't think I'll see the damage undone in my lifetime.'

'Is there work here?' I asked him.

'There was, but we lost 1,300 jobs to Mexico once NAFTA got through. That was mainly in auto parts and clothing. An accountant told me that the profits they're making in Mexico are almost the same as what they made here, but for that little margin they've left the town wounded. A Super Wal-Mart closed a lot of the businesses. The small farms and businesses and entrepreneurs were what formed the foundation of America, and they're getting killed off. A town has a better chance if it's on an interstate, but unfortunately we're not.'

He handed us each a calendar and address book put together by the town's merchants.

'Tell them you got that from a redneck from Mississippi,' he said.

Advocates of NAFTA (the North American Free Trade Agreement) said it would turn Canada, Mexico and the United States into a major unitary force in world trade, that it would raise standards generally in the region and provide new opportunities, that manufacturers from the United States would benefit from new unrestricted markets, and that, in any case, free trade is a necessary and dynamic principle in a world growing ever more compact. What in fact happened is that industry fled to the lower wages of Mexico, and the United States became an importer of products that they had previously exported. 'The US had large net sales of computers *before* NAFTA but had net payments to Mexico of −$3.8 billion for those high-tech goods in 2000,' wrote the compellingly named economist Charles W. McMillion. 'The large US net export losses to Mexico since NAFTA are concentrated in autos, machinery, electronics, apparel and furniture. US net export gains are largely in agribusiness and bulk commodities such as cereals and organic chemicals. Even the few manufactured goods with net export gains are concentrated in packing and boxes of plastic, paper and styrene largely destined briefly "in bond" to Mexico's Maquiladores and quickly back to US consumers.' Shareholders' dividends marginally improved, and more money gathered at the top, while unemployment rose and towns slowly died. Of 'supercapitalism' in the post-regulatory era, Tony Judt wrote: 'Regulatory structures set in place over the course of a century or more were superseded or dismantled within a few years. In their place came increased competition both for global markets and for the cataract of international funds chasing lucrative investments. Wages and prices were driven down, profits up. Competition and innovation generated new opportunities for some and vast pools of wealth for a few; meanwhile they destroyed jobs, bankrupted firms and impoverished communities . . . Abundance . . . may be the American substitute for socialism; but as shared social objectives go, shopping remains something of an underachievement.' After NAFTA, the United States in its trade relations with Mexico began to behave as the south traditionally had towards the north, as a colony to the imperial centre, exporting raw materials and importing manufactured goods.

We drove out of town and along a dirt road to look at a field of cotton. The topsoil here, brought by flooding rivers through the ages, is up to fifty feet deep. Much of the richest of all cotton-growing land did not become viable until after the Civil War, when the wilderness was cleared and levees were built to control the spring floods. Ex-slaves came out of the scrubland of the hills and into the Delta, which then saw the quickest and most extensive development of the sharecropping system. Sharecroppers got a fifteen- to forty-acre plot of land, seed, tools, a mule and a loan to cover their living expenses until the crop was sold in the autumn, when they were allocated what they were told was their share. They lived in a plantation shack, worshipped at the plantation Baptist church and bought supplies with scrip at jacked-up prices in the plantation store. Martin Luther King met sharecroppers in the 1960s who had never seen American currency. Children went to school up to the age of around fourteen in one- or two-room unheated plantation school-houses with time off for field work. Some children attended school only when it rained. 'In 1938,' wrote Nicholas Lemann, 'the average American teacher's salary was $1,374 and the average value of a school district's buildings and equipment per student was $274. For schools in Mississippi the figures were $144 and $11.'

Just before Christmas the planter would tell the share-croppers what their share of the yield was, an amount that had been reduced by equipment costs, the repayment of loans and any other arbitrary thing the planter might wish to deduct. Average interest was twenty per cent. It could reach as high as thirty-seven. Often the sharecropper could find that after working the fields all year he owed the planter money. A Yale anthropologist named Hortense Powdermaker, who spent a year in the Delta in 1930, estimated that only a quarter of the planters were honest in their accounts to their tenants. Questioning the 'settle', as it was called, could bring about a whipping. Sheriffs deferred to planters on questions of law involving tenants.

I turned the car around and headed back towards Greenwood. We stopped at a wooden shack. A wheel-less pickup truck was sinking into the earth. I saw the silhouette of someone inside move into the frame of the window, and then beyond. I thought to knock on the door and ask about this life so distant from my own, but couldn't find the temerity and drove on. Another story left unheard.

We got onto 49 going north, passing a town called Money. In 1955 a fourteen-year-old black boy named Emmett Till came down from Chicago to this place to spend some time with his sharecropper great-uncle, Moses 'Preacher' Wright. On the evening of 25 August he went with his cousins into a store belonging to Roy and Caroline Bryant, a white couple in their early twenties. Roy Bryant was driving a cargo of shrimp from New Orleans to San Antonio and his wife was alone behind the counter. On a dare, it seems, Emmett Till asked her to go out with him. He might have whistled at her as he was leaving the shop.

Roy Bryant heard about it when he got back. He and his half-brother J.W. Milam, both former soldiers, took Emmett Till from Preacher Wright's house in the middle of the night, drove him around for hours in the back of a truck, pistol-whipped him and shot him in the head with a .45. Then they tied a cotton gin fan with barbed wire around his neck and threw him in the Tallahatchie River. He was found three days later.

Milam and Bryant, to the surprise of many in Mississippi, were arrested, but the jury, twelve white males, stayed true to tradition and acquitted them. A grand jury declined to indict them for kidnapping. Milam lived until 1980 and Bryant until 1994, both of them dying from cancer. Months after the verdicts came in, knowing that under the laws of double jeopardy they were safe from any further prosecution, they gave an interview to a journalist from *Look* magazine. Milam described how they were only trying to frighten Till, but he wouldn't be frightened. With a gun in his hand he asked him, 'You still as good as I am?' and Till answered, 'Yeah.' This assertion of equality was a poison that Milam felt he had to purge with gunfire. 'What else could I do?' he said to the journalist. 'I'm no bully. I never hurt a nigger in my life. I like niggers – in their place – I know how to work 'em. But I just decided it was time a few people got put on notice. As long as I live and can do anything about it, niggers are gonna stay in their place. Niggers ain't gonna vote where I live. They ain't going to school with my kids. And when a nigger gets close to mentioning sex with a white woman, he's tired of livin' . . . Me and my folks fought for this country, and we got some rights.'

Medgar Evers, a black veteran of the Battle of Normandy, became a field worker for the National Association for the Advancement of Coloured People in the Delta and in the early 1960s conducted an investigation into Emmett Till's death, posing as a cotton picker to get information. A Molotov cocktail was thrown into his home and a car tried to run him down. Finally he was shot in the back on 12 June 1963 and died from the wound. Bob Dylan wrote songs about both men and came to Greenwood with Pete Seeger for a voter registration rally, singing 'Only a Pawn in Their Game'. Three years later, Stokely Carmichael came to Greenwood on a freedom march and shook up the south with his first mention of 'Black Power'.

We met 49 East again at Milner City and took it north to Tutwiler. In what remained of downtown we looked at a mural on the old railroad station depicting a field hand with a guitar and W.C. Handy, a black composer from Alabama whose first inspirations were, he said, the sounds of 'whooperwills, bats and hootowls', flowing water in a woodland and 'the song of every songbird and all the symphonies of their unpremeditated art'. In 1902, while waiting for a train to Memphis, Handy had fallen asleep on the platform in Tutwiler and awoke to the guitar music of the field hand beside him. 'His face', he said, had 'the sadness of the ages'. He had a knife pressed to the neck of the guitar and produced a long, thin wail of a note while he sang 'Goin' where the Southern cross the Dog'. This referred to the intersection of the Southern Railroad and the Yazoo and Mississippi Valley tracks further to the south. It was, said Handy, 'the weirdest music I had ever heard'. This, according to one legend, is where the blues was born. W.E.B. Du Bois wrote of slave songs the year after Handy was in Tutwiler, 'They are the music of an unhappy people, of the children of disappointment; they tell of death and suffering and unvoiced longing toward a truer world, of misty wanderings and hidden ways.'

In the town were the Silver Saver Shop, the O and J Package Store and the Tallahatchie County Ministerial Alliance. Eighty-seven per cent of Tutwiler is black. Steve went over to speak with three boys who were sitting under a tree, and after a while I followed. They wore immaculately pressed, brightly coloured shirts and finished each sentence with the word 'sir'. This made us both uneasy and put them out of reach. One said he was planning to be a truck driver, another to go to college to study art.

'What's the main form of work around here?' I asked.

'Social security, sir,' said a boy named Nathan.

A little later, in the Cat's Head Music Shop in Clarksdale, a man behind the counter, who was from Ohio, said that social security had replaced the plantation system in the Delta. 'You still go to the Man for everything,' he said. 'Only in this case it's the government.'

A long Cadillac drove slowly through Tutwiler, raising dust and a cloud of insects. This was the mayor, the boys told us, an employee at the state penitentiary at Parchman just a few miles to the south-west, a maximum-security prison for 4,380 inmates, including men sentenced to die. Elvis Presley's father did time here for forgery. The bluesman Son House was here, as was Bukka White, who wrote 'Parchman Farm Blues'. Convicted sharecroppers continued to pick cotton on the prison farm while incarcerated here. Mose Allison sang about throwing an eleven-foot sack of cotton with a twelve-gauge shotgun at his back. In 1972 Parchman was renovated following a decision by federal judge William C. Keady that it violated the Constitution and was an affront to decency.

We pulled back out onto Highway 49. The crossroads here is one of those where it is believed that the bluesman Robert Johnson sold his soul to the Devil in order to improve his skill on the guitar. He had gone out into the world with a small talent, was met with indifference, went back home and sequestered himself with a guitar and, when he came back out again, was hailed as a wonder. Everybody wanted him, including, it seems, a woman whose husband poisoned him with doctored whiskey in a juke-joint near Greenwood. Another Delta bluesman named Johnny Shines had gone on the road with Johnson, even though his family warned him that up in St Louis there were 'student traps', holes in the ground you'd fall into and then be sliced up for experiments by medical students. Up in Canada, they said, the people followed you around with big eyes in the centres of their foreheads that saw everything. The origin of this could be the Cyclops, but the eye that sees everything is also an all-American image introduced by the Puritans, who carved it into the pulpits of their churches to remind the congregations of the tireless scrutiny of God. The eye made it onto the back of the dollar bill, set in a pyramid.

Just north of Tutwiler was the private prison the man in Natchez had told us about, new and sparkling and parked beside Highway 49 like a liner in a dock. The companies that build and run private prisons belong to an organisation called the American Legislative Exchange Council, which helps states to draft tougher sentencing laws to fill their jails. The union for prison workers has the same interest and also funds the lobbyists. The 'three strikes' law, whereby a person with two felonies on his record must receive a mandatory minimum sentence of twenty-five years upon conviction for a third, has been a great generator of revenue for private prisons. Lobbyists pay the politicians, the politicians declare themselves tough on crime and propose more police and more jails, and the media portrays sections of society as bestiaries of serial killers, drugged psychopaths and rapists. According to an article in *Mother Jones* by Vince Beiser, homicide rates between 1990 and 1998 dropped by half, but reporting of homicides on the three major networks rose fourfold. Crime was the fear that filled the historical gap between the Cold War with the Soviets and Arab terrorism. In one case, a homeless black man with two previous convictions was being fed by a priest. He went one weekend to get his meal, found the priest out but the window open, went in, cooked himself a meal and was arrested for trespassing. For that he got twenty-five years. There are two million people in jail in America; 3,300 new prisons were built in the 1990s to accommodate them. Crime rates have fallen, but the prison population has quadrupled. Per capita spending on prisons has risen six times faster than spending on education. One private prison company, the Corrections Corporation of America, saw its share price rise from $4.12 per share to just under $45 between January 1995 and August 1997. A person's child can enter this system early and stay in it, more or less, for the rest of his life.

We kept going on 49. Big Joe Williams wrote a song about it. There are songs about 51 and 61, the two other north–south highways of the Delta, and many more about the trains that travelled between New Orleans and Memphis. Just before Clarksdale we passed what was the Hopson plantation, where, on 20 October 1944, the first production-ready prototype of a mechanical cotton picker was demonstrated. Hopson's calculations showed that picking a bale of cotton with this machine cost $5.26, while hand-picking cost $39.41. Up to then plantation owners sent their agents to Chicago to try to lure back sharecroppers with promises of reforms; after they saw the machine they did what they could to get those who remained to leave.

When newly freed slaves were given the vote and government jobs during Reconstruction in the 1870s, a former Confederate general named Lush Alcorn from Clarksdale, who had been both a governor and a US senator and was enough of a liberal to have his plantation burned by the Ku Klux Klan, appeared at a county convention with several other white men bearing arms, declaring the black officials in the state incompetent and corrupt and that sensible relations between the races had to be restored. At the same time, a former slave and Union Army soldier named Bill Peace raised his own militia of armed black men to defend the gains that had followed the Civil War. Alarms went up around the county, provoking a former Confederate general named James K. Chalmers to form a white militia, which confronted Peace's men at the Sunflower River in Clarksdale and harried them from the county. More white militias were formed, the federal government refused to send troops to maintain the Reconstruction administration, the governor was impeached, blacks were prevented from voting in the 1 November 1875 election and those who held state jobs were expelled, new Jim Crow segregationist laws were passed and Mississippi became the model for the other southern states in a system of segregation that lasted three-quarters of a century.

When we got to Clarksdale we went into a place called the Ground Zero Blues Club, owned by the actor Morgan Freeman, hoping for a sandwich. The kitchen, we were told, was closed, but three black ladies just finishing up their work

pitied us and gave us plates of chicken, greens, corn muffins and beans. John Lee Hooker, Howlin' Wolf and Robert Johnson all lived in Clarksdale. Bessie Smith died in a hospital here after a car accident in 1937. James Baldwin said that after listening to her records in a small village in Switzerland, he found the voice for *Go Tell It on the Mountain*, his first novel.

Muddy Waters, born McKinley Morganfield, was born in Rolling Fork, but was raised on the Stovall plantation outside Clarksdale by his grandmother. He derived his singing style from Son House and his bottleneck-style guitar playing from Robert Johnson. Carter Stovall, the son of the plantation owner, saw a white man recording Muddy Waters on the porch of his grandmother's shack in the summer of 1941. The white man was Alan Lomax from the Library of Congress. 'Certainly no white person in the Delta would ever have dreamed', wrote Nicholas Lemann in *The Promised Land*, 'that in the long run the blues music Muddy Waters played at jukes on Saturday nights would stand as the Delta's great contribution to American culture, while the writings of William Alexander Percy [a plantation owner and poet] would be a near-forgotten artefact of a peculiar regional way of life.' Two years later Muddy Waters went up to Memphis and caught the Illinois Central to Chicago, where he worked on a loading dock at a paper factory, played Delta music with an electric guitar and thereby established one of the main foundations for rock and roll.

Next to Ground Zero is the Delta Blues Museum. A young black man named Chris was serving behind a stack of post-cards on a counter. I bought one with Howlin' Wolf on it and told him about how I'd worked a whole summer on the West Side of Chicago just two blocks from where the man on the postcard played every week.

'I kept saying to myself that I'd go, but never did it. I never saw him that summer. In fact, I never saw him at all,' I said.

'The tragedy of procrastination,' said Chris.

'Where are you from?' I asked him.

'I'm from right here. People don't think I'm from Clarksdale, but I am.'

He told me he was thinking of going to college, but hadn't made the move yet. 'For now I read the dictionary. I like complicated words.'

'"The tragedy of procrastination" is pretty good,' I said.

'Tell them you heard that from a twenty-two-year-old black guy from Mississippi,' he said, a near-perfect replica of what the liquor-store owner had said to me in Greenwood, offering an address book rather than a phrase.

We drove through this town split by railroad tracks and out onto 278 going east. We left Coahoma County and entered another called Quitman. Somewhere between the Tallahatchie River and Batesville, Steve saw a dog splattered on the road and asked me to stop. I did so slowly, so as to get far enough from the dog not to have to smell it or think about it. I looked back at one point and saw him bent over and astride the dog, pointing his camera with concentrated purpose into his vast wound.

'How can you bear to do that?' I asked him when he got back.

'I'm used to it,' he said. 'This one was full of maggots, though.'

We passed Interstate 55, which runs from New Orleans all the way to Chicago. The flat Delta land gave way to wooded hills, the wooden shacks with old washing machines and mattresses on the porch to brick homes with well-tended lawns, black to white and the patched, bumpy country lane to a broad highway, smooth, guard-railed and freshly painted. The difference in the road was perhaps similar to the difference between the 'separate but equal' drinking fountains or railway-station waiting rooms in the pre-civil-rights south.

We arrived at Oxford, home for all but his first three years

to William Faulkner, and the principal campus of the University of Mississippi. It is the American town in its perfect form, immaculate, serene, slow in rhythm, a courthouse square in the centre with fine brick buildings around its perimeter, including Neilson's, established 1897, the south's oldest department store, and Square Books, one of the nation's finest bookstores, whose owner, Richard Howarth, is at the time of writing serving his second term as mayor of the town. Grand trees and elegant houses line the streets radiating from the square. Faulkner used to stroll down to the square in the evenings from his home, called Rowan Oak, to have a drink with his hunting friends. He never bought the first bottle of whiskey, they said, but always bought each subsequent one thereafter. A novelist friend of mine named Lamar Herrin came down here in a journey of homage a year after Faulkner's death and met these elderly men. 'We called him the Count,' one of them said. 'He'd always reply, "Count, No-Count." He'd come up here to this square and look out to the horizon for a while. We always knew not to disturb him then.' Samuel Beckett and Socrates also had a propensity for entering into trances in public places and had friends who understood to leave them alone at such moments. The men in the square went with Faulkner once to Memphis and, when they went looking for him early in the morning to go back to Oxford, they couldn't find him. Finally they went back to their car. Just as they were about to pull away, one of them looked down from the window and saw Faulkner's feet sticking out from under the car. He was sound asleep. 'Another two seconds and we'd have a few less books to remember him by,' one of them said to Lamar. His relationship to the people of the town was in general uneasy. Some didn't like his depiction of it in his books. Others thought him a kind of extra-terrestrial. When the Irish writer Patrick McCabe came to Oxford, Square Books sent a driver to meet him at the airport. 'Understand you're a writer,' the driver said. 'We had a writer once in Oxford, Mr William Faulkner. He wrote some very perplexing books.

There were some sentences in them you could wrap three or four times around this here airport.'

In 1962 a black student named James Meredith won the right in the Supreme Court to enrol in the then all-white University of Mississippi, the governor, Ross Barnett, having declared 'Never!' in answer to a question about when Mississippi schools would be integrated. Barnett was a member of the Ku Klux Klan. 'The Negro is different because God made him different to punish him,' he had said. He passed laws reducing workers' rights in order to attract industry and spent $300,000 having gold taps installed in the bathrooms of the governor's mansion. Waiting for Meredith to arrive at the university were US marshals, National Guard troops, state-highway patrolmen, the US Army and a white mob. A riot broke out on the evening of 30 September, during which 160 people were injured and two died. Meredith entered the university, completed his degree and at the graduation ceremony wore a badge saying 'Never' turned upside-down.

When we got to Rowan Oak we found it closed for refurbishment, but the curator was there and he let us walk around inside. With the walls painted and all the furniture in temporary storage, it seemed a more cheerful place than when I saw it intact in 1992, with everything as it was at the moment of Faulkner's death. There were a few mementoes of his travels, and over the walls of his study he had written a plot outline of *A Fable*, but it was otherwise formal, remote, devoid of the personal, the 1950s appliances anachronistic in this plantation-style, Greek Revival house, with a stable and woodland outside. It was difficult to imagine being happy here. Faulkner's relationship with his wife was evidently broken. They slept in different rooms. He'd once said that the perfect place for a writer to live was in a brothel, for it was quiet in the morning and there was a lot to do at night. Rowan Oak would seem to have provided him only with the former.

*   *   *

We left Oxford on 278, passing the southern edge of the Holly Springs National Forest, and stopped for a sandwich at Tupelo, named for its sweet-gum trees. Both Nick Cave and John Lee Hooker wrote songs about a cataclysmic flood that once hit this industrial town. Elvis Presley was born in a two-room shack here, built for $180 by his father, grandfather and uncle. The Elvis industry in Tupelo includes a museum, memorial chapel, a Walk of Life, a Story Wall, a statue of Elvis at thirteen and a replica of the car in which the family migrated to Memphis. The exhibits and gift shops were maintained by devout middle-aged women handling Elvis dolls and alarm clocks as if they were the bones of a saint. When they speak of the King, they lean close to you and whisper, as if to emphasise their devotion.

In 1933 Tupelo became the first place to receive electricity from the Tennessee Valley Authority, a massive New Deal state capitalist project that Roosevelt said was the achievement of which he was most proud. At the time Roosevelt took office, thirty per cent of the Tennessee Valley residents had malaria. The soil was exhausted, the forests had been depleted by fires and excessive logging and there were families living on a hundred dollars per year. The idea of Roosevelt and his planners was to deconcentrate population in the north-east by spreading cheap electricity, and therefore industrialisation and jobs, through the country. In the Tennessee Valley area the plan also included the control of floods, the replanting of forests, the education of farmers in the use of fertilisers and crop rotation and the placing of two hundred thousand people into unionised government jobs. Roosevelt declared that the nation's energy resources would remain in public hands as long as he was president.

Barry Goldwater proposed selling the TVA in 1964. The right's campaign to undo the New Deal finally began to produce results in the 1990s, when some states privatised and deregulated the generating and supply of energy. To this end Enron gave company jobs to Bush, Sr administration cabinet members and advisors, paid out millions in campaign contributions, helped write Vice President Cheney's national energy plan in 2000 and paid conservative journalists such as William Kristol, Irwin Stelzer, Lawrence Kudlow and Peggy Noonan to promote the company line in their columns. Seeking deregulation in Pennsylvania, they paid the former head of the Christian Coalition, deemed a superb lobbyist, $10,000–$20,000 per month to head their campaign, until Enron finally collapsed.

Because of the TVA's success in bringing industry and increased wealth to some of the poorest sections of Appalachia and the Deep South, State Department officials and even presidents such as Truman and Johnson believed that TVA-style projects could be the most effective form of American aid to the Third World. Dams and electrification schemes were proposed for the São Francisco Valley in Brazil, the Yangtze River in China and the Mekong River Delta in Vietnam. But free-market theorists such as Milton Friedman prevailed in this and other global economic debates in the 1990s, and a model of business-friendly tax, environmental and labour law, native stock exchanges, an economy oriented towards export and austerity regimes drawn up by the International Monetary Fund in the end superseded New-Deal-style, state–private infrastructure projects. The TVA nevertheless survives, and the federal government remains in control of most hydroelectric power generating.

Deregulation was sold as a basic principle of free enterprise, which was said to be godly, American and better for consumers because it allowed for open competition. But in the case of Enron it meant that the company had an unrestricted ability to manipulate the market. 'This was like *The Perfect Storm*,' an Enron trader named James Barth said. 'First our traders were able to buy power for $250 in California, sell it to Arizona for $1,200, then resell it to California for five times that amount.'

We went south from Tupelo on 45 to Columbus, then turned east on 82 and crossed into Alabama. We passed a place called Coal Fire, and another called Reform. Near Gordo ('Fat' in Spanish), Steve saw in a dirt lay-by a wooden trailer with an American flag painted on it. He asked me to stop so that he could take a photograph. Next to it was another trailer with a man sitting outside in a collapsible chair selling bumper stickers and Rebel flags. I waited in the car while Steve took the picture, then watched him from around fifty yards away as he read the display of bumper stickers and finally entered a conversation with the man in the chair. This could last a while, I thought, and it did. I got out and crossed the road.

The man was in his fifties, grey-haired, with a Fu Manchu moustache and his right leg pumping up and down as though to a frantic techno beat. His eyes had a predatory animal

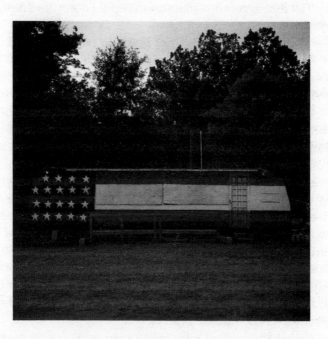

glint and his hairline was just an inch or so above his brow. He looked like Wolfman. 'We would have picked our own cotton if we knew what would happen,' read one of the bumper stickers. 'Cowgirls' foreplay: GET IN THE TRUCK, ASSHOLE!' read another. 'I got one here I got to keep hid,' he said to Steve. He lifted the edge of a Rebel flag that had a snarling pit bull imprinted on it. Underneath was a small sign that read, 'White Power, Ku Klux Klan'.

'Are you involved in that?' asked Steve.

'Damned straight,' he said. 'Since I was thirteen. And my daddy before me.'

'What does that involve?' asked Steve.

'I read the material, stay in touch with other members. Sometimes we have demonstrations.'

'What's the objective?' I asked.

'Get the niggers out, plain and simple. I don't have nothing against them. I just want them out.'

'Well, you know that's not going to happen,' I said.

'I know. In time there'll be no white and black. It'll just be America. I can't really tell you why I want them out. "White power", it just has a certain ring to me.'

He told us he'd been in the military twice, serving in Korea, Egypt and Vietnam, where he'd killed people. 'I wanted to go to Iraq, chase down Saddam Hussein. But they wouldn't let me. Said I was too old and too crazy. I've got three felonies, you see. I went into a town hall to register my car and the metal detector went off. It picked up the gun I was carrying. I got caught one other time, too, for possession of a concealed weapon. Then I killed a nigger in a bar in Houston. He came in coked up, asked me for ten dollars. I refused and he went for me with a straight razor. I put five shots into his chest. He tried to get up and I put another one into him. That was what got me sentenced, that last shot. I did three years, fourteen days.'

He said he wasn't allowed to own guns now – 'except a replica Colt, because it's classified as an antique. But I've got eight other illegal ones inside the trailer there.'

His father stepped through the trailer door, a duplicate of the son, including the moustache, except that his hair was white rather than grey. 'Killer dog inside,' he growled, and moved on to the other trailer.

'Killer dog?' I asked.

'I've got a Rottweiler,' the Klansman said.

'Do you have any children?' I asked.

'I've got a daughter down in Texas. She's just about to turn eighteen.'

'That'll be a celebration,' said Steve brightly.

'Damn right. I won't have to pay child support no more.'

'There's that, I suppose,' said Steve.

'I'll tell you something,' he said. 'If my daughter ever had a black boyfriend, I'd shoot both of them. I mean that.'

His wife then appeared at the trailer door and came down the steps. She was an emaciated woman wearing large glasses and a tracksuit, her cheeks sucked in and her mouth clamped shut, like a purse with the strings drawn.

'Dog ate mah teeth,' she said with a light whistle, then moved away.

'We know that for a fact,' said her husband. 'We found pieces of her dentures when the dog relieved himself.'

We left him there in the shadow of the trees. As I sat in the car writing down what he had said, two teenage black boys passed us, crossed the road and moved past the lay-by where the trailers were. The Klansman suddenly leaped out of his chair, raced over to them and began gesticulating. The boys stepped back and held their palms up as if to say, 'We don't want any trouble.' He carried on his tirade for a while, then went back to his chair, the leg driving his frenzied rhythm. The boys walked slowly on up a side road by a field.

'What do you suppose he said to them?' I asked Steve.

'I don't know,' he said. 'He looked angry.'

'I'm going to ask them.'

'No!' he said. 'He's insane. He's got a trailer full of guns.'

'I'll wait until they get further up the road. He won't notice us going by.'

I caught up with the boys as they were about to enter a park, where a basketball game was going on.

'Excuse me,' I said. 'Can you tell me which road I take to Tuscaloosa?'

'Just go back to that crossroads and turn left,' one of them said. 'That'll take you all the way to Tuscaloosa.'

'Thanks,' I said. 'Do you mind my asking you what that man said to you back there?'

They didn't expect this, and would rather I hadn't asked it. They looked down, stirred the dirt by the side of the road with their shoes, then the boy who had given me directions said, 'He just wanted to know if we wanted to buy anything.'

The Klansman's gestures wouldn't have accommodated any form of salesmanship, but I wasn't going to learn the true story of what he had said. It could even be possible that he had a genuine grievance. What was clear, though, was that the boys, when asked to reveal something to a white man, chose disguise. It's a life, it seems, in which you have constantly and exhaustingly to act out a role of guilelessness in order to avoid confrontation, a full forty years after civil rights were established in law.

'And I'm gonna put white hands / And black hands and brown and yellow hands / And red clay earth hands in it,'

wrote Langston Hughes in 1940 of the music he would compose for Alabama:

> Touching everybody with kind fingers
> And touching each other natural as dew
> In that dawn of music when I
> Get to be a composer
> And write about daybreak
> In Alabama.

In a half-vacant concrete strip mall in Tuscaloosa we had an Indian meal served by the owners, a tall, slender, bejewelled couple with the manners and elegance of Mogul aristocrats. Outside in the parking lot were dented pickup trucks with gun-racks and dogs in the back. We took 69 south past Greensboro, then turned east on 80. We got to Selma, where black people attempting to register to vote were met with police violence in 1965. One protester was shot dead by a state trooper. On Sunday, 7 March 1965, six hundred demonstrators intending to march to the state capital of Montgomery were battered by police on Edmund Pettus Bridge, named after a Confederate soldier who entered the war as a private and left as a general. Selma's grandest hotel is the St James, by no means the only one of that name in America. It may be the one Bob Dylan is looking out the window of in his song 'Blind Willie McTell', for the past that comes flooding into his mind at that moment is made up of the sights and sounds of whips cracking on the chain gangs, slavery ships and falling martyrs amid the sweet magnolias.

The southern states lost 288,000 lives in the Civil War, fought by them primarily to maintain their rights to have the service of slaves. They lost the war, but won the right to legally practise segregation for the next ninety years, with a brief interruption for Reconstruction. Poll taxes and literacy tests kept black people, and poor whites, from voting. Jim Crow laws clinically separated them from white society. Black people stepping over the lines that existed in the minds of

Klansmen and their supporters were dragged through the streets from the backs of cars, banged into jails by racist judges, whipped, strung up from trees, shot, castrated and burned alive. No northern legislator looked after their constitutional rights. When in the 1960s southern black people tried to take matters into their own hands in pursuit of the right to vote, go to school or have lunch where they wanted, mayors and governors set police and dogs on them. White people who came down from the north to help were thrown into jail, driven from towns or in some cases shot. In 'Blind Willie McTell', Bob Dylan sang of seeing a sign in the south declaring that all the land from New Orleans to Jerusalem had been condemned.

The liquor-store owner in Greenwood, Mississippi, referring to slavery, said, 'I can't keep paying for things my great-grandfather did.' His point is reasonable, but what if the crime continues to be committed? Does anyone pay then? Republicans have known for decades that they stand a better chance of winning elections if the black vote is low. In 2000, George Bush received just nine per cent of it. Republicans have over the years sought various means, both crude and sophisticated, to repress the black vote. In 1981, during the race for governor in New Jersey, Republicans hired police officers to patrol black neighbourhoods at election time, having put up signs that the 'Ballot Security Police' would be monitoring voters. In 1986 Republicans in Louisiana hired an agency to challenge the legitimacy of 31,000 mainly black voters, having suggested in one of their planning documents that 'this could keep the African-American vote down considerably'. In 1990, during Jesse Helms' run for senator in North Carolina, Republicans sent 150,000 'voter registration bulletins' into black neighbourhoods, falsely stipulating that multiple identification documents would have to be produced to cast a vote and that voters would be ineligible if they had been living in their precincts for less than thirty days. Son Kinon, a Republican state official, mailed three thousand leaflets to black people in Dillon County, South Carolina, saying, 'You have always been my friend, so don't chance GOING TO JAIL on Election Day! . . . SLED [South Carolina Law Enforcement Division] agents, FBI agents, people from the Justice Department and undercover agents will be in Dillon County working this election. People who you think are your friends, and even your neighbors, could be the very ones who turn you in. THIS ELECTION IS NOT WORTH GOING TO JAIL!!!!!' More recently, John Pappageorge, whose surname could be the nickname of a funk singer, but who is in fact a white Republican from Michigan, said at a local party meeting, 'If we do not suppress the Detroit vote, we're going to have a tough time in this election.' Detroit is eighty-three per cent black.

In the 2000 presidential election Republicans decided that Florida was the crucial state for the electoral-college results and tried systematically to nullify the black vote there. Polling stations in black neighbourhoods closed early or were moved without notice. Antiquated voting machines in black neigh- bourhoods resulted in ninety thousand votes being spoiled, more than half of them having been cast by black people, even though they only account for eleven per cent of Florida's population. The governor of the state was Jeb Bush, and Katherine Harris, the Secretary of State, who was in charge of elections, was at the same time George Bush's campaign chairwoman in the state. She allocated $4 million of state money to a database company called ChoicePoint to draw up a list of anyone who was a felon (or even a suspected felon) so that they might be purged from the voting register, as felons are not allowed to vote in Florida. Texas supplied lists of their own felons whom they believed had moved to Florida. Harris instructed ChoicePoint to be very liberal in their interpretation of who was a felon – similar names, similar birth dates, similar social-security numbers would suffice; just an eighty per cent match was necessary. 173,000 people were removed from the electoral rolls. In Miami-Dade County, two-thirds of those removed were black. Many of these people had never committed a crime and weren't aware they'd been excluded until they turned up to vote. They couldn't petition to be reinstated until after the election was over. Of black Floridians who managed to vote, nine out of ten voted for Gore. George Bush allegedly carried the state by 537 votes, giving him a victory in the electoral college, even though he lost the popular vote. When the Democrats sued, the case quickly escalated to the Supreme Court, where the Republicans wanted it, for it was crowded with their party's appointees. The court ordered the recounting of the vote, which would have resulted in a victory for Gore, to be stopped. Justice Antonin Scalia issued this opinion with his vote: 'The counting of votes that are of questionable legality does, in my view, threaten irreparable harm to the petitioner [Bush], and to the country, by casting a cloud upon what he [Bush] claims to be the legitimacy of his election.' That is, the recounting of votes that would result in the true victor of the election (Gore) taking office would be prejudicial to the interests of the candidate (Bush) who lost. So the recounting must be stopped.

Scalia later declared at the Pew Forum on Religion and Public Life that the Constitution, divinely inspired, indicated that the state was an instrument of God. 'That consensus has been upset by the emergence of democracy,' he said, adding, 'The reaction of people of faith to the tendency of democracy not to observe the divine authority behind government should not be resignation to it but resolution to combat it as effectively as possible.' Scalia was nominated by Ronald Reagan and approved in the Senate by a vote of ninety-eight to zero, ostensibly to protect the Constitution, the fundamental document of American democracy, one of the tenets of which is the separation of Church and state.

Is there a price to pay by those so covetous of power that they would get it by excluding from the right to vote southern black people, who had won it in the face of beatings and lynchings and shootings? George Bush, of course, became president. His brother remained governor of Florida and Antonin Scalia stayed in the Supreme Court. Katherine

Harris became a Congresswoman and has been spoken of as a future Republican presidential candidate. Jimmy Carter, who with Gerald Ford had been asked to make recommendations so that what had happened in Florida in 2000 would not be repeated, warned in the *New York Times* that the 2004 election was likely to have similar abuses, such as candidates' campaign managers also serving as state election officials. During that election, police with guns and dogs raided a black Baptist church in Jacksonville, Florida where citizens were attempting to register to vote, claiming that they suspected irregularities were taking place. It was an image from the era of Jim Crow.

'As a nation we began by declaring that "all men are created equal,"' wrote Abraham Lincoln to Joshua F. Speed in 1855. 'We now practically read it "all men are created equal, except the Negroes." When the Know-Nothings get control, it will read "all men are created equal, except Negroes and foreigners and Catholics." When it comes to this, I shall prefer emigrating to some country where they make no pretence of loving liberty – to Russia, for instance, where despotism can be taken pure, and without the base alloy of hypocrisy.'

We arrived in Auburn, the 'Village of the Plain' as some there like to call it, after the line in Oliver Goldsmith's 'Deserted Village' – 'Sweet Auburn! Loveliest village of the plain'. Auburn, it seemed, was booming, at least according to statistics it provided about itself. Since 1980 the economy had grown 220 per cent and the population sixty-five per cent. There had been a 1,200 per cent increase in industrial jobs. It had a small red-brick downtown area with clothing stores from a previous age and a drugstore with a soda counter. The bars where the young congregated had the look of being naturally and effortlessly integrated, something I had seen elsewhere in the south, particularly in university towns, but less often in the north. The rest of Auburn was a large suburban sprawl set prettily in gentle hills and woodland.

A Methodist college opened here in 1859 and evolved with time into Auburn University, where Mal Gynther is Professor Emeritus of Psychology. He is the father of a friend of mine from Valencia, Dana Gynther, who was in Auburn with her two daughters for the summer visiting her parents. They put us up for a couple of nights, before Steve flew back to the destruction he'd left behind in England and I went on to Florida.

The American motel, even those down near the bottom of the range where I was generally staying, tends to afford you the opportunity to relax. I'd seen a cockroach walk out of a crack in the tiles in a Ramada Inn in Oxford, Mississippi; the place in Medford, Oregon was a dump for transients and Miss Mridu Shandil's Route 66 Motel in Barstow, for all its oddity and charm, was just hanging on to plausibility once you entered the room; but most of them are clean and spacious, with a television, desk and two vast beds. There is nearly always an ice machine in the hall, even if you're in a dry county. But everything in it reminds you of its anonymity. There's nothing to detain you. The American home, on the other hand, if it is inhabited by those of middle income or above, tends to be commodious, well appointed and full of things to do. The refrigerators are better stocked than any I have seen elsewhere. At the house of Mal and his wife Ruth, I had a room full of books with birds twittering in the woodlands outside, a phone, food, company, the use of a washing machine, no check-out time. After around 4,500 miles and a dozen motels I sank into this with the mindlessness and lack of awareness of time one feels when in a steambath.

Dana took Steve and me to a dinner in a house of a friend of hers. It was made of grey planks and was built on a hillside with a tree trunk as its architectural model, decks, ponds, staircase and rooms twisting around the central axis of the high-ceilinged living room. As in an Escher drawing, you were sometimes going down in this house when you thought you were going up. There was a long table full of bottles of wine, candles and bowls of pasta, with conversation percolating among the ten people seated around it. Pieces of it reached me: '. . . her brother-in-law, whose underwear I'm not allowed to fold . . .', 'As she listened to the patriotic songs in *Yankee Doodle Dandy* over in Atlanta the lady next to her said, "I'm just getting chill bumps all up and down my arms!"', 'He's in a perpetual state of indignation. That's part of his charm, don't you think?', 'You've just got to see the War Eagle Supper Club!', 'Every single woman in that family has had plastic surgery', 'I hear when they teach Faulkner in California the students say, "I don't get it. I'd just leave"', 'The Floribama Bar on the way to Panama City – that's where you got to go!', 'Georgia is trying to steal Alabama's water!', 'I don't know who made Michael Jackson the standard of American beauty.' Steve was at the other end of the table, looking like he was at his own birthday party.

The house belonged to Dana's friends Joe and Mary. Joe, from Boston, was still astounded by the south, though he had been in it for fifteen years; Mary was from Auburn, where she taught primary school. Her father, like Dana's, had taught at Auburn. He was a professor of heptology and Alabama gentleman who had written a book entitled *The Reptiles and Amphibians of Alabama*, a copy of which, signed, I am looking at as I write. Here you will find, among many others, the bird-voiced treefrog, the red-eared pond slider, the eastern coachwhip, Beyer's waterdog, the slender glass lizard, the Mississippi mud turtle, the three-toed amphiuma, the mountain chorus frog, Fowler's toad, the broad-headed skink, the western lesser siren, the mud puppy, the dusky pigmy rattlesnake, the American alligator and the hellbender. Anyone, I would think, would like to see a hellbender some time.

There came a time when the stage was cleared, the room silenced and the attention directed to Bob by Mary, who said, 'So tell us, Dad, what you would do to protect me if I was in trouble.' He looked at her petitioningly, suddenly weary, as if to say, 'Do I have to?' She looked at him as she might if waiting in a classroom for a child's answer.

'If ever my daughter was in financial difficulties,' he began in a gently oratorical cadence, as if wheeling himself out for a recitation, 'I'd do everything I could to assist her. If she was in trouble with the law, or in poor health or had fallen into the use of drugs, I'd be there for her with the finest legal or medical assistance I could find.' He paused for a moment here. 'But if she ever came home with a black man, that would mark the end of my relationship with her.'

A roar went up and one by one they lit into him, as they had before, I supposed, and as he knew they would. It seemed a kind of party trick, performed reluctantly, but it perhaps went to the heart of the matter. White attitudes to black people in the south were perhaps less about fear of the other, or the dehumanising of those they exploit, or moral judgement, as they were about sexual hysteria. Gunnar Myrdal, who travelled all around the south in the 1940s and wrote a book called *An American Dilemma*, concluded that the fourth most important aspect of segregation for whites was the denial of the vote, while the first was 'the bar against intermarriage and sexual intercourse involving white women'. David Cohn, a southern lawyer-businessman of the time, wrote of black people, 'Sexual desire is an imperative need, raw and crude and strong. It is to be satisfied when and wherever it arises . . . We do not give the Negro civic equality because we are fearful that this will lead in turn to demands for social equality. And social equality will tend toward what we will never grant – the right of equal marriage. As a corollary to these propositions we enforce racial separation and segregation. It is the sexual factor . . . from which social and physical segregation grows.' Southern whites could see black people as many things, but one, perhaps the one that stirred them the most, was as pure human embodiments of carnality, possessed of a dark, occult sexual power. They looked at black people and saw the id, or, even worse, their wives' ids, and were terrified and revolted. When Dionysius wants to punish the Apollo-worshipping King of Thebes for ignoring him in Euripides' play *The Bacchae*, he drives the women of Thebes, including the king's mother, into an orgiastic frenzy in the hills. What torments Hamlet more than the murder of his father is the thought of his mother in sexual abandon with his uncle in the 'rank, unseam'd bed'. The women had to be kept from black men to keep the bloodlines clean, but also because, having been driven out of their minds by a force for which they were not prepared, they might never come back.

Mary began to talk about her Aunt Luanne, her father's half-sister.

'She was the fun aunt, the free spirit,' she said. 'But she had cold, cruel eyes.'

She had been Miss Albany, Georgia and married young to a man who killed himself when they divorced. Her next husband was a tennis pro with one arm, with whom she designed a tennis racket that purported to be 'all sweet spot'. She divorced him too, this time on the pretext that they spent too much time together. She drank her way through her glamour years and, when her looks began to diminish and she woke up naked on the kitchen floor, she quit. She was already cured by the time she went to Alcoholics Anonymous in the hope of meeting a rich doctor.

'She met a man named Dick Ball instead,' said Mary. 'I didn't make that name up. Her first husband had only one testicle and the second only one arm, so when Dick Ball proposed to her, she had him stand naked in front of her so that she could ascertain if he was "a whole man". She started her own business, an advertising agency. She called it Read and Mount. I said to her, "Are you running an advertising agency or writing a sex manual?"'

The marriage to Dick Ball didn't survive, either. She went through a period with crystals and channelling, and then moved on to Christianity. She eventually came to Auburn to live with her mother and to be near Bob, whom she considered the family patriarch, following Leviticus in this, as she also did in her business decisions.

'Her mother was terrified of the Internet,' said Mary. 'She

thought the mouse could get loose and cause all sorts of problems, like El Niño. Anything that could just move a picture of Luanne's head and place it on the body of a rat had to be an abomination.'

The next morning for breakfast Mal gave me the most perfectly succulent peach I'd ever eaten. He told me that at the beginning of his academic career he'd conducted a correspondence with Timothy Leary, who became the world's most renowned proselytiser for LSD, but was then an outstanding clinical psychologist. Years later, in the mid-1980s, Leary went on a speaking tour with the Watergate burglar Gordon Liddy and arrived at Auburn, where Mal and one of his daughters had dinner with them. Liddy had been an FBI agent, a prosecuting attorney, an undercover operator for Richard Nixon and eventually, like Oliver North, an ex-criminal turned American celebrity, acting in television dramas, riding with the Los Angeles Hell's Angels, learning to parachute with the Israeli military, and participating in the reality show *Celebrity Fear Factor*. As a child he'd cooked and eaten a rat to get over a phobia. One would imagine that this is known because he himself revealed it, which is perhaps odder than the act itself. In the early 1960s he'd organised the arrest of Timothy Leary, but now they were friends and making a fortune with their travelling show.

'How was the dinner?' I asked Mal.

'Fine. I enjoyed talking with Leary very much,' he said. 'My daughter spent most of it listening to Liddy tell her how to strangle a man with his bare hands.'

I drove Steve then to Atlanta to get his plane back to England. On the way he noticed one more flattened southern rodent and got out of the car to photograph it.

From Florida to Baltimore

Just as I sat down on a stool in a bar off Highway 19 on the Florida Gulf coast, a man came out of the gloaming and said, 'You're in my seat,' from about a foot above me. His upper body looked like a sack packed with rocks. I moved one stool to the left and looked straight ahead. The place was on the point of evacuating. Television screens all around the walls showed sporting events, from professional wrestling to cricket. The customers were ninety per cent male, the serving staff all female, all in mini-skirts, all wiping down tables and paying no attention to anybody as people made for the door.

I looked at a menu. I still had time to order, the barmaid said, if I did it quick. I told her what I wanted and looked from the corner of my eye to the right at a hand coming towards me. 'I'm Dennis,' said this living piece of sculpture, 'but they call me Chop.' The bar stool was like a golf tee beneath him.

He told me he was from Ohio and was a roofer in St Petersburg, but had trained with Secret Service and CIA operatives to be a personal bodyguard. 'Mostly I worked for executives. It was pretty tedious much of the time, checking out hotel rooms in advance for devices, looking under their cars to see if someone had attached an explosive. The service cost one hundred dollars per hour, but their employers treated these people like they were very delicate, very expensive instruments of some kind. There was the worry that something could happen to them when they were in a foreign country, or that someone they'd knocked over or offended along the way might try to attack them. I'm under contract not to divulge anything about them, but I can tell you I saw at first hand some pretty strange sexual tastes. One other group I looked after was women going through divorces. They were scared of their husbands.'

His father had been in the military and was a Golden Gloves champion boxer, while he himself had been a bony, awkward, weak child with a tendency to trip over sidewalks and embarrass himself. He took up power lifting and martial arts in the hope that his father would come to respect him. I watched the muscles in his arms twitch as though animals were running around in them.

'If you threw a punch at me now,' he said, 'I'd stop you. But my movement would be so minimal you'd barely notice it. Your punch would look very slow to me. That's martial arts. I got involved with several different martial arts, studied under several masters. Some of these involved no physical contact. They were forms of meditation. I went deeply into this. I got to the point where I could leave my body and then control it as though it were a puppet. I could see everything. I had 360-degree vision. And great power. A master taught me how to disable an opponent without touching him. I could mess up his insides, make him sick, by vibrating. That may be difficult for you to accept, but I am as certain of this and as familiar with it as you are with your own name.'

When Michael Jordan seized the basketball from the hands of Karl Malone with seconds left in the sixth game of the Utah Jazz–Chicago Bulls NBA finals series in 1998, he knew he would have one chance at a shot that would win the championship for his team. He later said that at this moment he knew where everyone was on the court and where they were likely to go, he felt that everything was moving with exceptional slowness and was certain that when the time came for him to make his shot, the ball would go through the hoop and the game would be won. He charged up the court with the Utah defence scurrying to assemble itself in front of him, faked right, pulled up above the free-throw line, leaving a Utah defender on the floor, went up high into the air like a dancing

Masai, released the ball at the peak of his leap and then, to the horror of the Utah fans, watched the ball fall into the basket. Magic Johnson said of him that his gift is in his control over his body and the slowness this brings to the passing of time in critical moments. 'Michael goes up with the ball and the defenders go up with him. He thinks, "Shall I shoot?" The defenders can't go higher and start to descend and Michael thinks, "Shall I shoot now?", but he's still in the air. It's all happening in the blink of an eye, but it's like he's floating there and has all the time in the world to decide, to take aim, to execute. Finally the defenders are nearly back on the floor and Michael makes his shot.' Who was I to say that Chop couldn't do it too, suspend himself outside his body, see all around him, the movement of time almost imperceptible as he rearranged the internal organs of his adversaries through vibration? As I ate my dinner at the bar we spoke of how artists tend to move in their working lives towards an economy of gesture, towards simplicity, and of how athletes speak of a wondrous slowing down of time in their most glorious moments and of how the capacity to slow time can bring not only increased efficacy, but also knowledge, and intimacy.

The barmaid appeared and told us that the hour of closing had arrived.

'Pity you can't stick around for a couple of days,' said Chop. 'We could keep talking.'

I'd come down from Georgia, meeting Highway 19 at Ellaville and crossing into Florida to the east of Tallahassee. I passed a pretty town near the state line called Monticello, which had a courthouse square. It was still the Deep South for a time, Spanish moss, broad green fields and white gospel music on the radio about being cleansed in the blood of the Lamb, but finally it gave way to palm trees, trailer parks and a long string of commercial detritus, jails, budget hotels and lap-dancing clubs. As the Federal Writers' Project observer said, 'Politically and socially, Florida has its own North and South, but its Northern area is strictly Southern and its Southern area is strictly Northern.'

I passed the Follow That Dream Pathway and the Goethe State Forest, then hit the coast where the Withlacoochee River empties into the Gulf. Just to the north of St Petersburg was Clearwater. In the middle of a May night in 1965 Keith Richards woke in his room in the Jack Tar Harrison Hotel here with the opening chords of the song that became 'Satisfaction' in his head. He'd heard 'Dancing in the Street' by Martha Reeves and the Vandellas and somehow it had mutated that night in his sleep into a new song. He got his guitar, played what he had heard into a tape recorder, went back to sleep and the next day wrote the song with Mick Jagger by the hotel pool. Clearwater later became a national gathering place for Scientologists, and the Church bought the hotel. Ruth Farrell, my first girlfriend as a near-adult, had passed from the mystical teachings of Ouspensky and Gurdjieff to marijuana and then to various hallucinogens until, her mind whirling and on its way down into an abyss, she fell for salvation on Scientology, which gave her structure and direction, two husbands and a profession as a management consultant for chiropractors and dentists in Clearwater. She died there of cancer while still in her forties.

Down the way in St Petersburg, Jack Kerouac, Apostle of the American Road, breathed his last on 21 October 1969, aged just forty-seven, but by then bloated, bitter, exhausted and sclerotic. I might never have set out on this journey had I not read *On the Road* at nineteen. I had been led to it by Ruth's older brother Jay, a seeker after higher planes who had led her to Gurdjieff and her chemical experiments. When he asked me what I thought of it I said, 'Everything looks different,' and it did – traffic lights, diners, trucks, railroad lines, clothes, drugstore signs, cheap hotels, docks, fields of corn, the mad and the down and out, all tinged thereafter with the elegiac melancholy and ecstasy of jazz. Before that, what I had known of the open road was from family holiday trips spent in the back seat of my parents' Oldsmobile. The road was a prison, the time to be served passed with sandwiches, quiz games and naps. 'There's the birthplace of Rutherford B. Hayes,' my mother might call out from the front, and I'd roll over again, hoping for sleep. *On the Road* changed that. Kerouac, Prince of the Beats, disavowed the title. Beat to him could mean hobo-beat, chewed up and spat out by quotidian life, with the open road the only home left; or it could be the pulse of music, the free and exuberant bebop jazz to which he tried to surrender. But above all it had its root in the word 'beatific'. Three years before the publication of *On the Road*, Kerouac walked into a Catholic church in Lowell, Massachusetts and felt 'wonderment in the bleakness of the mortal realm . . . the potent and inconceivable radiancies shining in the bright Mind Essence . . .' He later said that he wasn't a Beat but rather a Catholic, and, at least in part, wrote out of the mystic Catholic tradition of visions and charisms, gifts of power and beauty freely given by God. After I read his book, what had been solid and inert became liquefied and radiant and full of possibility.

I drove on the toll bridge over Tampa Bay and then stayed on Interstate 75 to Sarasota. I watched a smooth rock band for a while with six other customers in a downtown bar and then found a $45 motel run by Russians. The sink was blocked, the television didn't work, there were pubic hairs on the bathroom wall and no cover on the air conditioner, so that its internal, dust-clogged circuitry was exposed along with swathes of yellow foam insulation that looked like solidified pus. I went back to the desk to ask for shampoo and was handed a bottle with 'Best Western' written on it, which was the name of the hotel on the other side of the road.

In the 1930s Sarasota was the site for the annual convention of the Tin Can Tourists of the World, an organisation of 30,000 mobile-home owners who gathered to discuss trailer-park conditions, pitch horseshoes, play cards, barbecue, lie on the white sand beaches of Sarasota Bay and dance outdoors to tunes coming from phonographs activated by the deposit of a nickel. By then, the high and the low had both taken to wintering there, the high arriving in the wake of Mrs Potter

Palmer, art patron and wife of one of Chicago's richest men, who first came to Sarasota in 1910. John and Charles Ringling, of Ringling Brothers Barnum and Bailey Circus, built mansions on the shore of the bay and made Sarasota the winter headquarters of their circus. In time the city had three newspapers, a symphony orchestra, an art association, a theatre, an unusually dense concentration of writers and, according to local historian Furman C. Arthur, 'a high opinion of its lifestyle'.

I came here when I was nineteen to visit my friend Jim Waldron for a week. He was then a first-year student at Sarasota's New College, an experimental, architecturally unsettling institution of white concrete I.M. Pei cuboids among the palm trees on the bay, which had been founded by civic boosters and Congregationalists, but had become a place where courses in Zen, Herbert Marcuse and guerrilla warfare were of more interest to its students than those in Flemish art or the novels of Jane Austen.

I came to Sarasota engulfed in a condition of forlorn romantic yearning, sustained at that point for five months as Ruth, after our first summer together, had gone to live in Tucson, Arizona with her brother Ed. It became a week of progressive disarrangement of the world as I had known it. The town itself started it, with its population of circus performers and the retired. In Chicago the streets were lined with taverns; in Sarasota it was retirement homes and funeral parlours. Fishermen far out in the shallow bay gave the impression of walking on water, and one of the dark, Gothic Ringling mansions on the shore looked like a place where ghosts walked and the rituals of the damned took place. I sat alone on a patch of grass surrounded by bushes one afternoon when a young American Indian appeared beside me as if out of the air and told me that it had been proph-esied that the white man was doomed and that the Indian would rise again to inherit the Earth. There was no doubt, he said, that this would come to pass. Then he vanished, like an apparition.

One night I was in a campus television room with Jim and his girlfriend Liz watching Jerry Rubin, then an aspiring revolutionary, but later an entrepreneur and trader, and a group of his insurrectionist Yippies take over the stage of a national talkshow and present their alternative version of the programme. The minute hand on the wall clock held still for each period of sixty seconds, then jumped one position back and two forward. Two students, both black males, came in, sat down and were immediately immersed in the broadcast and the clock with the vaulting minute hand. They seemed to be speaking in tongues. Afterwards, Jim and Liz went back to their room and I walked with the two students to the other side of the campus amid the night sounds of frogs and cicadas and wind blowing through the palms. 'We're tripping,' the smaller of them said. 'But that's nothing to me. I control it. It's like a piece of music that I play.'

We stopped in a courtyard outside their room. The smaller one stayed with me while the other went upstairs. It was around eleven o'clock. Some people moved silently in the shadows. In another courtyard a student stood rigid against the trunk of a palm tree for the next hour.

The one who had stayed behind told me that he had been a military policeman in Vietnam and was the recipient there of a revelation that the Second Coming of Jesus was going to happen in Sarasota. He was not the only one who thought so, he said. There were several friends of his, some of them students at New College, others who had come on a pilgrimage there, who also believed this. He himself was now a student of art.

'You know what you're doing standing here talking with me like this?' he asked.

'What?'

'You're saving my soul. Right now in that room up there there's an orgy going on. I'm supposed to be there, but talking with you is keeping me back, keeping my soul clean.'

He told me that a female student who lived in the ground-level room next to where we were standing was an agent of the Devil. He told me he knew that as an absolute certainty.

'Do you know her?' he asked.

It happened that she was the only person – other than the ones I had been with that night – that I did know. I'd met her the day before. Some time around two o'clock she came out of her room barefoot in a nightdress and robe, walked up to where we were standing and joined us without saying a word. My companion looked at her and began slowly to quake from the feet up, in a kind of rising convulsion that had him shaking and gagging until the force of this threw him to the ground. She watched his feet kick spasmodically a few times like a dying animal, then she walked back into her room as if floating on a small cloud.

'I told you, man,' he said. 'I had to beat back the evil that was coming out of her. It was mortal combat.'

We walked then through the night and into the morning. He showed me a stack of his paintings that were stored in a shed on the shore of the bay, then we watched fishermen walking in the still water in a rose light. I remember a self-portrait of his in oil, one half of his face darkened, foul and sinister, the other innocent and radiant. There was a solemnity when we parted, as though we'd entered into a spiritual pact.

I went back through the campus to the room of the woman who'd stood by us in the night. It was around seven o'clock in the morning. I tapped lightly on the door and she immediately appeared, dressed as she had been before. She invited me in. I sat next to her on her bed and began to talk, but when I couldn't keep my eyes open, she told me I could sleep in the bed of her room-mate, who was away for the week. I lay down and for a moment watched her read a novel sitting up against the wall, then closed my eyes. When I woke around three hours later she was in exactly the same position.

I got up and walked over to her to say goodbye.

'When you were sleeping,' she said, 'you got out of bed

and went down on your knees. I watched you crawl across the room towards me. When you got to my bed you lifted the sheet and put your hand on my stomach. You didn't move. You just held it there. After a while you crawled back across the room and got back into bed.'

I couldn't imagine how that could have happened, but then everything that was happening to me in Sarasota was unfamiliar. I didn't see her again while I was there, but now and again I'd pass friends of the young man she appeared to bring so close to physical crisis. Each time they'd nod at me gravely, as though I shared their secret knowledge. Sounds and objects seemed less distinct as they moved towards me in the heavy air. Whatever fabric linked me to the world and made it seem proportionate and sensible was being stretched to a gossamer fineness. I couldn't discover the cause of this.

I had arrived in Sarasota not only weighed down by Ruth being far away in the desert, but also having lost myself somewhat. Life was somewhere, but I couldn't quite reach it. The Catholic Church had carried me until I was seventeen. It provided metaphysics, cosmology, ethics, a past and a future. I'd served Mass and at thirteen bore a pin that declared my membership in the Future Priests' Club. Then it turned septic. It suddenly seemed a monstrous lie, a conspiracy created to deny me my freedom. I drove it out of me with invective. The epoch and some of the people around me seemed to offer substitutes – mystical systems, radical politics, visionary poetry, the works of Pythagoras, Heraclites, William Blake, Schopenhauer, Sri Aurobindo, Karl Marx and Malcolm X, among so much else. I tried to assemble these things into a vast and intricate cathedral of thought, as hierarchical and rigid and carefully constructed as the Church had once seemed to me. But I couldn't do it.

One late morning in Sarasota I sat on the edge of the bed in the room of Jim and Liz reading the poetry of Thomas Merton, Zen-influenced Cisterican priest. They were somewhere else, perhaps down the hall preparing food. I tried to catch the rhythm and the meaning of Merton's words, but they eluded me. I would read three or four lines, then stop and start again. It was as though the words were out of order. I couldn't get them. I sat for a while in the fall of sunlight from the window, and began again to read. For a moment I received the words as though I was inhaling them. Then something seemed to give way within me and I was over-whelmed by a feeling whose nature and power I had never known before. It was as though a surging river had come crashing through the walls of the room and swept me up in it, demolishing all the petty constructions of thought I had been trying to make through analysis and engulfing me in the sheer force of what seemed like life itself. I had never felt such a thing before. It was serious and it was fast and I stayed in it for a time. I had no fear. Then I was thrown free of it as if onto a shore. The room was silent. A minute or two had passed, perhaps, since I had begun again to read. I looked around. The little lamp beside the bed, the pens on the desk, the bedframe, the pillow, Liz's shoes – they all seemed so funny to me then. I was in the world as if for the first time, thrown there by the wading fishermen in Sarasota Bay, the clock that jumped, the tripping art student, the proph-esying Indian and the words of Thomas Merton. What had happened? Where had this thing come from? I didn't know, but nor did I look for words then to describe it. It was fresh and it was alive, and it seemed that once it had arrived I would not go back to what I was in the moments and years before. That was all that I could, or would, wish to absorb then. Words, highly proximate and somewhat diminishing, came later, when I tried to describe it. I had found the life I had sensed was there, after looking in the wrong place. There were no absolutes, no certainties. There was just movement. I had only to be in it, without impediment or fear. This was a liberation, an unexpected gift in what seemed an unlikely place.

Thirty-three years later I was back. I drove through the arch that once marked one of the entrances to Charles Ringling's estate, then walked through the palm courts and along the shore of the bay. I thought I had found the spot where I had stood for hours talking with the man who had come to Sarasota to wait for Jesus, the part of the shoreline where we'd watched the fishermen in the dawn and the room where I'd read the poetry of Thomas Merton. But I couldn't be sure. I never again felt what I'd felt in that room, but I'd lived since in its effects.

'The general wildness, the eternal labyrinths of water and marshes, interlocked and apparently never ending, the whole surrounded by interminable swamps. "Here I am then in the Floridas," thought I,' wrote James Audubon in 1831. 'The state with the prettiest name, / the state that floats in brackish water,' wrote Elizabeth Bishop. 'A certain liquidity suffused everything about the place,' wrote Joan Didion of its principal city, Miami. 'The buildings themselves seemed to swim free against the sky.' John and Sebastian Cabot saw it from their boat in 1498, but thought it too inhospitable to come ashore, the idea of shore there in itself indefinable. Southern Florida has certain points in common with southern California – palm trees, sunshine, provisionality, a lack of focus, real-estate development from intermittent booms spread over land that provides no mineral, transport or industrial basis for urban life. As Joan Didion said, it can barely be called land.

I went south along the coast, then crossed the wateriest place of all, the great swamp known as the Everglades, a mangrove and sawgrass waterland with live oak, pawpaw, wild lemon, strangler figs and orchids. Caribbean flamingos, roseate spoonbills, pelicans, herons, egrets and hawks are among the many birds that live here. Five million of them were slaughtered in 1886 to provide feathers for women's hats. It's the home of the Florida panther and America's only crocodiles. Indigo snakes and rattlesnakes are natives of the Everglades, but many Burmese pythons, once household pets, have been surreptitiously released into it. A ranger once saw a python wrap itself around an alligator in an attempt to strangle it, but the python didn't last long. 'On the highway,' a Federal Writers' Project observer stated, 'especially in the early morning after night traffic has taken its toll, lie the mangled corpses of snakes, which in large numbers crawl out of the swamp to sleep on the warm road, and the bodies of raccoons and other small animals crushed when blinded by headlights. These provide breakfasts for flocks of yellow-headed red-cheeked buzzards which look like turkeys from a distance and remain on the road until a car is almost upon them.' A flattened snake on a swamp road being eaten by a buzzard with red cheeks could have been the prize of the trip for Steve.

I went into the Miami airport to wait for my daughter Aoife, then twenty-three, to arrive from London. She had visited my father in Chicago during the final three years of his decline and returned for his funeral in 1993. This would be her first time back since then and her first time in America outside Chicago. She had taken to the way homes were arranged, the ease of manner of the people she met, the entertainments, the beaches, the food and the way waiters took orders directly from children rather than looking first to their parents. She was to be with me up the east coast to New York. Many beaches on the way, I had told her. I watched her come through the door into the arrivals area, having somehow left childhood even further behind during the month and some since I had last seen her.

We had a meal of rice and beans in a Cuban restaurant in South Beach, then went to the Indian Creek Hotel. As with Steve, my accommodation would intermittently improve during the time I was with her. This was a stylish place of pastels, tactfully placed accoutrements in open spaces and a tropical courtyard with a swimming pool, set on the edge of a region that had become a living museum of Art Deco and Streamline Moderne architecture.

Henry and Charles Lum bought 165 acres of Miami Beach in 1870 to farm coconuts. John Collins, a farming Quaker from New Jersey, came later to work the land and then began to build a bridge from the island that was Miami Beach across Biscayne Bay to the mainland, but ran out of funds before he could get there. One of the epoch-making entrepreneurs of America, Carl G. Fisher, completed it for him in exchange for two hundred acres of Collins' land. It thus became 'the longest wooden bridge in the world', at least according to Fisher. Fisher dredged the bay, built residential islands and opened the legendary Flamingo Hotel on the beach, taking Miami Beach from mangrove swamp and coconut farms to elite tourism in a decade. Will Rogers said of him, 'Fisher was the first man to discover there was sand under the water . . . [sand] that could hold up a real estate sign. He made the dredge the national emblem of Florida.'

Fisher was born in Indianapolis, Indiana in 1874, the severely astigmatic son of an alcoholic father, who abandoned him and his mother when he was a small child. He left school at twelve to help support his family, working in shops and selling tobacco and sweets on trains. Eventually he opened a bicycle repair business. He drew the attention of the public and the police by dropping a bicycle from the tallest building in Indianapolis. From bicycles he moved on to cars, opening what is believed to be the first dealership in the United States. He fixed a white Stoddard-Dayton car to a hot-air balloon and flew it over Indianapolis, and later built the Indianapolis Motor Speedway, where the first Indianapolis 500 was run on Memorial Day, 1911. His connections in the motor industry led to an offer from a patent holder to manufacture acetylene car headlights. He sold this business, which was making virtually every headlight in America, to Union Carbide for millions.

In 1912, railroads went in all directions around America, but roads were local routes linking rural areas and generally made of dirt. Fisher saw that the expansion of the automobile industry depended on circulation and conceived the Lincoln Highway, a 3,300-mile road that traversed America from Times Square in New York to Lincoln Park in San Francisco. It was financed by car manufacturers, Teddy

Roosevelt, Woodrow Wilson, Thomas Edison and a group of Eskimo children from Anvik, Alaska, who had heard about it from their teacher and sent fourteen cents. Dwight Eisenhower travelled on it in 1919 in an Army convoy and later added to the literature of the American road with a chapter in his book *At Ease: Stories I Tell to Friends*, called 'Through Darkest America with Truck and Tank'.

Fisher then turned his attention to north–south routes and built the Dixie Highway, a network that gathered in motorists from as far north as the Upper Peninsula of Michigan and brought them all the way to the point at which the Collins Bridge from Miami Beach met the land. People came to his casinos and hotels, but it took a while before they began to buy residences. He distributed to the press pictures of millionaires and bathing beauties on the palm-lined white sand beaches, and in one instance photographed his pet baby elephant Rosie caddying for Warren G. Harding, the rotund, golf-obsessed president. Gradually his promotional élan, his Dixie Highway and the expansion of the motor-car industry that he had helped to establish engorged his real-estate empire. By 1926, he was worth $100 million. Then a hurricane blew down Miami Beach, the stock market crashed, the Depression virtually ended tourism and his attempt to create another Miami Beach at Montauk on Long Island went bankrupt. He settled into a cabin alone on Miami Beach and in a final spasm of entrepreneurship built the Caribbean Club on Key Largo, a fishing retreat for 'men of modest means'. His ex-wife later wrote of him, 'He wasn't interested in money. He used to say he liked to see the dust fly.'

The Art Deco and Streamline buildings appeared after the hurricane and Fisher's vanquishment, along with trains, cars, pencil sharpeners, toasters, radios and vacuum cleaners designed in the same style, all with long lines over which air could flow effortlessly. 'Amid the miseries of the Depression,' wrote Robert Hughes in *American Visions*, '– the sense of being stuck in a hopeless economic jam, of tension, friction, social overheating, collision – the streamlined effect displayed an iconography of effortlessness and control . . . When times are bad, some Americans idealize the past . . . [but] more Americans were idealizing the future, through the medium of hopeful packaging based on streamlines.'

Aoife wanted to sleep, so I went out alone. I hadn't missed having a beer at night in the whole of the journey, apart from in Jacksboro, Texas, which was in a dry county. I found a place called Club Deuce that looked acceptable, then crossed the road to a cash machine set into the wall of a Latin fast-food stall. Two men were drinking coffee in the open air. I took out a hundred dollars and, as I was walking away, one of them called out, 'Are you a writer?' That was one of the more unexpected questions I'd heard anywhere up to then. I thought of walking away and into the Club Deuce, but for what? I hadn't an hour when I had to be anywhere. And then there was the prospect of another unheard story if I kept walking. So I went back.

'Why did you say that?' I asked.

'It was a guess,' the man said.

He was Bill Cooke, a Vietnam veteran of around sixty who had a nose like something grown in a laboratory. His companion was Dax Balladares, a Nicaraguan thirty years younger. They were photographers who had become acquainted through the Internet and met a couple of evenings per month. I sat down with them and ordered a lemonade.

'I'm a kind of paparazzi, among other things,' said Bill. 'The celebrity count around here is high, but the competition is brutal. I struck it lucky once, when Madonna was here to do her pornography book. Paparazzi were flying around the city like military patrols looking for guerrillas, but I happened to see a hand-made sign marked "Crew" with an arrow in an alley in a quiet neighbourhood. I followed it and there she was naked in a back yard. I shot her with a long lens through a bush, sent the prints to Europe and didn't have to work for two years.'

Dax swam across the Rio Grande and into the United States when he was a boy. His father was a Sandinista-supporting journalist who fell foul of the regime when it was collapsing and was blacklisted; he got a job as a caretaker in an apartment building in Miami, but had a stroke. Dax and his mother were looking after him at home.

'I shot pornography for a while,' he said, 'but got bored. Now I do fashion. Miami is the place for it, particularly South Beach. I have never seen such a concentration of beautiful women anywhere. It's the mixture of the races, I'm convinced.'

'You're damned right,' said Bill.

I asked them about South Beach.

'By the 1980s it was a place of old people's homes and crack houses,' said Bill. 'The paint was peeling, dealers were living in the hotels, lowlifes had inherited the streets. They made *Scarface* here, which annoyed the Cubans, and then *Miami Vice*. After that gay people and designers started to move in and refurbish the apartment buildings and hotels. This produced a great revival of the area. Some of the best nightclubs in the world are here. That's the real-estate agent's American Dream – first a slum, then gays and bohemians make it look pretty and original, and finaly the rich, the fashionable and the beautiful move in. By then, of course, neither the former slum dwellers nor the bohemians can afford it any more.'

It was a place of the sun and the night when my father stopped here with his friend Dan Glasson on the way to Cuba for a holiday in the 1930s. He told me they were having a drink in a hotel bar and met Walter Winchell, the inventor of the gossip column.

'What was that like?' I asked him.

'We had a very interesting conversation,' he said.

Winchell had become one of the most famous journalists in America by purveying the salacious in a witty, slangy style that included words he'd invented himself, such as 'belly laugh' and 'pushover'. He incurred the displeasure of the gangster Dutch Schultz by using the latter term to describe the blondes Schultz kept company with. At the time my father met him, Winchell was anti-fascist and pro-labour, but he turned after the war and became a supporter of Senator Joseph McCarthy. He was always one of America's great hangers-out, having his own table and even a hamburger named after him at the Stork Club in New York. I knew of him as a child because Winchell was the narrator for a tele-vision series called *The Untouchables* about 1920s gangsters and the heroic policemen who hunted them.

One night not long after my father died I was having dinner with Dan Glasson and his wife. I raised the subject of the trip to Cuba.

'I heard you met Walter Winchell,' I said.

'That's right, we did,' he said. 'Your dad told you?'

'Yes.'

'What did he say?'

'He said you met in a hotel bar and had an interesting conversation.'

He laughed. 'That's correct,' he said, 'but only accounts for about ten per cent of what happened.'

Dan said that he and my father had driven down from Chicago and stayed for three nights in Miami in an apart-ment over a garage belonging to parents of a friend of theirs. They'd been out until dawn the first two nights and, when Dan came back to the apartment early on the third evening, he found my father asleep on his bed. Dan took a shower and began to get dressed. 'What are you doing?' my father asked when he woke. 'I'm going out,' was the answer. There was a brief silence, then my father said, 'I'll be ready in five minutes.'

As they stood at the corner of the bar with their first drink of the evening, Walter Winchell, at the apex of a small entourage, entered the room. As he passed, my father said, 'Walter, how good to see you! You remember Dan Glasson, don't you?' Winchell halted, considered, then stepped up. 'Of course I do,' he said, a professional lie. They spoke for a while, then Winchell asked them what they were doing later. 'Your father said it just happened that we hadn't any plans. Winchell told us he had some things to do, but that he'd be back later with some musicians, showgirls and anyone else he happened to meet and found interesting. He came back as he said he would. Your father was out on the dance floor all night long. He was the last to leave. The sun was up.' As Stalin blanked out disgraced Politburo members from photographs, so parents tend to excise the rakishness from their youth.

Bill and Dax escorted me to a bar they recommended on Washington Street called the Playwright, then walked on. I got the last drink with some vampiric-looking goths in Club Deuce, the only people I'd seen in Miami up to that point without suntans.

The next day Aoife and I sat on the beach in front of the house where Gianni Versace, entering his gate one morning in July 1997 after buying some magazines, was shot dead by a serial killer named Andrew Cunanan. Bodies formed in cosmetic-surgery theatres, gyms and in some cases, no doubt, effortlessly by nature, dallied on café terraces, glided on roller skates or strolled in the sand. A light breeze stirred the palms, waves fell with a whisper on the shore and in the distance were merengue music and the sound of stilettos hitting the pavement. The lifeguard stations were painted in the colours of 1950s sports cars. 'The entire tone of the city, the way people looked and talked and met one another,' wrote Joan Didion of late 1980s Miami, 'was Cuban. The very image the city had been presenting of itself, what was then its new-found glamour, its "hotness" (hot colours, hot vice, shady dealings under the palm trees) was that of pre-revolutionary Havana, as perceived by Americans. There was even in the way women dressed in Miami a definable Havana look, a more definite emphasis on the hips and décolletage, more black, more veiling, a general flirtatiousness of style not then current in American cities.' People had long been coming to

Miami, as they had come to New Orleans, to sin, but the characteristic vegetation was the palm tree rather than Spanish moss, the culture shaped by body worship rather than voodoo, and the Caribbean influence that of Cuba rather than Haiti, making the European antecedents Spanish rather than French.

As Joan Didion points out, 'Many Havana epilogues have been played in Florida, and some prologues. Florida is that part of the Cuban stage where declamatory exits are made, and side deals. Florida is where the chorus waits to comment on the action, and sometimes to join it.' When Francis Drake took St Augustine in 1586 and other British forces overcame Havana, the Spanish handed over the whole of Florida in order to get Havana back. José Martí raised money and an expeditionary force in Florida in the late nineteenth century to take Cuba, but it was the sequence of intrigues, coups and a revolution in the 1950s that made Miami such a Cuban city. 'The exiled Fidel Castro Ruiz came to Miami in 1955 for money to [establish a base in] the Sierra Maestra, and got it, from Carlos Prío,' wrote Joan Didion. 'Fulgencio Batista himself came back from Florida to take Havana away from Carlos Prío in 1952, but by 1958 Fidel Castro, with Carlos Prío's money, was taking it away from Fulgencio Batista, at which turn Carlos Prío's former prime minister tried to land a third force in Camagüey Province, the idea being to seize the moment from Fidel Castro, a notably failed undertaking encouraged by the Central Intelligence Agency and financed by Carlos Prío, at home in Miami Beach.'

There are white Miamians who try to overlook the Cubans, thinking of their city as a kind of Phoenix or Austin with beaches, but Miami is nearly sixty per cent Hispanic, with Cubans dominating. A few of them trim roses and wipe down tables in restaurants, but they also run banks, own some of the most expensive properties in the city and have occupied positions of political power at all levels, including the office of mayor. The Cubans have given Miami music, a distinctive cuisine and a certain sultriness of style unique to it, but also drugs, assassinations and spies. Many of the trails from the killing of President Kennedy appeared to lead to Miami, which by that time had the largest CIA installation in the world, outside of its Langley, Virginia headquarters. A Senate Select Committee report said there were between three and four hundred CIA case officers there, each controlling between four and ten Cuban 'principal agents' who in turn ran between ten and thirty 'regular agents', yielding a figure of up to 120,000 CIA operatives working out of Miami, making it one of the largest employers in the state. They had boats, planes, hundreds of pieces of property, fifty-four front businesses and control of harbours.

I had often wondered why Cubans – loud, rich, politically connected, armed and dangerous though some of them may be in Florida – should be able to hold the national government to ransom with respect to its Cuban policy. Nearly all of them were concentrated in just one county, yet while rapprochement was going on with the Soviets and the Chinese, the United States was placing embargoes, financing invasions and engaging in outlandish assassination attempts on the small island of Cuba. But evidently all has not been as it seemed in Miami. While the colossal covert-action apparatus kept spewing out plots, the Kennedy administration was making promises to Moscow not to invade Cuba. By the time Kennedy was assassinated, 'the notion of invading Cuba had been dead for years,' according to Arthur Schlesinger. When I was in Cuba in 1997 a Frenchman suggested to me that the American embargo suited both Castro and the American government, for it made Castro look heroically defiant in the face of its huge, bullying neighbour, solidifying his power and thereby sustaining a stable, if alien, administration on an island just miles off the Florida coast. Money was despatched, invasion plans fomented and arms bought, but it seems that all this covert activity was set up in a way that it could produce no concrete results. The Cuban agents were to be kept active for intelligence-gathering purposes rather than for a *coup d'état*. The Miami Cubans, dreaming of a triumphant return, have a highly developed sense of betrayal. With respect to the American government and its intelligence services, it is perhaps not misplaced.

We left the beach in the late afternoon and went north, passing Hollywood. It was once mangrove swamp and salt marsh, but a frenetic real-estate sales campaign in the 1920s resulted in its homes being bought from their blueprint plans long before they existed. Twenty-one buses travelled around the country picking up prospective buyers with offers of free hotel accommodation, drinks and entertainment. The Federal Writers' Project observer wrote, 'They were driven about the city-to-be on trails blazed through palmetto thickets; so desolate and forlorn were some stretches that many women became hysterical, it is said, and a few fainted.' European aristocrats were given free sites and champion tennis players, swimmers and golfers gave exhibitions. 'Auctions were popular', the report continues, 'whenever sales lagged. Patrons were attracted by blaring bands, free banquets, vaudeville shows and the drawing of lottery tickets. Doctors, dentists, merchants, barbers, and motormen abandoned professions, trades and prosperous businesses to become real-estate salesmen.' My friend Robert Gregory, who grew up here, told me that an alligator came up out of a waterway behind his house and ate a neighbour's dog. The swamp, it seems, is not so deeply buried.

We stopped for the night at Delray Beach, surprisingly chic in the coastal detritus, the last stop for the night being the Da Da Club, where I had the unwelcome experience of listening to a rapper extol the virtues of his penis for a quarter of an hour while I was sitting next to my daughter. I wouldn't have taken to it if she hadn't been there, either.

On Magnolia Avenue in St Augustine is the Fountain of Youth Park, open every day except Christmas. It was at or near this spot that Juan Ponce de León, a conquistador from Valladolid who had been with Columbus on his second voyage, is said to have arrived in 1513, naming the region 'La Florida' and establishing what is the oldest continuously inhabited European settlement in the United States. It had until then been Seloy, a village of the Timucua tribe.

Ponce de León is said to have sailed from Puerto Rico, where he had been governor, looking for the Fountain of Youth. Alexander the Great had searched for it in East Asia. Medieval romances were written about it, and the Polynesians believed it was located in Hawaii. An Arawak chief named Sequene led an expeditionary force from Cuba to Florida looking for it and never came back. The legend grew. Lucas Cranach the Elder painted a Fountain of Youth in 1546. His and other renderings of the fountain have a Dionysian look, a wooded glade with the old and grey being drawn up to one side of a pool filled with naked women and with feasts and dancing of the young taking place on the other side. Accounts of Ponce de León's search for the fountain didn't appear until after his death, when Antonio de Herrera y Tordesillas' history of the Indies was published, incorporating a memoir by Hernando de Escalante Fontaneda, which declared that that had been Ponce de León's objective. Ponce de León had probably come to Florida looking for gold. Nevertheless, after Dr Louella Day McConnell, also known as Diamond Lil', arrived from the Klondike and bought citrus orchards in St Augustine, she began to charge admission to people who wanted to drink from her spring, thought to be rejuvenating. This is now the town's Fountain of Youth Park. This dream of restoration is what in part drove the Florida real-estate boom. Now, on the other side of the peninsula at Palm Harbor in Tampa, is the Fountain of Youth Institute, where Dr C. Randall Harrell offers 'The Complete Solution' of sand, sun, surf and surgery. They carry out facelifts, tummy tucks, nose and eyelid procedures, chin and lip augmentation, collagen and Botox injections, thread and forehead lift, liposuction, cosmetic dentistry and breast lifts as well as breast implants. 'The great explorer Ponce de León of Spain spent a lifetime searching for the legendary fountain of youth,' they declare. 'Four hundred years later [*sic*] he would be pleased to know that his search would have ended in Palm Harbor at Dr C. Randall Harrell's Fountain of Youth Institute®.'

Going north along the coast, I was again in the Deep South. Latin music gave way to country and western, with a freedom song about 'this little piece of land' – that is, the United States – the guitars twanging and the voice seeming simultaneously to suggest the wounded, the righteously accusatory and the coy. Around Jacksonville, an illustrated billboard declared, 'Thank God for George W. Bush, Tony Blair and Our Military'. Florida's market for lap-dancing clubs continued to be healthy, it appeared. 'We Dare to Bare,' said a sign. 'You're the Kid, We're the Candy Store,' said another. On the radio was a report about the Justice Department examining which laws would need to be passed to suspend elections in the event of a terrorist attack. Truck drivers, it continued, had been enlisted as vigilantes against terrorism. We crossed into Georgia and hit a spectacular monsoon that strafed the car. It seemed to rock under the force of it and we couldn't hear each other speak. Afterwards, the road steamed.

We drove into Savannah. The air filled with silver and gold as the low sun hit waterdrops falling from the high trees. Clouds bearing the smell of dry earth newly wet rose around us, a scent that perfumers in India try to recreate with clay and sandalwood oil, calling it 'the monsoon scent'. Square succeeded square for miles, all of them grand, as we headed for the river front. It was like Bloomsbury, only unterraced and more stately. Much of eighteenth- and nineteenth-century architecture was evident in the houses. When you see Savannah you wonder how the same country could contain Medford, Oregon. How did so many people have so much money?

Here they produced indigo and silk. Rice came later, cultivated by West African slaves who had grown up with the same strain. Savannah became a conduit for the deerskin trade. Eli Whitney invented the cotton gin when he was tutoring the children of War of Independence general Nathan Greene on his Mulberry Grove Plantation near Savannah, vastly extending the land that could be put into cotton production. A considerable amount of it was exported through Savannah. By 1820, $18 million in goods was passing through the city annually.

James Oglethorpe, an English general, made the street plan. He had arrived aboard the *Anne* in 1732 intending to found a refuge for the English poor, particularly those who had been in debtors' prisons, somewhere south of the Carolinas. This would coincidentally provide a base for an English attack on the Spanish in Florida, which came to pass in 1739 as part of the War of Jenkins' Ear. Oglethorpe made friends with Tomachici, chief of the Yamacraw, when he arrived. He immediately banned slavery. Huguenots, Sephardic Jews, Greek Orthodox and Irish Catholics all arrived in this haven, and such was its genteel international ambience that Savannah, Georgia's first capital, was in part modelled on Paris. But slavery meant money and slavery duly arrived in Georgia in 1751.

America's oldest black church, the First African Baptist Church on Montgomery Street, has diamond-shaped holes in the floor to ventilate tunnels for slaves escaping to the Underground Railroad. When General William Tecumseh Sherman arrived in Savannah on his March to the Sea in December 1864, he offered the town as a present to President Lincoln, thinking to incinerate it, but Lincoln said it should be left intact and the freed slaves granted land. This produced Sherman's 'Field Order #15', which allocated forty acres and a mule to former slaves, courtesy of the government. 'Nurses with white children, little shoeshine boys, peddlers with push-carts, farmers with ox carts – all are part of the Negro scene,' according to a Federal Writers' Project reporter. 'Others drive little musical ice-cream carts, bakers' wagons with shrill bells, and trains of yellow garbage trailers that wind through this motley traffic like Chinese dragons. Throughout the city sound the cries of hucksters, unintelligible to the visitor unaccustomed to the dialect of the 'Geechee Negro. All day these hucksters shamble through the streets with great baskets of fish, vegetables and flowers balanced on their heads.' Savannah now is nearly two-thirds black.

We had dinner in a place overlooking the river called Kevin Barry's, named for the Irish Republican medical student hanged by the British in 1921. Alleyways and staircases led down to the riverbanks, the cobbled harbour made from the ballast of sailing ships. Aoife was too tired to continue, so she went back to the hotel to sleep. My short subsequent tour of the bars was fruitless, perhaps because Savannah is a university town. I sat on barstools and at tables wondering if I would receive a conversational gesture, but none arrived. The bars strove for a distressed harbour-front look and achieved it, but the clientele appeared to be the young and upwardly mobile, rather than sailors. I saw a dark place just before reaching my car and went in. It had one customer, a Thai barmaid, a spotlight, stage and chrome pole, but no dancer.

The next day we crossed over the state line into South Carolina. After Coosawatchie we got onto Highway 17 going east. In a roadside store I stood behind a black woman paying for an electrical earpiece, but when she saw the total came to $6.66 she added a fifty-five-cent glittering plastic ring.

'No one around here wants that number on their heads,' the woman at the till said when the customer left. 'We get a lot of sales that way.'

Somewhere on the way into Charleston a new voice appeared in the car, deep and guttural and with exaggerated vowels and sentence ends that rose in pitch. It was Aoife pretending to be a married, unemployed Liverpudlian describing his day – pub lunch, ten or fifteen beers, home for a nap, wipe down the work surfaces in the kitchen with a wet towel before his wife gets back for a break in her twelve-hour work day, a chip butty for the children – 'They get their nutrition, like, from the school lunches, don't they?'

– then back to the pub for the football. 'A lot of me mates are envious, but I say they're back in the Dark Ages. "Let the wimmen do the work if they want to," I tell them.'

We arrived in Charleston in the early evening, its historic district a peninsula in the shape of the state of Illinois, pointing southwards in a multi-river estuary. The first shots of the Civil War were fired here when Fort Sumter, under the command of Major Robert Anderson, was subject to a barrage directed by the Confederate General Pierre Beauregard, who had been a student in Anderson's artillery class at West Point. On Rainbow Row in Charleston there are houses of many colours, with shuttered windows and iron balconies made by slaves from Barbados. Like Savannah, with which it was (and is) in competition, it drew migrants fleeing oppression in Europe and also had a significant population of free blacks. America's first theatre building appeared here in 1736, its first museum in 1773, and it now had the country's only 'Liveability Courts' created in 2002 to adjudicate on matters concerning housing, noise, animal control, waste and the environment. Tourists thronged the streets, moving at grazing pace. During the day they have the choice of Civil War, architectural, black history and folkloric tours, the last featuring stories told in the local Gullah dialect, by cruise, trolley, horse and carriage or on foot. It seemed a good place to pass a winter, as some of America's wealthiest citizens once did.

In the darkness, we headed into the interior of South Carolina on Interstate 26, then to the north again on Interstate 65. The map was full of town names for this region, but the world outside the window seemed increasingly a wilderness. We got off looking for gas around Santee, but on the overpass I could only see a few dim street lights and what seemed a forest beyond. Along the road I saw an illuminated sign and drove over. There was an office, a row of barrack-like rooms and facilities, it said, for recreational vehicles. It was an all-male world there as far as I could see. Some low fires burned in pits and barbecues in the parking lot. The police had a man against a wall. Someone came out and complained of a snake in his room. I passed four men crouched over pieces of meat cooking on a fire. They looked at me with what seemed malevolence from faces covered in hair, their T-shirts smudged with charcoal and dirt. They could have been a string quartet on tour for all I knew, but lit up by the flames on this dark night, they looked like a diorama in a natural-history museum, cooking pieces of mastodon in front of their cave. It was worse than Tres Piedras, New Mexico, by far.

We crossed Lake Marion, created in the 1940s by the Santee Cooper Hydroelectrical and Navigation Project, for which 12,500 workers made forty-two miles of dams and dykes and cleared 177,000 acres of swamp and forest. The lake was named for Francis Marion, the legendary guerrilla leader of the War of Independence known as the Swamp Fox, whose home, Pond Bluff, was inundated by the Santee Cooper Project. Marion, a frail child the size of a New England lobster at birth, according to a friend, was first a sailor, then joined the British campaign against the Cherokee. Of this, he later wrote: 'The next morning we proceeded by order of Colonel James Grant, to burn down the Indians' cabins. Some of our men seemed to enjoy this cruel work, laughing very heartily at the circling flames . . . Poor creatures! thought I, we surely need not begrudge you such miserable habitations. But, when we came, according to orders, to cut down the fields of corn, I could scarcely refrain from tears. For who could see the stalks that stood so stately with broad green leaves and gaily tasselled shocks, filled with sweet milky liquid and flour, the staff of life; who, I say, without grift, could see those sacred plants sinking under our swords with all their precious load, to wither and rot untested in their mourning fields.' Marion became a member of the South Carolina Provincial Congress in 1775, and when the revolution broke out he developed a form of warfare involving intelligence-gathering, local knowledge, surprise, stealth, imagination and an untrained, unpaid army. This would come into its own early in the twentieth century, first in South Africa and then in Ireland. While British forces under Colonel Banastre Tarleton burned homes, Marion offered receipts for requisitioned supplies, the sums involved being repaid after the war by the state government.

We came off the interstate just after the lake at Summerton. There was a choice of hotels, and I picked the Best Value Inn, which cost $44 and had the feel of a correctional institution. Huge men with beards and the sleeves cut off their denim jackets stood around a stencilled NASCAR vehicle on a trailer. The two mattress bases in our room had reddish-brown stains that seemed to mirror each other as they extended from the head to the foot of the beds, as though someone had been laid out on the floor between them and opened with a knife. The complimentary breakfast the next morning was a long way away along concrete paths and stairs. Aoife stayed in the room. When I got there they told me I couldn't have any food unless I produced the voucher I had been given when checking in the night before. I went all the way back and got the voucher, but when I returned and looked at what was offered – pale, grey scrambled eggs in a metal tray, grits, bacon in gelatinous grease – I couldn't face eating any of it, hungry though I was. Even the toast put me off.

'I'll have an orange juice,' I said to a belligerent-looking woman holding a metal spoon.

'Orange juice is fifty cents!' she shouted, then stared at me out of tiny eyes, her mouth clamped shut. Everyone else knows, she seemed to be saying, that orange juice costs fifty cents at the Best Value Inn.

'All right,' I said. 'Forget it.'

Thereafter, all the way to New York, Aoife would call out in a bar or hotel room or from a prone position in the back of the car when I thought she was asleep, 'Oran' joos is feeiftay sayents!', in summation of the south, or of me.

South Carolina was the first state to ratify the Articles of Confederation, the precursor to the Constitution, and the first to secede from the Union during the preliminaries to the Civil War. Reconstruction, as elsewhere in the south, enfranchised freed slaves and provided many of them with land, but the freedmen were sold out in the Compromise of 1877, which allowed Republican Rutherford B. Hayes to assume the presidency after a close and disputed election, on the condition that federal troops protecting the Reconstruction reforms be removed from the south. Reconstruction Republican regimes fell and the south became Democratic, controlled by a coalition of pro-business, anti-big-government and anti-expansion Bourbons and a group known as the Redeemers. The Redeemers had a programme to purify the south of high taxes, corruption, government spending on infrastructure and schools and misguided attempts to impose equal rights for black people, thus giving a theological tone to southern right-wing politics more than a hundred years before this force realised itself in the presidency of George W. Bush. The Reconstruction period became known as the 'Tragic Era' in the Dunning School version of history, formulated by a Columbia University professor named William Archibald Dunning, who declared black people too confused, too easily led to be given the vote. The Dunning School's version of post-Civil War history prevailed in southern school textbooks into the 1960s. In South Carolina, 'Pitchfork' Ben Tillman, governor from 1890 to 1894 and a US senator from 1895 until he died in 1918, took part in the Hamburg Massacre in 1876, during which seven members of a black freedom militia were killed in the western part of the state by a white group known as the Red Shirts. He called a state constitutional convention in 1895 that enacted Jim Crow laws and later said of his efforts to prevent black people from voting, 'We have done our level best ... we have scratched our heads to find out how we could eliminate the last of them. We stuffed ballot boxes. We shot them. We are not ashamed of it.'

Sixty per cent of the population of Summerton, site of the Best Value Inn, is black. A quarter of all people there live under the poverty line. Europeans speak of the vast differences between, for example, Sicily and Milan, Galicia and Catalunia or Donegal and Wexford, but I have never been anywhere in Europe to equal the remoteness from what might be thought of as the mainstream of American life as the interior of South Carolina, in its cultural practices, its poverty and its wildness. It seems to be not only a different place, but also of a different millennium. Nevertheless, this state produced some transcendent Americans, including Dizzy Gillespie, Jasper Johns, James Brown and Joe Frazier.

My decision the night before to take the interstate out of Charleston kept us on 65 up past Florence and Dillon into North Carolina. It was my worst error in road choice in the trip. I longed for Highway 17, which had been so pleasing going into Charleston and which would have taken me out of it again along the coast through the Francis Marion National Forest, North Carolina and Virginia nearly all the way to Washington. I finally met it again at Williamston, North Carolina, and drove north, the names in this region nearly all English – Plymouth, Hamilton, Windsor, Darden, Woodard, Askewville and Burden. I was entering the mid-Atlantic shoreline states, the final ones of my journey, and leaving the Deep South – this place of vendettas, baroque speech, military recruiting, superstition and courtliness, where dandyism and coquetry are flamenco-like in their elaboration, where nearly everyone feels betrayed by someone and where all of America's, and much of the world's, popular music was invented. The air clarified in the Atlantic winds.

We stopped at Edenton, named state capital in 1722, on Albemarle Sound. Edenton has been preserved in several stages – colonial, antebellum, Victorian and mid-1950s. In 1775, fifty-one Edenton women publicly pledged not to drink British tea, then a near-revolutionary act, for it was an attack on the colonial taxation system. Thirty-eight years later Harriet Jacobs was born in Edenton of mulatto slaves. Her mother's owner taught her to sew, read and write, but when she was twelve she was passed on to Dr James Norcom, who raped her over a period of ten years and refused her permission to marry Samuel Sawyer, a white lawyer who eventually became a senator and who was the father of her two children. He'd sell her children if she tried, he told her. When she was twenty-three she escaped, hiding in a tiny space in her grandmother's attic for seven years. From there she could sometimes hear and see her children. She got away from Edenton on a boat, disguised as a sailor, stopping in Philadelphia and eventually New York, where she worked as a housemaid for the abolitionist Nathaniel Parker Willis and wrote *Incidents in the Life of a Slave Girl*, which Horace Greeley serialised in the *New York Tribune*, excising the sexual abuse but stirring northern opinion against slavery nevertheless. She was finally reunited with her children in Boston and survived by thirty-five years the ending of slavery by Lincoln's Emancipation Proclamation.

We walked out onto a pier, the day bright over the sound, which was frothing in the wind. At its far end were the Outer Banks, a two-hundred-mile-long ribbon of sand in the ocean that can shift southwards by up to twenty feet in a year. Here in the dunes of Kill Devil Hills near Kitty Hawk, bicycle-manufacturing bachelor brothers Orville and Wilbur Wright made the world's first powered flight – ten feet high, 120 feet long, twelve seconds in duration at 6.8 miles per hour. Having watched birds and bicyclists and using scientific data extending back to Leonardo da Vinci, they solved the 'flying problem' through their development of three-axis pilot control, involving wing warping for roll, forward elevation for pitch and a rear rudder to control yaw, or lateral movement. They had worked this out with a glider the year before, but it was the addition of their shop mechanic's aluminium, fuel-injection engine that resulted in what has generally been accepted as the invention of the aeroplane.

To the south and west of Kill Devil Hills is Roanoke Island, where in 1585 a gold-seeking expedition despatched by Sir Walter Raleigh and composed primarily of soldiers who had been involved in colonising Ireland established the first

English settlement in America. They were still there in 1587, but when a third expedition arrived the island was empty. No historian has ever solved the mystery of what happened to the settlers, nor why they carved the name of the local Indian tribe into the stockade.

Raleigh had earlier sent an exploratory expedition under Philip Amadas and Arthur Barlowe, which arrived at the Outer Banks in 1584. Barlowe later wrote that the Indians 'in their behaviour [were] as mannerly and civil as any in Europe' and that Granganimeo, brother of Chief Wingina, greeted them with 'signs of joy and welcome, striking his head and his breast and afterwards on ours to show we were all one, smiling, and making show the best he could of all love and familiarity'. They returned to England with tobacco, potatoes and two Indians, Manteo and Wanchese. Manteo was baptised and was beginning to assume the manners of an English gentleman by the time he went back to Albemarle Sound, but Wanchese hadn't at all liked what he had seen in the Elizabethan court. Each has a town named for him on Roanoke.

When William Least Heat-Moon was in Manteo, which he thought was listing towards the quaint, a woman called the Duchess, who owned a restaurant there, said to him, 'If you want the real yesterday, go to Wanchese. They haven't seen neon light down there yet.' I was in Wanchese with the writer Mark Richard for an afternoon in 1992, by which time modernity of a sort had hit it. Wheelhouses were shut up, winches were rusting in the grass, nets disintegrating in heaps. Boats were in dry dock, the paint peeling. Fishermen with angry looks and nothing to do sat on crates. 'Wanchese is on the brink of extinction,' said Mark. 'The inlet you enter it through is filling up and the fish have gone.' He'd fished on a boat owned by a man named Punk Daniels when times were better. 'It could be the most brutal work sometimes,' he said. 'You'd be exhausted, cold, with fish poisoning all over your hands. You'd be pulling up the most disgusting things with the nets – oil cans, plastic, all kinds of other junk thrown from ships, livers, rotted eyes, ovaries, skinless organs of fish by the shovelful. A friend of mine named Marshal told me he pulled up a human finger once. It's a nightmare world down there at the bottom of the sea. But, you know, I loved it at the same time. You'd come in with your catch and have the most almighty feeling of accomplishment.' We passed Marshal then, who knew the pathways, the currents, the stories of all the houses. His own family had been there for generations and his Somerset accent had held since they had first come from England centuries before. Mark asked him about various fishermen he'd known. 'He's in New Bedford . . . he's gone to Alaska,' were the answers. 'No fish any more.'

We left Edenton on 17, bypassed Elizabeth City and after Morgan's Corner entered the Great Dismal Swamp, a 110,000-acre wildlife refuge of forested wetlands, which extends to the suburbs of Norfolk, Virginia. Formed, it is believed, by the last great shift of the continental shelf, its base is made of peat. In the centre of the swamp is Lake Drummond, formed, scientists think, by a meteor and containing exceptionally pure, amber-coloured water kept free from bacteria by tannin from the trees. It was prized on sailing ships, where it was kept in kegs, maintaining a freshness long into the journeys.

George Washington visited the swamp in 1763 and proposed draining it and digging a canal to link Chesapeake Bay and Albemarle Sound. The trees could be harvested and the land used for farming. There was far too much water for the swamp to be drained, however, and Washington eventually sold to the father of Robert E. Lee his share in the consortium that was developing the project. It was later a stop for slaves on the run, travelling on the Underground Railroad. Up to a thousand slaves were thought to have hidden in it. The sun was going down as we passed the swamp, the waterways among the trees lit up blue, silver and gold.

We went around Norfolk, the world's largest naval base, to the south and east and got into Virginia Beach in the darkness. We drove around and around looking for a room and finally found one at a Day's Inn, run by Ajay Patel, one of the 8,400 members of the Asian-American Hotel Owners' Association, who collectively own thirty-seven per cent of America's hotels. After Mr Patel arrived in the United States in 1995 he got a job as a hotel gardener. He then became part of a consortium that owns a further five hotels and manages seventeen others. 'How do you come here one day and the next day own hotels?' he said. 'We don't go to restaurants. We don't go on vacations. At the beginning, we live in the hotel with our families so we can keep an eye on everything. And we work really hard.'

We then went into the strip along the waterfront, a kind of Costa del Sol resort on the Atlantic, with promenade, beachwear shops and surfer bars. It was a Saturday night and Virginia Beach was thronged, the volume high, cocktail-fuelled. Here can intersect, often with disastrous consequences, farmers, holidaying American youth on the rampage and sailors from Norfolk steaming in with the war-cry, '*I want to fuck, I want to fight, I want to eat dynamite!*' When I was at a dinner table in Virginia Beach with Mark Richard he said to all who would listen that they should beware coquettish women in bars where such people congregate. 'They play the mood of the men like it was a tune,' he said. 'They have emergency ward written all over them.'

Much of Virginia Beach is built on sand of uncertain stability. The shoreline is provisional and tending to recede. People can sit in their waterfront houses during a storm watching walls of green floodlit water moving towards them over sand and breakwalls and crashing into their plate-glass windows. They know that in time their houses will be taken by the sea.

Virginia Beach is at the mouth of Chesapeake Bay, America's largest estuary, a drowned plain into which 150 rivers flow. Slave ships entered here and troop ships now go out to war from the naval yards of Norfolk. On the slender finger of land across from Virginia Beach live guinea men of lawless ways who still speak Elizabethan English.

We went up to Cape Henry and past the First Landing State Park, where the Virginia Company settlers arrived on 26 April 1607, before they moved on to Jamestown. We crossed the mouth of the James River at Norfolk and got back onto 17, passing little towns with such names as Saluda, Mascot, Church View and Jamaica. I drove on through rolling cornfields. The afternoon light was soft, the earth fragrant after rain. We entered King and Queen and then Essex counties, the Rappahannock River to the right. 'The clearness and brightness of the sky', wrote Robert Beverley of Virginia in 1705, 'add new vigour to [the] spirit and perfectly remove all splenetic and sullen thoughts.' The road can make you feel many things, but just then it was peace and admiration. There was no other place I felt I would rather be, no wish for it to end.

I thought Aoife was asleep, but she started laughing at me as I tried to describe this sensation into a tape recorder. She then produced a Glaswegian woman advising her husband on the subject of cosmetic surgery. This was followed by an immaculately rendered African in a basso profundo voice ordering a pint of Carlsberg and two packages of cashew nuts in a London lap-dancing club. Indignant about the price compared to his local, he is offered a sarcastic, inaudible explanation. 'I know this is not Wetherspoons,' he replies, still indignant. 'I seen de ladies walking!' Finally, a young woman from a New Zealand sheep farm, who comes to London looking for bedazzlement and meets a commodity trader who lives with one woman, sees others and has very little time to offer. She wonders if this is a good prospect, then decides to give it a chance. 'We meet on Wednesdays for dinner, twice a month. Then we go to a hotel until midnight, when he has to leave. I pay, but I think that's a good thing, don't you? We don't have to be conventional. He says he's faithful to me now that he has his priorities right, and for that I'm grateful. He won't see me any more often than that because he says he wants to keep the relationship *fresh*.'

Other Virginia counties include Prince George, Isle of Wight, Sussex, Charles City, King William and Surrey. The English who landed at Plymouth in Massachusetts were Puritans fleeing Royalist persecution; among those who came to Virginia after 1650 were Cavaliers fleeing persecution by Puritans who had come to power with Cromwell. The Puritans were year zeroists who conceived of themselves in biblical terms as having been delivered into the Promised Land; the Cavaliers were spoiled dandies down on their luck and on the hunt for easy riches. 'They must have cut ludicrous figures, trudging through the salt marsh of the Chesapeake in their embroidered doublets and silken hose,' wrote Robert Hughes in *American Visions*. 'Sir Walter Raleigh is said to have taken jewels worth 30,000 pounds with him.' The Virginia colony they arrived at had long been a catastrophe. Of the 8,500 settlers shipped there by the Virginia Company since 1607, only 1,200 remained by 1625. The Virginia colonists stole from and murdered Indians, instituted forced labour and indentured servitude and attempted to replicate an English feudal aristocratic system that would survive in part due to the maintaining in ignorance of the masses. 'I thank G-d', wrote Sir William Berkeley, who became Governor of Virginia in 1642, 'there are no free schools nor printing, and I hope we shall not have these [for a] hundred years; for learning has brought disobedience . . . and printing has divulged [it] and libels against the best government. G-d keep us from both.'

The Puritans, on the other hand, were revolutionaries. Out of oppression and corruption they had come, into a natural paradise granted them by God in which all would be perpetually new and in which all men could remake themselves, be whoever they wished to be and live in amity and universal brotherhood. The vastness of the natural gift in itself gave scale to the vision. 'The scene which that country presents to the eye of the spectator, has something in it which generates and encourages great ideas,' wrote Tom Paine in the next century. 'The mighty objects he beholds, act upon his mind by enlarging it, and he partakes of the greatness he contemplates.' The Puritans' authority lay in the Old Testament and their objective was to remake the world by creating their exemplary 'city on the hill'. They and the virgin land of America were a match made by God. The pilgrims would arrive at their apotheosis through godly diligence, good works, contemplative gravity, reforming zeal and an absolute, pure belief in both equality and private property. 'The experience that was had in this common course and condition', wrote William Bradford in his Pilgrim history, 'may well evince the vanity of that conceit of Plato's and other ancients, applauded by some of later times; – that the taking away of property, and bringing into a commonwealth, would make them happy and flourishing; as if they were wiser than God. For this community (so far as it was) was found to breed much confusion and discontent, and retard much employment that would have been to their benefit and comfort.'

The Declaration of Independence and the Constitution had as their sources already existing laws, particularly English laws, but their democratic passion and sense of the exemplary, of a glorious, divine experiment being acted out before the eyes of the world, were Puritan. *Novus ordo seclorum* – a new order of the ages – is the message on every dollar bill. 'The American is a new man, who acts upon new principles; he must therefore entertain new ideas, and form new opinions,' wrote a farmer named J. Hector St John de Crèvecoeur in 1782. 'From involuntary idleness, servile dependence, penury and useless labour, he has passed to toils of a very different nature, rewarded by ample subsistence – This is an American.' 'We are the world's best, and last hope,' said Thomas Jefferson, who believed that this hope could only stay alive through periodic revolutions against banking and caste interests and the tendency of governments to centralise power, an idea later arrived at by Leon Trotsky.

The Puritan influence, so definitive of early America, has endured. Much of America's conservatism is Puritan. Free-market capitalism has its roots in a Puritan conception of individual liberty. There is the abhorrence of relativism, the acceptance of authority because that authority has been placed there by God, the idea of an unadorned, unmediated relationship with God translating into deregulation and the primacy of the individual over any generalised, collective responsibility. The separation of Church and state derived in part from the Enlightenment, but it was also an essential prerequisite for those who had suffered from persecution by an established Church. Overly centralised power to the Puritans suggested Popery, decadent aristocrats and tyrants. It must always lead to corruption. Now the enemies of liberty in the minds of many Americans are Washington and the United Nations. State rights are championed. Tax in itself is seen as a symbol of decadence. A Puritan personal style of simplicity, directness and modesty, allied to a righteously avenging wrath when wronged, is expressed, or aspired to, or imitated by many American conservatives.

The Puritan faith in the perpetually new is what lay behind the choice of Washington as capital. All European capitals exist in places where power and money accrued. Washington at the time was a tract of mostly uninhabited mosquito-infested land with a few tobacco farms up near the top of Chesapeake Bay. The revolutionary leaders created a separate constitutional entity called a district from land allocated by Maryland in which to place the capital, so that no state would be unfairly favoured by its location. They also wanted a clean slate for the capital, for they believed that was the nature of the country. George Washington, too embarrassed to refer to it as anything other than the Federal City, chose the site, but the city was primarily the invention of Thomas Jefferson. That it would be located in the south was decided at a dinner attended by James Madison and Alexander Hamilton that had been convened by Jefferson, and the city's layout and style were directed by him.

Jefferson came to collect visual art with the profligacy of a J.P. Morgan, but regarded the serious study and development of it in America as premature. 'Painting. Statuary. Too expensive for the state of wealth among us,' he wrote. Architecture, however, was different. Architecture could foster and serve a democratic vision. Jefferson, says Robert Hughes, was, in addition to everything else he did, 'the greatest American-born architect of his time', designing at least seven houses, including his own at Monticello, the Virginia state capitol building, a church and the University of Virginia at Charlottesville. His inspiration was ancient Rome, filtered through France, where he served as American minister to Paris from 1784. He was appalled by the buildings he saw in Virginia, full of 'barbarous ornaments' and 'maledictions' carried out by artless workmen and, worst of all, inspired by the English, whose general sluggishness he attributed to an excessive ingestion of beef. France, however, produced ecstasy. 'Oh!' he said of the Halle aux Blés. 'It was the most superb thing on earth!' Pierre Rousseau's Hôtel de Solm made him 'violently smitten'. 'How beautiful was every object!' he wrote to his friend Maria Conway, of Paris generally. In France at the time rococo was being jettisoned in favour of neo-classicism, 'the mature architectural speech of the Enlightenment', according to Robert Hughes.

Jefferson discovered the Federal style, the architecture of the new democracy, after seeing the Maison Carrée at Nîmes, a Roman temple from the time of Augustus, which he used as the basis for the Virginia capitol building in Richmond, of which he said, 'We wish to exhibit a grandeur of conception, a Republican simplicity, and that true elegance of proportion, which correspond to a tempered freedom excluding Frivolity, the food of little minds.' This was to be carried over to the new capital, for the design of which he commissioned Pierre Charles L'Enfant, a French military engineer who had fought in the War of Independence. L'Enfant designed a monumental city of broad avenues and streets radiating outwards from traffic circles, the whole being diamond-shaped. Others were to affect the city before its first stage was completed, including James Hoban, an Irishman whose design for the White House was based on Leinster House in Dublin.

When Alexis de Tocqueville came to America in 1831 he was stunned by how fundamentally democracy had established itself. Instead of the divine right of European kings and the *droit de seigneur* of aristocrats, there was the sovereignty of the people. And the people, he found, exercised their sovereignty in a living governance of activism through voting, participation in local associations, the rejection of hierarchies and the forming of a government that taxed little, maintained the smallest of armies, was responsive to the people's will and in which even the president got up and poured the drinks for his guests. 'Once again,' he wrote, 'my intellectual world totters and I am again lost and desperate in a powerful tide which shakes or inverts every truth on which I have based my beliefs and conduct ... We are travelling towards unlimited democracy ... No effort to stop this movement will do any more than bring about brief halts ... In America a free society has created free political institutions. In France free political institutions will have to create a free society ... It is no longer a question of obtaining from [Americans] suggestions about topics we are ignorant of but of re-examining in conversation with them almost everything we already know.'

François-René de Chateaubriand, a relative of de Tocqueville's who travelled in America forty years before him, wrote of the nature of freedom he found there: 'There are two types of personal liberty. One belongs to the infancy of nations; it is the daughter of manners and virtue – it is that of the first Greeks, the first Romans, and that of the savages of America. The other is born of the old age of nations; it is the daughter of enlightenment and reason – it is the liberty of the United States which replaces the liberty of the Indian. Happy land which in the space of less than three centuries has passed from the one liberty to the other almost without effort, and that by a battle lasting no more than eight years ... The United States has ... [a] safeguard: its population occupies only an eighteenth of its territory. America still inhabits solitude; for a long time yet her wilderness will be her manners, and her enlightenment will be her liberty.'

Behind liberty and equality for many Americans then and now was God, their originator and their guarantor. 'This august dignity I treat of,' wrote Herman Melville in *Moby-Dick*, 'is not the dignity of kings and robes, but that abounding dignity which has no robed investiture. Thou shalt see it in the arm that wields a pitch or drives a spike; that democratic dignity which, on all hands, radiates without and from God, Himself! The great God absolute! The centre and circumference of all democracy! His omnipresence, our divine equality!' There is much of the Bible in the tone and content of Melville, as there is in Hawthorne, Whitman, Faulkner, Steinbeck and Bob Dylan, pillars of the national literature.

Aoife and I came into Washington in the darkness. Charles Dickens called it the 'City of Magnificent Intentions', citing 'spacious avenues that begin in nothing, and lead nowhere; streets, mile long, that only want houses, roads and inhabitants; public buildings that need but a public to be complete; and ornaments of great thoroughfares, which only lack great thoroughfares to ornament'. In its outer avenues it still has a vacant, not quite completed feel to it. Washington's population reached its height in 1950 with 802,178 people and has been falling since. It now has just under a quarter of a million fewer people than it had then. We got into the area of monuments, all floodlit and silent, but couldn't get near enough to the White House to see it. When I came here with my parents as a child we parked fifty yards away from the gate and strolled up unhindered. Now the roads are blocked and the crash barriers are up. It seemed a bunker awaiting a siege. Jefferson's 'Republican simplicity' and 'true elegance of proportion' now has the look of paranoia.

My father, used to the Chicago grids, couldn't find his way around Washington, and neither could I. I parked without knowing where I was. We went out onto a large intersection overlooked by office buildings and sat at a pavement table outside a bar. Next door a queue began to form for entrance to a gay disco. At the table next to ours were three men and a woman, all in suits, all in their late twenties and all, I thought, with expressions that said, 'It's all a game and only we know the rules.' It was a look of which I had seen the first, not yet blossoming buds in the corridor of the Yale Law School. But perhaps I was imposing this on them.

Or perhaps they were lobbyists, in which case the look would have fitted the job. In 2005 there were 34,750 registered lobbyists in Washington, double the number in 2000. In this five-year period, annual government expenditure went up $0.5 trillion to $2.29 trillion, while spending on federal lobbying went up $0.5 billion to $2.1 billion. Firms were charging up to one hundred per cent more for their services than they had five years before and were paying starting salaries of $300,000 per year for new lobbyists. Many are former politicians and Congressional and White House aides. Nearly half of all departing legislators become lobbyists. One lobbyist said he receives around twenty invitations to political fundraising events every day, with several more arriving by email. The catering business in Washington has boomed. In the same year, 2005, there were 39,186 lobbyists registered in individual states. In New York there were twenty for each state legislator.

Dick Romano, the Chicago area stockbroker who told me about the process of determining executive wages, came to Washington as a board member of NASDAQ in order to try to persuade politicians to support its wish to be classified as a stock exchange rather than just a stock market. If they were an exchange, they could become a publicly listed company and raise capital through stock issues. He reported to NASDAQ's Congressional liaison office, where he met the lobbyist who was to guide him on his tour of Congresspersons' offices. Different lobbyists, he was told, have special access to different legislators. Money had been handed over to the lobbyist, the lobbyist took his fee and distributed the rest to the politicians' re-election campaign funds, and Dick got his list of appointments.

Each politician he saw was a member of the Financial

Services Committee, but had wildly different degrees of knowledge of the issue. One, Pat Toomey from Pennsylvania, he found very well informed and articulate, but another, a Congressman from the Chicago area, had no idea what Dick was talking about. When Dick finished his pitch, the Congressman asked one of his advisors, 'How will this play in the "hood" [meaning constituency]?' He got his estimate, then asked the lobbyist, 'What do you think of it?' The lobbyist, who had been paid well to support the proposal, said, 'I think it's a very good idea.' The Congressman thought for a moment, then said, 'Write a letter to the Securities Exchange Commission supporting it and I'll sign it.'

If there is a difference between this process and the business practices of the oldest profession, I can't see it, except that the service provided by the politicians might be less reliable. You could never be sure that you would get what you were trying to buy.

It has been said that the term 'lobbyist' was first used to describe the people who thronged the lobby of the Willard Hotel in Washington seeking to influence President Ulysses S. Grant, who used to have brandy and a cigar there, but it was in use as early as 1820. It evolved into a professional, non-partisan 'influence for hire' service, but entered a new era when Republicans won the Congressional election of 1994. House majority leader Tom DeLay compiled a list of four hundred lobbying firms, divided into 'friendly' and 'unfriendly' categories according to how much money they had donated to each party. The market stall was open, influence could be had, but there was a new price tag, and it was not only a question of cash. Republicans also demanded of the corporations seeking favours that they purge their Washington offices, and even the lobbying firms they hired, of Democrats. 'If you want to play in our revolution,' said DeLay, 'you have to play by our rules.' Republicans set about filling federal executive branch posts and judgeships with party loyalists, but the lobbying firms were of special importance, for they were placed at the intersection of money and political power.

Republican Senator Rick Santorum from Pennsylvania held Tuesday-morning meetings with other Republican law-makers and a group of around twenty-five of the most important lobbyists, the objective being that each new vacancy in a lobbying firm be filled by a Republican. Many of these could be Republican politicians who had lost elections or had decided to leave office for the more lucrative career of lobbying.

This really was a revolution. The making of money was an objective, but at the root of this transformation was ideology. The formerly non-partisan agencies who controlled the flow of money from the corporations into the political campaign funds were now coming to be controlled by Republican Party loyalists, dedicated to a low-tax, privatising, free-market, anti-regulatory agenda that was being pursued as though it derived from a religious revelation. These principles generally coincided with the interests of the lobbyists' clients, but not always. The corporations could be told, 'You can have x, which is what you want, but in order to do so you must support us on the issue of y.' The Republican Party was building a base for its ideology that could be maintained beyond the loss of electoral power. If power in America had passed from the people (eighteenth and early nineteenth centuries) to big business (late nineteenth and early twentieth) to central government (1930s and 1940s) and then to multinational corporations (1990s), it was now moving towards a single, highly motivated, evangelical and ideological political party. They were able to exercise tremendous leverage through the lobbying agencies. Though there was a Republican president in office who had lost the popular vote and had to rely on being appointed by the Supreme Court, and though Republican control of the two houses of Congress was held by only a slender margin, the party was able to pursue and successfully enact a radical agenda of two huge tax cuts for the most wealthy at a time of war; of a reversal of labour, environmental, civil libertarian and other regulatory protective laws that had evolved from the New Deal and been part of a national consensus into the

1980s; of a rearrangement of the constitutionally prescribed balance of power through a new concentration on the executive branch; of systematic cutbacks in public services; and of war-making against countries that had posed no direct threat to the United States. Much of this was against the expressed wishes of the populace and contrary to what they had voted for. But the populace had been taken out of the equation. Control of the lobbying firms and the money flow gave the party control not only of the legislators, but also of the corporations who were hiring the lobbying firms, for they could be directed on whom to support and what to tacitly approve in exchange for the particular legislative prize they most coveted. The party enfranchising of the lobbying industry also had the effect of routing more money into Republican accounts. Corporations previously tended to spread their bets fairly evenly between the parties. Donations to Republicans soon reached a level of two to one over those to Democrats. A prolonged Democratic majority could change the money flow, but perhaps not the principle.

Washington, the Unpardonable, the Disqualified, the Place Name Which Is Itself an Expletive. It could be called the City of Mirages. The tricks have long been in the process of being perfected. Woodrow Wilson railed against the Money Trust, a group of Wall Street banks, in his campaign for the presidency. Americans in general loathed the Money Trust, and candidates who campaigned against it were often voted in, as was Wilson. It was later discovered that the Money Trust had financed him, and was in turn facilitated by him when he was in office. Karl Rove, the principal engine behind the politicking of George W. Bush, began his political career at nineteen by joining under a false identity the campaign staff of a Democratic candidate for Illinois state treasurer, stealing one thousand sheets of paper with the candidate's letterhead on them and then having imprinted on them an invitation to FREE FOOD, FREE DRINK, WOMEN AND A GOOD TIME FOR NOTHING. These were distributed at homeless shelters and rock concerts. Later, running the campaign for the Republican candidate for governor of Texas, Rove planted a listening device in his own office and called a press conference, holding up the device and expressing sorrow at how low his Democratic opponent had sunk. A police investigation later discovered that the device hadn't even been connected. Rove was a reader of Niccolò Machiavelli. His predecessor, Lee Atwater, declared that he read *The Prince* every year. Machiavelli wrote, '[The Prince] should seem to be all mercy, faith, integrity, humanity and religion. And nothing is more necessary than to have this last quality . . . Everybody sees what you appear to be, few feel what you are.' Almost no one has said, as Hamlet did, 'I know not seems.' In recent times a proposal to end the forty-hour week has been called the Family Flexibility Act, another to loosen carbon-emission controls the Clean Skies Act, and another in favour of the timber industry the Healthy Forest Initiative, all of it without serious protest. The lying is so blatant you could almost think it is a form of entertainment for the practitioners, as with bullies who keep stepping up their perse-cutions to see how much their victims can take.

'A nation which asks nothing of its government but the maintenance of order is already a slave at heart – the slave of its own well-being, awaiting but the hand that will bind it,' wrote de Tocqueville, an enthusiast for American democracy, but also aware of its fallibilities. 'By such a nation, the despotism of faction is not less to be dreaded than the despotism of an individual. When the bulk of the community are engrossed by private concerns, the smallest parties need not despair of getting the upper hand in public affairs. At such times, it is not rare to see upon the great stage of the world, as we see at our theatres, a multitude represented by a few players, who alone speak in the name of an absent or inattentive crowd: they alone are in action, whilst all others are stationary; they regulate everything by their own caprice; they change the laws, and tyrannise at will over the manners of the country; and then men wonder to see into how small a number of weak and worthless hands a great people may fall.'

* * *

American politicians have had more than two and a quarter centuries to learn how to be unaccountable, and they have succeeded. The United States, I believe, cannot legitimately call itself a functioning democracy. Barely half those entitled to vote do so. People are alienated and dispirited about politics, and with good reason – politicians take bribes and lie with spectacular openness and without any legal or, in most cases, electoral consequences. Is there any way back? Not, I would say, without certain fundamental reforms.

Any interference in citizens' rights to vote or to register to vote, as happened in Florida, should be treated as a serious federal crime carrying a jail sentence, as should the lack of enforcement of this law by any local bodies.

Voting should be limited to representatives at city, county, state and Congressional levels, as well as the presidency. There should be a non-partisan, professional civil service and legal system. Almost no one but party activists and their own relatives knows who the judges, county comptrollers, attorneys general and so on are who appear on the ballots.

Ballots should be made of paper, and verifiably recountable, rather than electronic.

Elected politicians should not be able to oversee the redrawing of their own constituencies to guarantee them their office in perpetuity, as happens at present.

Tax loopholes should be closed. Many of the large corporations are paying no tax at all, having made large political campaign contributions to legislators in order to obtain this advantage. Hewlett-Packard doubled their lobbying budget to get a tax cut in their $14.5 billion in profits from foreign subsidiaries, and succeeded. 'We're trying to take advantage of the fact that Republicans control the House, the Senate and the White House,' they declared. The deficits that are accruing from decreased tax revenues are rendering the government dysfunctional and the economy in general unviable. The American War of Independence was fought over the issue of taxation without representation. The present system is a case of representation without taxation.

The Electoral College should be dispensed with. I haven't met anyone who understands why the president should not be elected directly by voting citizens.

Government should be limited to the management of the economy, the maintenance of public order and safety, national security and the provision of services. Issues involving the individual conscience, such as homosexual marriage and abortion, have overwhelmed and distorted the political process.

The private financing of political campaigns should be illegal. If this were done, there would be a massive and instantaneous cleansing of the system. The population generally would be the body to whom the politicians would be accountable. Many necessary reforms would follow from this – fair taxation, better schools, a cleaner environment, less war, an improved infrastructure, better conditions for workers, an economically healthier middle class, less poverty, better relations with other countries, fairer justice, renewed civic energy. Arizona has a system for its state legislature whereby candidates who raise a qualifying amount of money only in quantities of up to five-dollar individual donations can then avail themselves of public campaign funds. The media can be required to provide a certain amount of broadcast time for each candidate. There is no issue faced by American democracy that is more urgent or central than this.

We left Washington going north and entered Maryland, which has the curious slogan 'Manly Deeds, Womanly Words'. We stopped for the night on the southern edge of Baltimore. There is a statue of Edgar Allan Poe, a Baltimore native, here, on which was inscribed an inaccurate quotation. A local citizen petitioned for years for it to be amended, and when he finally ran out of patience he did it himself with hammer and chisel. He was arrested and brought before a magistrate who, sympathising with his literary scrupulousness, gave him a suspended sentence.

New York City

We bypassed Baltimore and continued north. That left 182 miles ahead and 15,064 behind. Much of the latter had been wilderness or near-wilderness – silent, grandiloquent and, if the mood was right, producing a feeling of glorious freedom. I could already feel it draining out of me, and would have liked to have staunched the flow. From here to New York it would be urban nearly all the way – cities spilling outwards towards each other, the road clamorous, over-looked, indifferent.

We crossed a corner of Delaware and then passed Philadelphia on its east side. Across the Delaware River was Camden, New Jersey. Walt Whitman was living here with his brother and sister-in-law in 1882, the year Oscar Wilde arrived in the country for a speaking tour. Wilde declared that the American poet he most wanted to meet was Whitman and sought an invitation through a publisher. Whitman sent a card letting it be known that he would be at home between '2 and 3½' on a given day. Wilde was twenty-seven and wore long Renaissance locks. He was inclined to dress in velvet, fur and breeches. Whitman was sixty-three and long into his poetic patriarch-hood. They had elderberry wine and a milk punch, the better to arrive at 'thee and thou' terms, as Whitman put it. They discussed poetics and beauty, with Wilde ever defer-ring in his views. Afterwards, Wilde said to the press, 'He is the grandest man I have ever seen, the simplest, most natural, and strongest character I have ever met in my life. I regard him as one of these wonderful, large entire men who might have lived in any age and is not peculiar to any people. Strong, true, and perfectly sane: the closest approach to the Greek we have yet had in modern times.' After they met again five months later, Wilde said to a friend, 'The kiss of Walt Whitman is still on my lips.'

We crossed into New Jersey at Trenton and got onto the Turnpike. New York seemed to be drawing us towards it as though through suction. Around halfway between Trenton and Newark was an industrial zone where Eric Schlosser encountered the virtuality of food. At East Hanover is the Givaudan corporation; at Teterboro, Haarman & Reimer and Takasago; and at Dayton, International Flavors and Fragrances. These, along with dozens of other similar manufacturing plants in the area, had their origins in the perfume industry and now produce two-thirds of the flavour additives sold in the United States. Around ninety per cent of the money Americans spend on food is used to buy processed food, according to Schlosser's *Fast Food Nation*, and all of that food uses flavours made in laboratories to replace what was taken out during canning, freezing and dehydrating. The flavours are produced by men and women in laboratory coats whose noses and palates are as refined as those of the best sommeliers. Methyl-2-peridylketone produces the flavour of popcorn, ethyl-3-hydroxybutanoate that of a marshmallow; 350 chemicals in tiny amounts combine to form the flavour of a strawberry. At International Flavors and Fragrances, Eric Schlosser was given some samples in the form of tiny drops from a bottle on white filter paper. 'I smelled fresh cherries, black olives, sautéed onions and shrimp. [The lab technician's] most remarkable creation took me by surprise. After closing my eyes, I suddenly smelled a grilled hamburger. The aroma was uncanny, almost miraculous. It smelled like someone in the room was flipping burgers on a hot grill. But when I opened my eyes, there was just a narrow strip of white paper and a smiling flavourist.'

At the northern end of the state the road was blistered and worn to a sheen like newly polished shoes. Houses crowded in on the borders of the highway, their back stair-cases and open windows making it seem as if they'd been filleted open. Soot clogged the girders of the bridges. This was a road that seemed exhausted by its daily burden. Jack Kerouac at the end of *On the Road* looked back from New Jersey at where he'd been and contemplated 'all that new land that rolls in one unbelievable bulge to the West Coast'. Here in the long approach to Newark the road was too crowded, too visible and too subject to repetition for it to suggest the mysteries and beauty he had written about.

In stalled traffic I watched through a chain-link fence beside the highway an elderly Jew and a young Latino screaming at each other by their cars in a strip-mall parking lot. The Latino was threatening to stave in the Jew's wind-screen with a plank of wood. The traffic moved me on before I could see how far they went. The road cleared amidst an elephantine sighing of buses and trucks and the whine of car tyres picking up speed. We passed Avenel, Rahway and Roselle, then Aoife produced her final performance of the journey, the testimony of a cockney woman of middle years with a twenty-one-year-old daughter, voice coarsened by cigarettes and disappointment and a little desperate with yearning.

'I said to my Rick when we was together, "Rick, if it's something personal with Tracey, leave it to me." Because we're mates, Trace and me, always was. Girl to girl, even when she was little. When she was coming up to thirteen she said to me, she said, "Mum, can I go on the pill?" "Course you can, darling," I said, and we went down the clinic. At the end of the day I didn't want her to be getting advice from somewhere else, did I, some kind of outside agency. Keep it in the family, I say. Rick's a toerag, he is. So's his wife. Can't stand her. Stuck up, with her BMW, her Givinchy whatsit and her seaweed baths. The tart. He sits in her house all day watching videos and cuts the lawn once a week. Never even called me on my birthday, did he?

'She's twenty-one now, Trace is. I been out to Ayia Napa

with her, and Magaluff. Her, me and six of her mates. We were out every night. Here in London I go clubbing with them every other weekend. They love it. "Your mum, she's a laugh, coming out in her stilettos and mini-skirt." It's not always plain sailing, mind. A bloke came up to Tracey and me in a club, must've thought we was sisters or mates. A bit of this, a bit of that. He was about twenty-three, I'd say.

I could see she was interested, but then he just blanked her. Asked me out to dance. It was me he fancied. I could see her standing there, poor cow. I felt so sorry for her. So I left her to it. I said, "Go on, babe." At the end of the day she is my daughter. He was tasty, though. Next time I mightn't be so generous!'

I looked at her there, laughing at her own last line. Where did she get these people – the Liverpool shirker, the stingy, voyeuristic African clutching his dignity in the lap-dancing club, the cockney mother in her fantasy of glittering eyes and faked bronze thighs under the disco strobe lights, and the one I heard about in instalments up the coast, the New Zealand ingénue with her fresh relationship? Shiftless, predatory men, women without guile. How had she come to know these things? One night at dinner she told me about the time before meeting her boyfriend, when men would ask her out and sometimes she'd go. How did you dress, what did you talk about? I asked her. She told me, but I couldn't quite get the picture. The child was in the way. But with her performances the child became an adult, the adult a friend and the friend the best of companions on the road.

We went around Newark, judged by *Harper's* magazine in 1975 to be the worst city in America. Connecticut Puritans founded it. Zinc electroplating and celluloid, the first commercially successful plastic, were developed here, the latter being used for billiard balls and dentures. An entrepreneur named Seth Boyden invented patent leather in Newark, which nuns later forbade girls in their charge from having on their shoes when wearing dresses, because of its reflective capacities. By 1870 Newark was producing ninety per cent of America's leather, bringing $8.6 million into the city in that year alone. By 1922 there were sixty-four theatres and forty-six cinemas. The painter Robert Rauschenberg is said to have disembarked from a bus from Texas and stayed in Newark for a month before realising it was not Manhattan, which is where he thought he was. After this Golden Age, Interstates 78 and 280 and the New Jersey Turnpike ploughed up neighbourhoods, white people headed for the suburbs, industry died as Latins and southern blacks arrived looking for jobs, huge housing projects concentrated the unemployed poor in tower blocks, and drug dealing and political graft were among the few growth industries. It became worse than East St Louis, Illinois, called by John Carvel of the *Guardian* an 'unplanned nightmare of deconstruction', where the traffic lights didn't work because the city hadn't the money to change the burned-out bulbs.

Cory Booker, the son of black civil-rights activists, played football at Stanford, was a Rhodes scholar and read modern history at Oxford, then graduated from the Yale Law School. After that, he went to live in Newark's Brick Towers, a slum in itself, where he organised tenants to fight for improved conditions. He participated in community action groups, operated free legal clinics and became a city council member. He went on a ten-day hunger strike against public drug dealing and was threatened with assassination by members of the Bloods gang who were serving time in New Jersey prisons. In 2002 he ran for mayor against Sharpe James, the most recent of three consecutive Newark mayors who were indicted on corruption charges. James, a black former physical-education instructor, declared that Booker didn't know how to be an African-American and he didn't have the time to teach him. A black Newark resident said of this, 'We tell our children to get educated, and when they do we call them white. What kind of message is that to send?' James also said Booker was Jewish, Republican and homosexual, none of which was true, though he had been a member of the L'Chaim Society, a group formed by a rabbi to reduce tension between American Jews and blacks. Booker's campaign advertisements were torn down by the police, businesses that held fundraising events for him were closed down and city employees who supported him were demoted. James was re-elected, but when Booker ran again in 2006, James, facing criminal charges, withdrew and Booker took seventy-two per cent of the vote.

Booker is a member of the Mayors Against Illegal Guns Coalition, an organisation headed by Mayors Thomas Menino of Boston and Michael Bloomberg of New York. They had aimed to recruit fifty mayors to this anti-gun group by the end of 2006, but got 225 instead. Arnold Schwarzenegger, an unlikely populist reformer perhaps, has introduced a radical environmental programme in California, with, among other things, the provision of fuel stations throughout the state for hydrogen-powered cars. More radical still is his proposal to provide health insurance for all uninsured Californians. This, if he can make it work, would be truly revolutionary, for it would be in effect an incipient state health service, a thing the legal profession, the insurance and pharmaceutical industries, the American Medical Association and their various lobbyists have mobilised all their power and money against each time it is mentioned. On environmental issues, such as the restoring of controls loosened by the federal government, he has sought alliances with other governors to build a national campaign.

Tony Benn has said that the last place anyone should look for the great reforming progressive ideas is in a national parliament. 'These things grow out of the needs of individuals or groups at the basic level of society. Pressure builds from underneath. An idea takes shape. It is explained to others, encouraged and taught more widely, and then a movement, sometimes very small, is organised around it. By the time it is noticed by those near the top it already has clarity and momentum. First the idea is ignored, then judged mad, and then dangerous. Forces are mobilised against it. Then there is a pause. After that, the notion is put about that everyone has been in favour of it all along, that it was in fact the politicians who first thought of it. Then a law is finally passed.'

Democracy itself is perhaps such an idea. If the Republican Party has found a way to bypass the public through the control of administrative positions, judgeships and the lobbying industry, then perhaps the public can reassert itself through the pressure it can place on city councils, state senates, mayors and governors, institutions and individuals more accessible to it than anything or anyone in Washington. Washington is unlikely to seriously reform itself, particularly on the single most important issue of campaign finance, but perhaps it can be made to move by pressure from below. Gun control, a higher minimum wage, social programmes for the poor, increased spending on education, improved infrastructure, regulation of financial institutions, environmental control, worker safety laws, campaign financing reform and a state-run health service are popular ideas in America, but the lobbying system in America prevents them from happening. Local governments, however, can be forced through public pressure to legislate for at least some of this. Washington could begin to feel the threat of redundancy. But this would require an animated body politic.

We went down into the Lincoln Tunnel and came up in Manhattan, gently pulsating in the late afternoon. Even if you've never been to New York before, it immediately offers you the comfort of familiarity. At the very least. We pulled up at the Chelsea Hotel. 'This hotel does not belong to America,' wrote Arthur Miller, who lived there for six years. 'There are no vacuum cleaners, no rules and no shame ... I witnessed how a new time, the sixties, stumbled into the Chelsea with young, bloodshot eyes.' Some of the people from that time were still there in the lobby, wizened a little, but still expectant and asking no one to forgive them.

A Latino bellhop in a T-shirt took us up to our room, a large one with two double beds and a balcony that looked out onto 23rd Street. 'I oughta tell ya that the balcony goes across to the room next door,' he said. 'That means that the people in there can come out onto it and over to your window here. So if you got your clothes off and you're gettin' down to business, just remember to close the curtains if you don't wanna be watched.' His brow furrowed and he inclined his head a little to the side, as if to say, 'Is there anything else I can help you with?'

Aoife whitened and fell back onto her bed. 'That's my *father*!' she nearly shrieked.

I'd been dreading this since Miami. At each hotel I'd been careful to say in an over-enunciated way that I wanted a room with two beds for 'my daughter and myself', while appearing nonchalant. I don't know what any of the desk clerks thought, but they'd betrayed no suspicions. At a gas station in Virginia I'd followed Aoife out the door after paying at the till, but was stopped by a nearly toothless, semi-bearded, wild-eyed young man in a pickup truck – the sort that provoked Jon Voight to petition Burt Reynolds before beginning their nightmare river journey in *Deliverance*, 'Can't we just go back to Atlanta and play golf?' – who said, 'You gotta tell me how you do it, man.' 'What's that?' I'd asked. 'Get yourself such a beautiful young woman,' he answered, with all the luridness he could find. But when I said, 'That's my daughter', he looked like I'd kneed him in the stomach. 'Sorry,' he said, and got back into his truck. For that I was grateful.

The man at the Chelsea, however, was unfazed.

'We've seen a lot worse than that here,' he said, and walked out with five dollars I'd rather have spent elsewhere.

Leonard Cohen, who stayed at the Chelsea and wrote a song about it, said, 'I love hotels, to which, at four a.m., you can bring along a midget, a bear and four ladies, drag them to your room and no one cares about it at all.'

The area was settled by Captain Thomas Clarke, a veteran of the French Indian Wars, who named it for the London barracks where old soldiers live in retirement. His grandson Clement Moore wrote 'A Visit from St Nicholas', better known as 'The Night Before Christmas'. The hotel, a Victorian red-brick, twelve-storey building with iron balconies, opened first as an apartment cooperative in 1884, and then as a hotel in 1905. It is in itself the repository of a rich history of American art, music and literature, housing at different times some of the most luminous of the country's literary saints and fallen angels. Mark Twain stayed in it and Thomas Wolfe wrote *Look*

Homeward, Angel there. O. Henry registered under a different name each night he stayed in it. Some of the great and frail of Europe found refuge there – Edith Piaff, Sarah Bernhardt, Brendan Behan and Dylan Thomas, who went into a coma in room 205 after drinking eighteen whiskies in the White Horse Tavern and later died in hospital. Vladimir Nabokov also stayed there. Edgar Lee Masters, author of the *Spoon River Anthology*, wrote eighteen volumes of poetry there, Arthur C. Clarke *2001: A Space Odyssey*, Jon Bon Jovi 'Midnight in Chelsea', Joni Mitchell 'Chelsea Morning' and Bob Dylan 'Sad-Eyed Lady of the Lowlands'. Dylan was a resident when his first child was born. Tennessee Williams, William Burroughs and Charles Bukowski stayed in the hotel. John Houseman, actor, impresario and co-founder with Orson Welles of the Mercury Theater, lived in the Chelsea, as did Virgil Thomson, who composed the music for Welles' all-black voodoo *Macbeth*, a Works Progress Administration-sponsored production that played at the Lafayette Theater in Harlem. Ten thousand people thronged the pavements on the first night. James Baldwin saw it as a schoolboy and was enthralled. Percy Hammond, the *New York Herald Tribune* critic, on the other hand, was both tepid about the production and patronising about the black cast, suggesting that whatever other virtues this 'noble race' might have, they demeaned Shakespeare, and that black actors should confine themselves to black subjects. Welles had hired an African dwarf witch doctor named Abdul with gold and diamond teeth to give authenticity to the rituals, and on the evening the review appeared, Abdul stopped him to ask if the critic was a bad man. 'Yes, he is,' said Welles, then twenty-one. 'You want I make beri-beri on this bad man?' asked Abdul. Welles told him to go ahead. Abdul said they would start drumming. 'Bad man dies twenty-four hours from now,' he said. Welles heard the drumming start as he left the theatre and was later told that it went on through the night. Percy Hammond contracted pneumonia before the show began the following night. He died the next day, a little later than had been predicted.

Among the visual artists who stayed at the Chelsea were Jasper Johns, William de Kooning, Henri Cartier-Bresson, Claes Oldenberg, Diego Rivera, Jackson Pollock and Robert Maplethorpe, who shared an apartment in it for a time with the singer Patti Smith. Art fills the staircase, the corridors and the lobby. Much of this had been bartered for rent. 'I consciously went after artists to bring them here,' said Stanley Bard, whose father had run the Chelsea and then passed it on to him. 'I found them interesting, stimulating. And they felt comfortable with me wanting to help them.' One of these artists was the Australian painter Brett Whiteley, who lived in the Chelsea in the late 1960s with his wife, Wendy, and daughter, Arkie, whom I met in London. 'I was three when we moved into the Chelsea Hotel,' Arkie told me. 'It gave me a very different kind of childhood. Jimi Hendrix and Janis Joplin used to babysit for me.'

There are parts of America where you can drive for miles without seeing a shop owned by an individual. The mall has superseded the town square and the mall is an arena only of franchises. Outside the Chelsea Hotel on 23rd Street were, on the different occasions I'd been there, a Chinese laundry, a fishing-tackle shop, a Jewish bank, a bar for fetishists, a second-hand guitar store and the El Quixote restaurant, its soft, golden light, low booths and jaded, career waiters bedecked in white all throwing you back into glamorous nights of half a century ago. A franchise store would be an aberration here. People walk in New York and are leaner than elsewhere in America. There is room on their faces for the play of thought and feeling to be visible. They have not been put in uniforms by Wal-Mart or any other arbiter of collective style. It's a city that asks for and expects the individual.

We walked down 8th Avenue past men in moustaches holding hands and stopped for a beer in the Corner Bistro on 4th and Jane. Two old men approached each other with arms out and embraced with leisureliness and gentility. This encounter could have been happening under an olive tree in a Greek village, so slowly did it unfold, but just down the road herds of taxis were whirling and honking around Sheridan Square and a little way beyond to the south was the financial capital of the world. Many Americans who have never been to New York assume it is a seething inferno of aggression, indifference and blinding speed. It seems to me, though, that the pace in general is a stroll, the manners incomparably considerate and the time available for others among the most ample in America. We passed hockey players on roller skates flitting past each other like mayflies, and the cafés and clubs where Bob Dylan, the falsetto maestro Tiny Tim and hordes of poets, comedians, magicians and folk singers did their turns and passed their hats in the bohemian innocence of the early 1960s. Outside an independent cinema around three hundred people were waiting to see a documentary called *The Corporation*, which analyses the nature of this modern phenomenon and how it functions in the world, including the means by which it successfully offloads its costs onto government bodies at local and national level. I'd seen similar crowds further uptown waiting to get into Michael Moore's *Fahrenheit 9/11*. When I was growing up, documentaries never appeared in cinemas. As both broadcasting and print media forsake deep research and analysis for propaganda, titillation or passivity, the documentary feature film offers one of the few remaining means for Americans to find out what is going on around them. Aoife and I walked on through the Village and went into the Pearl Oyster Bar on Cornelia Street, where I had red snapper and mussels, one of the finest meals I've had anywhere. We had a final drink in a bar on 7th Avenue, where an Italian Albanian spoke of the 2,500 olive trees he left behind and of the beauty of European Islam.

Down in the lobby in the morning, Stanley Bard hooked the arm of a passing Victor Bockris, a writer who lived in the hotel, and introduced him to me. I knew he'd moved among the more visible peaks of the 1970s New York underground world, working with Andy Warhol at the Factory and writing books about William Burroughs, Keith Richards, Lou Reed and Patti Smith. He'd acted, he told me, in *Cocaine Cowboys*. I'd read a small book he'd written about Muhammad Ali, an unlikely match, one would think. He'd phoned Ali's training camp at Deer Lake in Pennsylvania before the fight with George Foreman in Zaire, was answered by the champion himself and invited over.

Bockris' father was English and his mother a Pole. Both were scientists. They moved to Philadelphia in 1953 when Victor's parents had been offered jobs at the University of Pennsylvania. He was four at the time. He returned to England alone in 1959 to attend boarding school at Rugby, yearning through the time he was there for America. 'There was rock and roll there,' he said. 'James Dean and Marlon Brando were the most famous Americans, unprecedented, iconic figures. You couldn't help but be drawn to America with all the drabness around you in Britain. You didn't just like America. You wanted to *be* American. This must have made the job of being an American diplomat that much easier.'

He'd found his cultural milieu in the period that spanned from the Beats to punk. 'When I began to write books I went back down the streets of the Beats where it all began,' he said. 'The Beats studiously used marijuana, Benzedrine and, occasionally, opium for research. They used them to produce visions. In these and later years we watched on black-and-white television the civil-rights movement move on to resistance to the Vietnam War. These were serious things, involving violence and death. Emotions were strong. There was a feeling that it was important, and it was. Protest brought down two presidents. But there was a curve to the 1960s. The drugs changed, for one thing. Pot, acid and amphetamines were replaced by cocaine, heroin, qualudes. Drugs became a business, and the counter-culture began to lose control of itself. Instead of being an axis for social concern, there was an entertainment culture. There were still a few highlights – Nixon was brought down and there was a final theatrical outpouring of the counter-culture. After that you got glam rock. "I'm gay, look at me," it seemed to scream. Anything for attention. It's sad to think now how naïve and pretentious it was. I was a foot soldier in that movement, and though some of it is embarrassing, I think of myself as having been lucky to have been there, particularly with Warhol. After he had survived getting shot in 1968 he cleaned up the Factory. There were no drugs, no debauched behaviour. The people were straighter. He put together a formidable team. He was the hardest-working person I ever met. He put in sixteen to eighteen hours per day. It gave him joy. But outside of that, all the little groups that had been stitched together to make the counter-culture were falling apart. You look at it now and you think: All of that effort that people made, some of them dying in the process, twenty years of demonstrations, all that striving and intelligence and passion, and what is the effect? This hideous conservative backlash, the right working itself up with its catalogue of things to resent. Why would a young person be persuaded to go out and do it again? I've lived here for forty years out of choice and it is the first time I feel like leaving the country. I feel embarrassed. There were such great authoritative figures that came out of the United States and transfixed the world. Now Lance Armstrong gets spat on at the Tour de France.'

Aoife and I went back down to the West Village for a late breakfast at the Paris Commune, one of whose owners, a South African named Hugo Uys, also had a line in luxurious clothing for dogs. Outside on Bleeker Street a girl in a checked dress, bobby socks and two ponytails was playing hopscotch on the pavement, a game I thought had gone the way of ice-cream parlours, schoolboys delivering newspapers and non-working mothers. But there it was on a West Village street. Perhaps things somehow endure in New York, I thought. Then I noticed just in front of her a man being dollied back on a wheeled cart recording her with a film camera. When this small actress finished her scene, a woman appeared from behind a tree to put more make-up on her face. Aoife and I went into the restaurant and studied the long, enticing menu. A waiter appeared silently as though a little breeze had deposited him there. 'Any ideas?' he asked in a way it seemed he hoped would not offend.

Later we walked uptown until we went our own ways, she into some shops and me into a cab to see the novelist Charles Newman at his apartment on West 61st near Lincoln Center. The driver was an African in robes. He was listening to the right-wing radio-show host Rush Limbaugh rail against the Clintons and was laughing so hard he could barely keep his eyes on the road. 'This guy's crazy, man!' he said. 'I can't wait until this programme comes on. It's the best entertainment of the day.' Rush Limbaugh was bellowing as if to a multitude. 'Do you find anything he says sensible?' I asked. He turned completely around to face me. 'Are you serious?' he said.

I first saw Charles Newman when he walked onto the stage of a university lecture hall to deliver the initial talk in his course 'Writers of the Last Decade', in which I was enrolled. I was twenty and he thirty-three. He wore a woodsman's shirt and blue jeans, had glittering eyes, a trim beard and a sardonic smile and was unlike any other professor I'd yet met, or ever would meet. He was a novelist, a category of being the equivalent of high priest to me then. *Time* magazine had said of *New Axis*, his first novel, that it 'taxes the vocabulary of praise'. Another novel, *The Promisekeeper*, was about to appear, and a little later *A Child's History of America*, a memoir of his travels through Prague, Paris, Greece, Spain, San Francisco and other regions in varying degrees of upheaval in 1968, 'that vintage year for revolution', as he called it. He'd taken a journal of stapled-together academic articles called *TriQuarterly* and, immediately upon assuming the editorship, turned it into one of the most important literary magazines in America. I went to him and asked for a job and he gave me one reading manuscripts. I couldn't have foreseen such an act of faith. I stayed there for two years and learned far more than a whole degree's worth of courses. More adjectives could accumulate around him than anyone else I knew. He was worldly, dazzlingly intellectual, potentially violent, skilled at political gamesmanship, athletic, raucous, libertine, moody, intimidating, mischievous, caustic, handsome, hilarious, self-destructive, charismatic, ever looking to the new and ever disappointed. He spoke elliptically, perhaps to keep the listener on an uncertain footing. When he bought a farm in the Blue Ridge Mountains of Virginia to produce prosciutto and raise Hungarian dogs, he gave me a room, rent-free, in his Evanston apartment on the edge of Chicago to stand watch in his absence. When he was back, he would write his books half-naked in black ink on yellow legal pads and drink vodka like it was tea. In the spring of my final year at university he thought me over-taxed by course work, responsibilities at the magazine and various part-time jobs and invited me to his farm for a few days' rest. Once there, he put me to work planting two hundred trees, digging a pond and planting a herb garden. I was at that last task, hair falling down onto my shoulders, when a car pulled up behind me and a Baptist minister got out to introduce himself and welcome Charlie to the parish. 'Any time you and Mrs Newman would like to come by the church, we'd be most happy and honoured to welcome y'all,' he said. I turned around, sweat running down my face onto little wisps of beard. 'I *do* beg your pardon, sir!' he trilled, and drove off then in a cloud of dust.

I saw Charlie sometimes in the decades after I left, in St Louis, London, Evanston and, usually, New York. In 2003 I sent him a book I'd written in which I mentioned his once having said to me, 'It takes ten years to learn how to write a sentence', something I thought at the time was a figure of speech, but which I found subsequently, in my case, to be accurate – assuming, that is, I've learned it. He called me in Valencia from somewhere near Biarritz, howling drunk and slurring words, but lucid and funny, as well as dazzlingly intellectual and mischievous and charismatic and all those other things that he had been. When I got to New York I thought I'd try to see him before the alcohol could obscure him, and arrived before noon.

He sat on a swivel chair in the shadows of his apartment, magazines, little notes, tobacco leaves and opened books around the tables and floor. His face was unlined, eerily angelic, and he had a paunch the size of a medicine ball emerging from an otherwise lean body. It was the first time I'd ever seen him assuming this shape. He'd once had a try-out for the St Louis Cardinals baseball team and had gone for long, daily swims in the years after. After his first wife, a Hungarian ballerina, shot herself in 1972 he'd married four more times, usually to beautiful Hungarians. Now he was living alone. He'd turned sixty-five, he said. He'd lost consciousness and fallen in St Louis. A stroke had been diagnosed. Also Parkinson's, some infections and damage to internal organs. His back was terrible. But he was better now, he said. Turning in his chair in the dim light, he seemed as much Gothic monument as man.

We went down into the empty streets, through a court-yard in Lincoln Center containing a Henry Moore bronze, and then to a Mexican restaurant. He ordered some food, and water to drink. He asked me what I was intending to do with this book. He'd put aside a book he was writing on the subject of education to start a series of letters to his dead ancestors on the subject of contemporary America. 'We're after the same thing, maybe,' he said. That might have been the first time I'd found myself placed by him on something of an equivalent level to himself. His intimidating ellipticism appeared to have become redundant. He was more open, more extending of himself. There was a tenderness to his tone and his gestures. It may have been a frailty derived from his fall and his ailments, or it may have been that any other manner was no longer of interest to him.

I told him the story I'd heard from Jonno Larsen in Missoula, Montana about the old woman who'd found herself sitting in a church next to the CEO who'd bankrupted the Montana State Power Company and many of its workers and asked him to leave because she didn't want to be in the way if someone tried to take a shot at him.

'One day she'll take a .38 out of her bag, put it between his ribs and pull the trigger herself,' he said. 'I saw Ken Lay who ran Enron declaring on television that he knew nothing beforehand about the collapse of his company. "I'd just bought four million shares," he said. "But you'd just sold twenty-four million," the reporter told him. I was glad to see them go and Arthur Andersen along with them, because I know how crooked these accounting firms can be. Then I met an old woman in a bank weeping because all her money had been tied up in Arthur Andersen stock.'

He'd studied at Yale and Oxford, and when he came back from England he'd wondered which would be less boring, politics or an academic life. He became a Congressional aide for a while in Chicago, then took a job at Northwestern University in the English Department. He had stayed in university life in different institutions since then, but had occasionally revisited politics, writing speeches for a Democratic politician from Missouri. I asked him what he thought of the people who were drawn to the political world.

'Truman's administration was probably the high point with respect to the quality of advisors,' he said. 'There were a few smart people around Kennedy, but if you read the Cuban Missile Crisis tapes you can see that Rusk and McNamara had their heads up their asses. There is nothing new in the present disasters. We've been making the same mistakes since the Spanish–American War. It was evident at the time. After the invasion of the Philippines, William James said, "We are now simply pirates." Woodrow Wilson displayed some of the same weaknesses as Bush. There was always the idea that no one could defeat the Marines. They didn't know that in Vietnam there would be a fifteen-year-old girl living for weeks in a tunnel on beetles who would come out and plug you between the eyes. The whole country is in denial, and one of the reasons for this is the unprecedented organisation of the media to keep us there. We are creating mujahideens all over the world, highly motivated fighters who understand our military, political, intellectual and spiritual weaknesses. If someone had said in 1950 that we'd lose two wars to Stone Age people, who would have believed him? And it seems there are more losses to come. We're going down. There's a great fall coming. With all that happened through the last century, we still had everything to play for. There were still good wishes towards us from the rest of the world. But not now. It's been the greatest, fastest and most profligate squandering of reputation, goodwill and resources in history.'

Would he stay? I asked him. Would he think of moving to Europe?

'I've been in Europe every year for the past thirty-five years, but this year I'm staying here. I want to watch it all unfolding. Tragic as it is, it's also hilarious.'

H.L. Mencken thought the same eighty years ago. 'And here, more than anywhere else I know of or have ever heard of,' he wrote in *On Being American*, 'the daily panorama of human existence, of private and communal folly – the unending procession of governmental extortions and chicaneries, of commercial brigandages and throat-slittings, of theological buffooneries, of aesthetic ribaldries, of legal swindles and harlotries, of miscellaneous rogueries, villainies, imbecilities, grotesqueries and extravagances – is so inordinately gross and preposterous, so perfectly brought up to the highest conceivable amperage, so steadily enriched with an almost fabulous daring and originality, that only the man who was born with a petrified diaphragm can fail to laugh himself to sleep every night, and to wake every morning with all the eager, unflagging expectations of a Sunday school superintendent touring the Paris peep shows.'

Charles Newman died of a heart attack in March 2006 in St Louis, aged sixty-seven. He left behind his unfinished book on education, the one composed of letters to his ancestors, a three-volume novel involving Pavlov, Freud and Marx that he had been writing for more than twenty years, and several students around America and elsewhere, myself included, on whom no one had had the degree of influence that he had. He was always cynical about education when he spoke of it with me, but he seemed to feel an instinctive connection with the student who could be lifted and carried by him onto another level, not through pedagogy, but rather through exposure to his mind, his tastes, his flights, his jokes, the way he searched for meaning. He seemed not to be able to avoid giving himself to this. At a time when I was experiencing a rising identification with books, he showed me the making of them, through the magazine he edited and the work he did himself. It was as if he opened a door and I could see this process happening. It would remain closed to me, as he said, for another decade, but the picture he showed me was nevertheless irresistible.

We woke up at four-thirty in the morning in the Chelsea Hotel so that I could drive Aoife to Newark Airport for her flight to London. I stayed on for a few days. I walked the streets and saw some of the people I'd been with the year before. Pat Mongoven and his girlfriend Barbara flew in from Chicago for two nights, and then out again.

One afternoon I took the subway to Brooklyn to see Julio Mitchel, a Cuban photographer I'd met in London. He'd had the idea when young of being a crusading lawyer, but went sideways into photography, initially driven by a fascination with its mechanics. He studied under a Viennese Parisian named Lisette Model, who had taught Diane Arbus. There is a book of his called *Triptych* with sections on war, terminal illness and sexual passion so raw and brutal and uncompromising that a kind of fog of singed flesh, disease and the dizzying odour of the 'rank, enseam'd bed' seems to hover over it. It is as though the pictures lack a mediating agency. The distance has been cut.

He was waiting for me at the top of some steps. We rounded a corner and entered Brooklyn Heights. I'd only ever been in Brooklyn once before, thirty years earlier, to deliver a Christmas present to the mother of a friend of mine named Lou in Coney Island. Lou's father was a Jewish ex-boxer, his mother a Puerto Rican beauty queen. He had been, he said, the only Jewish altar boy in New York. By the time I went to see his mother she was a widow with three more children, living above a shoe shop beside some elevated train tracks. I walked up to her apartment, delivered the present, saw the bedroom where Lou had set fiendish traps with which to incinerate the cockroaches that had plagued his youth, then walked along the Coney Island boardwalk, Russian Jews in scarves and overcoats seated on beer crates and huddled together under the arches of food stalls closed for the winter. Bearded ladies and midgets and other unusual spectacles from the freak shows in the amusement parks strolled the streets, buying their groceries during their off-hours. I saw a man with his right eyeball hanging from its socket down to his collarbone at the end of a long pink-fleshed sheath. I passed Nathan's, the nation's archetype for hot-dog stands, then went into Odd Ball Pets, full of emaciated, trembling dogs calling out to passers-by for deliverance from this place and, in the centre, a moulting llama in a pen he could barely turn around in, and, beside him, a platypus.

Manhattan is a chaos of styles, its buildings relating anachronistically one to the other, the whole of it looking at times as though it's held together by string and plasters and rubber bands. Brooklyn Heights is almost uniformly nineteenth-century, stately, elegant, leafy, peaceful. There are grand brownstone mansions, carriage houses and houses built of wood by sea captains. Julio took me around the neighbourhood. Walker Evans lived here, and Thomas Wolfe. Truman Capote wrote *Breakfast at Tiffany's* and *In Cold Blood* in a basement flat in Willow Street. There was a building at its corner with Middagh Street that Anaïs Nin called the 'February House' because of the birthday month of a disproportionate number of its residents, which included W.H. Auden and Carson McCullers. Arthur Miller lived in the same building as Norman Mailer and met Marilyn Monroe at a party nearby.

'You'd see Mailer striding along with his boxer's swagger,' said Julio. 'Then he came to need two walking sticks.' Walt Whitman edited the *Brooklyn Daily Eagle* and, in Fulton Street in 1855, printed the first ten pages of *Leaves of Grass*. Hart Crane, whose father was the inventor of the enduring mint sweet with the hole in the middle known as the Life Saver, studied the Brooklyn Bridge from here. He lived in a street called Columbia Heights, where one afternoon Federico García Lorca came to visit him. Lorca had arrived in New York in 1929 and was immediately stunned by the city's 'extrahuman architecture and furious rhythm. Geometry and anguish', but was truly lured only by Harlem. He was in Manhattan on the day the stock market crashed and saw the corpse of a man who'd leaped from a hotel window. When he told the story in Spain he multiplied the corpses. On the day that he came to see Hart Crane he was accompanied by a Puerto Rican named Angel Flores. Crane came to the door, drunk. Behind him sailors were sprawled around the floor. Lorca entered, Flores withdrew and the door closed.

We went up onto a promenade overlooking the East River, Brooklyn Bridge to the right, the bay with the Statue of Liberty in it to the left and lower Manhattan straight ahead. 'A mighty woman with a torch, whose flame / Is the imprisoned lightning and her name / Mother of Exiles,' wrote Emma Lazarus of Liberty in the sonnet engraved on the statue's base, which then goes on to invite the world's poor and tired and huddled masses to the refuge of the New World. Thom Gunn, looking at her in 1973, thought her 'hard, but hard like a revolutionary'. Maxim Gorky, like millions before him, passed by the statue on an immigrant boat and saw a fellow passenger point at her and say to a little boy, 'That is their god.' There has been so much traffic and dumped industrial waste and sewage here that in the small bays to either side of me, Gowanus to the left and Wallabout to the right, up to a foot and a half of sludge accumulates each year, rotting in the summer heat and sending up to the surface basketball-sized bubbles filled with gas, making the water seem to 'seethe and spit', as Joseph Mitchell put it in his book *The Bottom of the Harbour*. Yet the vista from this spot is undeniably one of the world's grandest and most dramatic.

Julio came here just under three years before, on 11 September.

'When I heard on the radio about the plane flying into the Twin Towers I came out here to see what had happened,' he said. 'There were people looking out their windows, and up on rooftops. We could see the flames, the sky blackening with smoke. Then I saw out of the corner of my eye to the left a low-flying dark shape streaking over the bay heading for Manhattan. I had a premonition, thought, "No, please", and then watched the second plane hit the building. You were there and not there. It seemed too impossible to have happened. But of course it had. For days there was a smell of burnt flesh in my apartment.'

In 1947, ninety degrees to the left of here on a boat next to the Statue of Liberty, Simone de Beauvoir looked out towards the Manhattan skyline over water that she said smelled of salt and spices and thought, 'What a field day a bomber would have!'

On the morning of the day I was to leave I went to University Place and 13th Street, just south of Union Square, site of labour rallies and Tammany Hall, to see Charles Strozier, a psycho-analyst and historian who is the author of a book called *Apocalypse: On the Psychology of Fundamentalism in America*. He'd written of the Civil War era as if it were a mind that could be analysed, and in his more recent book had done the same with the rise of Christian fundamentalism, with its focus on the end of the world. He was tall and blond-haired and looked like a surfer just arrived in from being blasted by a sea wind. He was from Georgia, where fundamentalism was booming, but had made his study in New York City, where it had a stronger presence than he had thought.

Apokalypsis in Greek means 'lifting of a veil' or an un-covering, but *apokalypsis eschatos* means 'revelation at the end of the world'. Its original focus was on God electing to disclose Himself, with whatever inherent destruction there was in that moment being of our preconceptions, rather than of the world itself. Afterwards, in the Christian tradition, it came to be associated with endtimes, as depicted in the visions of St John of Patmos in the Book of Revelation. Knowledge of the Apocalypse was believed to have been bestowed by God upon a prophet. It was mysterious, powerful, unerring, mystical. There were lakes of fire, hideous lesions, eagles, seven trumpets and seven veils, crashing skies, the flapping of giant wings, beasts with numbers rather than names. There would be the righteous and the damned, and this would be the time of their separation. This was the purifying fury of God before the establishment of His millennial kingdom. 'I want to die shouting,' sing the saved in 'Amazing Grace'.

The Apocalypse is most clearly defined in the Book of Revelation, but it is present elsewhere in the Bible in various forms, including the warning: 'And ye shall hear of wars and rumours of wars: see that ye be not troubled: for all *these things* must come to pass, but the end is not yet. / For nation shall rise against nation and kingdom against kingdom; and there shall be famines, and pestilences, and earthquakes, in diverse places. / All these *are* the beginnings of sorrow' (Matthew 24:6–8); the description of the final destruction: 'the heavens shall pass away with a great noise, and the elements shall meet with fervent heat, the earth also and the works that are therein shall be burned up' (2 Peter 3:10); and the glorious aftermath, which is the point of it all: 'Then we which are alive *and* remain shall be caught up together with them in the clouds, to meet the Lord in the air: and so shall we ever be with the Lord' (1 Thessalonians 4:17).

There has been a millennial aspect to apocalypticism. Henri Focillon, in his book *The Year 1000,* said that the monks ceased their work of preserving human knowledge in the monasteries as they awaited the end of the world in the year 1000. When it didn't happen, they began again the copying of manuscripts, thinkers wrote treatises, architectural projects were resumed and economic activity increased. Columbus thought the end of the world would happen in 1650 and that it was up to him to convert the world and to acquire enough gold to finance an expedition to recover the Holy Sepulchre from the faithless. The end has been foreseen repeatedly by prophets without honour and those with hordes of devotees at their backs, beginning at least as long ago as Zoroaster in the fifteenth century BC.

A biblical conception of American history has been present since the Puritans, but in his book Charles Strozier follows a more recent line of righteous, apocalyptic fundamentalism that begins in the anti-slavery movement, with slavery being conceived as the national sin and abolitionist John Brown's raid on Harper's Ferry in 1859 being described by Frederick Douglass as having 'attacked slavery with weapons precisely adapted to bring it to the death . . . Like Samson, he has laid his hands upon the pillars of this great national temple of cruelty and blood, and when he falls, that temple will speedily fall to its final doom, burying its denizens in its ruins.' The Civil War was extolled in biblical terms as a cleansing, with a preacher named George Ide declaring, 'The cause of our country and the cause of religion, the cause of humanity, the cause of Eternal Right and Justice, are so intimately blended in this crisis, that you cannot separate them. The triumph of the Government will be . . . the triumph of pure Gospel.' This righteous national cause hardened into an ideology in opposition to the relativism and permissiveness of modernism and began to become a mass movement at the time of potential absolute annihilation from nuclear weapons.

'The fact of death haunts the psyche,' Charles Strozier said to me. 'It can produce a yearning to transcend, for immortality. Ninety-six per cent of our genes are like those of porpoises or baboons. But one of the ways we are distinct is that we can imagine our deaths. This can make the apocalyptic an endemic part of the psychic structure. The hope about death is that it is a beginning, and this is what the

apocalyptic is all about. There is vengeance against the faithless, great violence, then revelation, redemption, the fulfil-
ment of destiny. This has been a part of human history for
a long time, but in the middle of the twentieth century, with
the bomb, then the awareness of environmental catastrophe
and now terrorism, we realise that we have the power to
create world-ending violence ourselves. It needn't be a divine,
inscrutable act. I think this has given a much greater urgency
to our innate sense of the apocalyptic.

'The idea of hope deferred in the apocalyptic can make
it particularly alluring to the poor, the oppressed or the
broken-hearted. Many of the people I met in my study had
catastrophic, traumatic pasts of crack addiction, alcoholism,
attempted suicide, rape. They were looking for redemption.
Redemption will come, they'd been told. They need only
believe. If you believe, you will be saved. You don't have to
prove yourself through good works. You need only give yourself to it. This can make you yearn actively for the end. The
present becomes a time of waiting. You survive it if you don't
fall, if you hang on to your faith.

'The person who formalised the beliefs which are current
in American Christian fundamentalism today was John Nelson
Darby, an Anglo-Irish minister who came to America as a
missionary in the 1860s. He had a biblical theory called
"premillennial dispensationalism". The dispensationalism part
of it is to do with his idea of the various ages of the Bible,
leading to endtimes, the end of human history and the establishment of Jesus' kingdom on Earth. Premillennial refers to
the time when the rapture begins. The rapture is when Jesus
is in the air uniting the bodies of the saints with their spiritual selves and lifting the faithful to be with Him. All the
saved will have their resurrection bodies. Some believe the
rapture will happen before the seven-year tribulation, or time
of destruction, some during it and some afterwards.
Premillennial theory has the rapture happening before. There
are huge debates about this. Freud spoke of the narcissism
of small differences. These religious debates can look like

that. I spent a lot of time with people who believe in the rapture. They are deeply devout people grappling with images of death, and you have to have respect for their journey. And, psychologically, the idea that at the end of human history the saved will be like Jesus after the Resurrection is profoundly alluring. The statistics are that now in America eighty per cent believe that they will be brought before God on Judgement Day, forty per cent that the Bible is literally true word by word, half in angels and a third in the rapture as described by Darby. It is all over the country, at all social levels, and it is going up the social scale. Christianity is changing under the force of this. The emphasis has gone from the Sermon on the Mount to the Book of Revelation. Fundamentalist Christians read the parts of the Bible which confirm their beliefs. The reference to the rapture is in Ephesians. They could tell you every hostile mention of homosexuality, but neglect the parts about the sin of greed. This is where America is increasingly crazy – millions of people with extremely fastidious, detailed beliefs about the end of the world, waiting for it, in fact praying to God to bring it about quicker. They see the Antichrist in the peacemaking activities of the United Nations and yearn for the great battle on the plains of Israel. They form a nearly seamless constituency and are extremely well organised. It is a world of mass mailings, media bombardment, databases, phone centres, the forming of political–religious coalitions. They concentrate on gay marriage, prayer in schools and abortion, rather than class interests. They vote themselves into poverty.'

In the concluding pages of his book Strozier writes, 'Endism in our culture embraces many forms, and partially touches everyone's life in its connection with death. Endism is an attitude as much as a myth, a sense of foreboding as much as a given story, an orientation to ultimate concerns as much as a commitment to a specific endtime narrative. Endism describes the future location and deepest yearnings of the self. Endism is process and vision. It cuts against all logic, is usually mystical, and may become magical.'

None of this touched me when I was growing up in America. I never even heard of such a thing. The Apocalypse, if it was anything, was a literary device rather than a reality. It never formed part of the imagery or the teaching of the Catholic Church, as I experienced them. We never read the Book of Revelation. I never heard it quoted by a priest. The colours in the church and the classrooms were pastel blues and whites, with just the soft, golden glow of the haloes and the blood-red of Jesus' heart. The faces on the statues were gentle, comforting, extending of an invitation. Jesus was the Good Shepherd. I remember waiting at home through the terrifying days of the Cuban Missile Crisis, but at no time did it seem a harbinger of a new biblical era, or something mystical or magical. It was a specific, secular moment. Everyone I knew of hoped that the country's political leaders would avert the catastrophe and save us. I wouldn't have been able to imagine anyone praying for the nuclear bombs to fall so that Jesus would arrive and bestow on us our resurrection bodies. The mood generally in those years was of expansion, of problems being solvable, of America as buoyant and confident and as a never-ending experiment, of the present as a wonderful time to be alive and the future likely to be better still.

You can still drive back and forth across America and never hear anyone speak of the Apocalypse, as long as you keep your radio tuned away from the Christian stations. But there are suburban churches the size of aeroplane hangars filled with congregations numbering in the thousands listening each Sunday to descriptions of the Apocalypse and arranging their emotions, their plans and the directions of their lives around it. It is on the airwaves and in people's letter boxes and, outside of money, is perhaps the single most powerful organising force in politics – greater than infrastructure, healthcare, schools, the environment or, needless to say, labour.

The sense of a great and terrible end is a powerful presence too in the secular world of America now. Everyone knows that our protective sky is full of holes and that our skin could be scorched from our bodies. 'God gave Noah the rainbow sign, / Said, "No more water / But fire next time,"' sang the gospel singers and, later, the freedom riders. In the meantime the great cities of the world are predicted to be deluged by water from the melted polar ice caps. Global warming, with its floods, scorched earth, wild tempests and drowned plains, is predicted to continue for at least a century, no matter what we do. Our lands will be deserts, we will gag on our poisoned air. The fish of the sea will die chemical deaths and all the other great gifts of creation will wither and fall. All this we will have wrought ourselves.

Unlike the Cuban Missile Crisis, the planes going into the World Trade Center on 11 September seemed more an image from the Bible or from another work of prophecy than a political event. The act of imagining the Western world being vaulted back to a barbaric, medieval-like time of chaos, terrified wandering and tribes rather than nation-states was immediately effortless. All that was secure – air, water, roads, office buildings, subways, homes – seemed suddenly vulnerable. Television presenters warned their listeners to beware even those they trusted. The government changed the colour coding for various levels of danger from terrorism like railroad switchmen with their signals. Laws sanctioning unprecedented invasions of privacy were passed. The citizenry was enlisted in vigilantism.

The Internet is full of commentators warning of economic apocalypse. Debt now runs through the American economy like a San Andreas Fault. The pattern of cheap credit, inflated land and housing prices, frenzied speculation followed by a reversal in property values is what happened in the period leading to the Depression, and it is happening again. Much of this has been taking place at the very basic level of the home. An institution makes an unsecured loan for a property to a person without a credit record, the debt is traded around different financial institutions until it becomes part of a large investment bank's portfolio, the recipient of the loan fails to make the repayments, the property is repossessed and, in a time of falling prices, is auctioned at a loss on the original loan. The person who took the loan loses the house, and the institution that bought the debt in the hope of profit begins, during a time of increasing bankruptcies and repossessions, to see the basis of their financial structure being undermined. Pension funds and institutional investors find themselves unable to sell on these packaged debts. A company called New Century Financial, carrying $23 billion in debt, saw its share value crash from $66 to nearly zero. In a time of globalisation, declining industrial output and job losses, the American economy has been driven by consumer spending, financed by credit cards and the remortgaging of homes. People felt secure in taking out these loans because property prices kept rising and interest rates were low. At the same time the structure of loaning changed. A government mortgage guarantor, called the Federal National Mortgage Corporation and generally known as Fannie Mae, was established in the 1930s to guarantee loans made by banks to Americans with low incomes. They bought the debts from the banks, repackaged them and sold them on as securities. By the end of the 1980s, Fannie Mae was in possession of thirty per cent of the American mortgage debt. The debts were classed by bank regulators as low-risk, the loaning banks had the incentive to make unsecured loans at no risk to themselves, Fannie Mae grew to control seventy per cent of the mortgage debt by 2004, and pension funds and other institutions were happy to buy debt in a booming housing market, people took out more loans to buy more consumer goods and the government could declare that the economy was surging because of the level of consumer spending. But a housing market based on speculation is highly vulnerable, and when prices fall the entire superstructure is susceptible to collapse.

At the top of the chain the government is operating at a deficit, according to Congressman Ron Paul, of $800 billion per year. How do they manage this? They simply create more money that has no basis in fact. M3, or the amount of new money supplied by the Federal Reserve to the American economy annually, used to be disclosed. It became a secret in March 2006. It is estimated that money is being added to the economy at a rate of twelve per cent per year. Federal treasury notes are sold, interest has to be paid, more money is created. Inflation is the obvious consequence, but the government excludes food, energy and house prices from its inflation-rate figures. Meanwhile, around $3 trillion in debt, dollar assets and actual dollar cash are held outside the United States, with China alone holding $1 trillion. As the dollar decreases in value, it becomes more expedient for those holding these dollars to use them in America to purchase American companies. More of the country's assets leak away. Accounting firms manipulate company figures to make them look healthier; stock values are inflated. The dollar loses more of its connection with reality. The economy becomes more virtual. Until, as the Bible speaks of it, there is a day of reckoning.

Bertrand Russell, writing of the rise and fall of the Greeks, said that in Athens as the concept of the city state was being defined, the individual citizen was granted a great deal of liberty, science checked the advance of religion, rationalism set the tone and the activity of philosophy was in the main exuberant, original and exploratory, concentrating on how the heavens and earth worked and of what they were made. Such thinking enabled them to declare that matter was composed of atoms and to place the sun at the centre of the revolving planets more than a millennium before such ideas were advanced again. As power began to consolidate and the Athenian empire extended, philosophy began to turn its attention away from scientific discovery and towards ethics. After the empire suffered defeats and came under the chaotic governance of Macedonian armies, citizens ceased to take an interest in public life, wages fell and free labourers became mercenaries, revolution was continuously feared, sycophancy towards the rich created an army of servers, advisors and courtiers seeking an at least temporary path to indolence and luxury, and the exercise of knowledge became highly specialised. The forces of Fortune and Luck bedazzled people. Others practised astrology in the hope of finding a pattern that would enable them to see into the future as their world was falling down around them.

'The majority of even the best philosophers fell in with the belief in astrology,' wrote Russell in his *History of Western Philosophy*. 'It involved, since it thought the future predictable, a belief in necessity or fate, which could be set against the prevalent belief in fortune. No doubt most men believed in both, and never noticed the inconsistency. The general confusion was bound to bring moral decay, even more than intellectual enfeeblement. Ages of prolonged uncertainty, while they are compatible with the highest degree of saintliness in a few, are inimical to the prosaic everyday virtues of respectable citizens. There seems no use in thrift, when tomorrow all your savings may be dissipated; no advantage in honesty, when the man towards whom you practise it is pretty sure to swindle you; no point in steadfast adherence to a cause, when no cause is important or has a chance of stable victory; no argument in favour of truthfulness, when only subtle tergiversation makes the preservation of life and fortune possible . . . Meander, who belongs to this age, says:

> So many cases I have known
> Of men who, though not naturally rogues,
> Become so, through misfortune, by constraint.

'This sums up the moral character of the third century BC, except for a few exceptional men. Even among these few, fear took the place of hope; the purpose of life was rather to escape misfortune than to achieve any positive good.'

This is the age, it would seem, through which America is passing, an Endtime of Empire – a lack of belief in state structures, a decline in voting, an unreality in the unit of currency, enemies without and within, false accounting, vast numbers of servers accumulating around the rich, the ingratiation of the press to the powerful, the ascendancy of marketing over product, a retreat into privacy, reduced intellectual activity, a lack of public forums, a clouded future, religion based on salvation rather than good works, the infantilising of adulthood with computer games and motorised skateboards, high anxiety, falling wages, casinos, crystals, angels, lotteries, private armies, seers, fanaticism. Gibbon observed that the least stable of the Roman emperors became more hubristic the more they failed in battle, waging more wars they couldn't afford and for which they hadn't sufficient soldiers. 'Total war,' declared Richard Perle of America's future.

In *Collapse: How Societies Choose to Fail or Succeed*, the anthropologist Jared Diamond writes that societies begin to fall when a power elite is so far distant from the rest of the populace that they can feel none of the effects of the incipient doom. A religious and regal caste among the Mayans continued to live and wage war as if resources were infinite, while the rest of the people starved due to depleted water and soil. As children know, Nero fiddled while Rome burned.

In the United States, manufacturing wages fell by one per cent between 1980 and 2004. In the same period the real income of the top one per cent of the population rose by 135 per cent. The family fortune of the founder of Wal-Mart is equal to the combined wealth of the bottom forty per cent of the American population. In a time of a plunging dollar, record bankruptcies and foreclosures, industrial flight and massive state deficits, the merchant bank Goldman Sachs, in 2006, paid its co-presidents $53 million each, its chief executive $54 million, its vice chairman $32 million, its chief financial officer $40 million and its departing chief executive $110 million for his remaining stock options and $51 million to repurchase stakes in private equity and hedge funds owned by him and his wife. He sold $500 million in Goldman Sachs shares to comply with federal regulations so that he could accept his appointment as US Treasury Secretary. The bank's

26,467 employees were paid $16.5 billion, an average of $622,000 each. Goldman Sachs then announced, 'The most important contributor to higher profit margins over the past five years has been a decline in labour's share of the national income.' Legislation was passed cutting taxes and saving the wealthiest people in the country many millions of dollars per year, making George Bush's administration the first in American history to cut taxes in a time of war. The Wal-Mart founder's family thereafter saved $91,500 per hour in taxes. Over the previous six years the country learned from the American Society of Civil Engineers that 'We are failing to maintain even sub-standard conditions' in the highway system; from the National Education Association that the country's public schools would need $268 billion to raise them to an acceptable level of quality; that power-grid main-tenance was falling year by year; and from a US Treasury report, officially suppressed, but later surreptitiously released, that the projected government deficit would be greater than the country's entire capital stock of industry and stock-market capitalisation value combined. As for investment in its future citizenry, it was learned that while in 1940 the pay of a male teacher was 3.6 per cent higher than that of college-educated males, it was now sixty per cent less.

Bill Moyers, once a church minister, then an aide to Lyndon Johnson and latterly a journalist, said in a speech to a national school organisation in 2006, 'Aristotle thought injustice resulted from *pleonexia*, literally, "having more" . . . Plato thought that the common good required a ratio of five to one between the richest and poorest members of society. Even J.P. Morgan thought bosses should only get twenty times more than their workers, at most. How quaint. In 2005 the average CEO earned 262 times what the average worker got . . . Those who look fondly on "worker discipline" that's been keeping wages down ignore the deep distortions built into a system in which capital is highly organised and workers are not.'

Moyers then tells the story of an East Los Angeles cleaner

named Maritza Reyes and the Earned Income Tax Credit. This credit, which was introduced in 1975, praised by Ronald Reagan and considerably expanded by Bill Clinton, is designed to assist the working poor. If your income is below a certain level, your tax liability is assessed as a negative amount and you receive what is theoretically a rebate, but is in fact a subsidy designed to bring you above the poverty line. Maritza Reyes was a single mother, living with her son in a shack behind her husband's house, and earning $7,000 per year as a cleaner. She'd applied for and received Earned Income Tax Credit, but after several years of this she was told by the Internal Revenue Service that she would be required to return all her tax credits, because after an investigation it had been discovered that she had been living at the same address as her husband and was therefore claiming fraudulently as a single mother. What had happened was that Republicans who had taken over Congress in the 1994 elections had begun to attack the Earned Income Tax Credit system as a form of welfare. It was difficult for them to be too vociferous about this as the system benefited the working poor rather than their favourite target, the non-working poor, so they accepted a compromise from Clinton that allocated $100 million to the IRS to investigate tax-credit fraud. By 2001, one out of every forty-seven applicants for the tax credit was being audited, compared to one out of 366 of those earning over $100,000. Over eleven years the auditing of the poor increased by one-third, while that of the wealthy declined by ninety per cent. Another amendment to the tax-collecting activities of the government greatly desired by conservatives, the repeal of the estate tax, was too contentious to be achieved, but a kind of *de facto* version of it was quietly accomplished in 2005, when the Internal Revenue Service removed fifty per cent of its auditors investigating inheritance.

'What is the visceral kick we get from punking on the weak?' asked Michael Moore in a speech I heard him deliver in Chicago. What is it, indeed? There is no evident economic sense in spending $100 million to recoup some thousands from working poor people. Perhaps the answer is that the motivation is both tactical and ideological, rather than economic. There is no people more easy to govern than the fearful, the debt-ridden and the demoralised. It is a good idea to keep them that way. The ideological motive would be more daunting still to overcome. The low-tax, low-regulation policy is perhaps not just about liberating big business and the rich to have more. Were it so, the discussion about it could take place on objective assessments of self-interest. But it appears to have had grafted onto it the vision of God and become a kind of cult. The free market is not merely a desirable economic principle; it is a kind of scripture. 'The best lack all conviction,' wrote W.B. Yeats in his apocalyptic poem 'The Second Coming', 'and the worst are full of passionate intensity.'

By no means do most Americans have a sense of an imminent end, whether that end would be from divine intervention, environmental disaster, economic breakdown or the end of the American empire. But most feel a precipitous decline, with two-thirds believing that life will be worse for their children than it has been for them. How does it feel when things begin irreversibly to slip away? You could crouch low, and wait for the blow to fall. You could run in all directions searching for a place to hide or escape. You could begin to pray, and not stop. Some might have the serenity to wait with acceptance. The religiously apocalyptic yearn for the end because at last their true spiritual life will be allowed to begin and they will be taken by God. But for all those who have this sense of the nearness of an end, whether religious or secular, the exercise of citizenship becomes a hopeless, trivial thing. Fundamentalists will campaign on issues of moral righteousness as they see them and ignore everything else. Others will be preoccupied with survival, or despairing. What point in anything, as Bertrand Russell suggested, if it is all to be washed away? Who could think of making the 'city on the hill', for who would be around to see it? What meaning could there be any more in the Great Experiment? What point declaiming that 'Every man should be president' as I did in my dream at the age of nine? Where could anyone find that springtime, impassioned, youthful love of the shapes and textures, air, water, land and humanity that Whitman displayed in his 'Preface to *Leaves of Grass*' as he contemplated 'the great psalm of the Republic'?

America has long been accustomed to think of itself as forever young, the world's exuberant, darling boy. But as an independent, democratic republic it has been around longer than any other country in the world. Now, to many, it has suddenly begun to feel old. 'I think our nation has grown old, very rapidly,' says an elderly citizen named Gaylord Freeman in Studs Terkel's book *American Dreams: Lost and Found*. 'We've lost a lot of the Dream. We're like people my age, whose world narrows. A young man comes out of school and he's interested in everything. Then he gets a job, and his world narrows a bit. He marries. Job, home, family. And it narrows a bit more. Finally he gets older. Through with his job, his family gone away, his ultimate concern is his bowel movement every morning. Our country is going through a great deal of that now.'

I left the Chelsea Hotel and took a taxi to the airport. We glided as if in a liner through empty, twilit streets in Queens. On the plane to London I read, ate and slept a little. When I woke a blood-red sun flooded the tumultuous clouds with its light. There was no bag to pack in a hotel room or car waiting in the parking lot to take me out onto the open road, with some little bar spilling its weak light onto the pavement waiting for me at the end of the day. On the open road you can be in your own time, expect nothing and be accountable to no one. In such a place everything can be a surprise. It was over now and I could foresee no time when I would have such an experience again, but I was somehow still in it, anticipating the long unravelling of the day in continuous movement and the unexpected. They had been days of freedom for me, and I felt grateful to have had them. 'Free as the road,' wrote the poet George Herbert, 'loose as the wind.'

When I first thought of making this journey I imagined that any account I would make of it would be a bitter dirge, such was the simple picture I then had of my country. I thought it had lost its way and was full of the depressed and paranoid. But I left that idea behind at the beginning, before I got out of New York state. America is too big and too various to be so glibly ensnared. It can give you flight if you move with its currents, but reduce you to the molecular if you think you are its master. I felt that mile by mile as I moved across it. What can you do with the play of light in the Catskills, Bud McKenzie and his twenty-six cowboy ties in Hibbing, Minnesota, the smell of humid earth in Monument Valley, the rattling comedy of Kenny the confused animal skinner in Glendo, Wyoming, the green-gold of plains grasses at dusk or my cousin David in his daily negotiations with his wounds from Vietnam, except to admire them, celebrate them and perhaps fall for them again, as I had with other such wonders of the American road when I first went on it thirty years before? Had the plane had to turn around, I'd have been happy to go back, at least for a while.

What the Puritans gave thanks for is still there, if a little maimed. America has unexampled riches in nature and in its people. It has also skewed and poisoned the world, it beats up and extorts from its own citizens, and in character it can be vengeful, covetous, aggressive, anti-intellectual, naïve and parochial. There are levels of vulgarity there lower than any other I have met. But every day on the road you will meet far more of the hospitable, the compassionate, the independent and the enthusiastically exploratory. Americans have a willingness to go a long way with you into an idea, a project, a friendship. They can respect privacy, be slow to judge and be capable of being transformed by a place, an event or a person. They are anti-classist, anti-unexplained authority. Familiar signs that I see in Spain that declare one thing '*prohibido*' and another '*obligatorio*' – and which are accepted there without demur – would rile Americans, or at least provoke them to ask for an explanation. They haven't been subjected to the crushing weight of a single, powerful religion, a totalitarian regime, an ideology or an aristocracy, and in consequence tend not to be burdened by a sense of the uselessness of action. The individual, they believe, is paramount, and free. Time opens to new possibilities. They can applaud things well done and lack envy, spite or easy cynicism. Cynicism in fact can shock them. The intellectual style, where it exists, tends to avoid intimidating Latin phrases, quotations of antique, received wisdom or superior-sounding accents and concentrates instead on an open, methodical search for an objective truth. An injustice can move and motivate them. They can be modest, patient, at ease with themselves and capable of amazement and of journeys into the unfamiliar. They also listen well. A society of people with such characteristics would be open, progressive and sane, like Greece's first democracy.

But somehow, as de Tocqueville warned, after having looked too long in the wrong direction, Americans have come to 'wonder to see into how small a number of weak and worthless hands a great people may fall'.

Epilogue

In the 1960s, Lake Erie nearly died. Algae two feet thick and miles wide drifted across its surface. Mountains of detergent suds and dead fish were heaped along the shoreline. Faecal coliform bacteria and industrial waste had turned it into a huge open sewer that could be smelled miles inland. Once one of America's most abundant suppliers of walleye, bass, muskie, blue pike and yellow and white perch, the lake came to contain trash fish, bacteria, algae and sludge worms; 2,600 square miles of bottom water had no dissolved oxygen in it and nothing lived there.

The lake, the warmest and shallowest of the Great Lakes, is fed from Lake Huron and Lake St Clair through the Detroit River, into which the automobile industry and Detroit municipal authorities had been dumping garbage for decades. Phosphorus produced the algae, which is what was suffocating the deep water, but many other chemicals from industry and agriculture as well as the paving over of filtering wetlands also contributed to the lake's illness. Some limnologists said that these factors in the mid-twentieth century had aged the lake by fifty thousand years.

In June 1969 petrochemicals in the Cuyahoga River, which passes through Cleveland into the lake, caught fire. This had happened before, but on this occasion *Time* magazine wrote of the river that 'oozes rather than flows' and in which a person 'does not drown but decays'. Governments on both sides of the lake finally began to move and in 1972 the Clean Water Act, the Canada Water Act and the Great Lakes Water Quality Agreement were passed. Two years earlier the

Environmental Protection Agency had been set up. The effect on Lake Erie of this legislation was rapid and dramatic. Within three years algae blooms vanished, oxygen was present again at the bottom of the lake, perch and walleye returned in vast numbers and people again began to use the beaches. For the first time in decades you could see stones on the lake bed through thirty feet of crystalline water.

Alcoholics, corporations, endangered species, the suicidal and married couples come back sometimes from near-death and thrive. What of the great behemoth that is America? Many would say that reports of its near-death are greatly exaggerated, and they may be right. Many previous generations have contained those who have declared theirs to be the last generation of all and yet the country is still there, still rich and still the most powerful in all the world. Millions press at its gates for entry. No culture has such extensive reach. Of the twenty best universities in the world, three-quarters are American. But its wounds have gone deeply into its psyche and its structure and are evident for the world to see. The political system that it constructed to be exemplary has been sold to corporations for small change. The American Dream of an ever-growing, ever more solid middle class has gone into reverse. A social and economic brotherhood and the offer of 'life, liberty and the pursuit of happiness' become unviable when the infrastructure is breaking down and when equality is endlessly prosecuted against in tax structures, voting practices and a distorted access to justice, education and healthcare. The country that proclaims itself a beacon of freedom and protector of the weak is known for its tearing up of treaties, its excusing itself from the tenets of international law, its practices of illegal detention and torture and its preference for endless undeclared war over diplomacy.

The psychiatrist Robert Jay Lifton has looked at contemporary America and diagnosed it as suffering from what he calls 'superpower syndrome', a condition composed of senses of omnipotence, entitlement, righteousness, paranoia and grievance at being misunderstood. Around this is constructed a Manichaean world view. Those afflicted with this syndrome feel they must control history lest evil come to dominate the world. Future attacks are imagined, rage is felt and retribution is taken. If a human model for super-power syndrome were sought, it could be the dictatorial, mid-twentieth-century parent fearful of religious, cultural and social collapse and in consequence trying ceaselessly to control his children. Against such parents were ranged all the life force and yearning for discovery of the young. Ceaseless effort resulted in ceaseless failure.

Variants of superpower syndrome have been around since power began to be concentrated. Sophocles and Shakespeare wrote of it. Hemingway had it explained to him by a jour-nalist who said that what united all dictators – whether of the right or the left – was a sense of their own indispens-ability and their paranoia. What is different now is that the destructive capacities available to the superpower can bring the world to an end.

Were the superpower a person, it could perhaps be drugged, Rolfed, primal-screamed or faith-healed out of its syndrome, but Lifton recommends that it start with looking at the consequences of its ailment. The project itself has to be seen to be inherently impossible to achieve. Wars waged in the name of order instead produce chaos. Governments imposed on reluctant people break down. The struggle to keep doing this is exhausting, for the superpower itself, for its citizens and for the rest of the world. 'In its efforts to rule the world,' writes Lifton, 'the United States is, in actuality, working against itself, subjecting itself to constant failure. It becomes a Sisyphus with bombs, able to set off explosions but unable to cope with its own burden, unable to roll its heavy stone to the top of the hill in Hades. Perhaps the crucial step in ridding ourselves of superpower syndrome is recog-nizing that history cannot be controlled.' If the struggle to maintain omnipotence is despatched, along with it can go the fear of weakness. To move on from this and imagine and enter the lives of others is to cease to wish to control them.

Complexity and variousness become more enticing than right-eous certainty. Flaws and vulnerability, in oneself and others, can be acknowledged and accepted. The sense of victimhood comes to be seen for the weakness it is. In this there is liberation.

American history has been at least in part a sequence of excesses and corrections, beginning with the insurrection against European imperial power and the subsequent establishment of democracy. Abolitionists rose against slavery and thirty years later populists did the same against Gilded Age barons. When the money frenzy hit a peak in the 1920s and short-circuited the economy, a New Deal of government help and regulation put it together again. Millions marched for civil rights for southern black people until those rights were finally guaranteed in law, and millions more did it again over the Vietnam War until it was brought to an end. Great figures from Tom Paine to Martin Luther King were involved in these corrections, but so too were trade unionists, folk singers, students, philosophers, farmers, war veterans, shop assistants, grandmothers, children and even bankers, business leaders and politicians moved enough by rage or pity or love to right an imbalance. The journalist Martha Gelhorn wrote of 'that life-saving minority of Americans who judge their government in moral terms. They are the people with a wakeful conscience, the best of American citizens . . . They can be counted on, they are always there. Though the government tried viciously, it could not silence them.'

The cleaner Maritza Reyes who was prosecuted by the tax authorities for fraud never had to repay the tax credits she had received. A student at the Chapman Law School who was working voluntarily at their legal clinic for the poor took her case, represented her at court against the government lawyers and won. 'If just one person had taken the time to listen to her they would have seen what the judge did,' he later said.

Acknowledgements

I received help, advice and hospitality from many people while on the road and in the researching and writing of this book, and I am grateful to them. They include Anna Godberson, Caryl Phillips, Bruce Shapiro and Margaret Spillane, Joe Giocco and Laralu Smith, Tim Hulse, William Kennedy, Patrick Mongoven, Marcie Mongoven, Lamar and Amparo Herrin, David Hawkins, Martin Hayes and Liz Roth, Robert and Jan Gregory, Tom Hayden and Barbara Williams, the Gynther family of Auburn, Alabama, Lawrence Friedman, Robert Gordon, John Heinz, David Danone, Jim Wood, Eric Schlosser, Dave Wallace, Nik Cohn and Da Rangaz, Stanley Bard at the Chelsea Hotel, Ellen Crain of Butte, Montana, Studs Terkel, Mike Dibb, Charles Beckett of Arts Council England, Ishmael Reed, Dick Romano, Tony Benn, Andreas Karrall, David Ashton, Michel Koven, Dominic Dromgoole, Jill Cutler, Anastasia Pease and Ana Sims. John Berger provided a single, valuable piece of advice. Derek Spiers, Daniel Bianchetta and Steve Pyke let me use their photographs. I received financial help at an early stage from the Authors' Foundation, which is administrated by the Society of Authors, and from Arts Council England, and I am grateful for this, too. Geoffrey Mulligan at Harvill Secker commissioned this book and has supported it at every stage since. Simon Rhodes supervised the general design of the book, and in particular the points of connection between photographs and text. Mandy Greenfield copy-edited it with acuity.

Some names in the text have been changed.

Certain books and articles were of particular importance

to me in writing on specific themes, regions or people. They were: Nik Cohn's *In the Heart of the World* (New York: Knopf, 1992) and *Triksta: Life and Death of New Orleans Rap* (London: Harvill Secker, 2005) for New York and New Orleans, and also his article 'The Day the Music Died' in the *Observer* (15 January 2006) for the information about Katrina and what happened to B during and after it; William Kennedy's *O Albany! Improbable City of Political Wizards, Fearless Ethnics, Spectacular Aristocrats, Splendid Nobodies and Underrated Scoundrels* (New York: Penguin Books, 1985) for Albany, New York; Nicholas Lemann's *The Promised Land: The Great Black Migration and How It Changed America* (New York: Knopf, 1991) for Chicago, Mississippi and sharecropping; Jerry Dennis' *The Living Great Lakes: Searching for the Heart of the Inland Seas* (New York: Thomas Dunne Books, 2003) for Lakes Superior and Erie; Ian Frazier's *Great Plains* (London: Faber and Faber, 1990) for the plains, both north and south, and Paul F. Sharp's *Whoop-Up Country: The Canadian–American West 1865–1885*, for just the northern plains; Michael Lind's *Made in Texas: George Bush and the Southern Takeover of American Politics* (New York: Basic Books, 2003) for Texas and the consciousness of the southern landowning class; Thomas Frank's *What's the Matter With America?: The Resistible Rise of the American Right* (London: Harvill Secker, 2004) for corporate pay and manipulation of government; Joan Didion's *Miami* (London: Granta Books, 2005) for the city of that name; Robert Jay Lifton's *Superpower Syndrome: America's Apocalyptic Confrontation with the World* (New York: Thunder's Mouth Books/Nation Books, 2003) and Charles B. Strozier's *Apocalypse: On the Psychology of Fundamentalism in America* (Boston: Beacon Press, 1994) for information about the apocalyptic sensibility. For the chapter entitled Interlude, I consulted Gore Vidal's long essay 'The Enemy Within', published in the *Observer* (27 October 2002); Kevin Phillips' book *American Dynasty: How the Bush Clan Became the World's Most Powerful and Dangerous*

Family (London: Allen Lane, 2004); Molly Irvins' and Lou Dubose's *Bushwhacked: Life in George W. Bush's America* (New York: Vintage, 2004); Jonathan Freedland's 'Bush's Amazing Achievement', published in the *New York Review of Books* (14 June 2007) and William Pfaff's 'Manifest Destiny: A New America', published in the *New York Review of Books* (15 February 2007). Information about the Montana Power Company came from Michael Jamison's 'Montana Is No Longer the Political Powerhouse', published in the *Montana Standard* (no date specified); about suicides from the Golden Gate Bridge, from Tad Friend's 'Jumpers: The Fatal Grandeur of the Golden Gate Bridge', published in the *New Yorker* (13 October 2003); about Ken Kesey, from Robert Stone's 'The Prince of Possibility', published in the *New Yorker* (14 and 21 June 2004); about the suppression of the black vote, from Farhad Manjoo's 'Voter Terrorism', published on salon.com, also Kevin Phillips (op. cit.) and Michael Moore's *Stupid White Men* (London/New York: Penguin Books, 2004); about lobbyists, from Jeffrrey H. Birnbaum's 'The Road to Riches Is Called K Street', published in the *Washington Post* (22 June 2005) and Nicholas Confessore's 'Welcome to the Machine', published in the *Washington Monthly* (July/August 2003); about a new type of capitalism, from Toby Judt's 'The Wrecking Ball of Innovation', published in the *New York Review of Books* (6 December 2007); and about the housing market, from Benjamin Wallace-Wells' 'There Goes the Neighborhood', published in the *Washington Monthly* (April 2004). Bill Moyers' speech, which includes remarks about economic equality and the particular case of Maritza Reyes referred to in the final two chapters, was delivered on 27 October 2006 in San Diego to the Council of Great City Schools.

There were other books that were of great value to me generally in both travelling and writing. These were: William Least Heat-Moon's *Blue Highways: A Journey into America* (London: Pimlico, 2001); Henry Miller's *The Air-Conditioned Nightmare* (New York: New Directions, 1970); Alexis de

Tocqueville's *Democracy in America*, translated by Gerald E. Bevan, with an introduction and notes by Isaac Kramnick (London: Penguin Books, 2003); Eric Schlosser's *Fast Food Nation: The Dark Side of the All-American Meal* (New York: HarperCollins Perennial, 2002); *The Rough Guide to the USA* by Samantha Cook, Tim Perry, Greg Ward, et al. (Rough Guides, 2002); *The WPA Guide to America: The Best of 1930s America as Seen by the Federal Writers' Project*, edited by Bernard A. Weisberger (New York: Pantheon Books, 1985); Robert Hughes' *The Epic History of Art in America* (London: The Harvill Press, 1997); *The Faber Book of America*, edited by Christopher Ricks and William L. Vance (London: Faber and Faber, 1992); Woody Guthrie's *Bound for Glory* (London: Penguin Books, 2004); and Simone de Beauvoir's *America Day by Day*, translated by Carol Cosman (Berkeley, California: University of California Press, 1995).

Penguin Books granted permission to quote from their edition of *Democracy in America: And Two Essays on America* by Alexis de Tocqueville, as well as *Travels With Charley* and *The Grapes of Wrath* by John Steinbeck. Permission to quote from *River Horse* and *Blue Highways* by William Least Heat-Moon and *American Visions: The Epic History of Art in America* by Robert Hughes was granted by The Random House Group. Permission to quote from *America Day by Day* by Simone de Beauvoir was granted by the University of California Press. William Kennedy, Nik Cohn, Nicholas Lemann and Eric Schlosser granted permission to quote from their work. The Federal Writers' Project manuscripts are kept at the Library of Congress in Washington.

Picture Information

Index

All American place names are listed under the entries for their states.

www.vintage-books.co.uk